CASES IN
MARKETING RESEARCH

WILLIAM G. ZIKMUND
Oklahoma State University

WILLIAM J. LUNDSTROM
Old Dominion University

DONALD SCIGLIMPAGLIA
San Diego State University

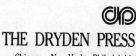

THE DRYDEN PRESS
Chicago New York Philadelphia
San Francisco Montreal Toronto
London Sydney Tokyo Mexico City
Rio de Janeiro Madrid

To Our Mothers:

Eleanor Zikmund

Alice Lundstrom

Lena Sciglimpaglia

Acquisitions Editor: Anne Elizabeth Smith
Developmental Editor: Paul Psilos
Project Editor: Brian Weber
Design Director: Alan Wendt
Managing Editor: Jane Perkins

Text Design by Alan Wendt
Cover Design by William Seabright
Copy Editing by Bernice Gordon Eisen

Copyright © 1982 CBS College Publishing
All rights reserved

Address orders to:
383 Madison Avenue
New York, New York 10017

Address editorial correspondence to:
901 North Elm Street
Hinsdale, Illinois 60521

Library of Congress Catalog Card Number: 80-65813
ISBN: 0-03-057636-9
Printed in the United States of America
2 3 4 5 6 7 8   090   9 8 7 6 5 4 3 2

CBS College Publishing
The Dryden Press
Holt, Rinehart and Winston
Saunders College Publishing

PREFACE

Many companies that hire marketing graduates complain that the trainees lack experience and cannot apply theoretical concepts to practical business situations. In many instances, the teaching of marketing research is one such subject that shares the fault. As the professors learn more sophisticated analytical techniques in their doctoral programs, they tend to focus their teaching efforts on analysis rather than on the nuts and bolts of the total marketing research program.

The purpose of this book of cases in marketing research is to introduce the student to the many facets of market and marketing research. Upon completion of the analysis of many or all the cases contained in this book, the student will be better equipped to reach decisions that require marketing research knowledge and to conduct research projects. For the instructor, the cases contain a wide variety of topics and situations that will bring to life theoretical and conceptual ideas discussed in marketing research texts. By using those cases, the instructor strongly enriches the learning process for students and provides them with the opportunity to develop and sharpen their research skills.

Cases in Marketing Research provides a wide variety of learning experiences. Cases range from the conceptual stage of problem definition in the earliest phase of marketing research to comprehensive cases that require a complete project design, execution, analysis and report. There are both short and long cases in each section so the instructor may chose from those that time, ability and depth of coverage require. Unlike the cases usually found in marketing research texts, the cases in this book tend to be considerably longer and have substantial information presented for analysis. In some cases there is excess information which requires that students sift through the data to find the relevant information which should be used in the decision–making process.

The vast majority of the cases in the book are new to marketing educators and reflect actual consulting experiences of the authors and contributors. The older cases were carefully selected for their ability to effectively ellicit tried and tested marketing research decisions by students. Overall, it has been our objective to present to marketing researchers, academic and professional, a comprehensive set of cases that is new, fresh and practical. The book can easily be used either for under-graduate or graduate marketing research courses through the appropriate selection of cases used by the class and the requirements set by the instructor as to the level of analysis.

We would like to acknowledge the assistance of numerous colleagues and insti-tutions that have made this book possible. In particular, we would like to recognize and thank Thomas Barry, Southern Methodist University; Phillip C. Burger, State Uni-versity of New York at Binghamton; Alvin C. Burns, Louisiana State University; David Chambers, San Diego State University; James W. Gentry, Oklahoma State University; Eleanor G. May, Tayloe Murphy Institute, University of Virginia; David J. Riebstein, The Wharton School of the University of Pennsylvania; Randall L. Schultz, University of Texas; Cynthia M. Taeuber, U.S. Bureau of the Census; Francis P. Tobolski, Sr., Container Corporation of America; Gerald Zaltman, University of Pittsburgh; San Diego Convention and Visitor's Bureau; Direct Mail/Marketing Educational Associa-tion; and the American Heart Association.

We would also like to thank the Arbitron Company, the *Journal of Economics and Business, The Public Opinion Quarterly*, U.S. Department of Energy, and the Dry-den Press for their generous cooperation in this endeavor.

Last, but not least, we would like to acknowledge the people behind the scenes. We would like to thank Joan Kirkendahl and Wanda Aldrich for typing the final man-uscript, collating the material, tracking down permissions, and prodding us to com-pletion; Bill Bearden of the University of South Carolina for his insightful review of the manuscript; and Brian Weber and Paul Psilos of The Dryden Press who made the actual publication of this book possible. And most of all we would like to thank our wives who spent cold and lonely nights as we pounded away on the typewriter.

Dr. William G. Zikmund   *Stillwater, Oklahoma*
Dr. William J. Lundstrom   *Norfolk, Virginia*
Dr. Donald Sciglimpaglia   *San Diego, California*
November 1981

CONTENTS

IV SAMPLING   97

V QUESTIONNAIRE DESIGN   121

VI ATTITUDE MEASUREMENT   151

VII FIELD METHODS AND CODING   177

VIII DESCRIPTIVE ANALYSIS   203

IX UNIVARIATE ANALYSIS   227

I

PROBLEM DEFINITION

1

BONITA BAKING COMPANY: (A)
PROBLEM DEFINITION

Frank Fortunada, Jr. is the sales manager of Bonita Baking Company. Bonita is a moderate-size regional bakery in Southern California, specializing in breads and bread products for markets, restaurants and institutional accounts. Established in 1910 by Frank's grandfather, Vito Fortunada, Bonita bakes and sells a number of well-known brands of bread under licensing agreements. Among these brands are Holsum, Butter-top and Hillbilly bread and rolls. Since his grandfather's retirement many years ago, Bonita has been run by Frank's father. To this day, everyone refers to them as Frank and Frank, Jr. (except in the latter's presence).

Frank Fortunada, Jr. has been involved in the bread business all of his life. As a boy he cleaned up at the bakery and later drove a route truck while attending high school. After serving four years in the U.S. Navy (as a baker), Frank, Jr. continued to work as a routeman while attending college on a part-time basis. A year after graduating with a degree in marketing from the local state college, Frank's father appointed him retail sales manager, in charge of sixty-five driver salespeople. Within two years, he was put in charge of both retail and commercial accounts. As such, Fortunada was the ranking marketing person at Bonita Baking, with his father in charge of operations of the bakery.

The Marketing Problem

About ten years ago, Bonita Baking introduced a line of specialty bread under the brand name of Bonita Health Bread. Specialty bread is made from special or mixed grain flour and is heavier than regular bread. National brands which have gained popularity include Roman Meal, Millbrook and Pepperidge Farm. Not only have specialty breads been a rapidly growing segment of the bread market, but it is a higher

Copyright © 1981 by Dr. Donald Sciglimpaglia.

gross margin product. Industry trade publications identified the specialty bread consumer as coming from upper–income households and as more highly educated than the typical bread consumer.

Fortunada knew that Bonita's specialty breads were high quality and that they should be selling well, but sales figures indicated otherwise. The Bonita Health line was apparently losing market share rapidly to the national brands and to another regional brand, Orowheat, which was the market leader. All, including Bonita Health, were actively promoted with consumer advertising, coupons and price deals. Also bothersome was the fact that many supermarket chains were also selling their own private brands of specialty bread. Fortunada's salespeople could offer no real insight as to why Bonita Health was doing poorly.

Fortunada decided to do something which had never been attempted at Bonita—to undertake some marketing research. He knew he would have trouble selling the idea to his father, but he also knew that he needed more information. Taking out a pad of paper, Fortunada began making notes as to what he would like to know about Bonita Health's position. Except for his own sales records and the trade publication reports, he decided that he knew very little.

Fortunada knew almost nothing about the size or growth rates of the specialty bread market in his area. He had no idea who bought his brand or those of his competitors, or how much consumers bought and how often. Except for his own experience, he really didn't even know who in the household requested specialty bread or who selected the brand. Another point that troubled him was not knowing the relative awareness of Bonita Health and its image among consumers. Lastly, since he hadn't been on a bread route in some time, Fortunada thought that he had better get to know retailers' attitudes toward the brands and the associated marketing practices.

Questions

1. How would you define the problem at Bonita Baking Company?
2. What are some of the major objectives of any research to be conducted with consumers?
3. What are some major objectives of any research to be conducted with retailers?
4. Why do you think that research has not been done previously at Bonita? Why will Fortunada have difficulty convincing his father of the need for research now?

THE SKOOL: PROBLEM DEFINITION

The Skool was a singles bar in Chicago's "Rush Street" area. The Rush Street area, located on Chicago's Near North Side by the Gold Coast, is approximately seven blocks long and three blocks wide, and is a popular area for evening entertainment.

The Skool once was one of the most popular spots on "Rush Street." There had always been wall-to-wall people on Friday afternoons, but lately, the crowds had begun to go elsewhere.

A marketing research consultant who patronized The Skool because it was two blocks from his home knew the manager, Karen Stein, well. After some discussions with The Skool's manager, the consultant sent a letter that proposed The Skool conduct some marketing research. (See Exhibit 1.)

Exhibit 1   The Skool's Marketing Research Proposal

Dear Karen:

Here is a brief outline of what I believe The Skool must consider if it is to regain its popularity on Rush Street. As you know, The Skool's management has changed the decor and exterior of The Skool, hired exceptional bands, and used various other promotions to improve business. In spite of this, a decline in The Skool's popularity has been evidenced. As these efforts have not brought back the crowd The Skool once had, I suggest The Skool undertake a marketing research investigation of consumer behavior and consumer opinions among Rush Street patrons.

I recommend this project because The Skool once had what it takes to be a popular bar on Rush Street and should still have the potential to regain this status. Most likely, the lack of patronage at The Skool is caused by one or both of the following factors:
1. A change in the people or type of people who patronize Rush Street bars.

Copyright © 1981 by Dr. William G. Zikmund. Names are fictitious to protect confidentiality.

2.   The opinion of The Sxlool held by people who patronize Rush Street has changed.

The problem for The Sxlool's management is to determine the specifics of the change, either in different people, or in the opinions of the regular patrons of Rush Street and The Sxlool.

Determining what type of information is desired by The Sxlool's management depends upon some underlying facts about the popularity of the bars on Rush Street. An assumption must be made concerning the questions, "Does the crowd (weekend and Wednesday patrons) go where the regulars go or do the regulars go where the crowd goes?" If you believe that the regulars follow the crowd, a general investigation should be conducted to test why the mass goes to the popular bars. If the assumption is made that a popular bar is popular because there are always people (regulars) there, the best method to increase business is to get a regular following which will attract "the crowd."

Of course, the optimal position is to appeal to both the regulars and the crowd. Thus, there are numerous areas for investigation:

■   Who visits Rush Street bars? What are the group characteristics?
■   What motivates these people to go to the various bars and thus, make them popular? For example, to what extent does the number of stag girls in the bars bring about more patrons? (Note: Remember that The Sxlool, Rush-up, Filling Station and Barnaby's had female waitresses at the start of their popularity. Could this have been a factor in their appeal?) How important is bartender rapport with the patrons?
■   What do drinkers like and dislike about The Sxlool?
■   What is the awarness among beer drinkers of Watney's quality? Do they like it? How does having Bud on tap affect a bar's popularity?
■   What image does The Sxlool project? Is it favorable or unfavorable? Has it lost the image it once had because it is trying to be the Store Annex, Barnaby's, Rush-up, and The Sxlool combined? Is the decor consistent? How can a favorable image be put back into Rush Street drinkers' minds? You might think The Sxlool can appeal to all Rush Street people, but you can't be all things to all people. A specialization of image and customers may bring back "the crowd" for The Sxlool.
■   How important is it to be first with a new promotion? For example, did Barnaby's idea of starting a wine and chicken feast make it the place to go to—at least in the short run? If a food promotion would go over, what should The Sxlool try?

There are many areas where The Sxlool would benefit if it conducted a marketing research survey. Of course, the above suggestions for investigation are not all–inclusive, as I have not had a chance to talk with you to determine which areas are the most important. If you would like to have me submit a formal research proposal to determine how The Sxlool can improve its business, I will be happy to talk with you any evening.

Sincerely yours,
Robert Millanes

Questions
1.   Has the problem been adequately defined?
2.   Evaluate the research proposal.

TLT (A): PROBLEM DEFINITION

"What this town needs is a reliable source of transportation between here and the Memphis Airport," said Jim Newman. "I've been in the travel business with Braniff for over ten years and I never had a sorrier time getting in or out of here on that blessed plane they call an airline."

This conversation took place on January 11, 1979, as Jim Newman, Bill Ranford and Knox Gary sat over lunch and tried to explore various business opportunities in Oxford, Mississippi. Newman, a former sales manager for Braniff Airlines, was now a managing partner of the largest thoroughbred horse breeding farm in Mississippi, his first love. Bill Ranford was a marketing professor at the University of Mississippi, located in the town of Oxford. Knox Gary, a retired U.S. Air Force Colonel, was presently involved as a real estate broker and also dabbled in the horse breeding business. All three had experienced difficulties with Republic Airlines in trying to make connecting flight to Memphis, Tennessee, some eighty miles northwest of Oxford.

"It seems to me," continued Newman, "that if we put together a limousine service between Oxford and Memphis, we could have a viable business which would provide us with some additional income and give the people of Oxford something which is really needed."

"I agree," said Ranford. "I am sick and tired of running up to Memphis to pick up relatives, faculty recruits for the University and for my own traveling that I do to conferences." "I have had my share of problems in bringing people into Oxford to look at real estate," added Gary. "Only two days ago, I was to meet a couple at the local airport who were interested in moving to Oxford and Republic cancelled the flight. I had to drive up to Memphis and pick them up. In addition to that, there's the time I left my car at the Memphis airport and somebody ripped off my hubcaps. I just hate the thought of making that drive."

All three agreed to think about the idea of a limousine service and to get in

Copyright © 1980 by Dr. William J. Lundstrom.

touch next week to further consider what they would have to do to initiate such a service. In the meantime, they also discussed the possibilities of a full-service car-wash, a janitorial service and a health club as other businesses that could be established. They were certain that any of these new ventures could be and should be profitable in a town such as Oxford.

Background
The City of Oxford

Many people consider Oxford to be atypical of the many rural towns that exist in the state of Mississippi. While Mississippi is known to have the lowest per capita income of any state in the United States, this generalization does not hold true for Oxford. Located eighty miles from Memphis (see Exhibit 1), it represents a combination of culture, industry and agriculture found in few other cities. Known as having been the home of William Faulkner, it attracts many visitors for the Faulkner Festival, various cultural events and the annual spring pilgrimage through antebellum homes.

The population of Oxford and the immediate surrounding area is approximately 25,000 inhabitants (not including students). A large proportion of these people represent professional and skilled worker families who are employed by local industries and firms or by the university. These figures also include a number of wealthy retired people who have returned to Oxford to spend their remaining days. Residents are served by the Tennessee Valley Authority for electric power and South Central Bell for telephone service (over ninty percent of the homes have telephones). Since Oxford has a very low crime rate and a high police-to-resident ratio, the use of unlisted phone numbers is almost unheard-of in the town.

Industry
The University

The University of Mississippi, affectionately called "Ole Miss," is the largest employer in the area. The University has 505 faculty members, 225 professional staff members, and 1,020 clerical and blue-collar workers on its payroll. In addition, the student body is composed of some 9,600 students who come from predominately middle- to upper-class family backgrounds. Known somewhat as a "good time" institution, students frequently party in other parts of the state or country.

Since the University places emphasis on research and publishing, faculty members receive encouragement to do the same. The results of their research productivity were frequently presented at academic conferences throughout the U.S. This required faculty to travel to these conferences by either car or plane. This type of travel was only part of the University's travel plans. Faculty recruiting was constantly going on to replace existing faculty or to fill new positions on campus. Additional travel was done by the administration and professional staff to attend seminars, give briefings and to carry out a myriad of other duties. For the majority of these people, Memphis represented the gateway to Oxford.

Light Industry

Oxford was not simply a university town. There was several divisions of major corporations that engaged in light industry and were headquartered in the city. Emerson

Exhibit 1   Map of Mississippi

Electric's Small Motor Division was the largest single employer (over 500 people) in town other that the University. In addition, Chambers Corporation, manufacturing drop-in stoves and oven units for Sears; Champion Building Product's Novaply Division, making particle board; and Kellwood Manufacturing, producing clothing, were also located in Oxford. These firms had a number of executives who traveled quite extensively to their headquarters or other regional operations. Infrequently, corporate jets were seen at the local airport but, due to lack of space, runway length and ILS (instrument landing systems), this was not the most frequently used form of transportation.

Government
Not only was there the University and light industry, but a number of state and federal agencies were present in and around Oxford. The U.S. government had located the U.S. Federal District Court in a new building just off the town square. The federal government had the Department of Agriculture's Sedimentation Research Laboratory, Hydrology Laboratory and the Soil Conservation Service, as well as the Southern Forest Service in Oxford. The state of Mississippi chose Oxford as the site for the Regional Rehabilitation Center and Regional Mental Retardation Center. Employees of these state and federal agencies did extensive traveling throughout the state and to Washington, D.C.

In short, Oxford was a unique city for such a rural setting. There were a number of diverse professionals who had to travel for their work. These travel plans were in addition to pleasure and business travel of these and other people residing in Oxford. (The city has a high proportion of medical doctors, lawyers and small business owners.)

Travel Market and Competition

Travel Market

The out-traveler from Oxford was typified as a businessperson representing the University, local business firms and federal or state agencies. Also, the pleasure market consisted of the occasional family trip during Christmas, spring or the summer holidays. There was some student market travel for the purpose of recreation and recruiting trips, but it was not a significant proportion of the total market.

The in-traveler to Oxford consisted of people calling on firms, governmental agencies or corporate recruiters. University business included visits by athletic recruits, visiting lecturers, performers and people attending continuing education programs on campus. Other in-travelers were visiting relatives and those coming for various lengths of stay, especially during the holiday season.

Travel information and reservations could be obtained through two sources. The first was a toll-free call to any of the major airlines serving the Memphis International Airport. The second source was World Travel Agency, the only active full-service travel agency in town that could handle all aspects of travel—airline reservations, rental cars and hotels. World Travel handled the major portion of reservations made going out of Oxford and was well respected around the vicinity for its travel advice.

Travel Competition

There were four ways that a person could travel from Oxford to Memphis and eventually arrive at the Memphis International Airport. These four modes of tranportation included Continental Trailways bus plus a taxi, privately chartered airplane, Republic Airlines or private automobile.

Continental Trailways made two daily trips from Oxford to Memphis with four stops en route. (See Exhibit 2 for a schedule and fares.) The buses did not stop at the Memphis airport but went to a central, downtown terminal located twenty some miles from the airport. A passenger would then have to get a taxi from downtown Memphis to the airport to make a flight. The cost of the taxi ride was between six and ten dollars, depending on the time of day.

An alternative means of transportation was to charter a private plane at the local Oxford airport. This service ran on prior request and could only carry three passengers with limited luggage per trip. This service was available if the weather was good but could be cancelled on short notice. The cost to the traveler was $48.50 per person for a one-way trip to the Memphis airport.

Scheduled airline service was available to Memphis and back on the newly formed Republic Airlines. Republic was the result of the merger between the regional carriers, North Central Airlines and Southern Airways. Republic's two daily departures and returns did not coincide well with connections in and out of Memphis and would typically result in layovers of from two to four hours in Memphis. (See Exhibit 3 for schedule and fares.) These layovers would be experienced only *if* Republic flew to or from Oxford. It was not uncommon for Republic to cancel a flight in Oxford or

Exhibit 2   Continental Trailways Bus and Fare Schedule

Oxford to Memphis

Lv 10:05 a.m. Ar Batesville 10:40 a.m.	Lv 6:00 p.m. Ar Batesville 6:35 p.m.
Lv 10:45 a.m. Ar Sardis 11:00 a.m.	Lv 6:40 p.m. Ar Senatobia 7:20 p.m.
Lv 11:05 a.m. Ar Senatobia 11:25 a.m.	Lv 7:25 p.m. Ar Memphis 8:00 p.m.
Lv 11:30 a.m. Ar Memphis 12:10 p.m.	

Memphis to Oxford

Lv 6:40 a.m. Ar Senatobia 7:15 a.m.	Lv 5:30 p.m. Ar Senatobia 6:05 p.m.
Lv 7:20 a.m. Ar Sardis 7:40 a.m.	Lv 6:10 p.m. Ar Sardis 6:30 p.m.
Lv 7:45 a.m. Ar Batesville 7:55 a.m.	Lv 6:35 p.m. Ar Batesville 6:50 p.m.
Lv 8:00 a.m. Ar Oxford 8:35 a.m.	Lv 6:55 p.m. Ar Oxford 7:30 p.m.

Fares

One-way	$10.40
Round trip	$19.80

Exhibit 3   Republic Airline Flight and Fare Schedule

Oxford to Memphis

	Lv 10:13 a.m.	Ar 10:43 a.m.
	Lv 5:05 p.m.	Ar 5:35 p.m.

Memphis to Oxford

	Lv 8:00 a.m.	Ar 8:30 a.m.
	Lv 3:05 p.m.	Ar 3:35 p.m.

Fares

One-way with Republic connection	$13.00
Round trip with Republic connection	$26.00
One-way no Republic connection	$42.00
Round trip no Republic connection	$84.00

Memphis for one of two reasons. The first reason was mechanical failure of the aircraft. Since the merger, Republic flew to 153 cities—more than any other domestic airline. Coverage of such an extensive market brought on an equipment shortage, so if one plane could not fly, another could not be found to replace it in enough time to make the flight. Secondly, the Oxford airport did not have an instrument landing system to guide aircraft during inclement weather. Therefore, a ceiling of 2,000 feet and visibility of one mile was required for a plane to land. After a period of time, Oxford residents became disenchanted with the service and began using their automobiles to get to the Memphis airport.

Driving one's own car to Memphis was the most common means of getting to the airport if one wanted to be sure to arrive on schedule. However, the rising cost of gasoline was starting to take hold and people thought twice about driving someone to the airport and returning home. This would cost approximately twenty to thirty dollars in gasoline if a trip back and forth had to be made. Alternatively, a person could drive to the airport and park the car for the period of the trip. Parking was currently four dollars per day for long-term or ten dollars per day for short-term parking. Hertz recently calculated that it costs an individual $.384 per mile to operate a mid-size car when all costs of operation are included.

Exhibit 4   Estimated Cost of Operating Limousine Service

Fixed Costs	Per Year	Per Month
Vehicle $11,000 ÷ 2 (2 year life)	$5,500.00	$458.33
License—ICC	450.00	37.50
Attorney fees	1,100.00	91.66
State tags	200.00	16.67
Advertising (pre-start)	500.00	41.67
Total	$7,750.00	$645.83

Variable Costs (2 trips/day–30 day month)	Per Month
Driver salaries	$900.00
Fuel	900.00
Maintenance	100.00
Advertising	50.00
Printing	50.00
Commissions to Travel Agency	100.00
Total	$2,100.00

The January 18th Meeting

"Well, what do you guys still think of the limousine business?" asked Newman. "Do you still think it is a worthwhile idea after you've had a week to mull it over?"

"I mentioned the concept to several different people," volunteered Ranford," and the majority of them think it's a great idea. They had several questions though that I couldn't answer at the time. These involved the frequency of service, times of the day it would run, how much it would cost and so on. These are definitely questions we're going to have to address before we can initiate service."

Gary Knox chimed in, "The initial reaction I have had from folks on the square has been quite good. They think the idea has merit but they asked some of the same questions Bill was asked. Do we have any idea of how much this little venture is going to cost us?"

"Funny you should mention that," said Newman. "I've done a little snooping around and talked to a few people. I ran an estimate of the start-up costs and here they are." (See Exhibit 4.)

"First of all, we must decide on the concept of the service we want to offer because that will determine the type of vehicle we will purchase of lease. If we decide to go with a customized van and executive comfort as we originally proposed, then we are looking at an $11,000 vehicle."

"Let's stay with that idea, Jim, since it is an hour and thirty minute trip," said Ranford. "Your bottom can get pretty sore riding on one of those hard benches for that long."

"Right," echoed Gary.

"OK," Newman continued. "Second, since we are crossing state lines we need to have an ICC (Interstate Commerce Commission) permit to operate. Zab, the attorney, knows a specialist over in Greentown who does this type of thing and he believes it should be no sweat to obtain it. Our other start-up costs will be for insurance, state licensing, commercial tags for the vehicle and advertising."

"Variable costs will involve gasoline, drivers' wages and maintenance of the vehicle. These costs will all depend on how many trips per day we plan to make between Oxford and Memphis. I made a preliminary estimate based on two round trips per day. So as you can see, the estimated breakeven costs for the operation are $2,745.83 per month.

"Let's see those figures again," asked Ranford. "I have my calculator here and I'll run the figures based on what we think we will charge each passenger. If we charge twenty-five dollars round trip, the breakeven is roughly 3.6 passengers per trip. At thirty dollars, it is three passengers per trip for the first year."

"That last figure sounds better," said Gary.

"Right," added Newman. "That corresponds to a fifty percent load factor which is slightly less than the airlines have to have to break even. Let's go!"

"Wait a minute, guys," Ranford interrupted. "I have seen this situation before in my consulting experience and it is contrary to what I preach in the classroom. Before we jump into this venture, we should determine what the demand is for the service, who our market will be, what times we should run, and how many trips to make among other things. With this information, we should be able to make a more intelligent decision. Now, let's get down to brass tacks and decide how we are going to do this feasibility study."

Questions

1. Define the research problem for TLT.
2. What information will TLT need to make its decision?
3. How would marketing research improve the decision–making process for the three men proposing to start TLT?

TULSA METROPOLITAN AREA PLANNING COMMISSION: DEFINING THE RESEARCH PROBLEM

The Tulsa Metropolitan Area Planning Commission has been Tulsa's planning and land use control agency since 1953. It performs advisory functions for elected officials on zoning, development and planning services and advice in Tulsa and portions of Osage County. In 1977, the commission investigated the possibility of conducting a mail survey to examine public use of the park system and determine the need for further development of park and open space land in the Tulsa metropolitan area. The description of research needs was sent out to several research consultants. (See Exhibit 1.)

Exhibit 1   Tulsa Metropolitan Area Planning Commision Survey

Proposed Scope of Planning Services
The Tulsa Metropolitan Area Planning Commission in conjunction with the City Parks Department, the County Parks Department, and the River Parks Authority, agrees to employ a consulting firm to perform the services outlined below as an element of the *Tulsa Metropolitan Park, Recreation, and Open Space Plan*. This survey deals with the element of the overall plan designated as the User Behavior and Opinion Survey.
Services of the Contractor
As a part of this study the consultant will perform the following services:
1. Review previous TMAPC reports and other pertinent park and recreation data from the Tulsa area.
2. In conjunction with TMAPC and the Park Departments, develop survey forms and techniques to determine how Tulsa citizens utilize park facilities and citizen needs in terms of land acquisition and facility development. Specifically, the consultant will:
    a.   Develop a random sample of the households in Tulsa County (and the five–mile perimeter in Osage County) for the survey. The sample will be geographically distributed throughout the ten municipalities and the unincorporated rural areas of the

Copyright © 1981 by Dr. William G. Zikmund.

county. The consultant will advise TMAPC on the size and composition of this sample.

   b.   Develop a mail survey form which can be sent to this representative sample.

   c.   Develop a complementary survey form which can be administered to junior and senior high school students.

   d.   Develop a complementary survey or interview form which can be administered to known recreation organizations in the metropolitan area.

3.   Coordinate the development of the survey forms with TMAPC and the Park Departments so that those agencies can arrange the tabulation of the completed forms.

4.   Assist TMAPC and the Park Departments in pre-testing the survey form so that problems may be resolved before the survey is mailed to the public.

5.   Formulate a system for tabulation of returned surveys and interviews for use by TMAPC.

6.   In conjunction with TMAPC and the Park Departments, analyze and interpret the tabulated results of the surveys and interviews.

7.   Prepare a camera-ready written report which incorporates the following:

   a.   Appropriate secondary data from relevant sources
   b.   Section outlining methodology
   c.   Results of the mail surveys
   d.   Results of the surveys interviews of recreation organizations
   e.   Results of school surveys
   f.   Analysis and interpretation of survey data
   g.   Appropriate accompanying graphs and charts.

8.   Be available to meet with TMAPC and city and county park agencies for a minimum number of meetings throughout the contract period.

Services of TMAPC

1.   TMAPC will designate a member of staff as a liaison with the consultant during the survey period.

2.   TMAPC will be responsible for printing the survey form(s) and for the costs of postage for the mail survey.

3.   TMAPC will designate staff members from TMAPC and city and county park agencies to administer the survey to local recreation organizations and to school students.

4.   Staff members from TMAPC, city and county park agencies will tabulate returned survey forms and return them to the consultant for analysis and interpretation.

5.   Staff members of TMAPC will be cooperative with the consultant in the performance of his contracted services and will be available for consultation with the consultant at reasonable times not in conflict with their primary responsibilities.

Questions

1.   Did the Tulsa Metropolitan Area Planning Commission follow the appropriate research procedure in defining their needs?

2.   Does the research project appear to be comprehensive?

3.   Should exploratory research have been conducted prior to the development of the proposal?

4.   What type of survey would you recommend?

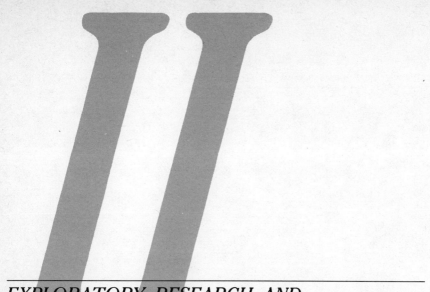

EXPLORATORY RESEARCH AND
SECONDARY SOURCES OF INFORMATION

5

CALIFORNIA FAMILY DENTAL CENTERS: SITE LOCATION USING AREA CENSUS DEMOGRAPHICS

California Family Dental Centers, Inc. was the invention of a San Francisco dentist, Joel Rosenbloom. Rosenbloom had been very successful in his private practice over the previous ten years. Prior to that he had worked at a dental clinic as an associate dentist. He had always wondered about the inconsistencies in attitudes regarding dental care in the United States. In his private practice, located in a suburban area of San Francisco, he saw only middle-upper and upper income patients. At the dental clinic, he used to see more middle or lower income patients, but only if the lower income families belonged to a dental insurance plan, or if supplemental payment was made by the government.

Statistics made available by the American Dental Society indicated that only about two-thirds of the American population sought out and received proper dental care. In a marketing sense, roughly one-third of the population are either infrequent or non-patients. According to the dental society, some of the major factors which inhibit greater utilization of dental services are: (1) lack of education or information concerning dental health, (2) fear of dentists, and (3) cost.

Rosenbloom felt that there was a need for a new type of dental care facility. The typical private dental practice has traditionally drawn from middle to upper income households. Dental clinics have been successful in reaching more middle to lower income households, but they rely on third party payment and have taken on an institutional, impersonal atmosphere. Some dentists tried to establish lower-priced dental offices in lower–income areas, but these were by and large poorly run and delivered inferior treatment.

It was with all of these things in mind that Rosenbloom came across the idea of California Family Dental Centers. He felt that it was possible to offer dental care to lower-middle and middle income households at significantly reduced costs, but in

Copyright © 1981 by Dr. Donald Sciglimpaglia.

surroundings similar to a private practice. He thought he could do this in two ways. First, he would have to generate sufficient consumer demand for the dental center's services. Through tight scheduling and other cost-efficient measures adopted from his clinic experience, he could minimize unused time and the total amount of time each patient would actually be with a dentist. Supplies could be purchased in bulk to cut costs, and laboratory work and other services could be performed on the site by dental center employees rather than being acquired externally. Volume, he reasoned, if efficiently managed, would generate economies of scale. This, in turn, could yield lower fees but, not coincidentally, high profits.

Second, Rosenbloom thought that it would be best to have the dental center office operate in such a way as to closely resemble a private practice. He planned to set up each center with one other dentist as his professional associate. Rosenbloom would arrange for financing, the facility, supplies and promotion under the California Family Dental Center name. The associate dentist would operate the center and take a share of the profits. Other dentists would be hired on salary plus a limited profit-sharing plan.

The overall objective of the concept would be to establish many individual dental centers, with Rosenbloom at the head of the entire organization and in charge of procurement, mangement methods and marketing. The day-to-day operation of the centers would be managed by his associate dentists.

Concept Development

Rosenbloom brought his idea to an account executive at a local advertising agency with whom he had occasionally played tennis. The agency was commissioned to develop a corporate identity symbol (Exhibit 1) and to prepare some preliminary brochure materials (Exhibit 2) based on information supplied by Rosenbloom. With the agency's help, he decided that his overall target market would be:
1. Lower-middle to middle income families without dental insurance
2. Senior citizens
3. Dependents of military personnel (military personnel receive free dental care but their dependents do not)
4. Lower income families who qualify for government dental assistance (e.g. welfare grants)

Rosenbloom wondered a little as to whether or not he should include all of these groups simultaneously in the target market for the dental centers.

Site Location

Time had come to test his concept. Rosenbloom now was in a position to select a site for the location of the first California Family Dental Center office. He knew that he wanted to locate in metropolitan areas with high growth rates. Rosenbloom did some preliminary analysis on a number of areas in California. Of interest to him were population and income figures as well as present competition. Rosenbloom personally knew a dentist in Detroit, Ben Turner, who wanted to move to the San Diego area, so Rosenbloom paid particular attention to that location. Turner had expressed interest in the dental center concept and was potentially an ideal candidate to open the first office.

Exhibit 1   California Family Dental Center Logo

Family Dental Center

Exhibit 2   California Family Dental Center Brochure

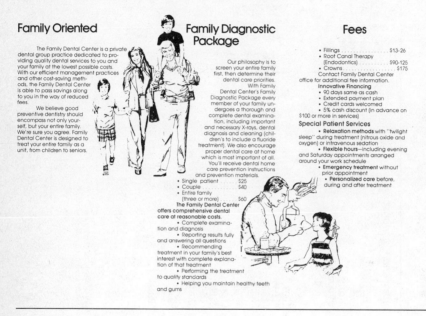

Family Oriented

The Family Dental Center is a private dental group practice dedicated to providing quality dental services to you and your family at the lowest possible costs. With our efficient management methods, and other cost-saving methods, the Family Dental Center is able to pass savings along to you in the way of reduced fees.

We believe good preventive dentistry should encompass not only yourself, but your entire family. We're sure you agree. Family Dental Center is designed to treat your entire family as a unit, from children to seniors.

Family Diagnostic Package

Our philosophy is to screen your entire family first, then determine their dental care priorities. With Family Dental Center's Family Diagnostic Package every member of your family undergoes a thorough and complete dental examination, including important and necessary X-rays, dental diagnosis and cleaning (children's to include a fluoride treatment). We also encourage proper dental care at home which is most important of all. You'll receive dental home care prevention instructions and prevention materials.

- Single patient $25
- Couple $40
- Entire family
  (three or more) $60

The Family Dental Center offers comprehensive dental care at reasonable costs.

- Complete examination and diagnosis
- Reporting results fully and answering all questions
- Recommending treatment in your family's best interest with complete explanation of that treatment
- Performing the treatment to quality standards
- Helping you maintain healthy teeth and gums

Fees

- Fillings $13-26
- Root Canal Therapy
  (Endodontics) $90-125
- Crowns $175

Contact Family Dental Center office for additional fee information.

Innovative Financing
- 90 days same as cash
- Extended payment plan
- Credit cards welcomed
- 5% cash discount (in advance on $100 or more in services)

Special Patient Services
- **Relaxation methods** with "twilight sleep" during treatment (nitrous oxide and oxygen) or intravenous sedation
- **Flexible hours**—including evening and Saturday appointments arranged around your work schedule
- **Emergency treatment** without prior appointment
- **Personalized care** before, during and after treatment

Preliminary research showed that the San Diego area was growing rapidly, but was already moderately saturated in terms of existing dentists (see Exhibit 3). Rosenbloom collected more information about the San Diego area since it appeared to suit his criteria and because of Turner's interest in moving there. (Some of the information available to him is shown in Exhibits 4 through 11.) He was troubled that some of the data were more recent than others, and that some data were for the entire county while the rest were for only the city of San Diego.

From the San Diego Dental Society he obtained a directory which showed the number of dentists in each geographical area. Rosenbloom compared these to population figures for a few areas in which he had initial interest. (These results are shown in Exhibit 10.)

Before proceeding further, Rosenbloom needed to know whether or not the San Diego area really was a good choice for his trial office and, if so, where he should locate the first Family Dental Center office.

Exhibit 3   Population per Dentist Figures—San Diego County and Comparisons

	Total Number Dentists	Population per Active Practitioner[1]	Population per Full-time Practioner[2]	Population per Total Number of Dentists	Households per Total Number of Dentists
San Diego County	1,115	1,909	2,163	1,443	516
Other Counties					
Los Angeles	3,994	1,932	2,241	1,737	
Orange	963	1,938	2,144	1,803	
Imperial	19	4,500	4,500	4,500	
Alameda	805	1,520	1,790	1,377	
Marin	149	1,540	1,784	1,437	
San Mateo	460	1,328	1,533	1,247	
Contra Costa	459	1,502	1,673	1,312	
San Francisco	919	964	1,205	718	
Santa Cruz	107	1,546	1,765	1,429	
Santa Clara	848	1,520	1,672	1,437	
Monterey	127	3,150	3,473	2,133	
California (total)		1,808	2,072	1,595	587
U.S. (total)		2,186	1,453	1,930	652

[1]An active practitioner is a dentist listing clinical practice as a primary or secondary occupation.
[2]A full-time practitioner is an active dentist involved at least 30 hours per week in clinical practice.
Source: American Dental Association.

Exhibit 4   San Diego County Population Projections by Statistical Areas

COUNTY POPULATION PROJECTIONS

BY STATISTICAL AREAS

No.	Major Statistical & Subregional Area — Name	July 1978	1985	1995	Percent Change 1978-1985	1985-1995	1978-1995
	SAN DIEGO COUNTY TOTAL*	1,598,928	1,973,433	2,354,254	23.4%	19.3%	47.2%
	CENTRAL MSA	**391,573**	**421,244**	**423,905**	**7.6**	**0.6**	**8.3**
01	Central San Diego	99,472	108,679	112,024	9.3	3.1	12.6
02	Peninsula	49,119	49,194	48,579	.2	−1.3	−1.1
03	Coronado	16,219	17,009	17,204	4.9	1.1	6.1
04	National City	38,460	40,695	41,452	5.8	1.9	7.8
05	S.E. San Diego	87,066	105,105	105,200	20.7	.1	20.8
06	Mid City	101,237	100,562	99,446	−.7	−1.1	−1.8
	NORTH CITY MSA	**406,917**	**518,911**	**605,755**	**27.5**	**16.7**	**48.9**
10	Kearny Mesa	126,424	139,721	134,009	10.5	−4.1	6.0
11	Coastal	71,352	73,017	73,272	2.3	0.3	2.7
12	University	23,770	42,346	40,768	78.1	−3.7	71.5
13	Del Mar - Mira Mesa	46,207	74,528	105,689	61.3	41.8	128.7
14	North San Diego	23,449	44,030	83,335	87.8	89.3	255.4
15	Poway	38,837	47,211	71,628	21.6	51.7	84.4
16	Miramar	780	754	725	−3.3	−3.8	−7.1
17	Elliot - Navajo	76,098	97,304	96,329	27.9	−1.0	26.6
	SOUTH SUBURBAN MSA	**174,076**	**224,431**	**310,716**	**28.9**	**38.4**	**78.5**
20	Sweetwater	22,770	39,258	72,415	72.4	84.5	218.0
21	Chula Vista	83,621	95,266	99,793	13.9	4.8	19.3
22	South Bay	67,685	89,907	138,508	32.8	54.1	104.6
	EAST SUBURBAN MSA	**295,049**	**353,613**	**436,703**	**19.8**	**23.5**	**48.0**
30	Jamul	4,581	5,748	17,568	25.5	205.6	283.5
31	Spring Valley	42,685	62,217	72,202	45.8	16.0	69.2
32	Lemon Grove	22,820	24,391	24,738	6.9	1.4	8.4
33	La Mesa	49,887	53,497	54,277	7.2	1.5	8.8
34	El Cajon	83,478	92,675	103,153	11.0	11.3	23.6
35	Santee	35,957	48,466	58,546	34.8	20.8	62.8
36	Lakeside	31,610	39,297	52,781	24.3	34.3	67.0
37	Harbison - Crest	7,934	8,810	11,849	11.0	34.5	49.3
38	Alpine	4,985	5,730	12,426	14.9	116.9	149.3
39	Ramona	11,112	12,782	29,163	15.0	128.2	162.4
	NORTH COUNTY	**320,613**	**441,234**	**559,175**	**37.6**	**26.7**	**74.4**
40	Escondido	73,676	103,253	115,513	40.1	11.9	56.8
41	San Marcos	21,840	38,219	50,261	75.0	31.5	130.1
42	San Dieguito	50,017	63,167	76,031	26.3	20.4	52.0
43	Carlsbad	30,217	57,184	91,035	89.2	59.2	201.3
44	Oceanside	64,525	78,775	105,826	22.1	34.3	64.0
45	Pendleton	12,082	11,687	11,232	−3.3	−3.9	−7.0
46	Fallbrook	19,114	21,522	28,179	12.6	30.9	47.4
47	Vista	40,906	57,775	69,872	41.2	20.9	70.8
48	Valley Center	5,926	7,101	8,510	19.8	19.8	43.6
49	Pauma	2,310	2,551	3,016	10.4	18.2	30.6
	EAST COUNTY	**10,700**	**14,000**	**18,000**	**30.8**	**28.6**	**68.2**
50	Palomar - Julian	N.A.	N.A.	N.A.	−	−	−
51	Laguna - Pine Valley	N.A.	N.A.	N.A.	−	−	−
52	Mountain Empire	N.A.	N.A.	N.A.	−	−	−
53	Anza	N.A.	N.A.	N.A.	−	−	−
54	Borrego Springs	N.A.	N.A.	N.A.	−	−	−

*Excludes military.
N.A. − Not available.
Source: San Diego County Comprehensive Planning Organization.

Exhibit 5   1970 Census Selected Housing and Population Characteristics by Statistical Areas

1970 CENSUS
SELECTED HOUSING AND POPULATION CHARACTERISTICS
BY STATISTICAL AREAS

Major Statistical & Subregional Areas*	Median Age (Years)	Median Education	Percent High School Graduates	Median Family Income**	Household Equipment Percent Households Having					Automobiles % Households Having		
					Clothes Washer	Clothes Dryer	Air Cond.	Dish-Washer	Food Freezer	0	1	2+
TOTAL COUNTY	25.6	12.4	65	$10,133	63	37	ï3	23	23	11	47	34
CENTRAL	**23.8**	**12.3**	**59%**	**$ 8,766**	**55%**	**25%**	**8%**	**13%**	**16%**	**19%**	**50%**	**31%**
01 Central San Diego	29.7	12.1	55	7,658	39	17	5	9	9	33	48	19
02 Peninsula	21.8	12.7	74	10,758	55	34	5	26	18	11	49	40
03 Coronado	22.7	12.8	77	10,415	62	39	5	29	19	11	57	32
04 National City	22.9	12.0	50	8,135	64	19	6	8	19	13	56	31
05 SE San Diego	20.6	12.0	52	8,535	74	31	8	8	28	10	51	39
06 Mid City	29.7	12.3	62	9,488	59	28	13	14	15	14	50	36
NORTH CITY	**26.6**	**12.7**	**77**	**12,331**	**70**	**51**	**8**	**37**	**24**	**5**	**43**	**52**
10 Kearny Mesa	23.3	12.5	72	11,392	79	53	5	29	29	4	41	55
11 Coastal	32.5	13.4	80	12,448	48	35	4	31	15	10	51	39
12 University	22.0	14.3	88	13,456	74	66	3	62	24	2	36	62
13 Del Mar - Mira Mesa	27.5	14.1	86	13,356	64	44	1	39	16	3	47	50
14 North San Diego	49.5	13.4	85	11,315	61	51	20	55	16	3	63	34
15 Poway	22.6	12.6	78	12,409	87	66	24	52	36	1	43	56
16 Miramar	21.7	12.5	79	6,889	100	100	0	81	100	0	52	48
17 Elliot - Navajo	25.8	12.8	82	14,513	93	75	19	60	32	1	27	72
SOUTH SUBURBAN	**23.5**	**12.4**	**60**	**9,653**	**65**	**37**	**7**	**21**	**25**	**7**	**51**	**42**
20 Sweetwater	21.4	12.8	79	12,805	9	69	8	54	35	1	32	67
21 Chula Vista	27.1	12.3	60	9,977	59	34	7	20	23	9	51	40
22 South Bay	25.1	12.1	55	8,326	67	34	6	14	26	7	55	38
EAST SUBURBAN	**27.8**	**12.4**	**65**	**10,877**	**70**	**41**	**32**	**25**	**30**	**6**	**41**	**53**
30 Jamul	27.2	12.4	66	9,943	79	32	21	14	55	1	32	67
31 Spring Valley	26.4	12.3	64	11,559	78	50	22	27	36	4	36	60
32 Lemon Grove	27.6	12.3	62	10,513	80	40	15	16	29	9	41	50
33 La Mesa	31.4	12.6	72	11,798	70	42	25	32	25	7	40	53
34 El Cajon	27.0	12.4	65	10,601	63	40	44	27	27	7	43	50
35 Santee	25.3	12.2	61	10,519	72	39	36	22	30	3	41	56
36 Lakeside	26.7	12.3	61	10,866	74	46	36	24	40	4	37	59
37 Harbison - Crest	28.0	12.1	53	9,194	68	35	26	14	45	3	49	48
38 Alpine	38.9	12.3	61	7,948	66	31	38	16	34	8	54	38
39 Ramona	39.6	12.2	58	9,128	79	30	35	14	38	13	53	34
NORTH COUNTY	**24.0**	**12.4**	**65**	**9,307**	**65**	**38**	**15**	**24**	**26**	**7**	**50**	**43**
40 Escondido	30.4	12.4	66	9,584	62	35	34	21	23	7	49	44
41 San Marcos	40.3	12.5	71	10,208	90	52	16	36	38	4	50	46
42 San Dieguito	31.2	12.6	71	11,238	68	41	4	32	24	7	44	49
43 Carlsbad	27.7	12.5	68	10,434	63	42	12	30	21	8	45	47
44 Oceanside	25.1	12.2	60	8,354	60	35	5	18	24	10	55	35
45 Pendleton	20.3	12.3	65	7,546	82	61	6	14	31	3	63	34
46 Fallbrook	32.8	12.4	67	8,179	69	40	21	30	28	6	46	48
47 Vista	31.5	12.3	62	9,073	66	36	9	26	29	7	50	43
48 Valley Center	39.1	12.4	64	9,496	63	40	49	37	36	4	58	38
49 Pauma	29.7	12.1	53	7,093	73	17	15	13	34	10	59	31
EAST COUNTY	**32.3**	**12.3**	**61**	**8,333**	**58**	**32**	**50**	**11**	**34**	**8**	**46**	**46**
50 Palomar - Julian	33.3	12.3	62	8,613	78	43	30	15	42	13	46	41
51 Laguna - Pine Valley	26.7	12.5	72	10,465	49	32	24	14	32	2	46	52
52 Mountain Empire	32.4	12.1	52	7,017	61	34	30	5	35	9	44	47
53 Anza - Borrego Springs	45.4	12.3	60	7,209	24	10	81	10	19	3	55	42

**Families are those households with related individuals living together.
Sources: U.S. Census, 1970; San Diego County Integrated Planning Office.

Exhibit 6   1975 Special Census Household Income Distribution by Statistical Areas

**1975 SPECIAL CENSUS
HOUSEHOLD INCOME DISTRIBUTION**

BY STATISTICAL AREAS

Major Statistical & Subregional Areas*	Median Household Income**	Total***	Less Than $5,000	$5,000-$6,999	$7,000-$9,999	$10,000-$14,999	$15,000-$19,999	$20,000-$24,999	$25,000 & Over
TOTAL COUNTY	$10,982	538,476	69,946	37,071	54,058	81,155	52,277	30,523	29,146
CENTRAL MSA	8,341	162,610	30,826	17,330	19,713	10,166	5,256	3,772	5,222
01 Central San Diego	6,665	51,661	12,523	4,150	4,583	4,576	2,056	980	1,020
02 Peninsula	11,109	21,793	2,751	1,435	2,003	2,694	1,716	1,234	1,733
03 Coronado	13,593	6,401	473	372	652	947	709	475	721
04 National City	7,789	13,306	2,272	1,571	1,820	1,750	731	289	147
05 S.E. San Diego	8,979	24,920	3,816	2,144	3,216	3,856	1,938	776	397
06 Mid City	8,141	44,529	8,991	3,837	5,056	5,890	3,016	1,502	1,204
NORTH CITY MSA	14,065	130,392	9,091	6,153	11,124	20,775	16,457	11,476	11,781
10 Kearny Mesa	12,778	42,957	3,570	2,443	4,409	8,116	5,808	3,497	2,302
11 Coastal	12,336	32,623	3,831	2,075	2,883	4,193	2,585	2,012	3,899
12 University	17,169	6,302	298	222	416	904	1,042	872	823
13 Del Mar - Mira Mesa	14,973	11,324	336	267	770	2,166	1,722	982	900
14 North San Diego	14,413	7,173	240	361	641	990	798	599	637
15 Poway	16,324	9,350	277	236	558	1,544	1,521	1,087	892
16 Miramar	11,032	192	0	3	48	46	16	4	4
17 Elliot - Navajo	17,021	20,471	539	546	1,399	2,816	2,965	2,423	2,324
SOUTH SUBURBAN MSA	10,831	53,305	6,621	4,269	6,417	9,280	5,587	2,685	1,839
20 Sweetwater	16,937	5,173	102	104	327	958	1,017	668	593
21 Chula Vista	10,433	29,462	3,786	2,200	3,405	4,888	2,947	1,424	962
22 South Bay	9,750	18,670	2,733	1,965	2,685	3,434	1,623	593	284
EAST SUBURBAN MSA	11,937	93,538	11,840	6,375	10,161	18,164	11,787	6,422	5,597
30 Jamul	13,209	1,259	95	50	86	146	108	82	81
31 Spring Valley	13,351	11,375	890	598	1,052	2,150	1,523	901	840
32 Lemon Grove	11,785	7,395	723	429	753	1,498	886	400	217
33 La Mesa	12,592	19,222	1,938	1,078	1,742	3,062	2,246	1,305	1,295
34 El Cajon	11,048	27,430	4,993	2,564	3,665	5,348	3,248	1,962	2,068
35 Santee	12,356	10,382	1,020	569	1,295	2,933	1,759	721	330
36 Lakeside	11,902	9,663	1,397	676	1,000	1,941	1,377	717	447
37 Harbison - Crest	10,319	2,599	282	157	236	484	278	134	104
38 Alpine	11,211	1,660	161	111	103	194	105	77	93
39 Ramona	11,232	2,553	341	143	229	408	257	123	122
NORTH COUNTY	10,382	95,328	11,061	6,586	8,737	12,787	8,055	4,572	4,590
40 Escondido	10,535	23,657	3,047	1,421	1,893	3,206	1,863	1,089	873
41 San Marcos	11,733	5,757	422	336	432	769	496	206	209
42 San Dieguito	13,407	14,713	1,361	761	1,089	1,648	1,380	1,028	1,409
43 Carlsbad	12,474	7,901	720	491	619	979	746	515	558
44 Oceanside	8,358	19,924	2,860	1,704	2,231	2,923	1,734	758	640
45 Pendleton	9,468	2,395	120	328	546	483	204	62	46
46 Fallbrook	11,104	5,819	512	311	359	574	373	227	260
47 Vista	9,751	12,844	1,833	1,114	1,400	1,993	1,152	625	494
48 Valley Center	11,278	1,712	106	78	116	176	88	51	75
49 Pauma	7,538	606	80	42	52	36	19	11	26
EAST COUNTY	9,612	3,246	499	172	286	430	224	111	114
50 Palomar - Julian	9,999	1,041	131	54	88	126	78	28	41
51 Laguna - Pine Valley	13,140	678	47	16	41	120	59	45	29
52 Mountain Empire	6,117	965	275	68	100	113	47	13	10
63 Anza - Borrego Springs	16,681	562	46	34	57	71	40	25	34

**Households include families, as well as persons living alone and two or more unrelated individuals living together. ***Includes non-responding households.
Source: 1975 Special Census — San Diego County.

Exhibit 7　1975 Special Census Household Population by Labor Force Status by Statistical Areas

1975 SPECIAL CENSUS
HOUSEHOLD POPULATION BY LABOR FORCE STATUS

BY STATISTICAL AREAS

Major Statistical & Subregional Areas*	HOUSEHOLD POPULATION**					
	Total***	Military	Employed	Unemployed	Adult Student	Not in Labor Force
TOTAL COUNTY	1,466,473	52,924	479,834	47,727	96,214	779,634
CENTRAL MSA	389,444	16,881	124,491	16,654	26,871	201,482
01 Central San Diego	100,604	3,324	34,212	5,380	4,902	51,911
02 Peninsula	49,060	2,058	19,818	2,686	3,533	20,695
03 Coronado	15,386	1,801	4,109	258	1,089	8,087
04 National City	37,836	2,848	9,648	1,463	2,106	21,612
05 S.E. San Diego	85,380	3,785	21,781	2,854	5,459	50,833
06 Mid City	101,178	3,065	34,923	4,013	9,782	48,344
NORTH CITY MSA	370,242	12,213	132,551	9,741	28,676	184,440
10 Kearny Mesa	126,571	4,527	46,253	4,024	10,076	60,658
11 Coastal	69,780	1,032	29,415	2,356	6,576	29,911
12 University	19,267	355	6,581	350	2,705	9,226
13 Del Mar - Mira Mesa	36,003	1,576	12,709	775	1,735	18,883
14 North San Diego	19,215	834	5,016	259	764	12,259
15 Poway	31,928	1,370	9,914	600	1,792	18,111
16 Miramar	791	194	47	3	33	511
17 Elliot - Navajo	66,687	2,325	22,616	1,374	4,995	34,881
SOUTH SUBURBAN AREA	163,552	10,721	44,290	4,723	10,690	92,074
20 Sweetwater	18,764	946	5,521	285	1,589	10,320
21 Chula Vista	80,018	3,818	24,646	2,564	4,943	43,581
22 South Bay	64,770	5,957	14,123	1,874	4,158	38,173
EAST SURBURBAN MSA	270,398	3,836	94,221	8,612	17,471	144,754
30 Jamul	4,052	21	1,289	105	309	2,319
31 Spring Valley	36,216	639	12,307	1,132	2,442	19,603
32 Lemon Grove	21,800	431	7,425	748	1,429	11,716
33 La Mesa	48,711	512	19,056	1,592	4,209	23,161
34 El Cajon	76,193	934	27,009	2,726	4,910	40,116
35 Santee	33,965	826	10,904	768	1,655	19,563
36 Lakeside	29,686	334	9,886	948	1,510	16,765
37 Harbison - Crest	7,447	80	2,470	223	337	4,207
38 Alpine	4,383	16	1,299	110	230	2,697
39 Ramona	7,945	43	2,576	260	440	4,607
NORTH COUNTY	264,084	9,177	81,733	7,772	12,161	151,410
40 Escondido	65,151	398	21,767	2,108	2,908	37,478
41 San Marcos	15,496	116	4,600	357	582	9,794
42 San Dieguito	39,318	182	15,326	1,485	2,427	19,507
43 Carlsbad	21,477	565	7,412	628	1,123	11,519
44 Oceanside	55,090	4,504	14,949	1,653	2,195	31,397
45 Pendleton	9,256	2,395	440	53	173	6,181
46 Fallbrook	16,203	344	4,818	342	782	9,827
47 Vista	35,341	664	10,410	1,027	1,642	21,443
48 Valley Center	4,765	7	1,429	69	206	3,039
49 Pauma	1,987	2	582	50	123	1,225
EAST COUNTY	8,611	86	2,518	209	331	5,427
50 Palomar - Julian	2,712	11	913	56	137	1,586
51 Laguna - Pine Valley	1,912	47	588	63	74	1,129
52 Mountain Empire	2,581	28	557	73	81	1,830
53 Anza - Borrego Springs	1,406	0	460	17	39	882

**Households include families, as well as persons living alone and two or more unrelated individuals living together. ***Includes non-responding households.
Source: 1975 Special Census — San Diego County.

Exhibit 8   Age and Sex Distribution—San Diego County

1975 SPECIAL CENSUS

AGE AND SEX DISTRIBUTION – SAN DIEGO CITY

Age	Male	Female	Total
Total Population*	401,862	368,482	770,344
Under 5 years	25,934	24,075	50,009
5 to 9 years	28,309	26,995	55,304
10 to 14 years	32,213	30,068	62,281
15 to 19 years	44,357	33,192	77,549
20 to 24 years	60,625	39,845	100,470
25 to 29 years	41,759	35,124	76,883
30 to 34 years	30,774	27,015	57,789
35 to 39 years	22,728	20,909	43,637
40 to 44 years	20,650	19,653	40,303
45 to 49 years	18,679	18,658	37,337
50 to 54 years	19,261	20,703	39,964
55 to 59 years	15,935	16,263	32,198
60 to 64 years	12,421	14,950	27,371
65 to 69 years	11,918	14,544	26,462
70 to 74 years	7,512	10,386	17,898
75 to 79 years	4,662	7,693	12,355
80 to 84 years	2,627	4,921	7,548
85 years and over	1,498	3,488	4,986

*Includes all military.   Source: 1975 Special Census – San Diego County.

RACE OR ETHNIC ORIGIN OF HEAD OF HOUSEHOLD – SAN DIEGO CITY

Race or Ethnic Origin	Number of Households	Percent
Total	273,816	100.0%
White	230,772	84.3
Black	18,647	6.8
Latino	16,565	6.1
American Indian	630	0.2
Filipino	3,258	1.2
Japanese	1,068	0.4
Chinese	767	0.3
Other Pacific Asian	630	0.2
Other	1,479	0.5

Source: 1975 Special Census – San Diego County.

AGE AND SEX DISTRIBUTION – SAN DIEGO COUNTY

Age & Sex	Total Population*	HOUSEHOLD POPULATION			Group Quarters Population*
		Total	Household Heads	Non-Heads	
MALE					
Under 5 years	53,875	53,805	159	53,646	70
5 to 9 years	58,297	58,182	18	58,164	115
10 to 14 years	69,570	69,261	28	69,233	309
15 to 19 years	68,604	66,319	4,215	62,104	2,285
20 to 24 years	76,392	74,543	42,407	32,136	1,849
25 to 29 years	70,070	68,526	57,560	10,966	1,544
30 to 34 years	53,990	53,203	49,186	4,017	787
35 to 39 years	42,794	42,526	40,493	2,033	268
40 to 44 years	41,209	40,954	39,206	1,748	255
45 to 49 years	38,126	37,918	36,405	1,513	208
50 to 54 years	39,218	39,006	37,499	1,507	212
55 to 59 years	32,792	32,577	31,479	1,098	215
60 to 64 years	26,220	26,994	24,981	1,013	226
65 to 69 years	26,025	25,672	24,748	924	353
70 to 74 years	16,638	16,318	15,540	778	320
75 to 79 years	10,228	9,864	9,271	593	364
80 to 84 years	5,755	5,299	4,782	517	456
85 years and over	3,210	2,722	2,265	457	488
Total	733,013	722,689	420,242	302,447	10,324
FEMALE					
Under 5 years	50,762	50,694	103	50,591	68
5 to 9 years	55,855	55,757	9	55,748	98
10 to 14 years	65,596	65,404	14	65,390	192
15 to 19 years	68,443	65,925	1,977	63,948	2,518
20 to 24 years	74,105	72,628	12,013	60,615	1,477
25 to 29 years	65,679	65,399	11,831	53,568	280
30 to 34 years	53,139	52,900	8,651	44,249	239
35 to 39 years	42,767	42,612	7,167	35,445	155
40 to 44 years	40,869	40,708	7,098	33,610	161
45 to 49 years	38,328	38,187	7,025	31,162	141
50 to 54 years	41,824	41,645	8,300	33,345	179
55 to 59 years	33,556	33,351	7,516	25,835	205
60 to 64 years	31,486	31,206	8,602	22,604	280
65 to 69 years	30,503	29,907	10,937	18,970	596
70 to 74 years	21,124	20,395	9,240	11,155	729
75 to 79 years	15,091	13,970	7,406	6,564	1,121
80 to 84 years	9,572	8,082	4,658	3,424	1,490
85 years and over	6,960	4,874	2,647	2,227	2,086
Total	745,659	733,644	115,194	618,450	12,015

*Excluding Military in Group Quarters.   Source: 1975 Special Census – San Diego County.

Exhibit 9   Population and Housing by Statistical Area—City of San Diego

POPULATION AND HOUSING BY STATISTICAL AREA
CITY OF SAN DIEGO

	Total Population			Housing, January 1980			
	January 1980	1985	1990	Average Household Size	Total Housing Units	Occupied Housing Units	Percent Single Family
ENTIRE CITY	**842,200**	**917,500**	**983,500**	**2.50**	**328,177**	**314,650**	**58.1%**
Military Areas	40,726	41,000	41,000	3.80	259	256	88.4
Civilian Areas	801,474	876,500	942,500	2.50	327,918	314,394	58.1
Public Housing	24,149	24,200	24,200	4.13	6,060	5,843	19.0
Private Housing	777,325	852,300	918,300	2.47	321,858	308,551	58.9
CENTRAL	**108,810**	**116,300**	**123,900**	**1.87**	**56,505**	**53,919**	**39.5**
Balboa Park	1,810	3,600	3,600	3.00	10	9	70.0
Centre City	8,000	9,400	10,900	1.20	5,356	5,100	6.3
Golden Hill	10,000	10,600	11,800	2.26	4,585	4,320	34.6
Hillcrest	14,400	14,700	15,100	1.62	9,130	8,590	29.6
Middletown	9,300	10,500	11,000	1.63	5,838	5,490	21.6
Mission Hills	8,700	10,000	10,700	2.08	4,252	4,130	62.8
North Park	26,800	27,400	27,100	1.74	15,895	15,360	37.9
South Park	15,100	15,800	18,300	2.30	6,698	6,470	66.1
Southeast S.D.-West	14,700	14,300	15,400	2.67	4,741	4,450	69.5
COASTAL	**156,780**	**166,200**	**169,900**	**2.09**	**61,272**	**58,115**	**49.2**
Harbor	33,280	39,000	39,000	2.17	296	295	9.5
La Jolla	28,200	30,100	30,800	2.35	12,427	11,670	68.1
La Playa	9,900	10,300	10,500	2.46	3,655	3,560	86.3
Loma Portal	12,200	12,500	13,000	2.43	5,157	5,010	75.1
Midway-Old Town	8,900	10,000	10,500	1.92	4,712	4,510	19.7
Mission Bay	6,800	6,800	6,800	1.79	3,977	3,800	41.1
Ocean Beach	19,300	19,200	19,800	1.94	10,441	9,950	44.7
Pacific Beach	38,200	38,300	39,500	1.96	20,607	19,320	36.0
EASTERN	**276,500**	**288,500**	**297,700**	**2.70**	**105,770**	**100,900**	**65.0**
Chollas Park	17,900	19,000	19,100	2.94	6,367	6,070	66.1
City Heights	17,300	16,000	15,800	2.29	7,997	7,540	64.2
Elliott	23,500	27,900	31,000	3.62	6,609	6,500	55.3
Encanto-East	21,100	23,800	26,500	3.69	5,874	5,720	89.5
Encanto-West	21,000	21,600	21,900	3.00	7,479	6,980	88.4
Montezuma	19,600	19,400	19,400	2.12	8,006	7,770	57.1
Navajo	35,600	35,900	35,500	2.87	13,031	12,340	66.4
Normal Heights	32,700	33,700	34,600	1.94	17,563	16,800	51.2
Paradise Hills	21,400	23,500	25,400	3.27	7,132	6,490	67.1
Rolando-Redwood	33,000	33,300	33,800	2.36	14,312	13,830	58.1
San Carlos	21,500	22,000	21,600	3.11	7,203	6,920	78.2
Southeast S.D.-East	11,900	12,400	13,300	3.00	4,197	3,940	70.1
KEARNY MESA	**159,600**	**170,300**	**172,200**	**2.71**	**58,948**	**57,565**	**59.5**
Clairemont-East	38,900	39,500	39,300	2.96	13,413	13,150	70.1
Clairemont-North	25,700	25,700	25,800	2.87	9,160	8,970	74.6
Clairemont-South	20,900	20,700	20,700	2.31	8,867	8,600	62.5
Linda Vista	22,600	23,600	24,700	2.68	8,301	8,070	44.2
Mission Valley	1,900	2,500	2,700	1.50	1,277	1,270	10.1
Montgomery	1,000	900	900	2.15	468	465	99.6
Serra Mesa	19,400	19,500	19,200	3.09	6,451	6,300	64.0
University-North	14,000	21,800	23,200	2.16	5,805	5,660	12.8
University-South	15,200	16,700	15,700	3.01	5,206	5,080	79.7
NORTH SAN DIEGO	**87,410**	**119,500**	**155,900**	**2.92**	**30,016**	**28,921**	**76.8**
Bernardo	16,600	23,400	30,900	2.39	7,219	6,960	75.8
Del Mar Heights	6,600	14,800	26,700	2.82	2,412	2,340	80.1
Los Penasquitos	16,100	23,100	30,000	2.82	6,024	5,710	64.2
Miramar	3,359	3,800	3,800	3.86	196	196	94.4
Mira Mesa	37,600	45,400	53,400	3.27	11,866	11,500	82.5
Pomerado	7,000	8,800	10,900	3.01	2,244	2,160	78.3
San Pasqual	151	200	200	2.75	55	55	98.2
SOUTH SAN DIEGO	**53,100**	**56,700**	**63,900**	**3.48**	**15,666**	**15,230**	**73.0**
Nestor	21,400	22,100	23,500	3.07	7,161	6,960	72.2
Otay	19,700	20,600	20,600	3.88	5,185	5,080	87.1
San Ysidro	12,000	14,000	19,800	3.76	3,320	3,190	53.0

Note: Projections based on Series IV estimations published in July, 1977; Series V to be published July, 1980.
Source: San Diego City Planning Department, State Department of Finance.

Exhibit 10   Area Market Potentials Based on San Diego County Dental Society Membership

	Number of Dentists and (Specialists)*	1975 Households per Dentist	1975 Population	1975 Population per Dentist	1985** Population (Est.)	1985 Population per Current Dentist
Clairemont/Kearny Mesa						
Clairemont	60 (19)					
Kearny Mesa	3					
University City	1					
Total	64 (19)	772	148,961	2,327	188,500	2,945
Mira Mesa/Del Mar						
Mira Mesa	8 (1)					
Del Mar	10 (2)					
Total	18 (3)	628	36,056	2,003	63,900	3,550
North San Diego						
Rancho Bernardo	8 (4)					
Rancho Penasquitos	1					
Rancho Santa Fe	3					
Total	12 (4)	562	19,215	1,601	37,000	3,083
La Jolla						
La Jolla	51 (14)	218	26,902	528	29,700	582
Pacific Beach						
Pacific Beach	27 (4)	701	37,840	1,401	44,300	1,640
San Diego County (total)	910*	626	1,488,857	1,636	1,981,300	2,177

*Only 910 of 1,115 dentists belong to Dental Society
**Based on different population estimates than Exhibit 9.

Exhibit 11   Projected Population Growth in Statistical Areas—City of San Diego

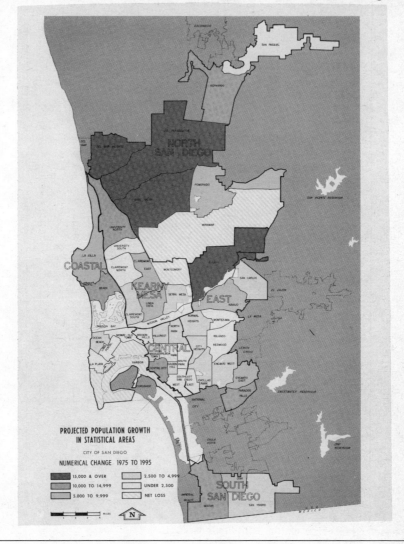

Questions

1. Based on the information given, does it appear that the San Diego area is a reasonable choice for the first dental center?
2. What household demographic factors and other statistics should Rosenbloom pay most attention to in selecting the actual site for the center?
3. What general area in San Diego County would you recommend based on the data available?
4. What other types of research could Rosenbloom employ to help determine whether the dental center concept is feasible?

TOBORTRONICS: USING SECONDARY SOURCES TO DETERMINE MARKET POTENTIAL

Tobortronics had just finished its sixth year of operations. A wholly-owned subsidiary of a major manufacturing company, Tobortronics had been set up to handle the manufacture and sale of an industrial production robot developed by the parent company. Primarily used for transferring heavy material, the robot had uses in machine loading and unloading, stacking, welding, and molding operations. Once its memory was "programmed," the robot would repeat an operation as often as desired. However, the robot's main attraction was that it could replace working people in a hazardous or noxious location, such as a forging operation. It easily performed such actions as picking up a piece of hot metal, moving the piece through a series of production operations such as tempering or cooling, and then stacking the piece at the end of the cycle; thus reducing labor costs and the possibility of industrial accidents.

Priced at $25,000, the robot sales of fifty units over the previous six years had not provided sufficient revenues to cover development, marketing, and manufacturing costs. Profits could be made only if the line were tooled up for mass production, which required an investment of an additional $3,000,000. Tobortronics' president, Mr. Masters, now faced a major decision: Should he drop the item or make the investment for mass production?

As part of the decision making, it was necessary to determine the potential market for the industrial robot over the next ten years. After evaluating the previous sales patterns, Mr. Masters asked his salespeople for information on the types of firms that either had purchased, or had indicated an interest in, the robot.

The major areas of information requested from the salespeople were:
1. The company's industry
2. The company's major products

Source: Reprint by permission from Eleanor G. May, *A Handbook for Business on the Use of Government Statistics,* Taylor Murphy Institute, The Colgate Darden Graduate School of Business Administration, University of Virginia.

Exhibit 1   Data on Industries Most Likely to Purchase the Robot

	Total Number of Establish- ments	Number of Establishments With:		
Major Product Group Selected Industries		20 or More Employees	50 or More Employees	100 or More Employees
Total for All Nine Major Groups	73,604	28,288	15,873	9,632
Rubber and Miscellaneous Plastics Products				
3011 Tires and inner tubes	182	110	84	72
3021 Rubber footwear	65	55	50	42
3069 Fabricated rubber products	1,189	671	441	270
3079 Miscellaneous plastics products	4,996	2,273	1,242	642
	6,432	3,109	1,817	1,026
Stone, Clay, and Glass				
3211 Flat glass	64	39	33	27
3221 Glass containers	120	112	110	109
3229 Pressed and blown glass	185	113	98	84
3231 Products of purchased glass	887	258	126	65
	1,256	522	367	285
Primary Metal Industry				
3321 Gray iron foundries	1,061	774	526	305
3322 Malleable iron foundries	81	75	66	60
3323 Steel foundries	296	248	201	159
3361 Aluminum castings	992	411	199	102
3362 Brass, bronze, copper castings	534	207	86	40
3369 Nonferrous castings n.e.c.	360	180	105	63
3391 Iron and steel forgings	272	189	138	100
3392 Nonferrous forgings	41	31	20	15
	3,637	2,115	1,341	844
Ordnance and Accessories				
1925 Complete guided missiles	65	59	57	52
1929 Ammunition	99	86	79	69
1931 Tanks and components	27	21	17	13
1911 Guns, howitzers, etc.				
1999 Ordnance and accessories n.e.c.	98	62	47	35
	289	228	200	169
Fabricated Metal Products				
3423 Hand and edge tools	667	252	146	87
3429 Hardware n.e.c.	1,041	484	293	194
3432 Plumbing fittings	214	90	62	42
3433 Heating equipment	533	258	161	110
3441 Fabricated structural steel	1,960	1,035	497	252
3443 Fabricated platework	1,465	784	403	194
3444 Sheet metalwork	3,054	811	312	121
3446 Architectural metalwork	1,377	198	71	38
3449 Miscellaneous metalwork	649	280	163	94
3461 Metal stampings	2,710	1,351	721	394
3491 Metal barrel drums, etc.	149	86	69	38
3499 Fabricated metal products n.e.c.	1,266	464	213	89
	15,085	6,093	3,111	1,653
Machinery, except Electrical				
3519 Internal combustion engines	155	96	76	56
3522 Farm machinery	1,618	661	354	211
3531 Construction machinery	651	358	255	181
3532 Mining machinery	212	110	64	38
3533 Oilfield machinery	360	174	113	69

Exhibit 1   Data on Industries Most Likely to Purchase the Robot–Continued

Major Product Group Selected Industries	Total Number of Establish- ments	Number of Establishments With:		
		20 or More Employees	50 or More Employees	100 or More Employees
Machinery, except Electrical (continued)				
3537 Industrial trucks and tractors	351	140	76	40
3541 Machine tools, metal cutting	903	338	193	119
3542 Machine tools, metal forming	350	168	95	58
3544 Special dies, tools, etc.	6,615	1,531	432	145
3545 Machine tool accessories	1,141	428	221	129
3548 Metalworking machinery	430	186	129	83
3551 Food products machinery	642	280	145	87
3552 Textile machinery	560	239	119	60
3559 Special industry machinery	1,129	486	279	156
3561 Pumps and compressors	660	299	202	142
3562 Ball and roller bearings	124	97	85	70
3564 Blowers and fans	287	129	74	50
3566 Power transmission equipment	513	303	190	112
3567 Industrial furnaces	255	117	61	38
3569 General industry machinery	758	346	186	92
3585 Refrigeration machinery	682	360	244	167
3599 Miscellaneous machinery n.e.c.	15,109	2,249	619	206
	33,505	9,095	4,212	2,309
Electrical Equipment and Supplies				
3612 Transformers	190	122	79	52
3613 Switch gear and switchboard apparatus	482	283	178	116
3621 Motors and generators	409	279	232	182
3622 Industrial controls	476	169	100	64
3631 Household cooking equipment	73	49	43	36
3632 Household refrigerators and freezers	36	25	23	19
3633 Household laundry equipment	35	28	26	20
3634 Electric housewares	290	143	114	86
3642 Lighting fixtures	1,213	524	281	151
3643 Current carrying wiring devices	375	185	114	72
3644 Non-current carrying wiring devices	174	105	80	47
3651 Radio and TV receiving sets	340	187	143	117
3661 Telephone and telegraph	106	63	47	42
3662 Radio and TV communication	1,296	782	543	389
3679 Electronic components n.e.c.	2,068	1,213	808	534
3694 Electrical equipment for internal combustion engines	269	132	92	62
	7,832	4,289	2,903	1,989
Transportation Equipment				
3711 Motor vehicles	181	130	111	103
3713 Truck and bus bodies	641	258	133	65
3714 Motor vehicle parts	1,674	785	523	375
3715 Truck trailers	179	108	73	54
3721 Aircraft	125	83	71	54
3722 Aircraft engines	255	202	149	118
3729 Aircraft equipment n.e.c.	893	547	387	265
3742 Railroads and streetcars	96	70	61	47
3751 Motorcycles, bicycles, and parts	91	33	25	20
	4,135	2,216	1,533	1,101
Instruments and Related Products				
3811 Engineering and scientific	667	282	169	96
3821 Mechanical measuring devices	661	285	174	125
3822 Automatic temperature controls	105	54	46	35
	1,433	621	389	256

3. The company's characteristics:
    a. Number of employees
    b. Number of shifts worked
    c. Degree of automation
4. The present and/or prospective product applications for the robot within the company:
    a. Nature of operation: that is, forging, molding, etc.
    b. How many robots were used, or needed, in the operation
5. Whether the company worked on a job shop or continuous production basis

The first two areas, industry and product information, would help Mr. Masters identify his broad market areas. The last three would help him determine whether there were any common characteristics among present and potential users of the robot.

Because of the high cost of the robot, Mr. Masters believed that small companies were not very likely to buy one. He also felt that those companies who were presently using automation in any part of their production processes would be much more receptive to the idea of using a robot.

Mr. Masters was particularly interested in determining whether the company worked on a job shop or on a continuous production process. Job shops generally produced customized products, usually in small amounts, and, because of the cost and reprogramming time required to change the robot for each new application, he thought that only those companies that made long production runs would find the robot practical. Using the robot in a multishift operation would also be more beneficial for a company, since the mahcine would replace people on each shift, thus doubling or tripling the resultant labor cost savings.

Next, Mr. Masters asked his design engineers to give him information about other technical applications that had not been reported by the salespeople. This information included the specific potential applications in consideration of the adaptability, speed, and strength of the robot, as well as the competition offered by other mechanized production systems in use in the industry.

After the salepeople and the engineers had submitted their reports, Mr. Masters spent several hours checking, analyzing, and summarizing the results. He found that the information supplied by his employees supported his concept of the market for the robot. Almost without exception, the companies that had purchased, or showed real interest in, the robot had at least fifty employees and used the robot in a multishift, long production run process.

Since the length and type of production processes varied greatly from industry to industry, Mr. Masters believed that if he had information on the number of companies who worked on multishift operating schedules, he could get a good approximation of his potential market, since multishift operations were more likely to be used in conjunction with long production run processes.

Again taking the information supplied by his salespeople and engineers, Mr. Masters consolidated and summarized the data on present and potential uses of the robot, assembling a list of 340 products and industries where the robot could be used. Although the *Standard Industrial Classification Manual: 1972* had been published, the 1972 *Census of Manufactures* had not. Thus, since only the 1967 *Census of Manufactures* was available, Mr. Masters decided to use the corresponding *Standard Industrial Classification Manual: 1967.*[1] This manual contained numerical codes and word descriptions for all manufacturing establishments in the United States, classi-

[1]U.S. Bureau of the Budget, Office of Statistical Standards, *Standard Industrial Classification Manual: 1967,* Alphabetic Index.

Exhibit 2 Standard Industrial Classification Manual

STANDARD INDUSTRIAL CLASSIFICATION

3481 Fly screening, made from purchased wire
2842 Fly sprays
3999 Fly swatters
3699 Fly traps, electrical
3651 FM and AM tuners
2899 Foam charge mixtures
3069 Foam rubber
2821 Foams, plastic made in chemical plants
2649 Foil board, made from purchased materials
3499 Foil containers for bakery goods and frozen foods
3497 Foil: cooper, gold, lead, magnesium and magnesium base alloy, nickel, platinum and platinum base alloy, silver, tin and zinc—not made in rolling mills
3497 Foil, laminated to paper or other materials
3352 Foil, plain aluminum
2631 Folding boxboard, made in paperboard mills
3079 Folding doors: plastic or plastic coated fabric, metal frame
3554 Folding machines, paper: except office machines
3962 Foliage, artificial and preserved: except glass
3231 Foliage, made from purchased glass
3551 Food choppers, grinders, mixers, and slicers: commercial types
2087 Food colorings
2654 Food containers, liquid tight, sanitary: made from purchased paper
3411 Food containers, metal: made from purchased materials
3551 Food packing and canning machinery: can cleaning, testing, soldering, filling, sealing, seaming, and labeling machines; vegetable grading, seeding, pitting, peeling, shucking, and silking; cutting, slicing, and chopping,

hulling, washing, steaming, mixing, and cooking machinery; bottling, boxing, wrapping, marking, hoisting. and loading machines; kettles, coils, pulpers, finishers, juice extractors, strainers, wilters, and similar machinery
2032 Food specialties, canned
2037 Food specialties, frozen
2599 Food trucks, restaurant equipment
2599 Food wagons, restaurant
3589 Food warming equipment, commercial
3639 Food waste disposal units
2037 Foods except fish, prepared: frozen
3842 Foot appliances, orthopedic
3949 Footballs and football equipment and supplies, except uniforms
3021 Footholds, rubber
2389 Footlets
2841 Foots soap
3141 Footwear, except house slippers and vulcanized rubber footwear (including custom work)
3141 Footwear, leather: with vulcanized soles
3021 Footwear, rubber or rubber soled fabric
3522 Forage blowers
3843 Forceps, dental
3841 Forceps, surgical
3599 Forges, fan
3542 Forging machinery and hammers
3392 Forgings: aluminum, brass, bronze, and other nonferrous metal—not made in hot rolling mills
3391 Forgings, iron and steel: light and heavy board drop and steam hammer, upset and press—not made in rolling mills
3391 Forgings, iron and steel: made in steel mills
3423 Forks: garden, hay and manure, stone and ballast
3914 Forks, table: all metal
3421 Forks, table: except all metal
2311 Formal jackets, men's and youths'

fied by the activities in which these establishments are primarily engaged. By using the alphabetical and numerical indexes of the manual, Mr. Masters began compiling a list of manufacturing industries by four-digit standard industrial classification codes. (See Exhibit 2.) Since many of the products on the salepeople's list were produced within the same industries, Mr. Masters was able to reduce the list by checking the industry description and list of products for each industry he identified.[2]

[2]U.S. Bureau of the Budget, Office of Statistical Standards, *Standard Industrial Classification Manual: 1967,* Industry Descriptions.

Exhibit 3   Industry Description for Primary Metals Industry

MANUFACTURING

Group No.	Industry No.	
336		NONFERROUS FOUNDRIES—Continued

3369   Nonferrous Castings, Not Elsewhere Classified

Establishments primarily engaged in manufacturing castings and die castings of nonferrous materials except aluminum, copper, and copper base alloys.

Beryllium castings
Castings, nonferrous metal except aluminum, brass, bronze, copper, and copper base alloy
Castings, precision: for industrial and aircraft use—cobalt-chromium, microcast process
Die castings, nonferrous metal except aluminum, brass, bronze, copper, and copper base alloy
Foundries, nonferrous metal except aluminum, brass, bronze, copper, and copper base alloy

Lead wheel balancing weights
Machinery castings, nonferrous metal except aluminum, brass, copper, and copper base alloy
Magnesium castings and die castings
Titanium and titanium alloy castings
White metal castings (lead, antimony, tin)
Zinc die castings

339   MISCELLANEOUS PRIMARY METAL PRODUCTS

3391   Iron and Steel Forgings

Establishments primarily engaged in manufacturing iron and steel forgings, with or without the use of dies. These establishments generally operate on a job or order basis, manufacturing forgings for sale to others or for interplant transfer. Establishments which produce iron and steel forgings and which are also engaged in fabricating operations, such as machining, assembling, etc., in manufacturing ...

... rolling mills

Axles, railroad: forged—not made in rolling mills
Bumping posts, railroad: forged—not made in rolling mills
Calks, horseshoe: forged—not made in rolling mills
Chains, forged steel: not made in rolling mills
Crankshafts, forged steel: not made in rolling mills

Horseshoes, not made in rolling mills
Locomotive wheels, forged: not made in rolling mills
Press forgings, iron and steel: not made in rolling mills
Railroad wheels, axles, frogs, and other equipment: forged—not made in rolling mills
Switches, railroad: forged—not made in rolling mills
Upset forgings, iron and steel: not made in rolling mills

3392   Nonferrous Forgings

Establishments primarily engaged in manufacturing nonferrous forgings, with or without the use of dies. These establishments generally operate on a job or order basis, manufacturing forgings for sale to others or for interplant transfer. Establishments which produce nonferrous forgings and which are also engaged in fabricating operations, such as machining, assembling, etc., in manufacturing a specified product are classified in the industry of the specified product. Nonferrous forgings are made to a considerable extent by establishments classified in other industries that produce forgings for incorporation, in the same establishment, into such products as machinery, motor vehicles, etc.

Nonferrous forgings, not made in hot rolling mills

Titanium forgings, not made in hot rolling mills

(See Exhibit 3.) For instance, Industry 3391—Iron and Steel Forgings, covered drop forgings, press forgings, and upset forgings. After grouping all the products into their respective industry classifications, Mr. Masters had a list of 100 possible industrial markets.

Next, Mr. Masters used the section on Selected Metalworking Operations from

Exhibit 4   General Statistics, by Employment Size of Establishment: 1972–

Item	Establishments (number)	All employees Number (1,000)	All employees Payroll (million dollars)	Production workers Number (1,000)	Production workers Man-hours (millions)	Production workers Wages (million dollars)	Value added by manufacture (million dollars)	Cost of materials (million dollars)	Value of shipments (million dollars)	Capital expenditures, new (million dollars)	End-of-year inventories (million dollars)
3412-- METAL BARRELS, DRUMS, AND PAILS											
ESTABLISHMENTS, TOTAL	157	10.2	98.9	8.1	16.7	71.2	188.8	273.5	461.3	8.4	65.9
ESTABLISHMENTS WITH AN AVERAGE OF-											
1 TO 4 EMPLOYEES E7	21	(Z)	.3	(Z)	.1	.2	.8	1.1	1.9	(Z)	.3
5 TO 9 EMPLOYEES E3	15	.1	.7	.1	.1	.5	1.8	2.2	4.0	.2	.7
10 TO 19 EMPLOYEES E2	22	.3	2.6	.2	.5	1.7	4.7	7.2	11.9	.4	1.7
20 TO 49 EMPLOYEES	31	1.0	8.0	.9	1.6	6.2	19.6	28.9	48.5	.8	6.3
50 TO 99 EMPLOYEES	32	2.5	24.0	2.0	4.1	17.0	48.6	80.0	128.7	2.1	14.8
100 TO 249 EMPLOYEES	33	5.1	49.7	4.1	8.5	36.9	90.0	132.2	221.3	3.8	36.4
250 TO 499 EMPLOYEES	3	1.0	13.6	.7	1.8	8.6	23.3	21.9	45.0	1.0	5.7
ESTABS. COVERED BY ADMIN. RECORD¹ .	16	(Z)	.3	(Z)	.1	.2	.7	.9	1.6	(Z)	.3
3421-- CUTLERY											
ESTABLISHMENTS, TOTAL	134	13.4	102.6	10.9	22.3	73.0	322.3	112.9	427.5	11.7	81.5
ESTABLISHMENTS WITH AN AVERAGE OF-											
1 TO 4 EMPLOYEES E9	36	.1	.6	.1	.1	.4	2.2	.8	2.9	.1	.5
5 TO 9 EMPLOYEES E7	18	.1	.8	.1	.2	.5	1.7	.6	2.3	.1	.4
10 TO 19 EMPLOYEES E3	11	.2	1.2	.1	.3	.8	2.4	1.1	3.5	.4	.6
20 TO 49 EMPLOYEES E1	19	.6	4.0	.5	.9	2.6	7.4	5.5	12.9	.3	2.1
50 TO 99 EMPLOYEES E1	14	1.1	7.5	.9	1.6	5.5	17.3	10.4	27.0	.5	4.9
100 TO 249 EMPLOYEES	25	4.0	26.8	3.4	6.7	19.6	55.7	38.2	91.5	1.6	20.7
250 TO 499 EMPLOYEES	5	1.6	11.8	1.4	2.7	9.3	22.4	13.8	35.8	.9	9.0
500 TO 999 EMPLOYEES	3	5.8	50.0	4.4	9.6	34.3	213.2	42.5	251.6	8.0	43.3
1,000 TO 2,499 EMPLOYEES	3	(D)	(D)	(D)	(D)	(D)	(D)	(D)	(D)	(D)	(D)
ESTABS. COVERED BY ADMIN. RECORD¹ .	40	.1	1.0	.1	.2	.6	2.3	.8	3.2	.1	.6
3423-- HAND AND EDGE TOOLS, NEC											
ESTABLISHMENTS, TOTAL	626	39.3	343.0	31.1	62.0	240.7	780.0	473.3	1 233.1	33.5	268.1
ESTABLISHMENTS WITH AN AVERAGE OF-											
1 TO 4 EMPLOYEES E9	215	.4	2.7	.3	.6	1.9	7.5	4.8	12.3	.3	2.8
5 TO 9 EMPLOYEES E7	69	.5	3.6	.4	.7	2.5	7.4	4.2	11.6	.3	2.3
10 TO 19 EMPLOYEES E1	87	1.2	10.1	1.0	1.9	6.5	21.0	13.0	33.5	.7	5.5
20 TO 49 EMPLOYEES	109	3.4	27.9	2.8	5.3	18.9	57.2	33.0	89.6	2.8	13.9
50 TO 99 EMPLOYEES	62	4.4	35.4	3.5	6.8	24.8	76.6	52.1	126.6	7.6	22.8
100 TO 249 EMPLOYEES	42	6.3	50.4	4.9	10.0	35.3	114.0	75.7	183.4	3.8	34.4
250 TO 499 EMPLOYEES	26	9.8	87.9	8.2	16.7	67.5	197.8	108.0	298.8	7.4	68.3
500 TO 999 EMPLOYEES	12	8.4	77.1	6.7	13.1	54.0	192.1	114.0	308.1	7.0	70.0
1,000 TO 2,499 EMPLOYEES	4	4.9	48.0	3.4	7.0	29.2	106.5	68.4	169.2	3.6	48.0
ESTABS. COVERED BY ADMIN. RECORD¹ .	221	.6	4.7	.5	.9	3.3	10.9	7.0	17.9	.5	4.2
3425-- HANDSAWS AND SAW BLADES											
ESTABLISHMENTS, TOTAL	91	6.6	56.7	4.9	10.0	37.5	127.5	70.6	194.3	6.4	46.4
ESTABLISHMENTS WITH AN AVERAGE OF-											
1 TO 4 EMPLOYEES E8	13	(Z)	.2	(Z)	(Z)	.1	.4	.2	.7	(Z)	.2
5 TO 9 EMPLOYEES	11	.1	.6	.1	.1	.4	1.0	.6	1.5	(Z)	.3
10 TO 19 EMPLOYEES E1	15	.2	1.6	.2	.3	1.0	2.9	1.5	4.4	.1	.6
20 TO 49 EMPLOYEES	23	.7	5.8	.6	1.1	4.0	11.9	6.8	18.6	.8	3.4
50 TO 99 EMPLOYEES	14	1.1	8.6	.8	1.6	5.8	17.3	7.0	23.6	.5	4.5
100 TO 249 EMPLOYEES E1	9	1.5	13.3	1.1	2.3	8.8	37.2	19.6	54.9	3.0	13.3
250 TO 499 EMPLOYEES	4	2.2	26.2	2.2	4.5	17.5	57.0	35.7	90.5	1.9	23.2
500 TO 999 EMPLOYEES	2	(D)	(D)	(D)	(D)	(D)	(D)	(D)	(D)	(D)	(D)
ESTABS. COVERED BY ADMIN. RECORD¹ .	16	.1	.5	.1	.1	.3	1.0	.5	1.4	(Z)	.4
3429-- HARDWARE, NEC											
ESTABLISHMENTS, TOTAL	1 054	100.2	903.9	79.1	160.3	634.1	2 026.2	1 265.7	3 243.7	91.5	536.5
ESTABLISHMENTS WITH AN AVERAGE OF-											
1 TO 4 EMPLOYEES E8	287	.5	3.7	.5	.7	2.6	10.2	7.4	17.7	.5	3.3
5 TO 9 EMPLOYEES E5	156	1.0	8.2	.8	1.5	5.2	19.5	14.9	34.1	.8	5.7
10 TO 19 EMPLOYEES	128	1.9	14.8	1.4	2.7	9.4	30.3	24.9	55.2	2.0	7.7
20 TO 49 EMPLOYEES E1	187	5.9	45.5	4.7	8.9	29.5	95.1	81.1	174.0	4.2	40.9
50 TO 99 EMPLOYEES	108	7.6	58.3	5.9	11.8	37.9	122.8	94.0	214.8	5.3	41.6
100 TO 249 EMPLOYEES	102	16.3	129.0	12.9	25.9	86.2	288.2	221.0	497.5	17.5	95.4
250 TO 499 EMPLOYEES	47	15.9	121.8	12.6	26.4	83.6	246.9	169.2	410.3	10.9	79.1
500 TO 999 EMPLOYEES	20	13.6	121.5	10.1	20.1	80.0	266.8	173.5	432.5	14.1	90.7
1,000 TO 2,499 EMPLOYEES	15	37.5	401.1	30.3	62.3	299.9	946.4	478.8	1 407.7	34.1	172.2
2,500 EMPLOYEES OR MORE	4	(D)	(D)	(D)	(D)	(D)	(D)	(D)	(D)	(D)	(D)
ESTABS. COVERED BY ADMIN. RECORD¹ .	317	.9	7.5	.8	1.4	5.1	18.5	12.9	31.4	.8	5.9

Note: The payroll and sales data for small establishments (generally single-unit companies with less than 10 employees) were obtained from administrative records of other government agencies instead of from a Census report form. These data were then used in conjunction with industry averages to estimate the balance of the items shown in the table for these small establishments. This technique was also used for a small number of other establishments whose reports were not received at the time the data were tabulated. The following symbols are shown for those size classes where administrative records data were used and account for 10 percent or more of the figures shown:

E1--10 to 19 percent   E3--30 to 39 percent   E5--50 to 59 percent   E7--70 to 79 percent   E9--90 to 99 percent
E2--20 to 29 percent   E4--40 to 49 percent   E6--60 to 69 percent   E8--80 to 89 percent   ED--100 percent

(D) Withheld to avoid disclosing figures for individual companies. Data for this item are included in the underscored figures above.   (Z) Less than half of the unit of measurement shown (under 50 thousand dollars or man-hours; under 50 employees).

¹Report forms were not mailed to companies that operated only on establishment—generally single-unit companies with less than 10 employees. Payroll and sales for 1972 were obtained from administrative records supplied to other agencies of the Federal Government. These payroll and sales data were then used in conjunction with industry averages to estimate the balances of the items shown in the table. Data are also included in the respective size classes shown for this industry.

the *Census of Manufactures*.[3] In this section the various operations involved in most metalworking industries are listed. Within each industry, data are given for both the number of personnel employed and the number of companies performing the operation. Because the cost of the robot was high, Mr. Masters believed that establishments had to have at least twenty employees before they would buy the robot.

[3]U.S. Bureau of the Census, *Census of Manufactures: 1967, Volume I, Summary and Selected Statistics.*

Exhibit 5   General Statistics on Primary Metals Industry

| Year | Establishments | | All employees | | Production workers | | | Value added by manufacture | Cost of materials | Value of shipments | Capital expenditures, new | End-of-year inventories | Specialization ratio | Coverage ratio |
	Total (number)	With 20 employees or more (number)	Number (1,000)	Payroll (million dollars)	Number (1,000)	Man-hours (millions)	Wages (million dollars)	(million dollars)	(million dollars)	(million dollars)	(million dollars)	(million dollars)	(percent)	(percent)
INDUSTRY 3391.--IRON AND STEEL FORGINGS														
1967 Census....	272	189	41.2	345.9	33.4	67.2	265.6	607.4	657.2	1,261.6	45.0	200.1	90	72
1966 ASM[1]......	(NA)	(NA)	41.3	346.3	33.4	70.6	269.4	594.9	687.0	1,273.1	34.6	210.8	(NA)	(NA)
1965 ASM[1]......	(NA)	(NA)	39.1	307.3	31.8	66.1	242.1	512.5	605.3	1,105.8	22.7	192.6	(NA)	(NA)
1964 ASM[1]......	(NA)	(NA)	36.6	276.3	29.5	60.2	214.4	440.5	531.9	961.2	*34.1	165.8	(NA)	(NA)
1963 Census[3]...	272	189	36.3	259.8	29.2	58.3	198.3	395.3	470.9	868.9	17.5	125.0	89	69
1962 ASM[1]......	(NA)	(NA)	40.9	282.1	33.0	66.0	214.1	456.5	484.0	928.8	14.6	142.6	(NA)	(NA)
1961 ASM[1]......	(NA)	(NA)	39.5	257.9	31.3	60.7	189.5	380.3	414.7	789.1	17.5	146.9	(NA)	(NA)
1960 ASM[1]......	(NA)	(NA)	41.0	261.7	32.8	64.2	197.3	393.7	470.4	854.8	15.0	141.4	(NA)	(NA)
1959 ASM[1]......	(NA)	(NA)	40.8	260.4	32.9	66.0	198.9	408.1	462.3	873.3	13.1	132.9	(NA)	(NA)
1958 Census[2]...	302	190	37.7	220.5	30.2	56.7	164.1	315.9	359.7	687.3	14.3	133.0	86	7?
INDUSTRY 3392.--NONFERROUS FORGINGS														
1967 Census....	41	31	10.1	87.5	7.4	16.5	61.4	154.4	178.0	333.1	32.4	72.2	67	5?
1966 ASM[1]......	(NA)	(NA)	9.6	77.8	7.3	16.1	56.5	145.6	178.1	311.4	16.5	68.1	(NA)	(NA)
1965 ASM[1]......	(NA)	(NA)	7.6	59.8	5.6	12.4	42.1	105.4	124.7	220.6	13.0	49.0	(NA)	(S?
1964 ASM[1]......	(NA)	(NA)	7.2	56.9	5.4	12.0	40.0	88.5	110.5	196.1	13.1	38.1	(NA)	(NA
1963 Census[3]...	34	19	6.3	47.6	4.6	10.1	32.5	71.4	93.4	165.1	4.7	34.3	69	5?
1962 ASM[1]......	(NA)	(NA)	*7.0	*49.0	*5.4	*11.1	*38.3	*78.1	*99.7	*175.3	*4.0	30.0	(NA)	(S?
1961 ASM[1]......	(NA)	(NA)	5.4	40.0	4.1	8.4	30.4	47.2	79.2	124.6	*4.7	28.1	(NA)	(NA
1960 ASM[1]......	(NA)	(NA)	*5.4	*38.4	*4.2	*7.8	*28.0	*43.2	*72.8	*116.6	*2.9	23.7	(NA)	(S?
1959 ASM[1]......	(NA)	(NA)	*4.7	*30.1	*3.6	*7.2	*21.6	*37.9	*65.6	*103.5	*1.3	21.5	(NA)	(S?
1958 Census[2]...	28	19	4.6	27.8	3.5	6.8	19.4	36.8	58.1	98.7	2.0	20.9	85	*
INDUSTRY 3399.--PRIMARY METAL PRODUCTS, N.E.C.														
		271	21.7	178.4				142.7	85.1	231.7	*9.7	15.0	(NA)	
1961 ASM[1]......	(NA)	(NA)	10.5	59.7	8.0	17.1	41.6	114.5	67.8	166.9	*7.0	13.3	(NA)	[S?
1960 ASM[1]......	(NA)	(NA)	10.5	59.7	8.0	17.1	39.5	104.4	57.9	161.6	*5.8	11.9	(NA)	5?
1959 ASM[1]......	(NA)	(NA)	10.1	56.1	7.8	16.2	37.6	100.0	56.3	158.5	6.3	11.5	(NA)	5?
1958 Census[2]...	581	149	9.8	52.7	7.4	14.8	35.1	90.7	50.1	141.2	3.6	14.4	98	?

Note: In 1967, 1963, and 1958, the number of companies in industry 3391 was 248, 248, and 287, respectively; in industry 3392: 37, 32, and 36; industry 3399: 868, 695, and 567. The 1967 company counts include the small companies whose data were estimated from administrative records. The number of such companies is shown in table 4.

Standard notes: - Represents zero.   (X) Not applicable.   (NA) Not available.   (D) Withheld to avoid disclosing figures for individual companies.   (S) Withheld because the estimate did not meet publication standards, either on the basis of the associated standard error of estimate or on the basis of a consistency review.   (*) These figures either have associated standard errors exceeding 15 percent or are not consistent with other Census series and related data. Thus, these estimates may be of limited reliability.

[1]Based on a representative sample of establishments canvassed in the annual survey of manufactures (ASM). These estimates may differ from the results of a complete canvass of all manufacturing establishments. The percentage standard errors of the 1966/1965 relatives for employment and value added for industry 3391 were 1 and 1, industry 3392 were 3 and 3, and industry 3399 were 4 and 3, respectively.

[2]Data prior to 1958 appear in Volume II, 1963 Census of Manufactures, in table 1 of the chapter devoted to this industry.

[3]The figures for 1963 are not strictly comparable with those for earlier years. Value added by manufacture for 1963 on a basis comparable with earlier years is $176.8 million.

Industries such as 3421—Cutlery, were therefore removed from the industry list because there were not enough establishments having twenty or more employees and that employed the production operations where the robot was useful. (See Exhibit 4.) By analyzing metalworking establishments on the above basis, Mr. Masters cut his final list to eighty-three industries with the best market potential. (This list is shown in Exhibit 1, and is arranged by major product groups.)

Mr. Masters' next step was to compute the total number of establishments to which the robot might be sold. He decided not to consider geographic distribution, and instead used nationwide figures. He was interested primarily in establishments that employed fifty or more, and 100 or more people. To obtain these figures, he used the statistics tables for each industry group in the *Census of Manufactures.*[4] From this publication, he took the number of establishments with over 100 employees. (See Exhibit 5.) To obtain the total of those establishments with fifty or more employees, he added the number of establishments in the category of fifty to ninety-nine employees to his totals from the above.

Mr. Masters decided to obtain the total number of establishments within each industry to compare them with his other figures. He also obtained the information

---

[4]U.S. Bureau of the Census, Census of Manufactures: 1967, *Volume II, Industry Statistics, Part 2, Major Groups,* pp. 25–33.

on those establishments with twenty or more employees, as he hoped that the production line process might eventually lower the price sufficiently so that smaller companies could afford the robot. He then added all his data by major industry groups to check with the grand total figures, shown in Exhibit 1.

Mr. Masters had found no information on the number of shifts worked by industry. He asked his salespeople for their judgment on how many of the firms that they visited typically operated more than one shift on a regular basis. Their opinion was that roughly forty percent used multiple shifts. Mr. Masters was then able to make his market size calculations. He believed that multiple shift companies with over 100 employees constituted his "most likely" market; that is, the market where he would make the majority of his sales. To make this calculation he took the total number of the establishments in the nine major product groups from Exhibit 1, and multiplied that figure by the estimated percentage of firms on multiple shifts:

> *"Most likely" market (over 100 employees)*
>
> 9,632 establishments (from Exhibit 1)
> x .40 (salespeople's estimate for multishifts)
> 3,853 potential customers

Mr. Masters thought that firms with 51 to 100 employees also were potential customers, but he was less sure of the profitability and adaptability of the robot to this size company. Therefore, he believed that a market projection including the figures on the 51 to 100 employee establishments would be "optimistic" rather than "most likely." When making this calculation, Mr. Master looked not only at the total market for establishments with over 50 employees, but also at the incremental market for establishments with 51 to 100 employees:

> *"Optimistic" market (over 50 employees)*
>
> 15,873 establishments (from Exhibit 1)
> x .40 (salespeople's estimate for multishifts)
> 6,349 potential customers

> *"51 to 100 employee" market increment*
>
> 6,349 potential customers with over 50 employees
> − 3,853 potential customers with over 100 employees
> 2,496 potential customers with 51 to 100 employees

Mr. Masters also wanted to see what his eventual market might be if he were able to reduce the robot's price through mass production. If the price could be lowered to the point where firms with only twenty employees could afford the robot, an additional 4,966 companies would be potential customers, resulting in a total market of 11,315 potential robot users:

> *"Lower price" market (over 20 employees)*
>
> 28,288 establishments (from Exhibit 1)
> x .40 (salespeople's estimate for multishift)
> 11,315 potential customers

"21 to 50 employee" market increment

11,315 potential customers with over 20 employees
− 6,349 potential customers with over 50 employees
4,966 potential customers with 21 to 50 employees

With these figures in mind, Mr. Masters now had to make his decision—could his salespeople sell a large enough share in these markets to justify the new production line?

Question

1.   Visit your library and update this information.

7

HOWARD GALLERIES: USING SECONDARY SOURCES FOR SITE LOCATION

As the cold winds of winter gave way to the soft, spring winds from the plains of Texas, Malcolm Howard's mind began drifting again to the vision he had held for the last twenty-eight years. Every spring, Howard thought of how he would give up his job as a representative for several North Carolina furniture companies and start his own furniture store. He believed he knew the business as well as anyone in Dallas, Texas, and could match his selection of lines with those of his prospective clients. Over the years, he had kept careful records of the price lines, styles, models, mix of room types selling at certain seasons, the manufacturers popular and unpopular with buyers and the ultimate customer. During this period, he had carefully set aside a very sizeable nest egg that he could use either for his working capital in the new store or for his retirement some ten years later.

Howard's friends would often ask him why he wanted to open a retail furniture store when he appeared to be doing quite well as a manufacturers' representative. Howard's response was always a wink of the eye and the pat response, "It's in my blood." While this wasn't only a subterfuge, Howard did know the margins in the furniture industry. As a representative, he would typically earn five to ten percent of the furniture's selling price to a retail outlet. However, as a retailer, the typical markup was 100 to 200 percent of the wholesale price. And, if a retailer could find and market closeouts on certain lines, the margins could be as high as 400 percent. Howard thought of how much more he could be earning and stashing away for his retirement if he had his own store. He realized that the store margins did not represent pure profit since there were additional inventory carrying costs, lease costs, utilities, showroom setups, insurance and the like associated with ownership. His own detailed pro forma income sheets, however, indicated that he could at least double his net earnings if he found the right location and marketed to the right segment of the population.

Copyright © 1980 by Dr. William J. Lundstrom

Howard's Furniture Store Concept

Malcolm Howard had been associated with furniture in one way or another all his life. Upon high school graduation, Malcolm went to work in his uncle's small furniture store in Bellefonte, Pennsylvania. His Uncle Walt and Aunt Patricia showed him the ropes of the business from repairing dents and scratches to waiting on a customer browsing and successfully turning it into a sale. Two years later, Malcolm was drafted and spent his service obligation in southwest Texas.

He fell in love with Texas and decided to make his home permanently in the Lone Star State. When discharged, he went straight to Dallas where he had spent a number of his military leaves and went to work for Weir's furniture in near north Dallas. Later, Malcolm became good friends with several independent manufacturers' reps carrying a number of furniture lines who convinced him to go to work with them. His success in the north Texas area provided him with a good income and a good following among the smaller stores in and around the Dallas area. In 1960, he set out on his own and established Howard's Furniture Representative, Inc. Initially the company carried only lines of furniture produced by small North Carolina firms which required additional sales effort to convince the retail outlets to carry the merchandise. Howard's hard work began to pay off and the firm grew slowly into a reputable and aggressive company. This attracted the attention of several larger manufacturers who wanted a more aggressive selling effort in Texas. By 1975, Howard was representing several lines of Thomasville, Hendredon and American Drew furniture in the north Texas region.

In late 1980, the dream of having his own store began to haunt him once again. He let this lie dormant over the winter until the winds of spring began to rustle the cobwebs of his mind. His only child, Lara, had just married at Christmas to Bradley Conley, son of a prominent Dallas physican. Brad had no desire to enter the medical profession and had expressed an interest in joining his father-in-law in the furniture business. Howard knew he could work the boy into and up in the rep firm and provide himself with the opportunity of operating the retail store.

Howard wanted to operate a store that would appeal to middle and lower-upper class families. His current line of goods would fit nicely into this market segment and he was sure he could get the manufacturers to allow him to sell these lines in his own retail establishment. (Most of the lines Howard carried were sold on a selective distribution basis and in stores that maintained a quality image.) In addition to the lines of furniture, Howard also wanted to include accessories, custom draperies, carpeting and he also wanted to have an interior designer for his customers. Thus, he could insure a full-service store and a start-to-finish capability for all his customers' needs.

A Time for Decision

Since Dallas had been his home for thirty years, the store would be opened there. Howard was no fool; he recognized that Dallas was one of the fastest–growing SMSA's in the country. A number of major corporations had recently moved their headquarters to Dallas and the state's central location in the U.S. made it an ideal distribution center. The housing boom in Dallas was primarily in a northern and northeasterly direction from downtown, so the store had to be situated somewhere in this general vicinity.

Howard knew he was not an expert in marketing research and store location but had some feel for the general market. Between his regular sales calls, he would scan the north Dallas territory for potential sites and vacant properties that could be prime candidates for his new store. One morning he saw an advertisement in the

Exhibit 1   Potential Store Location Sites on Census Tract Map

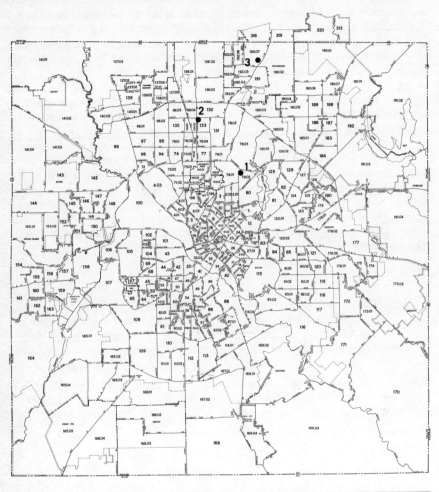

Southwest Edition of the *Wall Street Journal* for a seminar on the "Dollars and Sense of Marketing Research," sponsored by the Cox School of Business at Southern Methodist University. After reading the ad, he called and reserved a place in the seminar which he attended two weeks later. Although much of the seminar subject matter was beyond his needs and comprehension, he did learn about the existence of U.S. Bureau of the Census data and he felt this data could be useful in making his decision as to where his new store should be located.

Where to Locate?

In his travels around Dallas, Howard had identified three potential properties for the store.

- *Location 1* was in northwest Dallas at a site previously used by a Safeway supermarket. It was on a major east-west thoroughfare surrounded by single-family houses and one of the largest concentrations of apartment complexes in Dallas.

■   *Location 2* was in north Dallas in the heart of an all residential, single-family housing unit community. The building had housed several smaller speciality stores but the owner was willing to convert it to one large store for Howard's showroom. It was located on a major north-south street in an open-air mall which had more than adequate parking.

■   *Location 3* was in far-north Dallas just south of the county line. The building was currently under construction near a freestanding K-Mart and would be ready to lease in six months. The building was just off the only north-south freeway going into downtown Dallas and could serve both north Dallas and the south portion of Collin County. There was extensive building of new homes in this area which would likely continue for the next five years.

Using the knowledge he gained from the research seminar, Howard went to the Dallas County Library and photocopied a number of pages from the census data on Dallas County. This information and the locations of the three sites on a census tract map of Dallas were the inputs he would use in choosing the location for the future home of Howard's Galleries. (This information is available in Exhibit 1, and the Dallas Census Report.)

Questions

1.   Develop a profile of the clientele you would expect to find in each location.
2.   Which of the three store locations is best suited for Howard's intended store?
3.   What other information would be helpful in reaching this location decision?

SUNCOAST NATIONAL BANK:
A FOCUS GROUP STUDY

Suncoast National Bank maintains its headquarters and twenty-three branch offices in the San Diego metropolitan area. As such, Suncoast National is one of the largest locally headquartered banks in the region. Most of the other major financial institutions located in the San Diego area (such as Bank of America and Security Pacific Bank) are headquartered in either Los Angeles or San Francisco.

The San Diego metropolitan area presently has a population of about 1.8 million persons. It is the second largest city in California and is the eighth largest metropolitan area in the United States. Figures from the U.S. Census show that the San Diego area grew roughly 35 percent in population between 1970 and 1979. Estimates indicate further growth of about 20 percent by 1985.

Newcomer Project

Steven Bennett, the marketing research analyst for Suncoast National, was impressed with these population growth figures. In recent years Suncoast had been losing market share to other banks and its management was looking to the marketing area to help retain its place in the market. Bennett's direct superior, Bob Redmund, had asked him to give some thought to any research that could be conducted to help him formulate Suncoast National's marketing strategy.

Bennett was aware of programs used by banks in other cities which targeted new people moving into the area. In particular, he was familiar with one such "new-comer" program conducted by a bank in Atlanta which was so successful that it had earned the bank an award from the Bank Marketing Association. No doubt, Bennett thought, it probably also earned its originator a substantial raise in salary.

As he understood it, the Atlanta program worked this way. The bank accumu-

Copyright © 1981 by Dr. Donald Sciglimpaglia

lated the names of persons about to move to Atlanta from elsewhere and names of persons who had moved there within a very short time. The names were obtained through Atlanta employers, the Chamber of Commerce, realtors and welcoming services such as Welcome Wagon and Hospitality Hostess. The bank offered each person a complete kit to help make their transition a little easier. Included in the kit were such things as maps, city guides, guides to services, bus schedules and discount coupons. Each person contacted was sent an engraved invitation which entitled him or her to receive a newcomer kit at one of the bank's branch offices. Reportedly, the Atlanta bank had been successful in converting into new customers many of those who accepted the invitation.

Since San Diego is a high-growth and highly mobile community, Bennett thought that such a program should be investigated by Suncoast National. Accordingly, he wrote the memo seen in Exhibit 1 to Redmund.

Newcomer Focus Group Studies

Bennett received approval to proceed with the project. He knew that, in addition to information that would be available from industry sources, he needed to know more about the feelings and experiences of newcomers. This would assist him in designing a better survey questionnaire for the mail study. Bennett was especially interested in knowing about the problems that were encountered in moving, how newcomers selected a new bank and what kinds of information newcomers thought would be useful to them. All of this would be thoroughly evaluated in the survey.

Bennett selected Professional Interviewing to conduct two focus groups to help find out more about problems experienced by newcomers. That firm, a local field interviewing company, was instructed to recruit twelve persons who had moved into San Diego within the last month for each of two group interview sessions. Bennett prepared the outline seen in Exhibit 2 for the interviews.

Paula Jackson, the owner of Professional Interviewing, was to be the group moderator. For the first group session, seven participants, six women and one man, attended. The transcript of that session is seen in Exhibit 3.

Exhibit 1 Suncoast National Bank—Interdepartmental Communication

TO: Robert R. Redmund, Vice President, Marketing
FROM: Steven R. Bennett, Marketing Research Analyst
DATE: July 21, 1981
SUBJECT: NEWCOMER RESEARCH PROPOSAL

Purpose and Background: That we live in a highly mobile society is reflected by the fact that approximately one out of five U.S. citizens changes residence every year.

As people relocate, their life styles are temporarily disrupted and certain "needs" become self-evident at their new locale. Among those needs are services provided by financial institutions.

The match between newcomers and financial institutions seems to be a natural one; however, many feel that the difficulty in reaching prospective newcomers outweighs the advantages of designing a newcomer program. Contrary to this belief, the newcomer is one of the best retail markets available to the bank. Rather than expand an entire marketing effort to redistribute the existing market, we should develop a program to tap this newcomer segment with the advantage being that we would have little or no competition from other institutions.

Exhibit 1 Suncoast National Bank—Interdepartmental Communication–Continued

The newcomer program will have to be based upon information. In order for us to identify, locate, and capture this market segment, we must understand the key issues of the newcomer segment, their needs as newcomers to San Diego, and what it will take to attract them to our bank. We must understand how newcomers learn about banks (and savings and loans), who in a family will make the banking decision, at what point do they decide on a bank, and what their profile is.

Research must be undertaken to provide us with the necessary information to design and effectively market a newcomer program.

Methodology: A survey instrument will be designed to gather the above information via mail questionnaire of prospective San Diego residents and newcomers to San Diego. Address lists will be generated by the San Diego Chamber of Commerce and from San Diego Hospitality Hostess. The survey will be conducted of those persons most responsible in a household for the banking activities and it will be designed to gather the necessary attitudinal and demographic information in order to maximize the success of a future newcomer program.

Focus Groups: To better understand the problems that newcomers experience, we need to conduct some focus group research. This research will result in our being better able to design a survey instrument which relates to the needs of this segment. I think that two or three group sessions should be sufficient.

Time Schedule:	*Completed By:*
Focus groups	*August 21*
Qustionnaire design	*September 7*
Pre-test questionnaire	*September 12*
Survey	*September 29*
Data Analysis	*October 5*

Exhibit 2 Newcomers Study Focus Group Outline
General Purpose: 1) to determine problems and inconveniences experienced in moving to San Diego or shortly after arrival, 2) to understand how initial banks were selected, 3) to determine problems associated with banking transactions.
Topics
1. Reasons for moving to San Diego
2. Problems in *planning* the move
3. Problems *during* the move
4. Problems *after* the move
5. How problems could have been corrected
6. Problems related to banking
7. How participants learned about various banks available in the city
8. How they selected initial bank
9. What banks could do to make move less inconvenient
10. What other groups or organizations could do to make the move easier

Exhibit 3 Newcomers Study Focus Group

Moderator I'm Paula from Professional Interviewing and I really appreciate your participation in this group session. As you can see, we are taping this session because after the end of this it would be impossible to remember what has transpired. First of all, we are here tonight to talk about your reasons for moving to San Diego. Let's start out by having each of you introduce yourself and state how you came about coming to San Diego. . .how you got here and where you're from.

Exhibit 3   Newcomers Study Focus Group–Continued

Mary   My name is Mary—and we came to San Diego because my husband works here, and I came from New York.

Brenda   Brenda Cole from Maine—was headed for Arizona but came to San Diego by chance. Came west because of the weather.

Marian   Marian from Kansas City—came here because my husband took a job here.

Lisa   Lisa, Pacific Northwest, read in a magazine that San Diego had the most perfect climate and wanted to get away from Redlands where it was all smog. Came alone by bus.

Anna   I'm Anna, from Sacramento area and I came to go to San Diego State, pre-med student.

Carolyn   Carolyn, from Virginia. My husband took a job in San Diego.

Roger   Roger from Los Angeles, came because of a transfer in the company and liked a smaller city.

Moderator   Undoubtedly, some of you had situations that arose when you got ready to come here, inconveniences that happened to you. They may have been major things or minor things, but no matter what, they were still problems that came about when you got ready to move. I'd like to talk about the problems and inconveniences you had in getting ready to come to San Diego.

Brenda   What do you mean by inconveniences?

Marian   Like changes of addresses in banks or your subscriptions?

Moderator   Things that disrupted your living the way you were living.

Marian   Taking my daughter, who is a senior in high school, away and leaving all her friends. She dispises it. That is an inconvenience. The move itself. The movers were late naturally. The furniture was broken. The claim is still not settled.

Moderator   You mentioned banking, was that a problem?

Marian   I've changed banks since I've been here. I don't like the banking hours here. In Kansas City, the banks were open just like department stores, day and night. So the banking was very easy. Here I started with Bank of America, but they were never open so I switched real quick.

Moderator   What do you mean they were never open?

Marian   They didn't open early, the one near me didn't open until 10:00 in the morning and is only open until 3:00 and we're used to 7:00 to 7:00 hours. I'm surprised by the banks. In such a big place, why not open longer and on Saturdays. I found a bank that is open Saturdays for my checking account. I've never seen such long lines in my whole life. With so many working in such a large population you would think they would accommodate more. You could wait an hour just to get a check cashed. I'm trying to get my account going, just to add a name. The drive-up is open, but they can't pass the card. I have to go inside and stand in the hour-long

---

Exhibit 3   Newcomers Study Focus Group–Continued

lines to do that, and I'm not willing to do that. I learned a long time ago that anything you open up, use the word *or* not *and.* Like Marty *or* Marian —not *and.* Then you don't have any trouble.

Moderator   Brenda, how about you?

Brenda   Trying to weed out what to bring or throw away. We brought only what we could take in the car. We have a few things in storage but not much. Like everyone, I feel the banks out here are the most horrendous situations I've ever seen. I've never found it so hard to get a check cashed. My husband, in his own bank, has to show his drivers license, and if you don't have a picture ID, you're out of luck. They are too untrusting, it's outrageous. I've been in many cities in many states and have never run into anything so outrageous in my entire life.

Moderator   Then your difficulty in cashing a check is your main difficulty in banking?

Brenda   Just everything. . .people's attitudes. Out here it's like everyone is for themselves, no one wants to help anyone else. Everybody is on their own. The last place I lived was a small town and the people were more willing to help you out. Most people I've run into out here are not willing to be helpful, especially the banks. I haven't been here long enough for firsthand evidence, but from what I've heard, even the residents have trouble. The lady I'm staying near has had to change banks three times in the last year.

Moderator   Lisa, what problems have you encountered?

Lisa   Well, not really very much. I take life as it comes, living day-to-day. I don't have any money in banks. I would never put money in a bank. Why? Because I don't like the way they do business. I don't like what they do with the money while it's in there. I don't like the interest they give you and I don't like the waiting in lines. I don't like anything about it. The banks aren't interested in us, they just want the money so they can use it.

Moderator   Carolyn?

Carolyn   The moving van gave us the most problems. Many of our things were damaged and many stolen. I don't know how to claim these items. We were delayed one day because the vans won't move less than five tons and we only had two. We paid for five. Also the banks . . . cashing out-of-state checks in your own bank. My husband applied for a Visa card here. Our credit is fantastic but we were denied the credit because they say they have no record of our credit rating. We could not transfer it out here, so fine, they won't use our money, we'll just keep sending it back to Virginia. The service charge out here is outrageous. I had a totally free checking account. No service charge, no minimum balance, everything was free. The checks were free. We figured it will cost about $40 a year to maintain a checking account.

Lisa   So she has the right idea not to put money in the bank, put everything in cash. Also your records are not closed. The government can get your records. They can come in and construct a whole lifestyle by your transactions, so if you want the whole world to know about you, where you bank, where you buy, where you borrow, what church you donate or go to, then just use a bank!

Carolyn   Another thing that surprised me is that when you buy a money order, even in the city, the banks won't cash it. That's wrong. This is just like cash. It was bought and paid for. Where can you cash them? You have to open an account and leave them there for so many days . . . in the city a couple of days, out of the city probably two weeks, and out of state up

Exhibit 3   Newcomers Study Focus Group–Continued

to eighteen to twenty days. A cashier's check is the same. Nobody trusts nobody. It took a friend about thirty days to cash a cashier's check. It was for $1,000 from Las Vegas so they couldn't cash it. The money is there so why can't they cash it? Travelers checks are not acceptable everywhere. Some stores and gas stations will not accept them.

Moderator   Anna, tell us about your problems.

Anna   You wouldn't believe it. Being a student, I have no credit cards, no credit. I have a driver's license and a military ID and it's impossible to cash a check without a credit card. Also, trying to find a place to live. I'm not twenty-one so they won't let you rent an apartment. They would not take my signature. I had to call my Dad and have him fly down, which is $50 one-way, and sign for me to get the apartment, and then fly back home. My parents send me money each month in a cashier's check, but I go through the problem all the time to cash it. I could get my parents to put me on their Visa card as a signer.

Roger   Couldn't you go to a bank and get a check guarantee card?

Anna   I've heard of it, but I don't have one. I have a military ID and a driver's license. I feel those two should be sufficient.

Moderator   Did you experience any other problems as you were planning the move?

Anna   Yes, getting into school. They sent my application to San Jose instead of San Diego State, so by the time I got it back it was too late to register and I had to go contract register and it cost me $40 more per unit. At the time I was taking fifteen units, so I dropped all but ten units. I paid $400 instead of $100 and after moving down here and everything, I couldn't move back home.

Moderator   Roger, how about you? When you were planning to move from Los Angeles?

Roger   I had no problems moving down as I moved all my own stuff so if anything was broken, it was no one's fault but my own. As far as banking, you just go down and open an account and hope the bank has interest in other personal accounts in California. Most banks don't. I don't feel San Diego is any different than Los Angeles. In transferring down here, Bank of America would not give me a check guarantee card here, even though my account was with them in L.A., because they say I have not established my record with them. I closed my account with them. I switched. Of course, I had the same problem, but I'd rather give them the chance and build my record than a bank that didn't consider my past twelve-year record where I held two existing loans. I think it's like a franchise, you should get the same service here that you did in the other place if it's the same bank.

Moderator   What bank do you bank with now?

Roger   Security Pacific Bank.

Moderator   Do you notice any difference?

Roger   No. No difference. They all have the same policy. Their cause is not for you. You put a large sum of money into their savings account, you don't ask them their life history, they just take your money and put it in there. Just try to borrow money or try to get your own money

Exhibit 3   Newcomers Study Focus Group–Continued

out . . . it seems to be a different story. The interest they pay you is nothing. They're using that to invest at a much higher rate. You're donating to their cause when you have money in the bank, but yet they're a necessary evil. I wouldn't feel safe with that money at home. I think you need a bank. It's a must! They need some of the starch taken out of them. There are exceptions, some managers are nice but they're very few. Most are VIPs and we are the peons.

Lisa   If we could figure some other way to handle our money that would put them down to size and then they wouldn't by VIPs anymore. They would be human beings and maybe they would treat us better.

Roger   Credit unions are an alternative to banks if you have one; they are good.

Lisa   Why do you feel credit unions are better than banks?

Roger   I think they are more concerned with the people that are in that organization. They make loans to people in their organizations. They come first, not just someone who comes in off the street. If you're not a member, you don't get a loan. They deal more with people who are willing to invest some of their savings with them. They in turn give priority to that person. When you borrow money from a bank, they decide whether it's a good investment or not. What is a good investment to one person may not be to another. If he has a past record of paying back money, they should give him the same responsibility. The money is there to lend. And money should be there to lend when they hold "X" amount of money in savings accounts. When they have money to build new branches and furnish them quite lavishly, then I think they've got money. The bank manager shouldn't feel like the money is coming out of his own personal checking account. Their business is making loans. They don't make it on checking accounts. Even if checking accounts aren't free, that $2 or $3 a month isn't paying the salaries, it's the loans. As an example, we took out a loan for $125,000 for constructing apartments in L.A. through a savings and loan. We were putting $25,000 of our own money into the S & L when they OK'd the loan. We then sold the land prior to construction, never used one penny out of the account, but it cost us for that loan . . . $10,000—it was never used. Not only the cost for the loan but there was the prepayment penalty on the construction loan. Now in personal loans, if I was to borrow that amount of money from someone here, they would not be allowed to do that.

Lisa   What makes a bank an exception? I don't understand, but there is nothing you can do. It's in the fine print, they are above the law.

Moderator   Let's talk about immediately after you all moved here . . . what situations you came up against and what inconveniences.

Marian   Finding the shopping areas and schools. It's pretty hard to find out which schools are for which districts . . . and which ones are good. We have found that the schools here are a little behind in their teaching. Getting your children to feel as though they belong in the new school . . . everyone is in their little cliques and no one wants new people.

Carolyn   I find the people here very unfriendly. It seems that it's each to themselves. The drivers here are wild. I need to get a new driver's license and, I think, California plates. I'm not sure.

Moderator   Brenda, how about you?

Exhibit 3   Newcomers Study Focus Group–Continued

Brenda   Finding an apartment was hard. Knowing what area is good or not. Getting the apartment is hard. They need your life history even though you have the first month's rent and the deposit. They expect you to take a motel for awhile. They feel their apartments are worth gold and you are going to destroy them or something.

Carolyn   They don't want to rent to people with children. I have only an infant but they don't want to rent to me. I think the best thing going on now are the people that are trying to stop these apartment owners from not renting to families.

Brenda   Oh yea . . . and I'd bet that some of you had trouble finding out where to pay your utility deposits for gas and electricity and for the telephone. I had to go to four separate places. We had to wait two weeks for our phone to be installed.

Moderator   If you had it to do over again, can you come up with any suggestions or other ways you may have handled the move to prevent some of these problems?

Brenda   I don't think I would move here. The weather is great, but that's about it. I've lived in a lot of big and little cities, all over, and the people around here are the hardest to get to know of anyplace I've lived. There is a housing shortage here for renting and buying.

Roger   There is no way to solve the problems of housing since it is a bureaucracy. If you could get the bureaucracy out of it, then private enterprises would take over and meet the demands of the people, but it can't be done.

Moderator   Well, thanks very much for coming in to participate. You've been very helpful.

Questions

1. What kind of information should Bennett attempt to get from banking industry sources about newcomer programs?
2. Do you think it was wise to have a group with both men and women included and with participants of various ages?
3. Did the moderator do an adequate job of getting at the information needed by Bennett?
4. Analyze the focus group transcript very thoroughly. Make a list of problems generated and ideas for the proposed newcomer kit.

HAMILTON POWER TOOLS (A): EXPLORATORY RESEARCH

Background Information

On July 13, 1978, Mr. Campagna, the marketing manager for Hamilton Tools, was anxiously awaiting his meeting with the marketing research firm. He felt the findings from the marketing research would change Hamilton Tools from a sales-oriented company to a firm that would adopt the consumer-oriented philosophy of the marketing concept.

For more than thirty years, Hamilton Power Tools had been marketing industrial products by catering to the construction and industrial tool markets. Their construction product lines included tools such as power trowels, concrete vibrators, generators, and power-actuated tools. Their industrial lines were primarily pneumatic tools: drills, screwdrivers, etc. One of their products, the gasoline-powered chain saw, was somewhat different from traditional construction and industrial tools. The chain saw line had been added in 1949, when John Hamilton, Sr., had had the opportunity to acquire a small chain saw manufacturer. Mr. Hamilton believed that construction workers would have a need for gasoline-powered chain saws. He had acquired the business in order to diversify the company into other markets.

During the 1970's, the chain saw market was changing rapidly, and Hamilton Tool executives began to realize they needed some expert advice. Mr. Campagna, marketing manager, felt a major change in Hamilton's corporate direction was on the horizon.

Mr. Campagna had been in the chain saw business for fifteen years. Reports from trade publications, statistics from the chain saw manufacturers association, and personal experience had led him to believe that the state of the chain saw industry

All names are fictitious to protect confidentiality. This case is a modification of the original case that appeared in William G. Zikmund and William J. Lundstrom, *Outstanding Cases in Marketing Management* (St. Paul: West Publishing Company, 1979).

in the last few years was composed of roughly the following markets: professionals (lumberjacks), farmers, institutions, and casual users (home or estate owners with many trees on their lots). The casual user segment was considered to be the future growth market. Campagna wished to insure that Hamilton would not make any mistakes marketing to this segment of "weekend woodcutters," who once or twice a year used a chain saw to cut firewood or to prune trees in the backyard.

In March 1978, when chain saw sales began to slow down because of the seasonal nature of the business, Mr. Campagna and Ray Johnson, the chain saw sales manager, had a meeting with John Hamilton, Sr. Although Mr. Hamilton believed they had been doing well enough in chain saw sales over the past decade, Mr. Campagna and Mr. Johnson were able to persuade the aging executive that some consumer research was necessary. After talking with several marketing research firms, Hamilton Tools hired Consumer Metrics of Chicago to perform two research projects.

The TAT (Thematic Apperception Test) research was completed the first week in July. Mr. Campagna arranged for a meeting with the marketing research firm the following week.

As Dale Conway and Frank Baggins of Consumer Metrics made their presentation of the results of the survey of chain saw users, Bill Campagna, the marketing manager, thought back to the day Consumer Metrics had originally suggested the idea of a TAT to Hamilton. Dale Conway had sold him on the idea with his argument that motivational research was widely used in consumer studies to uncover people's buying motives. Conway had mentioned that Consumer Metrics had recently hired a bright young M.B.A. The young M.B.A.—Baggins, as it turned out—had specialized in consumer psychology and marketing research at a major state university. Conway had thought that Frank Baggins was one of the best qualified people to work on this type of project. Since Hamilton Power Tools had had no previous experience in consumer research, Campagna had been eager to proceed with the in-depth Thematic Apperception Test.

Mr. Conway told Mr. Campagna, Mr. Hamilton, the owner, and Mr. Johnson, the sales manager, that, in the TAT, respondents are shown a series of pictures and are asked to tell their feelings concerning the people in these photographs. He told Mr. Campagna that, while the present study was exploratory, it could be used to gain insights into the reasons people buy. He also suggested that the test would be a means for gaining the flavor of the language people use in talking about chain saws, and it could be a source of new ideas for writing advertising copy.

Mr. Campagna remembered that he had not thought this project would be very worthwhile; however, he realized he did not know that much about the consumer market. During the initial meeting with the research firm, it had been proposed that an exploratory research project be conducted in the states of Illinois and Wisconsin to obtain some indication of the attitudes of potential casual users toward chain saws. The researcher had suggested a TAT. Mr. Campagna did not know much about this type of research, and he needed time to think. After a week's deliberation, he called Mr. Conway and told the researchers to go ahead with the project.

At the meeting, Mr. Conway and Mr. Baggins carefully presented the research results. (See Exhibits 1 through 4 for the TAT used by the researchers.) They pointed out that, in the TAT study, several screening questions were asked at the beginning of the interview. The findings of this study are based on those respondents who either planned to purchase a chain saw in the next twelve months, owned a chain saw, or had used a chain saw in the past. The presentation closely followed the written report submitted to Mr. Campagna. The findings were as follows.

Research Findings

The first photograph (Exhibit 1) shown to the respondent was a picture of a man standing looking at a tree. The interviewer asked the respondent the following question:

> *I have a problem which you may find interesting. Here's a picture of a man who is thinking about the purchase of a chain saw. Suppose that such a man is your neighbor. What do you suppose he is thinking about?*

After the respondent's initial answer, the following probing question was asked:

> *Now, if he came to you for advice and you really wanted to help him, what would you tell him to do? Why do you think this would be the best thing for him to do?*

Initial responses seemed to center around what the man would do with the tree. Many respondents were concerned with saving the tree because they had interest in the tree. It seemed there was some pride in having a tree that beautified the owner's property. Some of the typical responses given are as follows:

> *He's thinking about cutting the tree down.*
> *Why cut a whole tree when you can save part of it.*
> *He could trim out part of those trees and save some of them.*
> *We lose trees due to disease and storm damage.*
> *Trees beautify property and make it more valuable.*
> *I don't like to destroy trees.*

Considering the alternatives to buying a chain saw was the next step many of the respondents took. Basically, the ultimate consumer sees the alternatives to the purchase of a chain saw as:

1. Using a hand saw
2. Hiring a tree surgeon
3. Renting or borrowing a chain saw

These alternatives were in the respondents' minds partly because they were concerned about the cost of doing the job. They seemed to be worried about the investment in a chain saw, about whether it paid to buy one for a small, single-application job. (Another reason for the alternatives came out in responses to a later picture.) Some quotations illustrating these points are as follows:

> *He's thinking how to go about it. He will use his hand saw.*
> *He doesn't have to invest in a chain saw for only one tree.*
> *He's thinking about how to get the tree down—the cost of doing it himself versus having someone else do it. Have him cut it down himself, it's not too big a tree. He'll save money.*
> *He's thinking whether it pays for a couple of trees. If it would be worth it. How much longer with an axe.*
> *He's thinking whether he should do it himself or get someone else to do it for him. Get someone who knows what he is doing.*
> *He's thinking he'll rent a chain saw for a small area and would buy one for a large area.*
> *The best way to get a job done. A chain saw is faster but a hand saw is cheaper. Depends on how much work he has to do.*

An interesting comment made by two respondents was, "He's thinking about Dutch elm disease." The area had recently been hit by the disease. The respondents were projecting their situation into the TAT picture.

Other statements were made concerning the ease and speed of using a chain saw. Some questions regarding the characteristic performance of a chain saw were raised in responses to this question; however, the second picture covers this area more adequately.

The second picture (Exhibit 2) showed two men in a store looking at a chain saw. The question asked went as follows:

Here is a picture of the same man in a store selling chain saws. Suppose he's a friend of yours—your next-door neighbor perhaps. Tell me what you think he will talk about with the clerk.

The issue most frequently raised was how the chain saw worked. An equal number of respondents wanted to know first how much it cost. Weight (lightness) was the next most frequently raised issue. Horsepower was of concern among many of the respondents. Other subjects they thought the man would talk about with the clerk were maintenance and the availability of repair, performance (what size tree the chain saw would cut), durability and expected life, safety (what safety features the chain saw has), and ease of starting the chain saw. In relation to price, the following comments were made:

Well, price is the most important, of course.

He's wondering how he will pay for it.

He's not considering price; price means nothing in regard to safety.

One individual was concerned whether the chain would come off the "blade." Individuals referred to the guide bar as a "blade" rather than a "guide bar." Various other issues were raised by respondents, such as:

- Ease of handling
- Length of blade
- Which was the best brand
- Whether it had direct drive
- Whether it had a gas protector
- Self-lubrication
- The warranty (guarantee)
- Ease of controls
- Specifications
- Availability of credit
- Possibility of mixing oil and gas

The third picture (Exhibit 3) showed a man cutting a felled tree with the chain saw. The question asked was as follows:

The man in the picture is the same man as in the last picture. He purchased the chain saw he was looking at in the store. Knowing that he purchased the chain saw, what can you tell me about him? Can you tell me anything about the character and personality of this man? A following probe was, "What do you suppose this man is thinking about while he's using his chain saw?"

A common response to the first part of the question was that the man was satisfied. Typical responses were: "He's pleased." "He's happy he bought the chain saw." "Lots of time saved." "He's happy with the chain saw; he made the right decision." Many favorable responses to the man actually using a chain saw were given, such as:

Sure beats bucking with an axe.

He's thinking about speed of getting through, time saved.

How much easier it is to cut a tree down with a chain saw over a hand saw.

He seems to be saying, "Why didn't I buy a chain saw sooner?"

Respondents in general seemed to think the man was using the chain saw for the first time. Very prominent in many respondents' answers was the fear of using a chain saw. It seems to be a major reason why people do not purchase one. Some additional comments were:

He's a little frightened. He doesn't know how to go about it, but he's willing to learn.

If he gets caught in that blade . . .

He's watching what he's doing—he could lose a limb.

He might be somewhat apprehensive about the use of it.

He looks scared of it.

He better think safety.

In general, as the test is designed to do, it made the respondents project their own personalities and backgrounds onto the character of the man. A wide variety of responses were given describing the man. He was described as a blue-collar working man, an office worker laboring after hours and on weekends, a somewhat wealthy man able to afford a chain saw, and a homeowner. A number of responses indicated that he was a "do-it-yourselfer," a man who liked to do things for himself, somebody who liked to "do his own thing." "Farmer" also received more than scattered response. Associations with an outdoorsman, a man who liked to keep in shape, were also indicated. He liked the out-of-doors. One quotation seems to sum it all up:

This seems to be his first job. He seems to be happy about it. He seems to think the chain saw will lighten his workload. He looks like he has not owned many power tools. He looks excited. He seems like he will be able to do a lot of cleanup work that he would not have been able to do without the chain saw. The chain saw is sure an improvement over the hand saw. It's faster, easier to use.

The fourth picture (Exhibit 4) showed a man and woman seated before a fireplace. The question read as follows:

Here's a picture of the same man [as] in the previous pictures, sitting and talking with a woman; what do you suppose they're talking about?

An analysis of the fourth picture in the projection test shows that respondents feel the man and woman in the picture are happy, content, cozy, enjoying the fireplace. The man is "enjoying the fruits of his labor." It comes out very strongly that the man who uses a chain saw is proud of himself after he cuts the wood. He thinks his cutting wood with a chain saw is a job well done. Some typical comments concerning this were:

He's very happy to cut his own wood for his fireplace—real proud of himself.

He's telling her how much he saved by cutting it himself.

They're talking about the logs; how pleased he is with himself.

He's thinking about the beauty of the fire, fire logs he, himself, sawed from their property.

The people projecting onto the picture seem to think that, because it is a job well done, purchasing a chain saw is worthwhile. Some additional comments were:

The man in the picture is saying, "The chain saw pays for itself. There's a $200 job and you will be able to use the chain saw afterwards."

Work's done and there's enough for winter and he has trees for winters to come.

What a good buy that chain saw was. Cut wood costs, save money.

The woman in the picture is also very happy; she's satisfied. Probably thinking about the future. But most of all she is very proud of her husband. This comes our very strongly. Some responses included:

The woman is looking to the enjoyment of the fireside and of the money saved because they cut their own wood. She might have questioned the investment before this, before sitting in front of the fireplace.

She is proud of her husband.

She is pleased the tree is down.

The woman is probably proud of the fireplace and starting the fire. He's probably thinking about the wood he sawed.

The man and woman are congratulating each other on finally getting around to buying a chain saw and cutting firewood.

She is complimenting him on his ability and on how handy it is to have a man around the house. She is also thinking that possibly it was easier for her husband to use a chain saw.

The woman doesn't care about the chain saw but she's satisfied.

A husband's concern over his wife's approval of this investment was also brought out by this picture. Evidently, men are worried that their wives will not see the value of a chain saw purchase. Also, there are implications that the man should be tired after using the chain saw.

After the presentation, Mr. Campagna was reasonably impressed. He asked John Hamilton what his opinion was. Mr. Hamilton said, "This is all very interesting, but I don't see how it can lead to greater profits in our chain saw division."

Questions

1. How should Mr. Conway and Mr. Baggins respond to Mr. Hamilton's question?
2. Is Hamilton investigating the casual-user market segment correctly?
3. What conclusions would you draw from the Thematic Apperception Test? Do you feel this is a valid and reliable test?
4. What specific recommendations would you make to Mr. Campagna concerning the casual-user chain saw market?

| Exhibit 1 | Exhibit 2 | Exhibit 3 | Exhibit 4 |

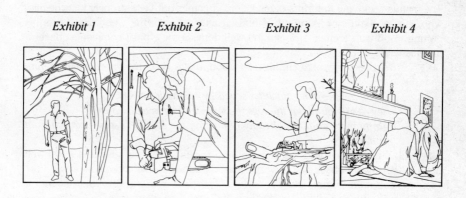

III

SURVEY AND OBSERVATIONAL RESEARCH

BONITA BAKING COMPANY (B): EVALUATING RESEARCH DESIGN

As sales manager at Bonita Baking Company, Frank Fortunada, Jr. has elected to undertake a research project concerned with Bonita Health Breads. Bonita Health is a line of specialty breads competing with national brands (such as Roman Meal and Pepperidge Farms) and regional brands (such as Orowheat—the market leader). Although the specialty bread segment was rapidly growing, the Bonita Health line has not been performing well. Most specialty brands (including Bonita) are actively promoted through television, radio and newspaper advertising, coupons and special price promotions.

Fortunada decided to undertake a research study to help him determine the source of the problem underlying the Bonita Health line's poor sales results. He was interested in ascertaining Bonita's relative position and image in the specialty bread market. Fortunada also needed to know more about the consumer profile of specialty bread users and how to reach them most effectively.

Fortunada solicited and received three separate proposals for the research study.

Proposal One–Consumer Research Analysts

The proposal from Consumer Research Analysts (CRA) suggested doing a two-stage mail survey to better understand the behavior of the specialty bread market. CRA had a reputation for doing sophisticated research for a number of consumer product areas. The proposal itself had been prepared by an associate of the firm who had recently completed an M.B.A. degree with an emphasis in consumer behavior. Excerpts from the proposal are shown below.

Copyright © 1981 by Dr. Donald Sciglimpaglia.

Statement of the Problem

Studies examining the process of adoption of products support the fact that consumers follow a general procedure that involves a series of stages:

Awareness   Before a person can consider purchase, the first requirement is that he or she be aware of the product's existence.

Interest   Often the level of interest is dictated by the need the consumer feels he or she has for a product. At other times, the mere awareness of the product stimulates interest.

Evaluation   At this stage, the consumer will determine whether or not the product should be considered for purchase.

Trial   In most cases the consumer will try the product—if possible—and form attitudes and further evaluations based on this trial.

Re-Evaluation   Attitudes toward the product are formed based on the trial.

Adoption   At this stage the consumer continues to use the product on a continuous basis or abandons it in search of another.

The problem to be studied here includes the determination of how many consumers (or potential consumers) currently are at each stage of this process, why they are there, and how they might be moved toward adoption of Bonita Health Breads.

Objectives

To determine the above, the following objectives will be sought:
1. Determination of levels of awareness of the product
2. Determination of attributes considered important in purchasing Bonita Health (or competitive lines)
3. Determination of number of individuals trying Bonita Health and evaluation of the same
4. Analysis of those attributes considered as important in evaluating Bonita Health bread (or competitive lines)

In addition, demographic and media viewing characteristics of the users and non-users will be provided.

Method

Preliminary evaluation of existing data will constitute the initial phase of the research. This procedure will utilize any existing sources of information that may provide insight into the problem.

The second phase will involve a two-step mail survey of consumers. The initial sample will consist of approximately 4,000 households selected from a city directory. The first survey will be used to identify the market profile for specialty breads and for Bonita Health specifically. A second (follow-up) survey questionnaire will be sent to those households identified in the first survey as Bonita Health and other specialty brand consumers. Its purpose will be to assess the objectives noted above.

Results

The results of the research presented will include a report covering:

1. Levels of awareness of Bonita Health, attitudes toward the same, and attributes considered salient in determination of these attitudes
2. Positioning of Bonita Health relative to the competition and relative strengths and weaknesses
3. Demographic and media-viewing characteristics of users and non-users

A copy of the computer output generated will be included.

Costs

The total cost of this project would be $8,000.

Proposal Two—Lancaster Associates

Another proposal was received from James Lancaster, a local management and marketing consultant. Lancaster's proposal was in the form of a letter to Fortunada in which he suggested using focus groups to research the problem. The essence of the letter proposal is shown below.

Dear Frank,

Thank you for allowing me to propose my research approach for the Bonita Health study.

I think that we need to really do an in-depth study of consumer awareness, attitudes and behavior regarding specialty breads in general and Bonita Health specifically. In this way we can get an understanding of the reasons behind the consumer purchase or nonpurchase of your product. I strongly feel that the way to do this is by using a series of focus group studies.

I propose to conduct four focus groups of roughly twelve specialty bread buyers each. The consumers would be recruited by phone to meet certain criteria. The panelist screening criteria include:

1. Total household income—$20,000 plus
2. Female head of household who is the principal shopper
3. Fourteen (14) plus years of education
4. Specialty bread users of the following breads:
   a. Bonita Health
   b. Orowheat
   c. Northridge
   d. Fresh Horizons
   e. Pepperidge Farms
   f. Millbrook
   g. Roman Meal
   h. Specialty store brands.

I will personally conduct the focus groups and provide a written summary report of the findings. The total cost, including recruiting and participant incentives, is $4,000.

Sincerely,
James Lancaster
Lancaster Associates

Proposal Three—Action Research

The third proposal came from Action Research. Dale Dash, the person that Fortunada spoke to on the phone, suggested that the most fruitful course of action would be to conduct what he termed an experience survey. He suggested that his firm would telephone roughly twenty bread department managers or store managers to determine their feelings about specialty breads and the Bonita line. In addition, Dash proposed that baking industry people in other parts of the country could be interviewed to get an understanding of what other regional marketers were doing to promote and market their brands of specialty breads. Dash thought that about ten baking industry marketing persons should be interviewed.

Dash told Fortunada that the total cost of the project would be between $1,500 and $3,000, although he could not say for sure. He indicated that he would be glad to give Fortunada a written proposal if he wished.

Questions

1. What are the strengths and weaknesses of each suggested approach?
2. Which (if any) proposal should Fortunada accept?
3. Write a short proposal which indicates how you would research this problem. You may want to refer to Part A of the Bonita Baking Company case for more information about the problem.

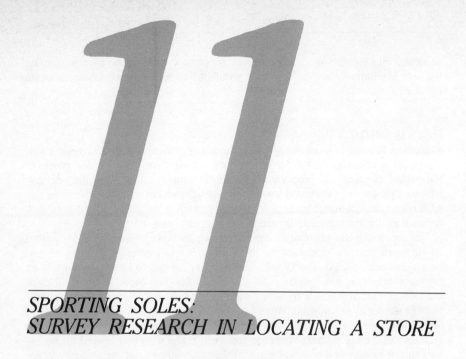

SPORTING SOLES:
SURVEY RESEARCH IN LOCATING A STORE

In September 1976, Greg Pickett, a former varsity track athlete in college, was considering opening a store selling a complete line of athletic shoes and accessories in Manhattan, Kansas. While there were several sporting goods stores in the area, none offered much variety in athletic shoes or clothing. The main competition would come from Brown's Shoe Fit which carried three brands: Adidas (about seven styles), Nike (about seven styles), and Converse (two styles). Other competitors carried only three or four brands, offering two or three selections per brand. Greg's store would offer considerably greater width and depth.

Greg's wife, Cindy, had been a store manager in the Athlete's Foot chain in Stillwater, Oklahoma, while attending college. After college they both worked in Manhattan for a couple of years, Greg as a newspaper sportswriter and Cindy as a physical education teacher. Together they managed to save a small amount of money. Also, Greg had impressed some of his business acquaintances to the extent that they were willing to provide him with financial support as an investment. Cindy was somewhat leery of leaving the security of their well-paying jobs to start a retail venture, especially since she did not have fond memories of her days as manager of the Athlete's Foot. The hours had been long and the pay little. Nonetheless, Greg convinced her that the opportunity was too good to pass up: financial backing was available, there was no real competition, and jogging, tennis, racquetball, and many other athletic leisure-time pursuits were rapidly growing in popularity. Part of the increasing demand was due to the opening of new facilities such as the Jay Hawk Racquet Club and the development of jogging and bicycling trails. Besides, Greg had realized that, while he was progressing satisfactorily in his job at the newspaper, he was too impatient to put up with the paper's editorial and promotion policies. Con-

Copyright © by Dr. Alvin Burns and James W. Gentry.

sequently, the Picketts made the decision to open a store, to be named Sporting Soles, in Manhattan, Kansas. Now their problem was to determine where to locate the store.

Background

Manhattan, Kansas, is a university town (the home of Kansas State University) with a population of about 30,000. Like most college towns, the demographic profile of Manhattan consists of proportionately more younger, lower–income, better–educated people (i.e., students) than other cities of comparable size which are not university towns. A rough map of Manhattan is shown in Exhibit 1, and Exhibit 2 summarizes the demographic breakdown of its four census tracts.

In appraising the information available, Greg used his knowledge of Manhattan sports trends and also discussed the location with an ex-teammate who was now an assistant coach at K.S.U. The Picketts felt that they needed to locate the store in an organized shopping area, as they did not expect Sporting Soles to draw sufficient numbers of customers as a free-standing store. A brief investigation into the locations of similar stores in other cities found them to be located in shopping centers or in the downtown area. After investigating the shopping areas in Manhattan, the Picketts found three primary shopping areas which had sites that offered the necessary square footage at a reasonable rent. These areas are shown in Exhibit 1 and are described below.

Aggieville   This area has a small shopping area just southeast of the campus, containing movie theaters, small specialty stores, a grocery store and many taverns. The area is in easy walking distance from the university's dormitories.

Westloop   This area contains the city's largest shopping center, located toward the western boundary of Manhattan (the city is expanding to the west, though). This shopping center offers a wide variety of goods, although it does not contain a large department store to serve as an anchor.

Downtown   An area reminiscent of downtown areas in most cities having a population of 20,000–50,000. The city commission has been dedicated to the maintenance of a strong downtown shopping area, as evidenced by zoning regulations that have prevented J. C. Penney's and Sears from moving out of the downtown area to Westloop or to other shopping areas.

Since the Picketts were familiar with Manhattan's geography but desired additional information concerning the town and the attitudes of the residents toward the shopping areas, they turned to secondary information. Census data, summarized in Exhibit 2, provided some insight into the town's composition. However, the census data available was somewhat out-of-date. Through Greg's ex-teammate, they were able to contact a summer marketing research class at the University that was seeking a topic for a class project. The Picketts agreed to reimburse the students' out-of-pocket costs in return for an image study of the three shopping areas.

Manhattan Shopping Area Image Study

A questionnaire was designed by the marketing research students to measure the importance of seventeen different criteria (shown in Exhibit 3) in determining where

Exhibit 1   Map of Manhattan, Kansas

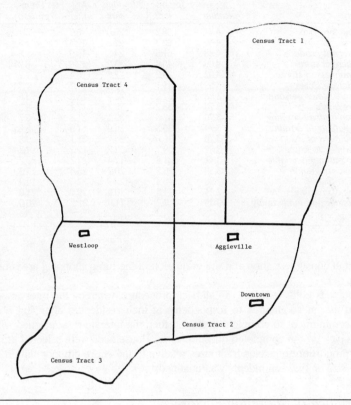

Exhibit 2   Summary of Manhattan's Population from 1970 Census Block Data

	Census Tract			
	1	*2*	*3*	*4*
Population	8,132	5,442	8,921	7,106
Percent Negro	4	9	7	1
Percent in Group Quarters	15	5	5	7
Percent under 18 years	10	4	15	20
Percent 62 years and over	7	20	12	5
Housing Units—Owned				
Number	1,200	732	1,390	1,406
Average Number of				
Rooms	6.0	5.1	6.8	7.6
Average Value ($)	18,700	14,300	24,100	29,400
Housing Units—Rented				
Number	2,173	840	1,814	1,316
Average Number of				
Rooms	3.6	3.4	4.0	4.6
Average contract ($)	98	94	110	136

Exhibit 3 Frequency Percentages of Importance of Variables

		Frequency Percentage				
Criterion	Mean Rating	Very Important	Important	Neither	Unimportant	Very Unimportant
1. Value for price	4.47	68.2	20.0	6.7	3.1	2.1
2. Prices	4.40	62.2	22.8	12.4	1.6	1.0
3. Variety of products	4.38	61.5	24.5	10.9	1.6	1.6
4. Quality of stores	4.09	45.4	33.0	12.9	6.2	2.6
5. Cleanliness of stores	4.02	49.2	22.6	16.4	7.7	4.1
6. Variety of stores	3.99	41.1	31.8	17.7	7.3	2.1
7. Friendly sales personnel	3.88	37.2	32.7	18.9	4.6	6.6
8. Store hours	3.78	33.2	35.2	17.1	8.3	6.2
9. Comparative Shopping	3.76	32.6	32.1	21.8	6.7	6.1
10. Availability of parking	3.74	39.3	26.0	17.9	5.6	11.2
11. Reputation of stores	3.70	36.6	24.7	21.1	9.8	7.7
12. Proximity to home	3.67	39.2	22.2	19.1	7.2	12.4
13. Free parking available	3.41	31.8	17.4	27.2	9.2	14.4
14. Traffic congestion	3.33	26.9	20.7	25.4	15.5	11.4
15. Advertising	2.98	12.4	22.7	32.5	14.9	17.5
16. Type of customers	2.54	11.3	10.8	29.7	21.0	27.2
17. Buildings and landscaping	2.49	7.7	11.3	32.2	20.0	28.7

Manhattan consumers shop and the evaluation of the three shopping areas on these criteria.

Data was collected using a call-back procedure, whereby the interviewers distributed the questionnaires to respondents at their residences after first obtaining verbal commitment to complete them and then the interviewers returned within an hour to pick up the completed questionnaires. Households were selected at random and in proportion to census tract sizes relative to the entire city population. A total sample size of 199 respondents was obtained.

Importance of Shopping Factors

Respondents rated the seventeen criteria as to how much influence they have on their shopping patterns using a five-point scale ranging from very important to very unimportant. A summary of the ratings is shown in Exhibit 3. Value for price, prices, and variety of products were rated as the most important factors. Closely following those criteria were quality of stores, cleanliness of stores, variety of stores, and friendliness of sales personnel. At the relatively unimportant level were criteria such as buildings and landscaping, type of customers, and advertising. The location factor (proximity to home) was found to rank twelfth in importance.

Evaluation of the Shopping Areas on the Criteria

Respondents were asked to rate each of the areas on a five-point semantic differential scale across the seventeen criteria. Exhibit 4 shows the mean responses for each area. Westloop was rated the best in terms of availability of parking, availability of free parking, prices, traffic congestion, buildings and landscaping, and store hours. Downtown was rated best in terms of variety of products, cleanliness of stores, advertising, quality of stores, variety of stores, availability of comparative shopping, reputation of stores, type of customers, and value for price. Aggieville was rated as having the best sales personnel and as being the closest to respondents.

Exhibit 4   Comparison of Shopping Areas

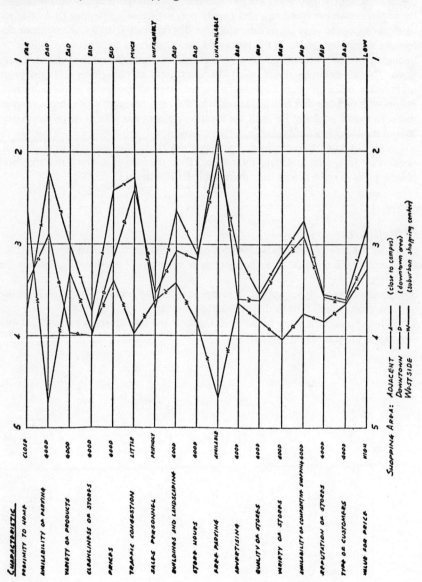

Along with the evaluations of each area, the respondents were asked to name the area at which they shopped most frequently. Fifty percent chose Downtown, thirty percent chose Westloop, and twenty percent chose Aggieville. To further investigate shopping area patronage, stepwise discriminant analyses were run to determine which differences in the perceived performance of the area were related to frequency of use. Three separate analyses were run, one for each of the shopping areas. This study broke down (most) frequent users as one group and infrequent users as the other group. In all three cases, proximity to home was the best discriminator—the variable that best explained why the respondents did or did not shop in that area most frequently. By itself, the location variable was able to correctly classify 80% of the shoppers for Aggieville, 64% for Downtown, and 80% for Westloop.

After obtaining the information summarized above, the Picketts were still undecided as to where to locate their store. They decided that more research and planning was needed before they made their final decision.

Questions

1. To what type of individual should Sporting Soles direct its marketing effort?
2. What characteristics of a shopping area should be considered in light of the target market?
3. Some of the analyses appear to present conflicting results. Which results make the most sense? Why is there a conflict?
4. Where should the store be located? Contrast the advantages and disadvantages of the three areas.

12

COTTON BANK AND TRUST: OBSERVATIONAL AND FOCUS GROUP RESEARCH

The Board of Directors meeting of Cotton Bank and Trust had just broken up. Donald Hitt was returning to his office and contemplating the first major change the bank would take in adopting an overall marketing strategy. The report from Bank Marketing Research had been valuable in pointing out the bank's weaknesses in relation to its competition in Delta, Mississippi. Now it was Hitt's responsibility to go ahead and begin a new marketing program that would put the bank in a competitive position for the coming decade.

Donald Hitt, the newly installed vice president and formerly of the large First National Bank of Memphis, was quite surprised and pleased at the receptivity the Board had for his plans to reposition the bank. They not only were receptive but they encouraged him to move as rapidly as possible in implementing the proposed changes. He remembered the large number of committees that even a simple proposal had to pass through at First National and was pleased that he had chosen to make the job switch to Cotton Bank and the relatively small town of Delta.

The First Proposed Change—Relocation

From Hitt's list of possible alternative courses of action, the Board chose to go along with Hitt's first choice of possibly changing the location of the main bank and erecting a building at a new site. Hitt's reasoning for this rather radical departure was twofold. First, the parking facilities were becoming increasingly overused and customers were becoming frustrated trying to find a place to park. Second, and more importantly thought Hitt, if the Bank is going to really change, it must have a new facility that is consistent with a progressive and aggressive bank. The present, cold

Copyright © 1981 by Dr. William J. Lundstrom.

gray building was just the opposite of what Hitt thought was needed for the bank's new image.

Hitt realized that a decision to move the main building could have a negative impact upon the bank. The downtown area, like many others in both small and large towns, was experiencing negative growth with businesses relocating away from downtown. If the bank chose this course of action, it could potentially lose some of its bigger downtown commercial accounts. On the other hand, staying in downtown would either require the entire remodeling of the old bank building or buying up existing downtown property, tearing it down and erecting a new building. The time for change was now. Hitt had to make his decision in the near future and he needed to know what the right course of action should be for the bank.

Before making an intuitive decision, Hitt felt it was necessary to get some hard facts to substantiate his choice. A quick call to Bank Marketing Research in Memphis was all that was needed. BMR would be down to Delta the following Monday to discuss the project with Hitt.

After Monday's meeting, Hitt and BMR had agreed to conduct a study. Rather than conducting a survey, BMR recommended using observational research combined with a focus group study. The observational study would involve a traffic count of passenger vehicles at the three proposed sites for the bank building. In addition, an inspection of the housing market and its relation to proposed locations would also be investigated. To study the proposed move ahead of time and get the reactions of bank trading area customers, three focus groups were to be conducted. The subjects for the three groups were composed of two groups of present Cotton Bank customers representing blue and white collar workers, respectively. The third group was represented by banking customers who did not bank at Cotton Bank. While the groups would focus on banking subjects and possible relocation effects, the actual name of the bank would not be revealed.

Bank Marketing Research told Hitt he could expect the results in about two to three weeks time. He felt confident that this study would give him the information he needed to start his proposed program. He returned to his office to begin the arduous wait. Three weeks later he was poring over the following report from BMR.

Cotton Bank and Trust Relocation Study
Traffic Flow

When one considers any real estate location, a traffic count and flow is usually done on the sites under consideration. Since this report is involved with picking potential alternative locations for the bank, a traffic count was undertaken for Wednesday, Thursday and Friday of the second week in April 1978, along Highway 4. Exhibits 1, 2 and 3 represent the traffic counts for each of the locations for the various time periods and days of the week.

The first site was the corner of Highway 4 and Front Street. It was thought to represent both the current location of the bank and any future locations that might be in the Front Street and Highway 4 area. It can be seen that there is no particular pattern to the traffic flow in this area. That is, we do not see any particular traffic patterns with people coming to and from work. We see relatively steady traffic at most hours of the day and for each day of the week with traffic steadily increasing from Wednesday to Friday. This type of traffic flow is common for downtown areas. The traffic generally builds from the beginning of the week to the end of the week. The total number of cars that passed by this location was 12,379 cars, with an average of 4,126 cars per day.

Exhibit 1   Downtown Traffic Count

Time	Wednesday		Thursday		Friday	
	East	West	East	West	East	West
Morning						
7:30–8:00	207	184	216	185	245	144
8:00–8:30	138	98	122	123	159	132
8:30–9:00	128	143	184	111	159	164
9:00–9:30	145	126	177	145	191	153
Total	618	551	699	564	754	593
Lunch Time						
11:30–12:00	237	170	215	195	298	236
12:00–12:30	210	182	299	191	292	240
12:30–1:00	162	204	281	156	203	203
1:00–1:30	223	160	194	128	223	183
Total	832	716	989	670	1,016	862
Afternoon						
3:30–4:00	125	125	128	100	143	151
4:00–4:30	147	141	121	118	156	165
4:30–5:00	129	165	129	178	170	205
5:00–5:30	130	171	117	146	166	189
Total	531	602	495	542	635	710
Grand Total	1,981	1,869	2,183	1,776	2,405	2,165
	3,850		3,959		4,570	

Total Cars 12,379

Exhibit 2   Branch Location Traffic Count

Time	Wednesday		Thursday		Friday	
	East	West	East	West	East	West
Morning						
7:30–8:00	206	275	210	270	220	255
8:00–8:30	128	140	125	145	123	200
8:30–9:00	108	155	133	140	119	195
9:00–9:30	146	140	176	180	172	155
Total	588	710	644	735	634	805
Lunch Time						
11:30–12:00	216	240	243	210	209	245
12:00–12:30	143	185	374	245	279	220
12:30–1:00	200	220	218	205	211	270
1:00–1:30	197	165	211	135	149	170
Total	756	810	1,046	795	848	905
Afternoon						
3:30–4:00	205	204	174	154	200	208
4:00–4:30	240	205	207	186	195	245
4:30–5:00	264	270	234	325	319	305
5:00–5:30	243	214	167	212	275	255
Total	952	893	782	877	989	1,013
Grand Totals	2,296	2,413	2,472	2,407	2,471	2,723
	4,709		4,879		5,194	
					14,782 Total Cars	

Exhibit 3   Bypass Location Traffic Count

Time	Wednesday		Thursday		Friday	
	East	West	East	West	East	West
Morning						
7:30–8:00	138	455	147	450	160	417
8:00–8:30	123	163	106	153	97	199
8:30–9:00	121	171	125	158	140	227
9:00–9:30	145	140	139	154	154	146
Total	527	929	517	915	551	989
Lunch Time						
11:30–12:00	201	170	200	143	212	166
12:00–12:30	213	157	235	185	306	200
12:30–1:00	207	141	113	139	206	208
1:00–1:30	138	150	147	150	183	162
Total	759	618	695	617	907	736
Afternoon						
3:30–4:00	259	201	239	170	245	245
4:00–4:30	261	210	236	200	260	295
4:30–5:00	406	215	435	350	445	337
5:00–5:30	231	167	262	237	275	300
Total	1,157	793	1,172	957	1,225	1,117
Grand Total	2,443	2,340	2,384	2,489	2,683	2,902
	Wed Total 4,783		Thur Total 4,873		Fri Total 5,585	

Total Cars   15,241

Exhibit 4 Locations of Traffic Counts

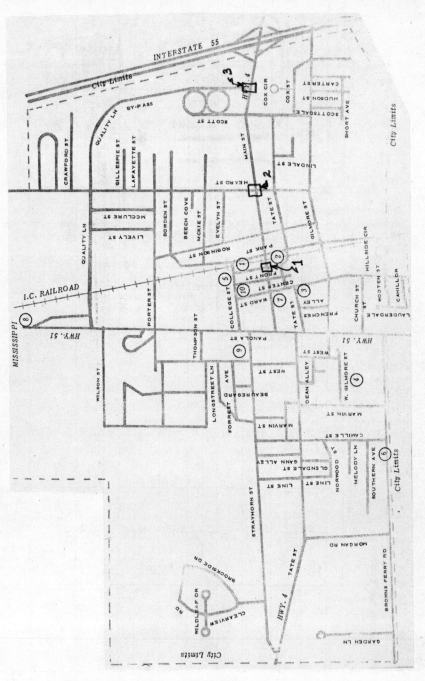

The second site was the corner of Heard Street and Highway 4. This site was thought to represent both the branch location that is currently in operation and any future mid-Main Street location. As can be seen in Exhibit 2, this location also does not have any particular pattern to its traffic. There is a relatively equal eastbound and westbound flow with no particular time period dominating the traffic flow. The traffic along the branch location is substantially better than the traffic along downtown since it had 14,782 cars pass this location over the three–day period, for an average of 4,927 cars per day.

The third location was the corner of Highway 4 and the bypass near the interstate highway. The traffic flow associated with this location was much different than either of the other site locations, as this location had traffic flows associated with people traveling to and from work. As one examines the time period from 7:30 to 8:00 a.m., we can see that westbound traffic is more than double the eastbound traffic for this time period. Likewise, if one examines the time period from 4:30 to 5:00 p.m., we can see the same workers returning home. Beyond this, we see a much heavier traffic flow associated with this site. There were 15,241 cars passing this corner during the study period, for an average of 5,080 cars per day. The traffic flow associated with this corner is the type most highly correlated with convenience. That is, it is located on a route that many blue and white collar workers will be taking to their employment. This type of location leads to increased visability for the firms locating along that area as well as having a high convenience factor for the persons passing along this route.

Housing Characteristics in Delta

While one can see the traffic flow as being heaviest in the bypass area and tapering off as it approaches downtown, another relevant consideration is the type of housing that is available in the various areas of the city. For this purpose, a housing characteristic study was done in the Delta area. As Exhibits 4 and 5 indicate, there were fourteen areas that were believed to be relevant to the location question. There are other areas which may be pertinent, but the designated areas were the ones with the highest housing density and most relevant to the study areas in question. There appears to be little difference with respect to the housing characteristics for any of the three locations. That is, all three locations are surrounded by lower, middle, and upper income housing. For the most part, the neighborhoods of Delta were middle-class neighborhoods whether they were white or black. Both the downtown site and the Heard Street site share the same characteristics with respect to the housing located within their proximity. The only location that might be superior, based upon housing characteristics, would be the third location on the bypass and Highway 4. This would be the result of people bypassing the downtown area and coming out on Main Street either at Scott Street or the bypass. This trend might be further accentuated if plans are completed to carry the bypass all the way around the city, further isolating the downtown area.

Exhibit 5   Type and Density of Housing in Delta

Area	Type	Density
1	Trailer Park, Lower Middle Class	High
2	New Structures Nice, Middle Class	High
3	Older Structures, Nice, Middle Class	High
4	Black Area, Middle & Lower Middle Class	Middle & High
5	Relatively New, Middle & Lower Middle Class	High
6	New Structures, Nice, Upper Middle Class	Low
7	Nice, Upper Middle & Upper Class	Low
8	Lower Middle Class	High
9	Lower Middle & Middle, Some Apartments	Low & Middle
10	Upper Middle & Upper, Older Homes	Moderate
11	Older Homes, Middle Class	Moderate
12	Black Area, Middle Class & Lower Middle	High
13	Lower Middle Class, Trailer Park	High
14	Middle and Upper Middle Class, Mostly New	Low

Distribution of Cotton Bank Customers

Before any decision is made with respect to moving the location of the main bank or opening a branch bank, an analysis of where the current customers of the bank are located is mandatory. Because of this, a study was undertaken to determine where the majority of the bank's customers lived with respect to the three branch locations. In order to do this, a random sample of the bank's customers was drawn from the 3,000 customers that have an account with the bank. The 400 randomly selected customers were then plotted on a map of Delta and Churk County.

The results of this study were quite interesting. It was found that two-thirds of all the customers of the Cotton Bank lived outside the city limits of Delta. One-third of the residents are domiciled within the Delta area. This result has several implications. First, the Cotton Bank and Trust is truly a county bank rather than a city bank. Second, this helped to explain why the new branch located at Heard Street and Highway 4 is getting two-thirds of all current demand deposits. Third, the bank must realize that its customers are traveling quite a long distance to be able to come to the bank, particularly to the downtown area. Fourth, this may truly call for a redefinition of the marketing effort being utilized by the bank at the current time. Fifth, it is quite an imposition for many of your customers to get to the bank when they live quite a distance from the downtown area.

Focus Group Interviews

In an effort to capture citizens attitudes about downtown banking and bank relocation, focus group interviews were held with three segments of the populations. Two groups consisted of present Cotton Bank and Trust customers representing blue and white collar workers, respectively. The third group was composed of non-Bank customers from the surrounding area. The results of these three group interviews in a condensed version of the conversations is presented in Exhibits 7 through 9.

Exhibit 6   Housing Areas

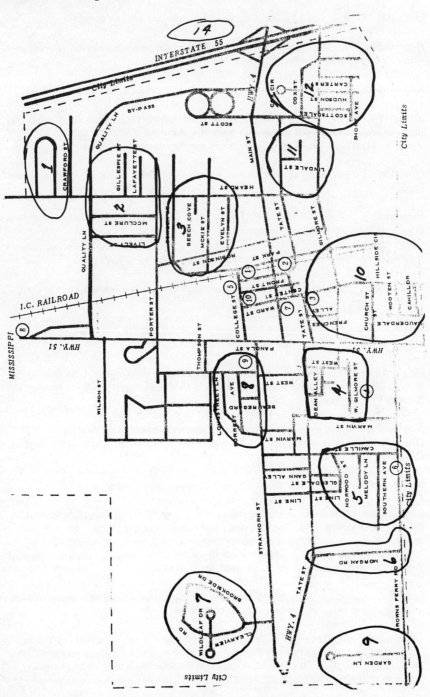

Exhibit 7 Low and Middle Income Blue Collar Workers

Question What do you think about the downtown area and how it's doing?

Respondent You have to make the place inviting for the people to come to. Business goes where it's invited. It goes where it's treated right.

Respondent The biggest problem downtown is finding a place to park.

Respondent Parking on the weekend is the most difficult. People don't like the fact that they can get a ticket parked too long in front of a store. But it is a city ordinance. I'm not against it. If I can't get what I need in two hours, then I'm spinning my wheels.

Question Do you think the store owners downtown are doing a good job of keeping their stores up?

Respondent I think they have done a good job in the last few years. They have done alot of work on the older buildings downtown.

Respondent They are a lot better looking than they were a few years ago.

Respondent A lot of people are shopping in the shopping center out-of-town.

Respondent One thing to be known about the plaza is that many people from out-of-town shop there. It doesn't draw a lot of local people. People from Olive Branch, Como, Holly Springs, Tunica, Sardis, within a sixty mile radius are coming to the plaza.

Respondent Five percent of the people in Panola County are shopping at the plaza. Downtown is hurting because of the plaza. A big reason is parking. Everyone is going to Walmart and Big Star.

Respondent I have to go an extra mile and a quarter to go out to the druggist at the plaza. (The druggist moved from downtown to the plaza.) That mile and a quarter makes a big difference.

Respondent I changed druggists when they (Walmart) moved out there.

Respondent A minimum amount of money could be spent to make the place (downtown) so much more inviting. If you don't believe it, just take a good look at it and you'd be looking at 1875 and 1880 buildings that haven't been changed one bit. There are buildings that are left unpainted and look as though they are about to fall down. You can't make progress like that. You have to take care of what you have; make the most of it.

Question One of the banks is thinking about moving into an outlying area instead of being downtown. What would you think about one of the banks leaving downtown?

Respondent We have banks in the outlying areas now. We are surrounded by banks. We got more banks that we got money to put in 'em. There is one at the shopping plaza. Cotton Bank has a branch bank. Other branch banks are in the area. Banks have made it very easy for people to do business with them.

Respondent I would vote against another bank moving out of downtown. It would make Delta a ghost town.

Exhibit 7   Low and Middle Income Blue Collar Workers–Continued

Respondent   When there was talk of building a new post office, they were talking about moving it out east. That got stopped right quick. You see where it is now. Fred's is keeping its second store in town.

Respondent   The Big Star was going to have two stores in the same area, but that didn't last but about two weeks. He closed one down.

Respondent   If you keep your prices right and don't try to make all your money off one man at one time, but take it out in dribbles, you can still stay in business. But when there is twenty percent difference between prices in 30 miles, that's ridiculous! Out of line! When you see the same grocery trucks driving up knowing the groceries come out of the same warehouse, don't anybody tell you that there's twenty percent more difference in hauling thirty miles. Also, some people get credit at some stores where I'm paying cash. My cash has been used all along to take care of these people. It's not right! Stores could cut their prices five percent, and they would see a marked increase in patronage.

Respondent   In some stores, you see items that have gone up more than five percent from one week to the next.

Respondent   I bought Lipton Instant Tea here (downtown) for ninety-one cents. I bought it thirty miles from here for sixty-nine cents.

Respondent   I had rather buy my groceries here, but they have to get the price down a little bit. Otherwise, I'll go thirty miles more and buy groceries for two weeks at a time.

Respondent   Big Star and Sunflower, in the city, keep their proces together. There is no competition.

Respondent   The stores are raising their prices on the *same* can of goods that has been on the same shelf or the warehouse in the back, but they keeping adding stickers with higher prices. That's wrong!

Question   Do you think if the banks stayed downtown, but also built a newer facility in the outlying area, that people would use it? This would be a larger facility with offices.

Respondent   Yes, people would use it.

Respondent   But they (people) like the downtown area.

Respondent   It would be just like Memphis or Jackson. Small, large, or medium-size town, the same thing happens everywhere. I don't know what you're going to do to get people to come back, you have to make it attractive, give a man more for his dollar. If the price is better in the downtown area, he will suffer that hardship of finding a place to park to shop where the price is better.

Respondent   You don't have a place to eat or buy groceries except in the outlying area.

Respondent   What Delta needs is a place to eat!

Questioner   It would seem then that the smart business people are probably going to continue to move out from downtown because they can't go it alone.

Exhibit 7   Low and Middle Income Blue Collar Workers–Continued

Respondent   I think that's true.

Respondent   Yes, I think the move is in that direction. It may not continue that way, but right now, its true.

Respondent   They can put up North Lee Drive out there and that would be it.

Respondent   I was walking behind Walmart this morning and there is plenty of acreage out there. Of course, the land is probably very expensive.

Question   What is the difference between the banks in town?

Respondent   Usually people grow up doing business with one bank. I started doing business with the Cotton Bank because my folks did business there, and my children will probably do that. Chances are, eighty or eighty-five percent of the people in this town do that.

Respondent   I've done business with both of them (banks), and I find them equally nice. They help people that need it.

Question   They are concerned with people and the county.

Respondent   Oh yeh! I think you'll find that true with a certain bank in Coldwater, too.

Respondent   They are one reason that this county has progressed so well. If you go around to other areas, you'll find that this area is well off economically. You wouldn't find another town this size that looks much better.

Respondent   Speaking about the banks, we have been fortunate in both banks. We've had the finest presidents and vice-presidents. Men in these banks seem to understand the needs of a person. They will sit down and talk to you about your needs.

Respondent   No bank will loan you money unless you have collateral. I don't care how congenial they are. That's the reason they are real sound.

Respondent   There are two motor companies downtown and one out on Highway 51. The one on 51 is doing well.

Respondent   Turner Motor Co. just built in the shopping center (3 years ago). They are doing well.

Question   What kinds of things concern you when you pick out the bank that you will do business with?

Respondent   The first thing that I would be concerned with is if they are federally regulated, that they are insured, and what kind of people will be helping you should you get in a tight fix. Would they give you a little extra time if you should run late on a note? Would they help you buy land that would run into quite a bit of money or would they ignore that type of loan for just car loans.

Question   Does anybody have their house mortgaged with a bank rather than a savings & loan?

Exhibit 7   Low and Middle Income Blue Collar Workers–Continued

Respondent   They make some of those.

Respondent   Five years and then they will renew it.

Questioner   I think they are beginning to do that more and more.

Respondent   They've done that for years for good customers.

Question   When do you do most of your banking? Do you go once a week?

Respondent   To cash a payroll check is when I usually go, or to make a deposit.

Respondent   I go twice a week.

Respondent   It is also handy to pay some of your utility bills there.

Question   Do you cash checks at the bank?

Respondent   I go every day for the business.

Question   Do you ever cash checks at the grocery store?

Respondent   If the bank is closed.

Question   Do any of you have any questions you want to ask of me while I'm here?

Respondent   What is the purpose of our discussion tonight?

Questioner   Well, we are trying to find out what you think about the downtown area and what we could do for the downtown area. At the same time, one of the banks is thinking of keeping their downtown branch but opening their main office elsewhere because there is no room to expand and no parking. They are concerned about people and they want to be sure that it would be best for the city to move out of the downtown.

Respondent   I think it would be fine. We have a bank that is opened until 6:00 now, and that helped a lot of people.

Respondent   A bank is a lot like a hospital. The business is going to be there. The people will come to it because it will be more convenient.

Question   Would it be better for you if they had better facilities in the outlying area?

Respondent   Better facilities really don't affect us because we do business with the teller. You will have the same window you will go to no matter what the facilities are.

Question   What about easier parking for everyone?

Respondent   That might help people.

Exhibit 7   Low and Middle Income Blue Collar Workers–Continued

Respondent   There are some people who want to do business with certain tellers. So he will come downtown if that certain person is there. I waited two hours to do business with a certain man in the Cotton Bank.

Respondent   If that man moved to the shopping center, I'd be out there too. A lot of people that can't drive come downtown.

Questioner   Thank you.

Exhibit 8   White Collar Workers

Question   We are interested in your feelings about Delta, shopping in Delta, and the convenience of doing everyday activities in Delta. We are interested in where you do your shopping and your feelings about the variety of products offered in Delta. Do you ladies leave town to do your shopping?

Respondent   I believe in Delta. I have a business in Delta. I believe in doing all my shopping here. If I expect people to do business with me, then I have to do business with them. If people come to me to ask for donations, then the least they can do is to keep their own money in town.

Question   What kinds of things are you forced to leave town for? Are there things that you can't get here?

Respondent   Groceries, sometimes, because of the prices. But I do most of my Kroger shopping here.

Question   Are *you* forced to leave to buy anything?

Respondent   As far as clothing is concerned, I go to Memphis because I get better prices there than I can get here. I agree with the shopping as far as groceries are concerned. You can buy groceries cheaper in Grenada, and the same man owns both Big Star grocery stores. My in-laws down there buy things three to five cents cheaper.

Question   What do you think of the downtown area in terms of shopping? Do you think it is being kept up well? Are the stores doing their best to keep people coming downtown to shop?

Respondent   I think you have invited the wrong people here. I think you should have invited strictly lay people that were not business peole.

Questioner   We have already.

Respondent   I don't think the downtown Delta area has tried to do nearly as much as they should have to keep up the fronts of their stores. The insides of the stores are generally in good shape, but over-all appearance of the town itself is not good. When I first came here from outside the county, I was really shocked with the appearance of the town. The area is convenient to a large city, an airport. North Mississippi is a good area to live in, but downtown Delta was awful. It has improved in the last ten years. A little money spent to improve the downtown would have an effect upon people just passing through. The business is moving; its going out yonder.

Exhibit 8   White Collar Workers—Continued

Respondent I was born and raised here. I've lived here for thirty-two years. I'm comptroller of a plant that does business with people from all over the country, Chicago, New York, etc. The downtown area definitely needs improvement. The town gives the impression of 100 years ago which is not the impression that a town of this size should give. The buildings need repair. The inside of the stores are good. We were talking about prices. If you had been here a year ago, you would have really thought the prices were high. The town has grown in the last couple of years and we have been able to bring in general commerce, more businesses, more competition. Because of this, prices are more competitive. The area itself is financially basically sound. With improvements and more money put into the area. But several things have to be done before that. In our instance, we would like to expand our operation, but we can't do it because we can't find the people available in this area to work second and third shifts to hire to expand our plants. We could put a couple million dollars into the area. People without the educational background are the ones looking for the jobs. The economy could be drastically updated which would help the businesses in the town. We need help to upgrade the educational facilities in this area.

Respondent We are caught up in the web of so many small towns in that, when the main drag of town was built, they didn't foresee fifty years from then. The way they build all the facilities was the way it was expected to stay for the next 100 years. There is not a lot to do about it as far as parking because they built up all around it as they were expanded without any kind of a program for the future. They have got themselves bottled in. All we can do is fix up and pretty up. They little parking we had is being taken up to build the municiple building.

Respondent Fred's left because they (city fathers) put the new municiple building where it is. The post office took parking in one end several years ago; now the parking is gone down here. Only in peak periods do you really have a problem. Saturday morning and Saturday afternoon is the peak.

Respondent I'm in the drug business, and out business is affected when the people get out of the doctor's office at 10:00 and all the parking spaces are filled. That's why we moved to the new shopping center. We just moved out there.

Respondent The people that go to Memphis for their shopping; I give them the devil for doing it. They are not thinking of their over-all best interest when they do so because the sales taxes they are paying up there and the cost of the trip, you're behind doing that.

Respondent This community is so small, but we have many good things going. Our band, for instance, Northwest Junior College, their paper, their radio station. All of these things take financing, and they always come to the businesses. That's fine. You have to turn somebody down eventually, but you try not to. It's hard to give to anybody that you know takes their business out of Delta. They are thinking of their pocketbook, at the moment, but they are not thinking of the future growth of the town.

Question In terms of banks in town, there is some thought of moving out of the downtown area. They are restricted in size and they need to expand; they need more parking. There is some thought that they might keep their buildings downtown but move out onto the strip. How would you feel about that?

Respondent It's gonna happen! It's going to hurt the businesses so bad when they do it. They probably want to go out there so they won't have to worry about all the traffic problems. It would really seem to me that it would take away the business downtown.

Exhibit 8   White Collar Workers—Continued

Questioner   They are not going to shut the banks down in the downtown.

Respondent   If they move out, even though you would consider this (downtown) a branch, the traffic will be cut fifty percent or more.

Respondent   The banks are supposed to be the leader of downtown, and they are doing just the opposite when they consider doing that.

Respondent   They are just like everybody. They can't grow or get bigger.

Respondent   When you say the strip, what do you mean?

Questioner   Well, there is a variety of places, and there is also room downtown. In order to stay downtown, they have to destroy a city block.

Respondent   How much they hurt downtown all depends on how much of their operations they are moving. If they move their loans, etc. out of town, it will hurt. If they simply move their teller services out, then it will not hurt much.

Respondent   The banks have a moral obligation not to move away from the people that really support them. I don't see how they could afford to think that they could move away.

Respondent   Delta is facing the same thing that Memphis faced. The downtown area is getting run down. It is not attractive to come to. It's inconvenient; parking is impossible; the traffic is unreal. So everything is moving out for everyone's convenience.

Question   What percentage of business is conducted downtown versus on the other side of the railroad track onto 55?

Respondent   A great majority would go out toward 55. Downtown, only if you can't find it out there.

Respondent   I wouldn't say that right now. The trend is moving that way, but I wouldn't say that right now.

Respondent   You go the strip first *knowing* you can't get a parking space downtown.

Respondent   Most of the grocery shopping is on the other side of the railroad tracks. The clothing business is on this side of the railroad tracks. Most people don't do much clothing shopping east of the tracks.

Respondent   We are in a building that is partly owned by someone else that will not sell. We don't want to spend money on somebody else's building. Other businesses are in that shape.

Respondent   Too many people who own the property outlying the city see that Delta is growing and are holding onto their land waiting for the price to go up. Therefore, we cannot enlarge because nobody will let go of the land. No large industry will come in because of the housing shortage. No one will sell land for housing. We can't progress!

Exhibit 8   White Collar Workers–Continued

Respondent   (Later) This town will double in size if we can get a few things to happen in respect to housing, parking, education, and upgrading downtown.

Respondent   People have been satisfied with the status quo. They really didn't want it to be a big town. The people that own the land sell the land on a very piecemeal basis.

Respondent   (Speaking of businesses leaving downtown). There are soon going to be more spaces downtown. Fred's and Ben Franklin are leaving. If I was Freds' and Ben Franklin, I'd beat myself to death to get out. I really would, and others are going the feel the same way. When those banks leave, then in my opinion, the whole thing is going to start to fold up.

Respondent   My reference point is Greenville. Businesses left the downtown to go to the malls. Downtown spent lots of money on building up the area, beautifying the area. The banks did not leave and the area has maintained its business and is flourishing.

Respondent   People are more concerned with their convenience than anything else, not necessarily price or anything else.

Respondent   Nothing will stop you from buying something quicker than not being able to park your car.

Question   Isn't it the same for a bank as for other businesses?

Respondent   Not necessarily. A bank will do business even though other businesses move out.

Respondent   Banks have enlarged in the last ten years.

Respondent   Banks are a necessity. If you have to be inconvenienced to borrow money, you will put up with a little inconvenience to do so where you won't take that little inconvenience to go to the grocery shop or clothing store.

Respondent   If your money is in one bank, you don't often think of taking it out and putting it in another one. Banks have prospered on that kind of business.

Respondent   A branch office of a bank is really the bank's way of being nice to their customers.

Questioner   Thank you for coming.

Exhibit 9   Non-Bank Customers

Question   We are trying to get your reactions to the shopping facilities in Delta and any problems that you see. Generally, how do you find the shopping? Is there much selection in the stores or do you think it is somewhat limited and would you like to see some changes made?

Respondent   For my day-to-day shopping needs I find the facilities to be adequate in Delta. I do find the prices to be somewhat higher than in other areas. For many of the big purchases, I have to do my shopping in Memphis.

Exhibit 9   Non-Bank Customers–Continued

Respondent   I agree. There seems to be a lack of competition in the area and prices are too high. I wish there were more stores to choose from.

Question   Do you have any problems with the parking?

Respondent   Sometimes. Especially in the downtown. Sometimes I have to drive around the block several times before I can find a parking place. This is really the case on Saturday mornings when a lot of folks come to town.

Respondent   Yeh. Sometimes it is a real problem and at other times it isn't too bad.

Question   Do you find any objections to shopping downtown, or is it adequate?

Respondent   I guess I would say it is adequate but not much more. It doesn't appear that the downtown stores really care about how their stores look. They should really fix them up.

Respondent   That's true. The downtown stores are not nearly as nice as those on the strip or in the plaza. They (the owners) don't seem to care about their stores. It is more convenient to do my business elsewhere.

Question   Where do you do your grocery shopping?

Respondent   I buy my groceries out in the plaza.

Respondent   Me, too.

Respondent   Ditto.

Question   What about using Walmart?

Respondent   Yes, I use it. There is also a shoe store over there that I go to.

Respondent   I do too. I think the prices are better out there than in the downtown.

Question   Do you think the plaza has been a plus for Delta?

Respondent   Yes, I think it is. When I grew up, we went to downtown Memphis to shop. Now I wouldn't go there because I was so surprised at how the downtown had changed. Delta is the same way. There is a blight on it (the downtown).

Questioner   The problem is that people have moved out and want to have the same type of facilities, but closer to home.

Respondent   Yes, I think you are right. I like to have things handy to my home.

Respondent   I also believe that people have tried to run away from the old days of segregation and want to shop in new places that don't remind them of the past. To my way of thinking, businesses generate taxes and we need more of them.

Respondent   Yes, we need to attract more business to Delta. It's good for our city.

Exhibit 9   Non-Bank Customers–Continued

Question   Do any of you bank downtown?

Respondent   Yes, I bank at People's Bank.

Respondent   So do I.

Respondent   I bank at Coldwater. I have done some business with Cotton Bank, and they seem to be real friendly. My daughter and son-in-law bank at People's and they really like it. I don't think they would change banks.

Question   A bank is thinking about moving its major location out of downtown and maintaining a branch there. What do you think about that?

Respondent   Our methods of doing business have changed. When the downtown was designed, they didn't take into account the amount of traffic there would be in the future. Therefore, parking has become a real problem. I can see why they would do that.

Respondent   I think it would be OK. But what would happen to downtown? The way things are going nothing would be left in downtown.

Respondent   Yes, that could be a problem. But there is no room to expand in downtown.

Question   Would you be inclined to perhaps change you bank if it was located out by the plaza?

Respondent   Yes.

Respondent   I would give it some thought.

Respondent   Maybe.

Respondent   I doubt it. I like my bank.

Question   What are your perceptions of the two banks in downtown Delta?

Respondent   They're both good banks and have done a lot for Delta.

Respondent   We built a church and we went to Coldwater. The note was turned over to Cotton Bank. It was a warm transaction. We've been thinking about phasing out the other account with this other place (Coldwater). Long time ago, people didn't think about having to be nice to you. But now, business is different. Things have changed. At one time you didn't have a choice, but now you do.

Respondent   I've never gone to People's Bank. As far as Cotton Bank is concerned, I couldn't say anything bad about it.

Question   It has a pretty positive image?

Respondent   Yes.

Exhibit 9   Non-Bank Customers–Continued

Respondent   I think so, too.

Respondent   As I said before, I think both banks are very good. It just depends on which one you go to first.

Respondent   Yep. I think that's the case. They're both pretty good.

Questioner   Thank you for coming tonight.

Questions

1. Based on the information in the case, develop three options—(1) staying in the old location, (2) moving to new location or, (3) building a new facility downtown—for Mr. Hitt.
2. Is there any other information you think Mr. Hitt should have in making his decision?

NATIONAL ENDOWMENT FOR THE ARTS: PROPOSAL FOR SURVEY RESEARCH

In 1979, the National Endowment for the Arts was soliciting research proposals for the development and testing of models for audience surveys. This project is described in the following paragraphs.

Broad Agency Goal

The National Endowment for the Arts is an independent agency of the Federal Government. The goal of the Endowment is to foster professional excellence in the arts in America, to nurture and sustain them, and equally, to help create a climate in which they may flourish so that they may be experienced and enjoyed by the widest possible audience. The Research Division supports this goal by conducting a limited number of research projects that provide data to assist in the development of the agency's policies and resource allocations. All research outputs from the project that may be supported by means of this program solicitation must be designed and formulated so that they are useful in support of the above goal.

Definition of Audience Survey

For this project, the term "audience survey" refers to studies that collect information by questionnaire or interview or by other appropriate research methods aimed at providing a description of the demographic characteristics, attendance-related expenditures, perceptions and reactions to the event or activity attended, anticipated future behaviors, and other information from persons who attend events and activities or use facilities of individual arts organizations.

Based on National Endowment for the Arts, Program Solicitation 79–4, May 1, 1979.

It is not intended that the methods and procedures to be developed and tested in this project will constitute a broad marketing approach or consumer demand approach to the understanding of the potential audience. However, the need to compare the characteristics and other information collected about the persons who attend performances or use facilities of individual arts organizations with characteristics of the non-attenders in the community may be an important aspect of an audience survey as defined here.

Project Objectives

Audience research by arts and cultural organizations has become increasingly common. Such organizations find audience data to be valuable in making informed policy and planning decisions as well as for supporting funding requests to public and private agencies. These agencies, in turn, often employ audience data in their own policy and planning decisions. A review of 270 audience studies had been sponsored by the Arts Endowment's Research Division and the results are now published as Research Division Report #9, *Audience Studies of the Performing Arts and Museums: A Critical Review.* The report generally concluded that audience survey quality and utility can be much improved.

The proposed project is intended as a step towards upgrading audience survey quality and utilization by providing models for questionnaires and survey procedures, as well as procedures for evaluating the results and comparing them to community populations. The project is to include experimental validation of the recommended methods and procedures, and the preparation of an audience survey manual for use by arts administrators and the researchers whom they may engage to conduct audience surveys.

Project Description

The project is to be conducted in two phases that overlap in time. Phase I will consist of the tasks necessary to develop model audience study questionnaires and procedures, and to prepare an audience survey manual. Phase II will consist of the testing of the models in cooperation with a group of institutions to obtain experience with the approaches and procedures that are recommended. Some of the tasks of Phase I and Phase II may be conducted concurrently, and the final tasks of Phase I, consisting of the evaluation of the results of the field experience and preparation of the manual, will take place after the field testing has been completed.

Phase I—Development of Models for Audience Surveys and Preparation of a Manual

Phase I is to consist of Tasks 1, 2, 3, 4, and 5. In these tasks, the awardee of the contract will conduct the research and development and the associated work necessary to establish a manual for the conduct of audience surveys.

Task 1—Review of Audience Survey Experience

As soon as possible following the issuance of the contract, the awardee will meet with the staff of the Research Division and will be provided with the latest available information relevant to this project. The awardee will become familiar with the collection of audience studies housed in the Arts Endowment's library. This collection includes 265 of the 270 items collected in the course of the critical review conducted for the Arts Endowment by Michael Useem, Paul DiMaggio and Paula Brown, and reported in Research Division Report #9, previously mentioned. Additional audience studies that have come to light subsequent to completion of the critical review study may also be included in the review.

Task 2—Development of the Work Plan
A work plan will be prepared utilizing the information acquired through interaction with the Research Division and review of audience studies. The work plan will be submitted for approval prior to commencement of the remaining tasks.

Task 3—Development of Questionnaires, Survey Procedures, and Instructions
As soon as the work plan is approved, the awardee will commence the preparation of models for questionnaires or sets of questionnaires and accompanying procedures and instructions. The questionnaires may be modular with standardized demographic sections, expenditure data sections, and other specialized components that may be combined in various ways with or without special questions for individual audience survey situations and objectives.

The modular sections should be designed to collect basic data which may be fundamental to most audience surveys. There may also be supplementary sets of questions which can be used as needed by arts organizations to meet special needs and conditions. The wording of questions and the layout and appearance of the questionnaires, both in the basic modules and supplemental sections, will be organized and developed to obtain the highest possible response rate, reliability, and validity.

Procedures and instructions will include sample selection, selection and training of survey personnel, pretesting and modifying questionnaires, distribution and collection of questionnaires, editing and coding procedures, data processing, analysis and interpretation, and presentation of results. Guideline procedures should be included to assist arts organizations in choosing contractors to perform part or all of audience surveys. Checklists should provide guidance on necessary steps in monitoring the progress of audience surveys done by outside contractors.

Task 4—Evaluation of Questionnaires, Survey Procedures, and Results
During the course of the field experience in the experimentation with the recommended models as part of Phase II, necessary information shall be collected to make possible an analysis and evaluation. Information for this analysis may be drawn from interviews with staff of the organizations that are host to the field trials as well as with attenders and non-attenders in the community. Matters of interest will include: How was the decision to participate in an audience survey made? Who advocated the decision and whose approval was required? Why were the audience data thought to be necessary? How does the envisioned utilization of the results compare with the observed utilization of the results?

The awardee shall assess audience reaction to the survey instruments and procedures. The awardee shall also assess the sensitivity of the instruments and procedures to identify characteristics unique to attenders as opposed to non-attenders. Information should also be obtained on changes in the host organizations' expectations for utilization of audience data and the steps taken as a result. Other matters found to be relevant may also be evaluated.

Task 5—Reports

The awardee shall prepare a final report that will consist of a number of sections. They may be completed as discrete volumes and submitted independently as they are ready. The sections shall include: (1) a report on each of the audience survey case studies, including the data collected from the audiences, and the analysis; (2) a general review of the project history, evaluation of the field experience and conclusions and recommendations regarding the utility of the recommended model audience survey designs and procedures; (3) a manual for the conduct of audience surveys written to provide guidance for arts organizations administrators and the researchers whom they may engage to conduct audience studies.

Each section of the report shall be submitted in draft form for review and comment. Five copies shall be provided for this purpose. Following receipt of comments and suggestions, the awardee shall complete the final report as a unit or in separate volumes and deliver twenty-five copies to the National Endowment for the Arts.

Phase II—Audience Survey Case Studies

Phase II shall consist of Tasks 6, 7 and 8. In these tasks, the awardee shall coordinate and administer the experimental use of the proposed models for the conduct of audience studies in at least five organizations. The selection of organizations to participate in the testing of Phase II will be done cooperatively with the awardee. The group of institutions will be a diverse set that may include a performing arts organization, a museum, an alternative space (visual arts), a media center (radio, video, film), a community–based arts organization (expansion arts), and some organization that presents free admission events such as street theatre or concerts in the park.

Task 6—Selection of Participating Organizations

The selection process for participating organizations will begin after the acceptance of the work plan prepared as Task 2. Nominations of organizations who may wish to participate will be received from the Arts Endowment's Programs including their Advisory Panels and from service organizations representing the major sectors of the arts and cultural community. The numbers, location, and kinds of organizations selected to participate in the project will be determined jointly by the awardee and the Research Division with consideration given to all project objectives and the costs of the possible audience surveys. The awardee will not approve any organization as a site independently and without concurrence by the Research Division Project Manager.

A minimum of five sites will be selected. Selection criteria will include: diversity of organization type and geographic location, type of organizational management decision to be made with the results of an audience survey (see Research Division Report #9), degree to which audience survey data is important in making the anticipated management decision, and prospects for effective use of the audience survey results by the organization.

Task 7—Initiation and Monitoring of Surveys in Participating Organizations

To simulate as accurately as possible the actual conditions under which the model survey questionnaires and instructions will eventually be used, participating organizations rather than the awardee should be primarily responsible for the day-to-day conduct of the surveys. The awardee will assist in the initiation of the surveys and training of the local personnel and will closely monitor their progress. The awardee will provide advice for questions and problems which may arise during the course of the surveys and provide the necessary guidance and instruction that may be required.

For proposal writing and budget planning purposes, it should be assumed that the awardee will make at least three visits to each of the participating organizations: (1) to complete necessary arrangements and train the staff, (2) to observe and instruct the survey staff at the time questionnaires are distributed and collected from the audience, and (3) when the survey results are evaluated by the decision–making group of the organization. For proposal writing and budget planning purposes, proposers should assume that there will be one organization in the West, one in the South, one in the North Central region and two or more in the Northeastern regions of the United States. Some additional visits to the sites may be required to discuss survey plans and procedures with the organizations' staff to assure that survey procedures are properly implemented, and to assess survey results and reactions to the survey instruments and procedures.

Some of the costs incurred by the participating organizations may be assumed by the awardee. Such costs will be negotiated by the awardee and may cover: contracts with individuals, research firms, or university–based researchers to conduct those parts of the work for which the participating organizations cannot provide their own staff or volunteers; the printing of questionnaires; and audience data processing. For proposal writing and planning purposes, the proposer should assume that necessary reimbursement or funding to the participating organizations will not exceed a total of $25,000.

Task 8—Preparation of Individual Audience Survey Reports
The awardee will prepare, for each of the participating organizations, a separate report summarizing the results of its audience survey and the conclusions and recommendations that are indicated by the data. These reports shall be provided to the individual organizations for their use and not made available for general distribution without their consent. The organization reports will, however, form part of the final report to the Arts Endowment (see Task 5).

Proposal Format
Each proposal should contain the following:
1. Cover page
2. Abstract
3. Narrative
4. Budget
5. Appendices

1. *Cover Page* The top page of the proposal should provide the information suggested by a sample format attachment. The use of elaborate binders and notebooks for proposals is discouraged and they may be removed and discarded by the Arts Endowment if the information suggested in the Sample Proposal Cover Format is covered from view.
2. *Abstract* The second page of the proposal should be an abstract of about 200–250 words. The abstract should avoid general statements about the project and consist of a brief description of the topics that are cited under Evaluation Criteria.

3. *Narrative* The narrative should be as concise as possible. While a maximum length is not specified, a limit of thirty pages is preferred. Additional details and supporting materials may be included in appendices. The narrative should include the following sections:

    a. *Introduction* Describe the special circumstances associated with the collection of audience data in different types of organizations, such as: performing arts, museums, alternative spaces, media centers, community–based arts organizations, and free admission open air events. Demonstrate a knowledge of the problems in conducting audience surveys for such organizations.

    b. *Survey design and data collection methods* Specify the details of conducting audience surveys of arts and cultural organizations. Include a general description of questionnaire formats, approaches to data collection, and data processing. Provide specimen questionnaires.

    c. *Personnel* Identify project staff, consultants and advisors. Describe their qualifications that are important to the proposal. Full vita should be included in an appendix. An appendix should include letters from consultants, advisors, and consortium organizations *(not to include organizations that may be hosts to case studies in Phase II)* indicating their knowledge of and agreement to be included in the proposal.

    d. *Management plan* Include a schedule of principal tasks with staff assignments. Show the necessary steps for achieving project objectives with estimates of time and costs to reach each step. Describe capabilities, facilities, controls, and experience in providing privacy to audience data that will be collected. Related information should be provided on resources, flexibility, and experience that enhance the capability of the proposer to undertake the project. Collaborative arrangements are encouraged; however, it is absolutely essential that there be a single focus of responsibility and the proposal should identify the person responsible for the planning, coordination, supervision, and integration of the work in the final product. This individual should be named on the cover page as the project manager. In the case of collaborating arrangements, the proposed method for coordinating the work should be described and a letter from an authorized administrative official of the collaborating organizations should be included as an appendix to substantiate their agreement to participate in the proposal if an award is made.

4. *Budget* The budget form to be used in applications for support through this Program Solicitation is Contract Pricing Proposal (Research and Development), Optional Form 60, October 1971, General Services Administration.

5. *Appendices* Detailed curricula vitae and supporting information that proposers wish to make available to the reviewers may be attached to proposals as appendices. Letters should be included from consultants, advisors, and collaborating organizations indicating their knowledge of and agreement to participate in the proposal.

Question

1. Outline a research proposal to satisfy the requirements of Phase I of this project.

IV

SAMPLING

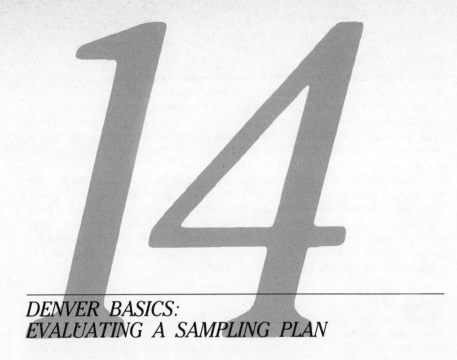

DENVER BASICS:
EVALUATING A SAMPLING PLAN

Denver Basics, a manufacturer and distributor of a line of soap products designed especially for skin care in high altitudes, was examining the sampling plan used by Rocky Mountain Research in a produce placement test.

Background

Denver Basics was formed in 1971 to develop a line of soap products that would be gentle and add moisture to dry skin. This problem was particularly acute for residents living in high altitude areas such as Denver, Salt Lake City and Sante Fe, as well as smaller surrounding communities such as Boulder, Colorado. The high altitude was extremely dry and caused skin to be dry and to crack. Other companies, like Scott's Liquid Gold, had already capitalized on the special needs for this problem and the time appeared ripe for Denver Basics to do so as well.

The founders of the company were two M.B.A. classmates at the University of Colorado, Boulder. Both Stan Willton and Philip Cather were finance majors but had enough marketing courses to realize that marketing research should always play a role in decision making. Upon graduation in 1971, they acquired some venture capital from their respective families.

The company, established in Denver, adopted the name of Denver Basics. The first product developed was a cocoa oil based, high-density bar soap. Rocky Mountain Research, a local research house, had been consulted in the selection of a name for this first product. The name decided upon was Aspen Cream and, since its introduction, it has been a great success, selling throughout the Rocky Mountain region and successfully competing with Caress and other oil-based soaps.

Copyright © 1981 by Dr. William J. Lundstrom

Present Situation

Denver Basics had developed and was now thinking of introducing a balsam-rich dandruff shampoo into their marketing territory. Before embarking on a total rollout of this conditioning antidandruff shampoo, the company called in Rocky Mountain Research to ask their valued opinion. The research firm proposed a product placement test prior to introduction to get consumer reaction and iron out any bugs in the product before proceeding with mass production. Willton and Cather accepted the proposal and went ahead with the placement test.

The results of the test were less than encouraging and caused a setback in the new product introduction. Willton and Cather could not understand the poor consumer reaction since they had thought the product through very carefully and spent considerable time and money on its development. Confused, they asked Rocky Mountain Research to present them with the sampling plan used in selecting the people for the test. The following is the procedure the research company used in choosing the participants for the shampoo test.

Sampling Plan

To accomplish the placement test task, it was believed that the sample should be representative of the general consumer population. That is, persons selected should come from the various income strata, racial groups, sexes, and age brackets that comprise the consuming public. Secondly, it was believed that consumer use is not limited to any one particular stratum or type of individual; although some groups appeared to be heavier users than others, the product use extends across all individuals. For these reasons, the selection procedure for the usage test was not limited by the exclusion of identifiable, demographic groups.

The sample was selected from residents of Denver, Colorado. Denver contained a large, heterogeneous population comprising all income levels and a mixture of Caucasian, black, and Mexican-American consumers. A larger metropolitan area was chosen over small communities, such as Boulder, Colorado, to avoid sampling from the rather limited range of income and racial groups that exist within their boundaries.

The sampling procedure employed was intended to capture a representative sampling by including a cross-section of the Denver population. Sample elements were stratified on the basis of income levels and racial groups. The selection of sampling areas was conducted by using 1970 census tract data for the city of Denver which was available for the demographic characteristics of income, race, age, and sex.

Census tracts were chosen that had large majorities of Caucasian, black, and Mexican-American elements. These tracts also included a balance of average household income distribution along a Warnerian classification of low, middle and upper-income families. This scheme was more readily employed with the Caucasian tracts which exhibited incomes throughout the lower to upper-income range. On the other hand, blacks and Mexican-Americans resided in tracts that would be considered low and middle-income areas. However, this income limitation portrays a minority income distribution that in all likelihood reflects the nature of their true distribution.

Once the pertinent census tracts were identified, individual residents were randomly selected from each individual tract. The number of individuals selected from each racial group represented an oversampling of minorities due to their possible resistance to participating in the study. The final sample of 510 thus contained over forty percent minority residents (see Exhibit 1).

The sampling procedure used the *Bresser's Directory* as the primary source listing the population elements and their location. The *Bresser's Directory* is an alphabetical listing of streets in the Denver metropolitan region with street addresses given in ascending order. In addition to the street address, the resident's name, telephone number, and age of the listing are given as well as the census tract in which each address is found.

By establishing a census tract's boundaries, the streets within that tract were identified by using a standard metropolitan street map of Denver, Colorado. Upon locating a street, the directory was employed to identify actual street addresses and occupants on that particular street. One sample element was selected from every second or third block until that street was exhausted—in most instances each street yielded only two or three names per census tract. Continuing, the next contiguous street was skipped, to avoid possible respondent interaction, and the following street was used for selection. This procedure continued until fifteen to twenty persons had been selected from that tract. A limit of fifteen to twenty persons was set so that a disproportionate number of individuals would not be taken from any one census tract.

Within block sampling it was attempted to vary the age of the listing, obtaining new, Fall 1979 listings as well as those that had been in service for ten years. In addition, females were selected from those persons listed with designated female Christian names or prefixed by "Mrs." A larger number of females were selected from primarily black neighborhoods than from the other neighborhoods to compensate for the fact that more black women assume the role of head of household. However, in none of the racial groups did the number of females selected exceed the number of males. This male-biased proportionality was maintained to balance the sexes in husband-wife households and the likelihood that the wife would actually be the one in the household to use the product.

To conclude, a sample of 510 residents from the city of Denver, Colorado, was selected to be representative of racial and income groups in the consuming public. In selecting a cross-section of individuals, the information acquired would give an indication of user product preference from not only one segment of the population but from individuals of varying socioeconomic strata.

Exhibit 1   Selected Sample for Item Selection—Race and Income Breakdown

Race	Lower Income	Middle Income	Upper Income	Total
White	62	194	45	301
Black	49	76	0	125
Mexican-American	38	46	0	84
Total	149	316	45	510

Questions

1. Evaluate the sample plan.
2. What reasons could explain why the results were negative?
3. Would an alternative plan be better?

15

METROPOLITAN CABLE TELEVISION COMPANY (A): SELECTING THE RESEARCH DESIGN AND SAMPLING PLAN

Metropolitan Cable Television Company (MetroCable) is a medium-sized cable television company serving a combination of communities and suburban areas in Orange County, California. Located immediately south of Los Angeles, this sprawling area is actually part of the greater L.A. metropolitan area, even though some areas served by MetroCable were nearly 100 miles from downtown Los Angeles. Although each year had seen increasing revenues, and total sales were now nearly $25 million, the management of MetroCable was becoming increasingly concerned as to whether or not this growth trend could be sustained. Indeed, a cursory analysis of customer data indicated that this year's revenues were not increasing at the rate seen in recent years. Management recognized that it was necessary to begin to be concerned about some things that previously had been only given lip service—namely, marketing research and marketing planning.

Cable Television Industry

The cable television industry, which today is a multibillion dollar business, began in a rather inauspicious manner. From the early days of television broadcasting, many areas of the country suffered from poor reception due to characteristics of the terrain (mountains, valleys, etc.) which interfered with the TV signal. In the mid-1950's, a frustrated television viewer who lived in such an area mounted a television antenna on a nearby mountain and ran a cable to his home in the valley. The experiment worked and soon the homes of his friends and neighbors were hooked up to this common lead from the mountain-top antenna. Soon other people who saw the dramatically improved television reception agreed to pay a fee to have their homes hooked up as well. Thus, the first cable television system was born.

Copyright © 1981 by Dr. Donald Sciglimpaglia

Most of the early growth in the cable television industry was generated by similar installations. In areas of poor television reception, due to terrain problems or due to distance from the broadcast signal, independent operators mounted a large centralized antenna and proceeded to establish a network of home subscribers. Many of the original cable operations were best described as "wire-stringers," an industry term referring to what they knew best how to do—lay wire or cable. From a business standpoint, many were small, underfinanced and relatively unsophisticated.

In spite of this lack of sophistication, the industry grew rapidly during the 1960's and 1970's. Cable systems became available in many large metropolitan areas as well as in more remote locations. By 1980, roughly 16.6 million homes in the U.S. (22 percent of all households with TV sets) were subscribers to some sort of cable system. Individual cable operators also grew rapidly. For instance, Mission Cable in San Diego, California, the nation's largest single operator, has 210,000 subscribers (about 50 percent of the market area's homes).

This growth period also saw profound technological and business changes in the industry. Some of the technological advances included the use of microwave and communications satellites to beam signals to cable operators. These signals included the broadcast of regular programming by so-called "super-stations" (such as WTTG in Atlanta) which could now be received throughout the country. Also broadcast by these new technologies were specialty programming such as Home Box Office (movies and entertainment specials), Cable News Network (twenty–four-hour news and special events) and ESPN (twenty–four-hour sports and entertainment programming). Another change in technology allowed some cable operators to offer two-way, interactive communications to subscribers (such as Qube in Columbus, Ohio). Still another allowed operators to offer service without using cable by broadcasting an electronically scrambled signal which was decoded by a receiving device at the subscriber's home.

At the same time, more and more local operators were either branching into new geographical markets or were being acquired by bigger cable operators to form "multiple system operators" (MSO's). Many of these MSO's, in turn, were being acquired by large, sophisticated, marketing–oriented firms such as Warner Communications and Westinghouse Corporation. So, too, was the market changing; subscribers, particularly in metropolitan areas where reception of local signals was not such a problem, were demanding more varied and more sophisticated program offerings.

MetroCable

MetroCable was founded in 1958 by Ross Hall, whose previous experience was as a technician at an early cable operation on the East Coast. Hall built MetroCable from a system having less than 1,000 subscribers in 1960 to one having over 100,000 in 1980. Much of this growth came from Hall's innate business sense (he made more right decisions than wrong), the rapid growth of the Orange County area, and some much–needed capital which was supplied by outside investors along the way. For all his success, Hall was primarily a "wire-stringer." He liked what he knew best, the technical side of the business, and gave little attention to marketing or business development, areas which he never thought were very important. By 1976 Hall had settled into semiretirement in a small beach community and became increasingly concerned with sailing, fine wines and modern art.

The marketing area at Metro was headed by Dave Chambers. Dave started with the firm while he was a student in business at the University of Southern California. He now had primary responsibility for advertising, sales and customer service. Much of his time and efforts were directed toward managing the twelve-person sales force that was used for customer contact. Dave's principal approach toward marketing was to generate enough leads for his sales force to try to close. Some were easily obtained, such as new apartment residents who could not use an outside antenna, while other leads were generated by more creative marketing strategies, such as seasonal special promotions or price incentives.

Service Offerings of MetroCable

MetroCable offered three types of services to subscribers: (1) regular broadcasts of stations transmitting from Los Angeles and San Diego which were rebroadcast over cable; (2) specialty programming which was available to cable subscribers as part of the service fee, and (3) Home Box Office (HBO) which was offered on an optional basis for an extra monthly fee. MetroCable program offerings are listed in Exhibit 1.

The basic cable service was priced at $9.00 per month for a single outlet after a $15.00 one-time installation charge. Multiple connections at a household were slightly higher (and about 43 percent of subscribers had more than one service connection). HBO was priced at $7.95 per month for a single set. Roughly twenty percent of MetroCable's customers subscribed to HBO. Average annual revenue per household derived from cable service was nearly $200 per subscriber in 1980. The remainder of Metro's revenue base was generated from advertising sales on its own Channel 1 and from other business.

MetroCable's Market

Dave Chambers was aware of a number of things that were occurring in Metro's market area. While the last decade had seen ever–increasing growth in new subscribers and in revenues, the customer base appeared to be leveling off at around 105,000 subscribers. While this was happening, Metro's market penetration was steadily declining. It now serviced about thirty-two percent of all households in its service area, down from nearly forty percent in 1975. In addition, the customer turnover rate had been accelerating. Chambers' sales efforts were barely sufficient to keep up with the number of customers who left the system, for whatever reason.

MetroCable enjoyed a virtual monopoly on cable service in its market area. No one else could string cable in the areas serviced since Metro had been awarded exclusive service rights by the local governing agencies. However, two new subscriber broadcast systems were now available to households in the MetroCable area. Both of these (ON-TV and Omega) broadcast specialty programming, mainly sports and movies, which could be received only by paid subscribers. These program offerings competed directly with MetroCable's HBO service and indirectly with its other specialty programming.

Research Problem at MetroCable

Since MetroCable had no formal marketing research position, most previous consumer research was normally commissioned and directed by the marketing manager. Chambers recognized that he needed some information to help him assess the effectiveness of the marketing program and the programming offered by MetroCable. He decided that it would be important to generate information regarding the following:
1.   Customer evaluation of MetroCable program offerings

Exhibit 1   MetroCable Program Offerings

Channel	Program Service
1	Metro-TV, movies, Madison Square Garden sports
2	KNXT (CBS) Los Angeles
3	KCST (NBC) San Diego
4	KNBC (NBC) Los Angeles
5	KTLA (independent) Los Angeles
6	XETV (independent) Tijuana/San Diego
7	KABC (ABC) Los Angeles
8	KFMB (CBS) San Diego
9	KHJ (independent) Los Angeles
10	KGTV (ABC) San Diego
11	KTTV (independent) Los Angeles
12	KPBS (PBS) San Diego
13	KCOP (independent) Los Angeles
14	KMEX (independent) Los Angeles (Spanish)
15	KCET (PBS) Los Angeles
16	XEWT (independent) Tijuana (Spanish)
17	Associated Press, financial news, NYSE quotes
18	TV program guide
19	Weather information
20	Home Box Office (optional)
21	Educational Community Services
22	Public access
23	Consumer shopping guide
24	C-SPAN, line coverage of U.S. Congress proceedings
25	ESPN, entertainment and sports programming
26	CNN, Cable News Network
27	Christian Communications, religious broadcasts

2.   Effectiveness of MetroCable advertising
3.   Effectiveness of sales activities
4.   Attitudes toward Home Box Office
5.   Demographic and household information

Chambers thought that it would be relatively simple to draw a sample of customers using the firm's computerized accounting system. He could have the computer select, for example, every one-hundredth account and print out that list. Or, it would be possible to have the computer use a random number generator and select the accounts at random. Although it would be more difficult, Chambers could have a data processing person write a short program which could select accounts by such variables as average monthly billing, area of residence, length of service or type of service used.

Chambers thought that he would like to gather information from about 500 customers, since this was a number frequently used in past studies. It would be important to have included in that figure roughly 100 HBO subscribers so that they could be analyzed separately. Chambers thought that he could do either a mail or telephone survey to collect the data. If the survey were to be done by phone, it would be possible to use MetroCable personnel which would hold expenses down, even though this would still be more costly than mail.

Chambers began to wonder about the pros and cons of using mail versus telephone to conduct the survey. For example, he knew that mail would probably have a higher non-response rate. This might not only affect survey accuracy but would also affect the number of accounts that would have to be generated by the computer for the initial mailing.

Once he settled on a choice between mail or telephone, Chambers needed a way to estimate the number of accounts to select in order to yield his desired sample size. In addition, he also needed to determine how the sample of accounts should be selected.

Questions

1. What are the relative advantages and disadvantages of using mail or using telephone surveying in this situation?
2. How should Chambers go about selecting the sample accounts from Metro-Cable's computer file?
3. If he were to conduct a mail survey, how could Chambers estimate the number of accounts to select?
4. What additional information could Chambers gain from surveying non-customers in addition to current subscribers?

16

STANDARD PHARMACEUTICAL COMPANY: SAMPLE SIZE AND PLAN DETERMINATION

Standard Pharmaceutical Company supplies generic pharmaceutical products to drug stores and pharmacies in twelve western states. Headquartered in San Jose, California, Standard last year showed sales of roughly $9 million.

General Pharmaceuticals

The pharmaceutical industry, a multi-billion dollar business in the United States, is divided into many product segments. One major differentiation is between what are called over-the-counter (O.T.C.) products and ethical pharmaceuticals. O.T.C. products can be purchased without a prescription, while ethical products can be sold only as prescribed by a physician. Ethical products are in turn divided into branded and generic pharmaceuticals. Branded products are those prescription-only pharmaceuticals which are sold under a company's specific brand name (e.g., Darvon). Generic products are the pharmaceutical equivalents of the branded products. Most states allow a consumer to have the generic equivalent substituted for a branded product, even when the physician's prescription called for the latter. In doing so, consumers generally can save considerably since generics are substantially less costly. California law, for example, mandates that a generic equivalent *must* be substituted if available when the consumer is utilizing state–supported medical assistance. For these reasons, the generic market has been extremely active in recent years.

Pharmacists have available to them a wide variety of lines of generic products to choose from. Some suppliers, including Standard, utilize a sales force to call on pharmacies and then ship orders direct from a central warehouse. Others utilize drug wholesale houses or direct mail "catalogue" selling.

Copyright © 1981 by Dr. Donald Sciglimpaglia

Standard's Management Question

Standard Pharmaceuticals, with a full-time sales force of eleven individuals, has traditionally stressed its wide line, the quality of its pharmaceutical products and the service offered by its sales force. Experiments with price promotions and special discounts have historically proved successful, but usually only in generating short-term demand. Overall, Standard's prices are about average for the industry.

Increasingly, however, Standard's sales force has argued for a more aggressive pricing policy and additional sales incentives. Standard's marketing manager, Darrell Evans, was interested in knowing more about how pharmacists selected the source of generic products, so that he would be better able to assess any potential changes in sales strategy. Evans elected to conduct a research study to try to determine the relative importance of different factors in a pharmacist's decision as to the source of generic products.

The Research Study

Evans decided to conduct a survey of pharmacists in his geographic market. After careful consideration, he came up with a list of twelve factors which he thought might affect the pharmacist's decision as to source of supply. These were:

1. Dependability of generic supplier in filling orders (frequency and quality of delivery)
2. Convenience of ordering from a supplier
3. Service or information provided by a supplier's sales force
4. Whether a supplier's products are priced competitively
5. Whether a supplier's products are the lowest-priced in the industry.
6. Special price considerations (cash discounts from list, volume discounts or deals)
7. Overall quality of supplier's product line of generics
8. Supplier's ability to offer full line of generic products
9. Supplier's trade journal or direct mail advertising
10. Physical consistency and appearance of supplier's products
11. Confidence established with supplier's sales representative
12. Whether supplier has product liability insurance

Evans' plan was to ask the pharmacist to rate each factor in terms of the pharmacy's decision regarding which supplier's generic products to purchase. Next, questions would be asked about present source of supply and satisfaction with the suppliers. Lastly, he would also ask questions concerning buying authority, relative size of the pharmacy and number of prescriptions filled per day for comparison purposes.

Standard's prior experience with surveys of this sort proved that pharmacists were often difficult to reach and interview over the telephone, particularly in large, busy pharmacies and that mail surveys, when properly conducted, were nearly as successful in generating responses. Evans elected to use mail for this project. Based on prior experience and on the incentive which he planned to use (a small digital desk clock), Evans thought that a mail survey would probably generate between a thirty and forty percent response rate. He planned to utilize the services of an outside mailing firm so that Standard's identity would not be known.

Sampling Problem

Evans had available to him a commercial directory which listed all the pharmacies in his market territory. In all, there were nearly 30,000. From sales records, it was possible to identify which were past and which were present Standard customers.

The directory also indicated the name of the person in charge of the pharmacy, the relative size of the pharmacy and whether it was an independent or part of a chain.

First, Evans needed to know how many of the 30,000 pharmacies he should sample. After reviewing an old textbook of his and discussing the problem, he decided that he would like to have a sample large enough so that the statistical confidence in the results was ninety-five percent. Evans was unsure as to how to translate this abstract notion into sample size, since the textbook always dealt with rather simple examples and his survey dealt with a number of variables. Also, in reviewing the material on sampling Evans read again a section on sampling methods. He wondered if he should draw a systematic sample or a simple random sample. Evans also questioned whether or not it made sense to stratify the sample and, if so, on what dimensions.

Questions

1.   How should Evans go about determining sample size? Make any necessary assumptions and calculate the number of questionnaires which should be mailed.
2.   What sampling method (systematic, simple random or stratified) do you suggest? Explain why.
3.   If Evans were to use a stratified sample, what variable(s) should be used to stratify on?

ARBITRON: RADIO AUDIENCE SAMPLING METHODOLOGY

The Arbitron Company is a subsidiary of the Control Data Corporation. It offers many marketing research services and has offices in New York, Chicago, Atlanta, Los Angeles, San Francisco, Dallas and Washington, D.C. One of the services in which Arbitron specializes is the measuring of radio audiences.

Arbitron uses a seven-day personal diary which is placed with a sample of individuals, twelve years old or older, within a local market. Each survey period consists of ten or twelve consecutive weeks with a separate random sample of individuals participating in each week of the survey period.

The Arbitron radio diary in Exhibit 1 is the data collection instrument for determining the time of radio listening, the station and the place of listening. The methods for selecting samples as described by Arbitron follow.

How Arbitron Measures Radio
There are many research measurement techniques which are used to gather data. Arbitron Radio has developed the current personal diary method of measurement after investing millions of dollars in research and testing.

Each year, Arbitron retests its current methods and experiments with new techniques that may be used to replace those in existence. This constant testing assures you, the user, that Arbitron is always using the best and most practical techniques available. For this reason, the techniques included herein are subject to change. An overview description of the present measurement techniques follows.

Defining the Geography That Is To Be Measured
Three different factors govern the geography that Arbitron measures for radio.

Copyright © 1977, 1981 by The Arbitron Company.

Metro Survey Areas   These generally correspond to Standard Metropolitan Statistical Areas (SMSA's) or Standard Consolidated Statistical Areas (SCSA's) as defined by the U.S. government's Office of Management and Budget subject to exceptions dictated by historical industry usage and other marketing considerations. The SCSA is a larger area which always encompasses a smaller SMSA and is implemented by Arbitron only upon agreement among subscribing stations within the market.[1]

Total Survey Area (TSA)   The Total Survey Area consists of all Metro counties plus all other counties in which there is significant listening to stations located in the Metro Counties in the TSA, but outside the Metro are called non-Metro counties.

When a market is measured for the first time, Arbitron uses 0.5MV/M signal contours of the market's AM and FM radio stations in conjunction with station performance in surrounding counties to establish the non-Metro. With the contour maps in place, Arbitron looks for counties in which ten percent of the Cume[2] listenership is to the stations home to the Metro being measured. Any county which meets this listenership level becomes part of the Total Survey Area. Exception: If a county which is in the Metro of another Arbitron measured market is contiguous to the Metro of the market being examined, the requirement for Cume listenership is five percent rather than ten percent.

Arbitron updates its Total Survey Areas once a year, in April, based on listenership during the past two spring surveys, and the past fall survey, in those markets where a fall survey was conducted.

Arbitron's ADI (Area of Dominant Influence)   ADI's are Arbitron Television's geographic market design which defines each television market, exclusive of others, based on measurable viewing patterns. Every county in the United States (excluding Hawaii and the portions of Alaska outside of the Anchorage ADI) is allocated exclusively to one ADI.

In addition to radio and television, other media, including newspapers, magazines and outdoor, provide estimates of audience delivery based on Arbitron's ADI's. Listening estimates in ADI's give radio an equal opportunity to compete for advertising dollars.

How Much Sample Should There Be?

All surveys are based on taking a sample and projecting the results to the total universe. A blood test requires a small sample of blood, not the entire supply in the body. A properly drawn sample, even if it does appear to be small, can be very representative of the universe, just as a blood sample can.

Market quotas or diary "in-tab objectives" are established for a market's Metro and non-Metro area based largely on the population of the market. The in-tab objective is established by the following formula:

$$\text{Standard Radio Markets:} \quad 1.5 \; \frac{2.055}{\sqrt{\text{Metro Population 12} +}}$$

$$\text{Maximum} = 4000$$
$$\text{Minimum} = 550$$

---

[1] In New England, SMSA's are defined on a "town" rather than a county basis. Where the SMSA represents sixty-five percent or more of the SRDS full-county definition for the market, Arbitron uses the SRDS full-county definition to define the Metro Survey Area; where the SMSA represents less than sixty-five percent of the population of the SRDS full-county definition for the market, Arbitron uses the SMSA to define the Metro Survey Area.

[2] Cumulative Audience Estimates.

Condensed Radio Markets: $$2.055 \sqrt{\frac{\text{Metro Population } 12+}{1.5}}$$

Maximum $= 400$

Minimum $= 250$

Sample Allocation

Allocation of sample among Metro counties is based on each county's percentage of total Metro population. The Metro receives a larger sample in order to project estimates for individual age/sex cells for each reported station. The non-Metro's sample size is for the purpose of adding listening estimates in these areas to the stations' estimates in the Metro.

Here is an allocation example:

Market: Your City, U.S.A.

Area	12+ Population	Quota
Metro	100,000	475
Non Metro	20,000	75
Total Survey Area	120,000	550

Metro Area	12+ Population	% of Total Metro Pop.	County Objective
County A	73,700	73.7%	350
County B	26,300	26.3%	125
Metro Total	100,000	100.0%	475

Non-Metro Area	12+ Population	% of Non-Metro Pop.	County Objective
County C	1,000	5	4
County D	6,000	30	23
County E	4,000	20	15
County F	6,000	30	23
County G	3,000	15	11
Non-Metro Total	20,000	100	76

Non-Metro sample allocation is usually more complicated than the above example. If the population in the non-Metro is relatively high in comparison to the Metro population, there may be higher objective in-tab quotas.

Placement Rates

The number of diaries placed is calculated based on Arbitron's experience in each county in getting back complete, usable diaries. Each county's agree rate, average household size, return rate and usability rate are taken into consideration to determine how many diaries should be placed to get back the proper number of "in-tab" diaries.

Market: Your City, U.S.A.

County	In-Tab Diaries Required	÷	% of Usable In-Tab Diaries of Those Originally Mailed	=	Diaries Mailed	÷	Persons per Household among consenting Households	÷	% of Households that consent to Participate	÷	% of Originally Designated Households in which Telephone was Answered	=	Household Listings Ordered
X	175	÷	60%	=	292	÷	2.4	÷	81%	÷	87%	=	173
Y	131	÷	61%	=	215	÷	2.2	÷	87%	÷	90%	=	125

Example: The number of household listings to be ordered is adjusted after each survey in order to compensate for over- or under-response rates.

The number of household listings to be ordered is adjusted after each survey in order to compensate for over-or under-response rates.

.Example:

Your City, U.S.A.
Metro Market Quota or objective: 475

	In-Tab Quota	Actual In-Tab This Survey	Actual In-Tab Last Survey	Actual In-Tab 2 Surveys Ago
Metro County A	350	400	390	388
Metro County B	125	130	127	125
Metro	475	530	517	513

In this example, County A is returning more diaries than the quota. The number of household listings may be adjusted downward. Response in County B is on target, and there will be no adjustment.

Example: In this example, County A is returning more diaries than the quota. The number of household listings may be adjusted downward. Response in County B is on target, and there will be no adjustment.

Drawing the Households That Will Be in the Sample

Sample quotas are recorded on a computerized tape which goes to Metromail Corporation, the nation's leading supplier of listed telephone households. Metromail then uses a sophisticated sample selection program developed by Arbitron to choose those households which will be asked to participate in the survey. It is virtually impossibel to exactly duplicate the Arbitron-selected sample households.

Listed telephones in each county are sorted into order by zip code. Business numbers are removed from the list. The computer counts the number of listings in each county and divides this number by the quota for the county in order to create an "interval". Within each interval, the computer generates a random number which corresponds to a household within that interval. That household becomes part of what is called the "designated sample."

Example:

	Households Needed	Listed Telephone Households	Interval
County A	121	25,400	210

The random telephone listing sheet can be seen in Exhibit 1.

Arbitron's Expanded Sample Frame

Arbitron's Expanded Sample Frame (ESF) is a universe which consists of unlisted telephone households. ESF is used in addition to normal sampling procedures in some Arbitron Metros.

What is an Unlisted Telephone Household? Unlisted telephone households are telephone households which do not appear in the current telephone directory. They are households which have requested their telephone number not to be listed or they are households where the assigned telephone number did not get listed in the directory because of the date of installation and the date of telephone directory

Exhibit 1 Random Number Listing Sheet
Household randomly selected within each interval of 210 households
The computer, in this instance, will count down 210 telephone listings and then generate a random number between 1 and 210. The number, let us say 67, signifies the residential listing to be included. A new random number is selected for each interval.

By design the sample selection system is geographically dispersed by zip code.

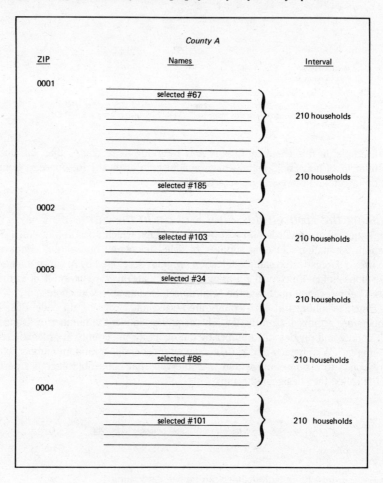

Household randomly selected within each interval of 210 households

The computer, in this example, will count down 210 telephone listings and then generate a random number between 1 and 210. The number, let us say 67, signifies the residential listing to be included. A new *random number* is selected for each interval.

By design the sample selection system is geographically dispersed by ZIP Code.

publication. These two types of unlisted telephone households have been labeled unlisted by choice and unlisted by chance. Arbitron's procedures reach both types of households.

Identifying Unlisted Telephone Households   An analysis is made of listed telephone numbers to locate those numbers which tend to be unlisted. Using a computer, and the published telephone directory showing all listed telephone households, an analysis is made of all telephone exchanges which contain residential telephone listings. For this analysis, a telephone exchange is defined as the first five digits of the seven–digit telephone number. For example, PA5-1234 is a listed household in the PA5-12XX exchange. All exchanges which contain five or more listings are considered for ESF sampling.

The computer identifies all 100 numbers in the PA5-12XX exchange (PA5-1200—PA5-1299). The telephone directory provides all listed numbers which are then deleted from the 100 numbers in the computer's memory. This deletion provides a group of remaining numbers which are unlisted or not assigned. The computer saves all of the "remaining" numbers for all residential exchanges in the metropolitan area. A systematic random sample is then drawn from the "remaining numbers." This provides all the numbers to be dialed for a given ESF metropolitan area sample. Where known, all commercial telephone numbers are deleted along with the telephone banks used for pay phones.

Getting Households to Participate (Areas Not Ethnically Controlled)

The listed telephone households are sent a letter telling them of their selection. The letter is followed by a call from one of Arbitron's 3,500 field interviewers who asks for their participation. (The first contact for residents in unlisted telephone households is the phone call.) If the household agrees, and more than eighty percent do, then the interviewer asks the number of individuals residing there who are twelve years or older. Diaries for each individual are mailed in time to arrive one or two days before the start of the week the household is to participate in the survey. Each survey week begins on a Thursday and ends the following Wednesday. No household participates more than one week. The Arbitron interviewer calls the household just prior to the beginning of the survey and answers any questions the household may have about participating. In the middle of the survey week the Arbitron interviewer calls the household to confirm that the diaries have been received and are being filled out. The interviewer also reminds the household to return their diaries at the week's end. These calls are part of a comprehensive diary security program designed to ensure the integrity of the sample and the estimates that are produced. As an incentive to get good response rates, premiums varying from fifty cents to five dollars are enclosed with each diary.

Arbitron's Ethnic Measurement

The 1970 Census under-represented millions of Black and Spanish-speaking people. If this can happen in a government-managed census that is supposed to account for all persons in the United States, than it can happen in a sample of the general population taken by an audience measurement company that is measuring radio listening.

Recognizing this possibility, Arbitron Radio has done the following about it:

1. Special interviewing procedures in high density ethnic areas

2.   Identification of the race nationality of respondents
3.   Weighting audience estimates by race

Special Interviewing Procedures in High Density Ethnic Areas   The important objective in measuring listening among Blacks and Spanish-speaking people is to (1) find them and (2) get them into the tabulated sample. In order to meet this objective, Arbitron Radio uses special interviewing procedures in high density Black and Spanish areas. Use of these procedures has resulted in a significant improvement in the response rate from people living in these areas and has resulted in a better representation of Black and Spanish-speaking persons in the tabulated sample.

Selection of Metros for Ethnic Measurement Procedures   The criteria for selecting the markets in which to implement special ethnic interviewing techniques are:
1.   Metros with twenty percent or more Black or Hispanic population;
2.   Metros with station(s) programming fifty percent or more to Black or Hispanic audiences can qualify if they have ten percent or more Black or Hispanic population or if they have a Black or Hispanic population of 150,000 or more.
     In selecting Metros, these criteria apply to each population group separately. That is, one does not add the Black population to the Hispanic population to determine if there is twenty percent penetration.
     When special interviewing began in 1967, the criteria above were not established as policy. Markets in which ethnic interviewing was done prior to 1970 continue to have these special techniques even though they may not meet the present criteria.
     Using these selection criteria, Arbitron now conducts special ethnic interviewing techniques in more than sixty radio Metros.

Selection of High Density Ethnic Control Areas Within Metros   The high density ethnic control area is essentially a geographic area. When a market qualifies for ethnic measurement, each qualifying county within the Metro area is examined on the basis of zip codes. If a zip code contains thirty-five percent or more Black or Hispanic population, that zip code area is designated as a control area in which the special interviewing techniques will be conducted. Usually, there are several zip code areas which form the control area of each Metro in which ethnic measurement is done.
The specific requirements that these Zip Code areas must meet are as follows:
1.   They must be within a county containing twenty percent or more Black or Hispanic population (10 percent if Metro has a station programming fifty percent or more to Black or Hispanic population); and
2.   They must contain thirty-five percent or more Black or Hispanic population; and
3.   The cumulative Black or Hispanic penetration across zip codes or census tracts within zip codes must equal ten percent or more of the Metro in-tab objective or sixty diaries, whichever is less.
Once a part of a county, or counties, is designated as a high density control area, this area is treated as a separate county. The results of interviewing from within this control area are projected only to the people living within the control area the same as results would be projected for a separate Metro county.

Special Interviewing Procedures in Black Community Areas   The telephone is used as a data retrieval procedure within high density Black areas selected on the basis of the penetration of the Black population. Interviews are conducted with persons age twelve and older in sample households over a seven-day period.

The Arbitron interviewer makes an initial call and finds a time convenient to household members when he or she may call on a regular daily basis. She then interviews each household member twelve years and older on a daily basis and records the results in a separate diary designated for each family member. In other words, the interviewer keeps the diary for the respondent and fills it out based on the information obtained in daily telephone calls. This procedure is followed for all households, irrespective of their race/nationality characteristics, in the high density Black areas.

Arbitron respondents to the telephone retrieval procedure are told *before* they listen that they are going to be asked about their listening at some time in the future. There is no attempt to ask persons, without any advance warning, about what radio stations they listened to in the previous twenty-four hours. People who are told in advance that they are going to be asked about their listening, can remember it better than people who were never warned ahead of time.

The telephone retrieval procedure is conducted daily over a seven-day period. There is no attempt to ask people what they listened to seven days ago. People who are contacted daily about their listening can be more accurate in telling what they did than people who are asked to remember—on a total recall basis without advance warning—what they did seven days ago.

In research conducted by Arbitron outside of high density Black areas, it was noted that response rate among Blacks, when interviewed using the standard diary procedure, was lower than those among non-Blacks. In other words, Blacks from outside of high density Black areas were responding at a somewhat lower rate than non-Blacks.

In order to do something about this, Arbitron extended the telephone retrieval procedure to include all Blacks living within the Metro area irrespective of whether or not they lived inside or outside of high density Black areas. This procedure is now being used in all metropolitan areas in which any kind of telephone retrieval procedure is used for high density Black areas.

Special Interviewing Procedures in Hispanic Community Areas   Within those control areas selected on the basis of Hispanic population, the technique used is personal placement, personal follow-up, and personal pick-up. People in sample households are given bilingual diaries by bilingual interviewers. These diaries are personally delivered to the household prior to the start of the survey and reviewed with the family members. During the middle of the survey week, another personal visit is made to the household to encourage continuation of the survey and to answer any new questions respondents may have. At the conclusion of the survey, the diaries are personally picked up.

Processing Ethnic Diaries   Diaries obtained through the special telephone and personal placement retrieval methods are edited and processed along with those diaries which were placed by telephone in non-ethnic areas and which were returned by mail. The same careful editing and processing control procedures applied to non-ethnic diaries is used to process the ethnic diaries. The population estimates used for projection purposes are based on updated 1970 Census data provided by Market Statistics, Inc.

Identification of the Race/Nationality of Respondents   In 1972, Arbitron Radio conducted considerable testing to determine the best way of obtaining race/nation-

Exhibit 2   Race/Nationality Identification Question

"Arbitron designed this survey to measure all segments of the population. Would
you please tell me how you describe your family? Is it Cuban, Mexican/American,
Puerto Rican, Other Spanish, American Indian, Black, Oriental, White or Other?"
(INTERVIEWER: CHECK APPROPRIATE BOX BELOW.)

☐ CUBAN   ☐ AMERICAN INDIAN

☐ MEXICAN/AMERICAN   ☐ BLACK

☐ PUERTO RICAN   ☐ ORIENTAL

☐ OTHER SPANISH   ☐ WHITE

                            ☐ OTHER_____
                                      (Please specify)

ality characteristics from respondents. After much experimentation, it was determined that the best procedure for obtaining race/nationality information was at the time of the diary placement in the placement interview.

Beginning with the April/May 1973 survey, the question in Exhibit 2 was asked in all Metro areas in which any kind of telephone or personal retrieval procedures were used.

This question was validated in several markets through face-to-face interviews of respondents who had previously given their race/nationality characteristic on the telephone.

Identification of the race/nationality of respondents will continue in every Metro area in which Arbitron has any kind of telephone or personal retrieval procedures. The question is asked of *all households* in the Metro, not just those households which fall within the high density Black or Spanish areas.

Processing the Diaries When They are Returned

Diaries are postage paid and are returned directly to Arbitron's Research and Production Center in Beltsville, Maryland. A Spring Sweep measures more than 170 radio standard markets plus over eighty "smaller" markets called "condensed radio markets." Over 240,000 different diaries are processed for a spring survey alone.

The First Diary Check   Diary processing begins with a "usability edit." The diary is checked for the following items:

- Timeliness—diary must be postmarked after last day of survey and received prior to cutoff dates (thirteen to twenty days after last date of survey week).
- Completeness—listening is recorded and/or "no listening" box checked on each day.
- Age/Sex—to be filled in, but, if not, an attempt is made to contact respondent.
- Proper County Assignment

The Second Diary Check—Crediting Slogans   Diaries containing slogans, frequencies or personality names are sent to special editors. This intermediate step takes place for all diaries requiring special attention. It is here that slogans, frequencies, personalities and multiple station conflicts (i.e., two stations have same slogan, frequency, etc.) are resolved.

These special editors check slogans against a master slogan list for the county from which the diary came. This master list is a compilation of slogans taken from facilities forms filled out by each station in the market prior to each survey, and is on a county-by-county basis.

A maximum of three slogans from each station are accepted for use in a slogan edit. When two or more stations have the same or nearly the same slogan, set procedures are followed in assigning listening, among them:

1.   Assign the slogan based on whether the entry is AM or FM.
2.   One percent slogan conflict rule criteria applied.[1]
3.   Re-call the diarykeepers when more than one station in conflict meets the one percent criteria.
4.   If conflict remains unresolved after callback, ascription is applied.[2]

Entries which name personalities or programs are checked against the program logs provided by each station for that particular market.

If a station carries any sports events, it is also important that this information be submitted on the sports log with team name (e.g., Tigers Football). This way, the station will receive credit for mention of any sports events covered.

When call letters are not present, Arbitron uses this priority in assigning listening: (1.) frequency, (2.) slogan, (3.) program/personality. If, for example, a respondent makes the entry, 94.5 News Radio, the station whose frequency is 94.5 would receive credit.

Final Diary Check   After the second diary check is performed, diaries are sent to one of Arbitron's three data-input minicomputers. These minicomputers perform certain edit checks on the key-to-disc operators' work which catch many types of errors.

Crediting Aberrated Call Letters   Arbitron's two huge Control Data 3500 computers collect the data input from the three minicomputers and perform basic logic checks and call letter legality tests prior to the actual market report calculations.

For instance, if station WXXX changed call letters six months ago from WYYY, any entries to WYYY would be automatically "flipped" to the new call letters.

If an entry is to WXXX-AM and there is no WXXX-AM but a WXXX-FM does exist, the computer will automatically "flip" WXXX-AM to FM or vice versa in specified counties.

If a station's call letters are often aberrated or "confused" by respondents and these aberrations meet automatic flip criteria, an automatic flip is entered into the computer to correct the respondent confusion. An example of this follows:

Correct	Actual Entry
WBER	WVER (sounds like V to respondent)
WLVE	WIVE (L is written as I)
WBER	WBRE (transposed call letters)

---

[1]The "one percent slogan conflict rule" basically establishes a cutoff point for resolving slogan conflicts. The cutoff is one percent of the previous year's TALO (total number of mentions) by county, by station. All "potential" conflicting station slogans are analyzed to determine whether they qualify for slogan conflict resolution. If only one of the two or more stations, "potentially" in conflict, received one percent or more of the mentions in that county, then that station will receive credit for any slogan entries in that county, thereby eliminating the need for a callback(s). However, if in another county, two or more of the stations "potentially" in conflict, receive one percent or more of the total mentions in that county, each is considered in conflict. Callback procedures are then instituted to determine proper listening credit.

[2]Ascription is a statistical technique that allocates radio listening proportionate to each conflicting station's diaries as calculated on a county basis using the previous year's TALO. Diary credit is randomly assigned automatically to a station based on its share of total diaries in that county.

In addition, the Arbitron Radio Department examines every set of call letters when processing a report in an attempt to assign aberrated call letters to the proper station.

Weighting   Weighting the sample can best be described as projecting the sample to represent the population. All these projections require a basic statistical assumption, that a sample can represent the universe. In its simplest form, here is how it works:

An in-tab of 1,000 diaries is actually the measurement of 7,000 days of listening.
(1,000 diaries X 7 days = 7,000)

Exhibit 3   Arbitron Radio Day

COUNTY "A"

	18-24 Men
Population	30,000
In-Tab	15
Value of each diary - Persons Per Diary Value (PPDV)	2,000

Questions
1. Critically analyze the procedures used by Arbitron.
2. How do these methods differ from methods used for telephone surveys? Other forms of data collection?

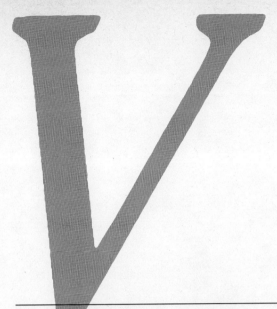

QUESTIONNAIRE DESIGN

SENAT BANK (A): QUESTIONNAIRE DESIGN AND EVALUATION

Mr. John White, pensively sitting at his desk in the town of Walkersville, Indiana, had recently been brought in as president of Senat Bank and was faced with the task of building up the deposits and depositors. He had come from Continental Illinois National Bank in Chicago where he was formerly vice-president and a trust officer with the bank. Seeking a slower pace of life, Mr. White accepted this position and the additional responsibilities of the presidency. Although he knew Senat Bank was nothing compared to Continental Illinois, he still faced many of the challenges that Continental had in the middle 60's. That is, Senat was a typical small town bank that only provided general banking services to the public. It had no marketing department; it didn't know anything about the marketing concept; and, its cold, mausoleum-like walls were typical of the banks of yesteryear. Thus, Mr. White knew he had a formidable task ahead of him; much like the transition that Continental Illinois went through. Continental's transition was that of becoming a modern, progressive, consumer-oriented bank when many of its senior officers did not know how to cope with such a drastic change in the basic philosophy of its management.

History of Senat Bank

Walkersville was a moderate–size town with a population of 62,000. It was located in northwest Indiana, some seventy-five miles from Chicago. The population in and around Walkersville was composed of people in a variety of different occupations. A considerable number of the people were employed in the steelworks of Gary, Indiana, and were represented by both blue-collar and white-collar professional workers. Other members of the community were employed by a local factory that produced major appliances under various private brand names. Also included were small mer-

Copyright © 1981 Dr. William J. Lundstrom

chants in the town of Walkersville who maintained commercial accounts with the bank. Another segment of the market was composed of the agricultural community, representing farmers in the immediate locale as well as agricultural supply houses such as International Harvester, Case, Purina and other seed and fertilizer businesses. Thus, Walkersville represented a mix of different professions and occupations not often found in a town of its size.

Senat Bank was formed in 1918 to handle the banking needs of the local farming and business community. The founders of the bank were Senator Lucius Atkinson, a distinguished member of the U.S. Senate whose abbreviated title became the name of the bank; Colonel J. B. Sanbourne of Spanish War fame; and, Thadeus "Tippecanoe" Tyler, a large Indiana landowner. The founding fathers chartered Senat Bank as a state bank and were strong believers in the boom times which followed the end of the Great War. Their projections were correct and Senat Bank grew from a meager capitalization of $100,000 in 1918 to a very prosperous bank of some $17 million in 1929. The Board of Directors had invested in Florida real estate and much of this prosperity was due to the increasing land value there. The bubble soon burst in November 1929; the board was asked to pay up the loans that were taken out in order to purchase the Florida real estate. Senator Atkinson put his personal fortune up as collateral against the loans and the bank managed to survive the Depression.

The rather flambouyant and risky bank dealings which took place during the Roaring Twenties gave way to a conservative fiduciary posture during the 1930's. Upon the death of Senator Atkinson in 1938, the bank passed into the hands of the Atkinson family and remained a closely held family–run operation for the next four decades. Agatha Atkinson and her sons Andrew and William assumed the key managerial positions in the bank and maintained control until John White was brought on board in 1980. Agatha, Chairman of the Board until 1962, retired from the bank and Andrew took over as chief executive officer. William became president and chairman of the Finance Committee. These moves had little effect upon the outlook of the bank and its operation remained the same until 1978.

In 1978, both Andrew and William attended a school of banking at a major university in the Midwest. During their stay, they were exposed to several courses in marketing. One, in particular, a marketing research course made them think of what they hadn't done in the past and the potential for what they could do at Senat Bank. This newfound knowledge, in conjunction with an introduction to the marketing concept, got the two brothers excited about the possibilities of making their bank more responsive to customer needs.

A Time of Change

The enthusiam shown by the Atkinson brothers was not entirely due to a rejuvenation of spirit due to the banking school. Senat Bank's competition had grown steadily during the past four decades. The principal competitors were Peoples Bank and Citizens National Bank of Walkersville. Peoples Bank was also a state-chartered bank like Senat while Citizens represented the only federally chartered bank and was under the control of the Federal Reserve System. While these may appear to be major differences, all three banks were insured by the FDIC and had the same security provisos.

During the past decade, both Peoples and Citizens Bank had exhibited a faster growth rate than did Senat Bank (see Exhibits 1 and 2). This did not go unnoticed by the Atkinson brothers who brought it to the attention of the Board of Directors.

Exhibit 1   Balance Sheet for Senat Bank (in 000's)

Assets	1980	1975	1970
Cash	$ 4,280	$ 3,927	$ 3,783
Securities	7,350	10,160	11,934
Loans	27,125	20,851	18,739
Buildings	1,107	983	994
Other Assets	209	537	610
Total	$40,071	$36,458	$36,060
Liabilities			
Demand Deposits	11,734	9,476	3,932
Time Deposits	24,056	23,471	23,216
Shareholders' Equity	3,530	3,092	2,717
Surplus	751	419	1,195
Total	$40,071	$36,458	$36,060

Exhibit 2   Abbreviated Balance Sheet for both Peoples and Citizens National Bank

	1980		1975		1970	
Assets	Peoples	Citizens	Peoples	Citizens	Peoples	Citizens
Cash	$ 1,917	$ 2,312	$ 1,577	$ 1,991	$ 1,278	$ 1,765
Securities	1,631	3,743	1,349	2,017	2,332	1,663
Loans	17,006	22,117	11,614	16,094	9,082	13,111
Total	$20,614	$27,172	$14,540	$20,102	$12,692	$16,539
Liabilities						
Demand Deposits	$ 8,107	$ 7,216	$ 6,957	$ 5,819	$ 5,512	$ 4,111
Time Deposits	12,507	19,956	7,583	14,283	7,180	12,428
Total	$20,614	$27,172	$14,540	$20,102	$12,692	$16,539

Realizing that they did not possess the experience necessary to make a major shift in bank policy and that the bank's position might be jeopardized if they didn't, Andrew and William proposed to the board that the bank take some drastic steps in adopting the marketing concept. The directors concurred that a change appeared to be necessary in order to attract more depositors and improve the growth rate of the bank. However, the previous conservative banking policies and thinking left the board in a quandary as to what course of action should be taken. It was finally proposed that if the bank were to seriously pursue this new course of action, then fresh management talent with previous experience in developing a strong marketing program would be needed. A search was undertaken for a new president and resulted in the hiring of John White. Andrew remained as Chairman of the Board, William became the newly created Vice-chairman and John White was made President and Chief Executive Officer.

Implementing the Marketing Concept Through Research

John White, who had been through a similar transition from staid banking practices to an aggressive marketing position, realized the value of conducting marketing research before any major marketing program was developed. His previous employer,

Exhibit 3   Research Proposal for Senat Bank

```
                              EXHIBIT 3
                    RESEARCH PROPOSAL TO SENAT BANK


                            May 20, 1981


         Mr. John White, President
         Senat Bank
         Walkersville, IN  47301

         Dear John:

              It was a pleasure to speak with you again and to know
         that High Performance Marketing Research can assist you in
         solving your current problems.

              After our discussion, and deciding a positioning study
         would be the best approach to take, I have put together
         what I believe will best give you the input you desire at
         a reasonable cost.  What High Performances proposes is:

         1.   A sample size of 250 persons.

         2.   Sample randomly selected using random digit
              dialing within the county trade area.

         3.   Use of standardized questionnaire that in-
              corporates the multiattribute model to deter-
              mine where the Bank stands against its
              competitors.  (The importance weights have been
              predetermined through many previous bank studies).
              The questionnaire is enclosed for your approval.

         4.   The data will be computer analyzed and presented
              in a report showing your position (image) relative
              to other banks.

              The estimated cost to conduct this study for Senat Bank
         will be $3200.00 ± 10%.  I believe that this study and cost
         are reasonable and will help to expedite your new marketing
         program.

              Thank you for giving High Performance this opportunity
         to be of service and we look forward to working with you on
         this venture.

                            Yours truly,

                            Jack

                            Jack Grisham, Vice President
                            High Performance Marketing Research
```

Continental Illinois, has embarked on several marketing efforts without having obtained research information, resulting in the loss of thousands of dollars as well as
their image in the banking community. Only then did the bank employ an outside
research firm which gathered data and showed why the programs failed. From that
point on, Continental never embarked on any new marketing program without first
conducting some phase of marketing research. By the time White left Continental, the bank had a full-time, in-house research staff headed up by a Ph.D. in marketing.

Realizing the folly of not conducting marketing research prior to making
changes in bank operations and marketing, White pondered how and what to do
first. Using his old contacts, he called Jack Grisham at High Performance Marketing
Research in Chicago. He explained his problem and the need for some direction in
changing the bank's performance over the next five years.

"Sounds like you need to look at your present strengths and weaknesses before

Exhibit 4   Telephone Questionnaire for Senat Bank

```
                                    FOR OFFICE USE ONLY
                                Job # 250-1 _____    (1-4)
                               Respondent # _____    (5-7)
                                  Record # _____     (8)

    _____
    _____
    Telephone Number _____ Date Interview Completed _____
    Interviewer _____
    _____

    TIME BEGAN _____
    ASK FOR AND INTERVIEW IF AT HOME:   Man of the house . . . . ▽
                                        Woman of the house . . . ▽
    Good evening, I'm Ms. _____ from High Performance Research, Inc.
    We're a professional research organization. We don't sell anything -- we
    just conduct various types of surveys for our clients. I'd like to inter-
    view you for a survey we're conducting today. I want to assure you that
    your privacy will be completely protected. First, I need to find out
    several things about your family.

    1.  Do you live in Clark County?
                                    Yes . . .▽
                                    No  . . .▽ > TERMINATE
    2.  Does any adult member living in your household have a checking account
        with any bank in Walkersville or Clark County?
                                    Yes . . .▽
                                    No  . . .▽ > TERMINATE
    3.  Are you able to sign checks for this checking account?
                                    Yes . . .▽
                                    No  . . .▽ > ASK FOR ANOTHER FAMILY MEMBER
                                                  WHO CAN.
    4.  Does any member of your household work for a bank, savings & loan, or
        credit union in Clark County?
                                    Yes . . .▽ > TERMINATE
                                    No  . . .▽
    5.  When you think of banks in Clark County which ones come to mind?   (9)
                                                                          (10)
        _____ _____ _____     (11)
                                                                          (12)
    6a. Which one of the following banks do you or would you most prefer to deal
        with?  READ LIST. CHECK ONLY ONE.

     b. Which of the following other banks do you or would you also consider dealing
        with?  READ LIST, EXCLUDING BANK MENTIONED IN QUESTION 6a.

     c. Which of the remaining banks would you just as soon not deal with? READ
        THOSE NOT MENTIONED IN 6a AND 6b.
```

	6a One Most Preferred	6b Others Liked	6c Don't Like	
Citizens Bank	▽-1	▽-2	▽-3	(13)
Peoples Bank	▽	▽	▽	(14)
Senat Bank	▽	▽	▽	(15)
Other _____	▽	▽	▽	(16)

you do anything, John," was Grisham's response on the phone. "You remember the positioning study we did for CI several years ago? Well, from the way you are painting the situation, I think that would be the Phase I research needed at this time."

"Jack, I think you hit the nail on the head," said White. "I'll leave the particulars of the study, sample size, sampling method and so on, in your hands, but send me a detailed copy of the questionnaire so that I can look it over before we conduct the study. Also, give me a rough idea of how you will do the study and how much it will cost. I'll run it by the other officers and then get back to you."

A few days later, White received a brief research proposal from Grisham and a detailed questionnaire for the proposed study (see Exhibits 3 and 4). After looking over the proposal and questionnaire, he wondered if the questionnaire would do the job that needed to be done to initiate a new marketing program. Since his formal schooling was in finance, he thought it looked very sophisticated and the results would provide many of the preliminary answers to his dilemma.

Exhibit 4   *Telephone Questionnaire for Senat Bank—Continued*

7a. What specific advertisements for local banks do you remember seeing or hearing recently? DO NOT READ LIST.

　　　　　None . .▢—▶ SKIP TO QUESTION 8.

b. FOR EACH BANK MENTIONED: Where did you see or hear the ads for _____?

	7a. Check All That Apply	7b. TV	WSAD Radio (Holly Springs FM 94)	Newspaper	Other		
Citizens Bank.	▢	▢-1	▢-2	▢-3	▢-4	(17)	(21)
Peoples Bank	▢	▢	▢	▢	▢	(18)	(22)
Senat Bank	▢	▢	▢	▢	▢	(19)	(23)
Other_____ .	▢	▢	▢	▢	▢	(20)	(24)

8. Which three of the following banks are you most familiar with?

　　　　　1. Citizens Bank. . . . . ▢　　　　　　　(25)
　　　　　2. Peoples Bank . . . . . ▢　　　　　　　(26)
　　　　　3. Senat Bank . . . . . . ▢　　　　　　　(27)
　　　　　4. Other_____ . ▢
　　　　　5. Other_____ . ▢
　　　　　6. Other_____ . ▢

9. Now, please think about only the three banks you are most familiar with ---
(READ NAMES FROM QUESTION 8) -- for a minute. I'd like your opinion based on your experiences or what you know or feel about each one, as to which one of the three is clearly better than the other two in various areas. Of course, you may not feel that one is better than the other two. So, for each area I name, please tell me whether you believe one of the three banks is clearly better than the other two; or that two of the banks are about the same but better than the third; or if you feel that all three are about the same. For example, in terms of (THE ONE CHECKED BELOW), do you feel that one of the three banks (READ NAMES FROM QUESTION 8) is clearly better than the other two? Or, that two are about the same and better than the third? Or, that all three are about the same? IF "ONE" IS CLEARLY BETTER, ASK "WHICH ONE?" ETC.)

	One is Clearly Better (WHICH ONE?) WRITE IN NUMBER	Two are About the Same and Better Than the Third (WHICH TWO?) WRITE IN 2 NUMBERS	All Three Are the Same CHECK BOX	
▢ a. Offers new services.	_____	_____ _____	▢	(28)
▢ b. Easy to obtain a loan.	_____	_____ _____	▢	(29)
▢ c. Attractive facilities.	_____	_____ _____	▢	(30)
▢ d. Makes fewest mistakes.	_____	_____ _____	▢	(31)
▢ e. Drive-up window service.	_____	_____ _____	▢	(32)
▢ f. Convenient to work	_____	_____ _____	▢	(33)
▢ g. Low interest on loans.	_____	_____ _____	▢	(34)
▢ h. Takes time to explain accounts and 　　　services	_____	_____ _____	▢	(35)
▢ i. Variety of savings plans	_____	_____ _____	▢	(36)
▢ j. Easy to get waited on.	_____	_____ _____	▢	(37)
▢ k. Hours open	_____	_____ _____	▢	(38)
▢ l. Sympathetic and understanding 　　　attitude when dealing with 　　　problems	_____	_____ _____	▢	(39)
▢ m. Convenient to shopping	_____	_____ _____	▢	(40)
▢ n. Quick approval on loans.	_____	_____ _____	▢	(41)
▢ o. Offers the most services	_____	_____ _____	▢	(42)
▢ p. Parking.	_____	_____ _____	▢	(43)
▢ q. Knowledgeable employees.	_____	_____ _____	▢	(44)
▢ r. Auto loans	_____	_____ _____	▢	(45)
▢ s. Service charge on checking 　　　account.	_____	_____ _____	▢	(46)
▢ t. Convenient to home	_____	_____ _____	▢	(47)
▢ u. Friendly employees	_____	_____ _____	▢	(48)
▢ v. Interest paid on savings	_____	_____ _____	▢	(49)
▢ w. Really wants your business	_____	_____ _____	▢	(50)
▢ x. Community-minded	_____	_____ _____	▢	(51)
▢ y. Personal interest in customers . .	_____	_____ _____	▢	(52)

Exhibit 4   Telephone Questionnaire for Senat Bank—Continued

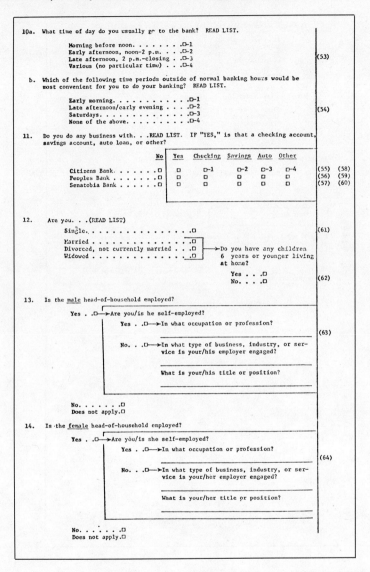

10a. What time of day do you usually go to the bank?   READ LIST.

        Morning before noon. . . . .□-1
        Early afternoon, noon-2 p.m. . . .□-2
        Late afternoon, 2 p.m.-closing . .□-3   (53)
        Various (no particular time) . . .□-4

  b. Which of the following time periods outside of normal banking hours would be most convenient for you to do your banking?   READ LIST.

        Early morning. . . . .□-1
        Late afternoon/early evening . . .□-2
        Saturdays. . . . .□-3   (54)
        None of the above. . . . .□-4

11. Do you do any business with. . .READ LIST. IF "YES," is that a checking account, savings account, auto loan, or other?

	No	Yes	Checking	Savings	Auto	Other		
Citizens Bank.	□	□	□-1	□-2	□-3	□-4	(55)	(58)
Peoples Bank	□	□	□	□	□	□	(56)	(59)
Senatobia Bank	□	□	□	□	□	□	(57)	(60)

12. Are you. . .(READ LIST)

    Single. . . . .□   (61)

    Married . . . .□
    Divorced, not currently married . . .□ ——►Do you have any children
    Widowed . . . .□   6 years or younger living
                      at home?
                      Yes . . .□
                      No. . . .□   (62)

13. Is the <u>male</u> head-of-household employed?

    Yes . .□——►Are you/is he self-employed?

          Yes . .□——►In what occupation or profession?
                                (63)

          No. . .□——►In what type of business, industry, or service is your/his employer engaged?

          What is your/his title or position?

    No. . . . . . .□
    Does not apply.□

14. Is the <u>female</u> head-of-household employed?

    Yes . .□——►Are you/is she self-employed?

          Yes . .□——►In what occupation or profession?
                                (64)

          No. . .□——►In what type of business, industry, or service is your/her employer engaged?

          What is your/her title or position?

    No. . . . . . .□
    Does not apply.□

Exhibit 4   Telephone Questionnaire for Senat Bank—Continued

15.   Into which of the following categories does your age fall? READ LIST.

        25 or younger. . .□-1
        26-35. . . . . . .□-2
        36-45. . . . . . .□-3   (65)
        46-55.. . . . . .□-4
        .56-65. . . . . .□-5
        66 or older. . . .□-6

16.   Which of the following best describes the approximate total income of your
      household last year?

        $9,999 or less. . . .□-1
        $10,000-11,999. . . .□-2
        $12,000-14,999. . . .□-3
        $15,000-19,999. . . .□-4   (66)
        $20,000-24,999. . . .□-5
        $25,000 or more . . .□-6

INTERVIEWER: Sex of respondent : Male. . .□-1   Female. . .□-2   (67)

              Race of respondent: White . .□-1   Black . . .□-2   (68)

                                                                LC   (69)

                                                                SES   (70)

        ┌─────────────────────────────┐
        │ TIME ENDED_____ │
        └─────────────────────────────┘

I hereby attest that this is a true and honest interview, and complete to the best
of my knowledge. I guarantee that all information relating to this interview will
be kept strictly confidential.

                            ───────────────────────────────
                                INTERVIEWER'S SIGNATURE

Questions

1.   Evaluate the research proposal.
2.   Will the questionnaire provide the information Mr. White needs?
3.   What are the limitations of this questionnaire? Does it fit the kind of research
     design Mr. Grisham proposes?
4.   What additional information would you recommend to be collected?

THE DR PEPPER COMPANY: INDUSTRIAL QUESTIONNAIRE DESIGN

> *"We are a sales company . . . The Dr Pepper bottler is the key to our success . . ."*[a]

> *"No matter how good a job we do, [consumers] can't get Dr Pepper unless you [bottlers] have made the sale to the retailer."*[b]

Background of the Dr Pepper Company

The Dr Pepper Company has had a long, interesting and dynamic history in the soft drink industry. Beginning in Waco, Texas, in 1885, Dr Pepper has risen from a local "soda" company to one of the top manufacturers and marketers of soft drinks, falling behind The Coca-Cola Company, Pepsi and virtually tied with Phillip Morris' 7-Up. Dr Pepper manufactures, markets and distributes soft drink concentrates and fountain syrups through 500 franchised bottlers throughout the United States and in several foreign markets. In finished form, the product appears as carbonated regular and sugar–free soft drinks in bottles and cans in food stores and vending machines, and as a fountain drink in fast-food outlets. Since its beginnings, Dr Pepper has faced reorganization, bankruptcy, and, in the 1970's, dynamic national growth.

In 1979, Dr Pepper generated earnings of nearly $24 million from sales of approximately $291 million. Virtually all of the firm's sales come from two brands of a single product: regular and sugar–free Dr Pepper. The company has production facilities in Texas, Alabama and Japan. It has wholly–owned bottling operations in Texas and Southern California; its national headquarters are in Dallas, Texas.

Prepared by Thomas E Barry, Professor of Marketing, Edwin L. Cox School of Business, Southern Methodist University, Dallas, Texas. This case was prepared with the approval of the Dr Pepper Company and the author is indebted to John Albers, Senior Vice President, Marketing, for his special assistance.

[a]W. W. (Foots) Clements, Chairman of the Board, Dr Pepper Company, Stockholders Meeting, April 15, 1980

[b]John R. Albers, Vice President, Marketing, Dr Pepper Company, National Bottlers Meeting, October 1, 1979

In early 1980 the Dr Pepper Company retained a marketing consultant to conduct a thorough marketing audit for the firm's national marketing operations. The
consultant was given the objective of:

> *. . . independently and comprehensively examining the marketing department's
> environments, planning and control systems and all marketing-related activities
> for the marketing of regular and sugar–free Dr Pepper brands.*

In thinking through the problems of Dr Pepper, the consultant decided that it would
be necessary to conduct three major surveys for the company. The first was a survey
of Dr Pepper's top corporate officers. The second was a survey of the two major
components of the company's outside marketing activities—bottlers and the company's advertising agency, Young and Rubicam. The third was a detailed internal
survey of the marketing department's managers. (An outline of the auditing procedure appears in Exhibit 1.) Of particular concern to the two top marketing officers at
Dr Pepper was the audit of the bottler franchise system, a system which is presently
in a state of dramatic change.[1]

The Beverage and Soft Drink Industries

Dr Pepper competes, in general terms, in the beverage industry, and specifically in
the soft drink industry. The beverage and soft drink industries grew during the sev-
enties although growth has slowed rather dramatically since 1977. Most analysts
believe that there is a softening of growth in the soft drink industry due to general
economic conditions, inflation, increased soft drink prices, unemployment problems,
poor weather conditions, fuel shortages and concerns about health and nutrition.

Beverage tonnage for 1979 was level, there was no increase; dollar volume was
up slightly except for ground and instant coffee. The soft drink industry was up
slightly in 1979 in unit sales, dollars and ounces. For the past four years the retail
price of soft drinks has continued upward. On a gallon basis, Dr Pepper cans (6-
pack) cost $2.93 compared to $2.09 for private label milk, $1.51 for private label soft
drinks and 19¢ for presweetened Kool-Aid.

The competition in the beverage industry is intense, particularly in the soft
drink industry. In both of these industries there has been a recent proliferation of
product and packaging alternatives available to consumers. Some observers of the
industry contend that soft drinks are now commodities with little brand loyalty,
heavy price discounting and decreasing promotional activity. There is likely to be an
intensified market share war among major brands given the almost universal availability of soft drinks.

U.S. consumers simply love soft drinks. The annual per capita consumption of
soft drinks in the U.S. is second only to that of water. For 1978, per capita gallonage
of soft drinks was 37.6 while water was 44.7 (an imputed figure). Coffee was a distant
third place with 27.8 per capita gallons annually. Other than milk and beer, competitive products such as tea, juices, powdered drinks and bottled water were below
eight gallons per capita. Soft drinks accounted for approximately twenty-nine percent
of the beverage industry in 1980 and industry analysts expect that figure to be 35
percent by 1990.

---

[1]The top two marketing officers are Frederick F. Avery, Executive Vice President/Marketing (now Executive Vice President
and Chief Operating Officer of Anderson/Clayton Foods) and John Albers, Vice President/Marketing (now Senior Vice Pres-
ident/Marketing).

Exhibit 1   Auditing Procedure for the Dr Pepper Company

I.   Marketing Environment (External Audit)
   A.   Macro Environment
       1.   Environmental Trends
       2.   Economic Atmosphere
       3.   Important Demographic Trends
       4.   Present and Future Technological Outlook
       5.   Political-Legal Atmosphere
       6.   Social-Cultural Trends
   B.   Task Environment
       1.   The Beverage Industry
       2.   Dr Pepper Markets
       3.   Distribution—Customers
       4.   Segment Trends
       5.   Customer Perceptions
       6.   Suppliers
       7.   Major Facilitating Agencies
       8.   Competition and Competitors
II. Organizational Environment (Internal Audits)
   A.   Marketing Systems Audit
       1.   Dr Pepper Marketing Information System
       2.   Dr Pepper Planning and Control Systems
       3.   Dr Pepper New Product Development System
   B.   Marketing Strategy/Productivity Audit
       1.   Objectives and Strategies
       2.   Adequacy and Priority of Resource
       3.   Productivity
   C.   Marketing Organization Audit
       1.   The Organization Chart/Structure
       2.   Job Perceptions
       3.   Departmental Interactions
   D.   Marketing Functions Audit
       1.   Distribution
       2.   Advertising
       3.   Brand Development
       4.   Sales
       5.   Sales Promotion

The main competitors in the soft drink industry include The Coca-Cola Company, PepsiCo, Phillip Morris and Royal Crown Industries. Crush International (recently purchased by Procter & Gamble) and the Canada Dry Corporation are also important competitors in the soft drink industry. Dr Pepper is without peer at present in the pepper category, a category which is the fastest growing in the industry. Mr. Pibb, a product of Coca-Cola, has had flashes of impact in various local markets, but at this point does not appear to be a significant threat to Dr Pepper although it remains a competitive brand since it has sales exceeding those of Kroger, Winn-Dixie, Safeway and A & P's combined private labels.

Dr Pepper is faced with heavy competition from giants in the industry who do not rely solely on the soft drink industry for sales revenue and profits. While Dr Pepper's profits are 100 percent soft drink generated, Coca-Cola's are seventy-five percent and PepsiCo's are thirty-three percent soft drink generated. Exhibit 2 provides a synopsis of Dr Pepper and its main competitors.

The Dr Pepper Company anticipates being a $500 million company with $50 million in diversified profits by 1985. The company plans, at this point, to stay in the soft drink industry initially and then move into related food industries.

The Bottler System

Critical to the efficient and effective distribution of Dr Pepper brands to ultimate consumers is the franchise bottler. The company distributes its fountain concentrate/ syrup through various channels of distribution; however, its primary customer is the bottler (wholly-owned or franchised). The firm ships approximately two-thirds of its product through its bottlers. Bottlers in turn bottle and can the concentrate and ship it as finished product to the grocery trade and vending operators. Bottlers also ship fountain syrup to fast-food chains in their franchised territories.

The Dr Pepper Company will also ship fountain syrup direct to fast food and convenience chains when it cannot get bottler support in a given market area. Additionally, the company will ship syrup through wholesale jobbers, third–party operators (e.g., Canteen, ARA, etc.), theaters (e.g., General Cinema) and military operations (vis-a-vis military broker specialists). Bottlers will also service such customers as jobbers, military operations and vending operators.

In roughly eighty percent of its franchised distributors, Dr Pepper brands are considered "secondary." That is, the vast majority of bottlers distributing Dr Pepper brands are also distributing brands for either Coca-Cola, PepsiCo or 7-Up. Analysis of interviews with top corporate officers at Dr Pepper (see the Top Management Questionnaire in Exhibit 3) indicates that these officers are very concerned about how bottlers perceive Dr Pepper relative to their "major" or primary brands. This perception involves not only brand image around product quality but the planning and execution of marketing programs for the bottlers developed by the Dr Pepper Company.

Consider the following comments made by Albers to bottlers attending the 1979 National Dr Pepper Bottlers Meeting:

With the strength we've demonstrated in the past decade and the Pepper powerful potential ahead of us, none of us can allow any bottler to sit on the brand and inhibit its growth.

What do I mean by "sitting on" the brand? Not giving Dr Pepper [its] share of off-pricing, in-ad features, in-store display or shelf space, selling our post-mix syrup to national accounts at a premium to subsidize your post-mix operation or increase your profit.

In the post-mix area, I understand the competition colas face. Many fast food accounts look at cola as a cola and many of their customers can't tell one from another. For that reason, most fountains only serve one and it's important for you to be the one cola that's served.

Let me give you an example of "sitting on" the brand in the retail grocery area. In a market where we have over a fifty bottle per capita and are number four in the market, our bottler recently conducted a promotion with three chains, set up to include all his major products. One display had approximately fifty cases Pepsi, three cartons 7-Up and three cartons Dr Pepper. A second had fifty cases Pepsi, eight cases Mountain Dew, four cases 7-Up and four cases Dr Pep-

Exhibit 2 Dr Pepper's Major Competition

Company	Volume (Millions of Gallons)		Net Sales (Millions of Dollars) (Total Company)		Market Share	
	1978	1974	1978	1974	1978	1974
Coca-Cola Company	1,998	1,546	4,338	2,614	36.3	34.7
PepsiCo, Inc.	1,281	925	4,300	2,409	23.3	20.6
Phillip Morris	386	340	6,632	3,011	7.0	7.6
Dr Pepper Company	360	234	271	156	6.5	5.2
Royal Crown Industries	259	240	391	227	4.7	5.4
Crush International	208	143	NA	NA	3.8	3.2
Canada Dry Corp.	159	151	NA	NA	2.9	3.3

Exhibit 3 Marketing Audit—Top Management Questionnaire

Classification Data
1. Name of Respondent ————————————————————————
2. Title of Respondent ————————————————————————
3. Length of Time with Dr Pepper (Years) ——————————————

Dr Pepper in General
1. How would you define, as specifically as possible, the business that Dr Pepper is in? What is DP's purpose or basic mission in this business (what does DP want to be)?
2. What would you say are the most important general business strengths of DP?
3. What are the most important deficiencies or weaknesses of DP today?
4. In order of importance what are two or three of the main business objectives of DP? And what are the strategies linked to meeting each objective?

    Objectives   Strategies

5. Do you see any major external threats to DP's attainment of its major business objectives now or in the near future? If so, what are they?
6. Do you see any major internal instabilities or threats (people, money, material, etc.) to the achievement of the objectives?
7. Assuming that DP stays on its present course of action, what is its future in the soft drink industry with respect to:
    a. market share:
    b. profitability:
    c. general corporate image:
    d. unit and dollar volume:
8. What is the main strength of DP in facing Coke, Pepsi and 7-Up in the next few years?
9. What about the main weakness of DP in facing these competitors?
10. Does DP, as an organization, have a planning focus? If so, does it focus on operations, strategic planning or both?
11. What types of control measures, if any, are used to monitor the progress of plans which are developed either at the corporate or functional level in DP? Do you consider these measures adequate?
12. Realistically, to what extent does interdepartmental (functional) cooperation exist in DP? (good, bad; a lot, a little, etc.)
13. In general, do you think that there is an adequate flow of information within and between functional areas (to the extent that managers get the information they need to meet their responsibilities and objectives)?
14. Most corporations are said to have a "personality." How would you describe the "personality" of Dr Pepper?

15. What is the single most important thing DP *should* do for:
    a.   its shareholders:
    b.   customers/users:
    c.   independent bottlers:
    d.   company-owned bottlers:
    e.   employees (all levels):
    f.   the community:
16. With "1" being low and "5" being high, how satisfied do you think each of the groups we just discussed is with the performance of DP?
    a.   shareholders:
    b.   customers/users:
    c.   independent bottlers:
    d.   company-owned bottlers:
    e.   the DP employees (at all levels):
    f.   the community (however you defined it above):
17. How would you describe the underlying management philosophy of the Dr Pepper Company? In other words, what words or phrases would describe how DP is run?
18. Given the resources of competition and the recent growth of DP, is it likely that the management philosophy will change in the near future?
19. Given these changes, what will be their impact on DP's plans, strategies and performance in the near future?
20. What do you see as the major requirements for success in the business in which DP competes?

The Dr Pepper Marketing Department
1.   In general, throughout the company, what are the impressions of the Marketing Department? Does it have an image which you could describe?
2.   What would you say are the strengths of the Marketing Department?
3.   What are the Marketing Department's weaknesses?
4.   Could you state what you think the main or core objective of the Marketing Department is?
5.   What do you believe to be the MD's core strategy in reaching its objective(s)?
6.   Do you feel that Marketing's main objective and strategy are the most appropriate (effective) for DP at this time?
7.   Looking at your major competitors, does DP's marketing program have a "distinctive competency" over its competitors? Does the marketing program do something better than all other competitors?
8.   Does DP have any major marketing opportunities (in terms of new markets, new products, etc.) facing it right now?
9.   What are the resource needs of the MD to capitalize on these opportunities? Are these needs realizable in the near future?
10. With "1" low and "5" high, give a quick rating of the MD re:
    a.   overall ability of its people:
    b.   the efficiency of the department:
    c.   the effectiveness of the department:
    d.   the commitment of the department:
    e.   ability of other areas to work with the MD:
    f.   respect of top management of the MD:

per. A third had fifty cases Pepsi only on display, and the grocery ad feature listed Pepsi, 7-Up and Dr Pepper. There is no way Dr Pepper can realize its growth potential in this market with that type of merchandising.

But if you're subsidizing your cola business with high-priced Dr Pepper syrup, then you're sitting on the brand.

Some bottlers are sitting on the brand by using the extra profit margins they obtain from in-store sales of Dr Pepper to promote their other brands. In some cases, profits from Dr Pepper are used to promote brands that have a much smaller share of market than Dr Pepper.

Dr Pepper, nationwide, is now one of the highest–priced soft drinks, and some secondary brands are even getting more shelf space than we are. That's not only sitting on the brand, that's hurting both your short and long-term growth position.

And some of you are sitting on the brand because you claim Dr Pepper just isn't a big factor in your market. When I hear that, I encourage bottlers to ask themselves why Dr Pepper isn't a big factor in their market. If they want to test the viability of Dr Pepper, all they have to do is put it in any fountain account.

By industry standards, and from a separate consulting report done for Dr Pepper, it can be generalized that Dr Pepper has historically enjoyed very strong relations with its bottlers. The bottling industry is, however, rapidly changing with small family-owned businesses beginning to be bought out by corporate-owned bottling operations. Packaging innovation in the industry has been prolific in the last five years and the number of multi-brand bottlers and variations in distribution are creating problems for Dr Pepper as well as its competition. As part of the total marketing audit, Avery and Albers wish to know more about their bottlers.

Questions

1. Evaluate the Top Management Questionnaire provided in Exhibit 3. What information would you *exclude* as being unnecessary, too sensitive, etc.? What information is lacking which you would want to *include?* Be specific.

2. Develop an instrument which can be used for auditing franchised bottlers of the Dr Pepper Company. What type of survey would you use? Why? What do you consider the most critical information which Dr Pepper management should capture from its bottlers? Justify your position.

SAN DIEGO CONVENTION AND VISITORS BUREAU: COMPARISON OF QUESTIONNAIRE RESULTS

Background

Tourism is one of the biggest industries in the San Diego area. Last year roughly twenty million persons visited San Diego as a destination. Total visitor spending is estimated to be roughly $1 billion annually.

Overall responsibility for stimulating vacation travel, tours, business meetings and conventions in the area is given to the San Diego Convention and Visitors Bureau (CONVIS). CONVIS is a semi-public marketing agency whose board members come from the hotel/motel industry, visitor attractions, restaurant operations, transportation carriers and public agencies. The CONVIS staff operates on a budget of roughly $2 million per year generated mainly through a hotel/motel occupancy tax and industry grants.

While much of the CONVIS budget is devoted to promotional activities, it maintains a staff position for a director of research projects. The current director, Lauri Sanderson, operates on a research budget of about $60,000 (roughly three percent of the overall bureau budget). Some of the major projects conducted by Sanderson include:

1. Publication of the Visitor Industry Digest—a monthly report of visitor activity in San Diego
2. Visitor profile study—an on-going monitor of visitor attitudes and expenditure information conducted on-site at major attractions (done by an outside firm)
3. Analysis of visitor information requests
4. Special studies done on an "as needed" basis.

Comparison of Research Projects

Sanderson was reviewing the preliminary results of a mail survey conducted by the visitor marketing department. A major portion of the visitor advertising budget was

Copyright © 1981 by Dr. Donald Sciglimpaglia.

Exhibit 1   San Diego Visitor Survey

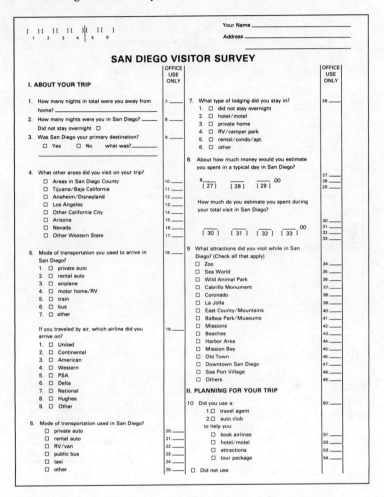

spent on magazine ads in national (e.g., Travel Holiday, Family Circle, Golf Digest), regional (e.g., Southern Living, New West) and local (e.g., Detroit Magazine) publications. Many of the ads included a coupon response format which allowed CONVIS to identify potential visitors. A mail questionnaire was sent to those potential visitors who indicated that they were actually planning a visit. The questionnaire was mailed so that it would arrive about one month after the trip's completion. A copy of the mail questionnaire is shown in Exhibit 1.

The advertising response survey was of interest to Sanderson because she had just completed a special project which contained some similar questions. Sanderson had been asked to conduct a survey of visitors in the downtown area. This was somewhat unusual because most of the visitor survey work was usually conducted at either an information center or at an attraction location.

Someone else at CONVIS wanted to know more about visitors to the downtown area of San Diego. It had been assumed that many would be there on business, but

Exhibit 1   San Diego Visitor Survey—Continued

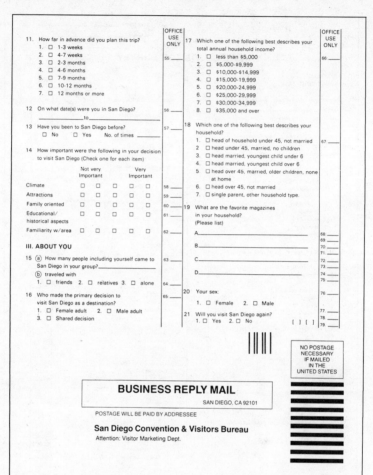

no one knew for sure. Additionally, it would be of interest to know what the downtown visitor did while in San Diego.

Sanderson drew up a survey form (shown in Exhibit 2). She then hired ten personal interviewers who were sent to various downtown locations. They were instructed to approach people at the location and ascertain if they were from the local area or from out of town. They were instructed to conduct fifty interviews each with visitors from separate parties.

Survey Results

Interestingly, 68.9 percent of those interviewed in the downtown visitor survey indicated that they were in San Diego on a non-business visit. Sanderson decided to analyze the results of these "pleasure" visitors separately. Those results were com-

Exhibit 2   Downtown Visitor Survey

1. Residence: City _____ State _____ ZIP _____
2a How many nights in total on this trip are to be spent away from home: _____
2b How many nights are you staying in San Diego County: _____
3. What type of lodging are you staying in while in San Diego County:

    _____ Hotel/Motel   _____ Rental/Condo

    _____ Private Home   _____ Other

    _____ Campground/RV park   _____ Day trip—not overnight

4. Are you here for: _____ Pleasure _____ Business _____ Convention _____
    Other _____
5. What type of transportation did you use to arrive in San Diego?

    _____ Personal car   _____ Air (which line) _____

    _____ Rental care   _____ Train

    _____ Van/RV/Motorhome   _____ Bus

                                       _____ Other (which) _____

6. What type of transportation are you using while here?

    _____ Personal/Friend's car   _____ Taxi

    _____ Rental Car   _____ Tour bus

    _____ Van/RV/Trailer   _____ Other (which) _____

    _____ Local Public bus

7. What attractions have you or will you visit while in San Diego: _____
    _____ _____ _____
    _____ _____ _____

8. Why are you visiting downtown?

    _____ Sightseeing   _____ Shopping   _____ To get information   Other _____

8a Did you visit: Grant Hotel Information Booth   Y   N   _____

                 Convention & Visitors Bureau   Y   N   _____

                 Chamber of Commerce   Y   N

9. How many people are in your visitor group all together?
    Under 18 years old _____   Over 18 years old _____
10. Which of these best describes you and your household?

    _____ head under 45/not married

    _____ head under 45/married/no children

    _____ married/child under 6

    _____ married/child over 6

    _____ head over 45/married/no children at home

    _____ head over 45/not married

    _____ single parent/other

11. Sex of respondent   _____ Male   _____ Female

12. Race of respondent   _____ White   _____ Black   _____ Latin   _____ Other

pared to the results from the magazine advertising visitor response survey. Some of the results are shown in Exhibit 3.

Upon inspection, Sanderson could tell that the downtown visitor was different from those responding to the magazine advertising campaign. One thing that was particularly intriguing was the difference in percentages between the two samples of those visiting various sites and attractions. Even if the samples were from two different segments of the overall visitor population, she wondered about the differences in the results. For instance, Sanderson thought, why did apparently 60.8 percent of the magazine visitor respondents visit Old Town and none of the downtown visitors? Further, she wondered which set of numbers was most representative.

Exhibit 3   Comparison of Survey Results

	Downtown Visitor Survey (Non-business)	Magazine Advertising Visitor Response Survey
Nights Away from Home (Median)	8.0	11.2
Nights in San Diego (Median)	2.2	5.6
Arrival Transportation (Percent using)		
Private auto	17.0	27.8
Rental auto	3.2	12.9
Airplane	42.7	52.1
Motor home/RV	10.3	2.7
Train	15.8	1.2
Bus	9.1	3.1
Other	2.0	0.2
Type of Lodging Used (Percent)		
Hotel/Motel	57.5	75.2
Private home	16.5	16.5
RV/Camper	16.5	2.0
Rental/Condo	2.0	2.2
Other	0.4	1.2
Day trip	7.1	2.9
Attractions Visited in San Diego (Percent visiting)		
Zoo	21.6	77.6
Sea World	26.3	55.5
Wild Animal Park	0.8	29.1
Cabrillo Monument	0.4	33.9
La Jolla	4.2	53.9
East County/Mountains	1.5	14.6
Balboa Park/Museums	15.1	51.0
Missions	0.4	31.7
Beaches	45.9	57.3
Harbor Area	3.1	67.1
Mission Bay	0.0	51.8
Old Town	0.0	60.8
Sex of Respondent		
Percent Male	58.7	51.7
Family Status (Percent)		
Head under 45/Not married	30.9	16.6
Head under 45/Married—No children	12.9	16.6
Married/Child under 6	11.3	6.5
Married/Child over 6	16.9	19.0
Head over 45/Married—No children	18.7	38.6
Head over 45/Not married	8.6	7.5
Single parent/Other	6.6	7.1

Questions

1. Look carefully at both questionnaires. Are there items or questions which can be improved?
2. Compare the results in Exhibit 3. Do the two samples appear to come from the same population?
3. What is the *major* reason for the differences in reported visits to the various sites in San Diego?
4. Which set of statistics (if any) is the most valid? Why?

SUNBELT ENERGY CORPORATION: QUESTIONNAIRE EVALUATION

Sunbelt Energy Corporation[1] is a multinational energy and chemical firm located in Houston, Texas. Sunbelt Energy Corporation is a diversified petroleum company engaged in the production and marketing of gasoline, motor oil, petrochemicals, and a number of other energy–related activities such as coal mining, uranium extraction and atomic power generation.

Late in 1973, the Arab Oil Embargo highlighted the fact that there was a finite amount of fossil fuel available in the world. The phrase "energy crisis" became commonplace. The public desired to attribute a cause to this problem. The news media began to raise questions about "oil companies."

On a quarterly basis, Sunbelt surveys the public to determine their attitudes towards business and energy, and towards oil companies. During and shortly after the 1974 energy "crisis," Sunbelt prepared the questionnaire seen in Exhibit 1. This questionnaire was used in a telephone survey consisting of a sample of 150 households selected by random digit dialing in each of the following five cities: St. Louis, Houston, Kansas City, Dallas, and Denver.

Exhibit 1   Market Awareness Questionnaire

A. First, we would like to know how you feel about big business in general. Would you say that you are _____ toward big business?

---

[1]This is a fictitious name in order to protect confidentiality. The data are adjusted slightly for the same purpose.

Copyright © 1981 by Dr. William G. Zikmund.

Exhibit 1   Market Awareness Questionnaire—Continued

(1) Very favorable, (2) favorable, (3) neutral, (4) unfavorable, (5) very unfavorable
(If 4 or 5) Why do you feel that way?
1. Too much power
2. Push out small business
3. Monopoly
4. Impersonal, don't care about people
5. Greed—too much profit—too high prices
6. Tax advantages, not enough taxes
7. Dishonest—cheat—rip off people
8. Other
9. Don't know or no answer
B. What does the phrase "the free enterprise system" mean to you?
1. Private ownership
2. Run a business like you want to
3. Freedom to sell the way you want
4. Able to advertise as you want
5. Freedom to go into business of your choice
6. Right to make reasonable profit
7. Right to go broke
8. Free economy
9. No price control
10. Invest capital and get a return on investment
11. Competitive system—supply and demand
12. Capitalistic system
13. Whole basis of country
14. Right to buy and sell what you want
15. Other
16. Don't know
17. No answer
18. Nothing
19. Equal opportunity for everybody
C. Why do you think companies or businesses should be allowed to make a profit?
1. Negative comment—overcharging
2. Provides employment—jobs
3. They risk their money
4. People won't invest if they can't make a profit
5. To better the economy
6. Negative—public good/public owned
7. Money back in business—reinvest
8. For their own good—better themselves
9. No profit—no business
10. For research
11. Provide incentive
12. To develop and grow
13. Make it possible to get rich—to make money
14. Improve products and services
15. That's the only reason for being in business
16. Encourages competition
17. No reason
18. Don't know or no answer
19. Other
20. Free enterprise system, American, capitalistic

Exhibit 1   Market Awareness Questionnaire—Continued

D.   How do you think the general public benefits from the profits companies make?
1.   Better economy—economic growth
2.   More and/or better products
3.   New inventions
4.   Community involvement
5.   Service
6.   Quality
7.   Benefits for employees
8.   More jobs
9.   Makes competition—lowers prices
10.   Better choice of merchandise
11.   They contribute to charities
12.   Pay taxes—build things in community
13.   For schools, roads, highways, dams, swimming pools
14.   None—no benefits
15.   Don't know or no answer
16.   Other
17.   Stock goes up, stockholder's benefit

E.   There has been a great deal of publicity given the fuel shortages which we have had in the past year. What do you feel was the major cause of these shortages?
1.   Companies holding back supply
2.   Too many cars
3.   People; people wasting energy
4.   Politics, the government
5.   Resources running out
6.   Large companies pushing out small ones
7.   Bad planning
8.   Alaskan pipeline needed
9.   Other
10.   Don't know or no answer
11.   No shortage
12.   To raise prices
13.   Oil embargo, foreign interference

F.   How do you feel about the oil companies? Would you say that you are _____ toward the oil companies?
(1) Very favorable, (2) favorable, (3) neutral, (4) unfavorable, (5) very unfavorable
(If 4 or 5) Why do you feel that way?
1.   Higher prices, profits
2.   Greed, cheating people, taking advantage
3.   No shortage
4.   Holding back supply, caused shortage
5.   Fuel shortage
6.   Too much power, should be regulated
7.   Other
8.   Don't know or no answer

G.   Do you feel that the oil companies told the truth about the energy crisis and the fuel shortage?
(1)   Yes
(2)   No
(3)   Other

Exhibit 1   Market Awareness Questionnaire—Continued

Why do you feel that way?
    1. No shortage
    2. To raise prices
    3. Too fast, sudden, over too soon
    4. Poor planning
    5. Didn't tell entire truth
    6. Holding back supply, in storage
    7. Politics, government
    8. Other
    9. Don't know or no answer

Demographics

H. Sex
    1. Male
    2. Female

I. Which of the following age groups do you fall in?
    1. Under 25
    2. 25–34
    3. 35–49
    4. 50–64
    5. 65 and over
    6. No response

J. And which of the following educational categories are you in?
    1. High school graduate or less
    2. Some college
    3. Completed college
    4. Postgraduate
    5. No response

K. An finally, simply for classification purposes, what is your total yearly family income?
    1. Under $8,000
    2. $8,0001–$10,000
    3. $10,001–$12,500
    4. $12,501–$15,000
    5. $15,001–$25,000
    6. Over $25,000
    7. No response

Question

1. Evaluate the questionnaire in Exhibit 1.

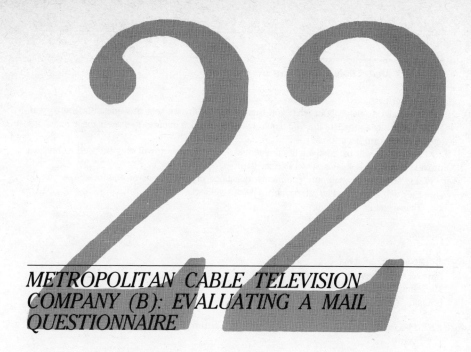

METROPOLITAN CABLE TELEVISION COMPANY (B): EVALUATING A MAIL QUESTIONNAIRE

Metropolitan Cable Television Company (MetroCable) is a cable television company servicing roughly 105,000 households in Orange County, California. Serving both local municipalities and unincorporated suburban areas, MetroCable currently enjoys the right of being the exclusive cable service supplier in its service area. The company offers rebroadcasts of sixteen television stations from the Los Angeles and San Diego areas. Additionally, it offers specialty programming such as Cable News Network, sports, community access, shopping guides and other information. For a separate charge, MetroCable also offers Home Box Office (HBO) which provides major movies and special event programs. Competition for HBO comes directly from two subscription broadcast services available from Los Angeles (ON-TV and Omega). These services offer households movies, special events and sports programming which are transmitted directly to the subscriber through use of an electronic decoder.

Dave Chambers, the marketing manager for MetroCable, had decided previously to conduct a research study of current subscribers. He hoped that the project would help him assess current program offerings and the effectiveness of marketing activities. Also of interest to him were attitudes of HBO customers and non-customers toward that service. Chambers listed the objectives of the study to be:
1. Customer evaluation of MetroCable program offerings
2. Evaluation of MetroCable advertising and sales efforts
3. Subscriber attitudes toward HBO
4. Collection of demographic and household information.

The Research Study

Chambers elected to select a sample of current subscribers to MetroCable service. After considering a number of alternatives, he decided to conduct a mail survey.

Copyright © 1981 by Dr. Donald Sciglimpaglia.

Exhibit 1   MetroCable Mail Survey Cover Letter

Dear Subscriber:

We really do care about what you think. That is why we sent this questionnaire to you. We would really appreciate it if you would take the next five minutes to answer these questions and mail the form back to us.

Your reply will be completely confidential. The information will only be used to help us provide better cable television service for you.

Please feel free to write any comments, questions or suggestions on the form. You can be sure they will all be read by MetroCable TV management.

Thank you for your help.

Sincerely,

David S. Chambers

David S. Chambers,
Marketing Manager
DSC/sjb

P.S.   Please use the enclosed prepaid envelope to return your completed questionnaire. Thank you.

Exhibit 2   MetroCable Mail Survey Questionnaire

1. Please indicate how many months you have been a subscriber to MetroCable TV service.
   _____ months

2. Please indicate the three most important reasons for deciding to subscribe to MetroCable TV services. Just place a 1, 2, and 3 (1—most important) next to the appropriate response categories.
   _____ Madison Square Garden sports
   _____ Availability of San Diego stations
   _____ Consumer Shoppers Guide
   _____ Improved reception
   _____ Christian Communications Network
   _____ Availability of Home Box Office (HBO)
   _____ CSPAN (House of Representatives proceedings)
   _____ Entertainment and Sports Programming Network (ESPN)
   _____ Other (Please specify)
   _____

3. Did you subscribe to MetroCable through a salesperson who came to your home or by calling the MetroCable office?
   _____ Salesperson at my house
   _____ Telephone call to MetroCable business office
   _____ Other (Please specify)
   _____

4. Do you remember having heard or seen MetroCable TV advertising?
   _____ Yes (Go to Question 5)
   _____ No (Go to Question 6)

5. Please indicate the type(s) of MetroCable advertising you remember. (Check appropriate responses)
   _____ TV
   _____ Radio
   _____ Billboard
   _____ Newspaper

Exhibit 2   MetroCable Mail Survey Questionnaire—Continued

_____ Doorhanger
_____ Direct mail

6. Who in your household made the decision to subscribe to MetroCable TV?
_____ Female head of household
_____ Male head of household
_____ Mutual decision
_____ Other (Please specify)

7. Overall, how would you rate MetroCable TV?
_____ Excellent
_____ Good
_____ Average
_____ Fair
_____ Poor

8. Why have you chosen not to subscribe to Home Box Office? (Check applicable responses)
_____ Previous subscriber . . . discontinued service
_____ Too expensive per month
_____ Not enough sports
_____ Movies are not current
_____ Installation cost too high
_____ Did not know about HBO service
_____ Friends have discouraged me
_____ Not enough entertainment specials
_____ Too many repeats of programs
_____ Programs are not offered at convenient times
_____ Too many R-rated movies
_____ Not enough R-rated movies
_____ Subscribe to ON-TV or Omega
_____ Other (Please specify) _____

a. How long have you been a subscriber to Home Box Office (HBO)?
_____ months

b. Why did you choose to subscribe to Home Box Office?

_____
_____
_____
_____

c. Please rate each of the following characteristics of HBO:

	Excellent	Good	Average	Fair	Poor
	1	2	3	4	5
Quality of movie selections					
Frequency of showings of the movies/specials					
Uncut versions of movies					
Lack of commercials					
Quality of entertainment specials					
Cost of the service					
Quality of service overall					

Exhibit 2   Telephone Marketing Questionnaire—Continued

The following questions are for statistical purposes only.

9. Including yourself, how many people live in your household?

    _____

10. Do you live in a:
    _____ House
    _____ Condominium
    _____ Apartment
    _____ Mobile home

11. What is the age of the head of the household?

    _____

12. What is the highest educational level completed by the head of the household?
    _____ Less than high school graduate
    _____ High school graduate
    _____ Some college
    _____ College graduate
    _____ Postgraduate training

13. Was the total 1979 household income:
    _____ Under $15,000
    _____ $15,000–$25,000
    _____ $25,000–$35,000
    _____ $35,000–$50,000
    _____ $50,000 plus

14. What is your zip code?

    _____

Using the computerized billing account system, Chambers selected 2,500 households (roughly 2.5 percent of all accounts).

Each household was sent a questionnaire with an enclosed cover letter and postage-paid return envelope. The cover letter and the questionnaire are shown in Exhibits 1 and 2.

Questions

1. Evaluate the cover letter Chambers used. Can you think of any ways to improve it?
2. Carefully evaluate the questionnaire. How could it have been improved?
3. What types of MetroCable subscribers are most (or least) likely to respond to this mail survey?

VI

ATTITUDE MEASUREMENT

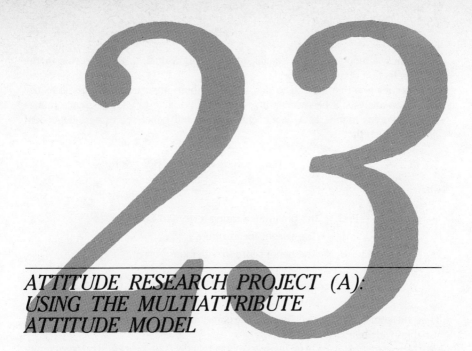

ATTITUDE RESEARCH PROJECT (A): USING THE MULTIATTRIBUTE ATTITUDE MODEL

A manager designing new products, repositioning existing products, and, in general, developing product strategy would like to be able to understand consumer behavior. More specifically, he is concerned with which product attributes are important to the consumer, and to what extent, in making a brand selection.

Much research has concentrated on the role of advertising and sales, but the determination of the importance of specific attributes could provide useful guidance as to which points should be stressed in the advertising. In addition, information regarding the role of the different product attributes in the decision-making process would illuminate what should be changed for existing products or avenues to follow in designing new products.

Importance Weights and Model Form

The major questions are: how to determine attribute importance weights for a particular product category, and what is the model which best represents the consumer's decision process?

There are several possible approaches to determine the importance of weights. One straightforward method would be to survey a representative sample of consumers and to simply ask them which attributes are most important to them. Unfortunately, a large number of studies have shown that most consumers are unable to describe accurately the importance of different attributes in their decision-making process.[1] This is generally because most individuals can recognize which attributes are important to them, yet they are not conscious of which attributes are significant in discriminating between brands. For example, an individual may consider price to be an important attribute, even when all brands are priced identi-

[1]See discussion by G. S. Day, "Evaluating Models of Attitude Structure," *Journal of Marketing Research*, Vol. 9, No. 3 (August 1972), pp. 279–86.

From *Cases in Marketing Research* by Randall L. Schultz, Gerald Zaltman, and Philip Burger. Copyright © 1975 by The Dryden Press, a division of Holt, Rinehart and Winston, Publishers. Reprinted by permission of Holt, Rinehart and Winston.

cally. Thus, although price is significant to the individual, it plays no role in the actual selection of any one brand.

Another possible method to determine attribute importance weights is to use regression analysis. If behavior is unknown, it is possible to use preference ratings of the different brands as a dependent variable and belief scores as independent variables, such that

$$\text{Pref}_i = \beta_{0i} + \beta_1 B_{1i} + \beta_2 B_{2i} + \ldots + \beta_n B_{ni} + \mu_i \qquad 1$$

where

$\text{Pref}_i =$ the preference rating for brand i
$\beta_j =$ The weight for attribute j
$B_{ji} =$ The belief score for attribute j on brand i
$\mu_i =$ a random disturbance
$n =$ the number of attributes

Thus, the coefficients (β_j) will indicate the contribution of the respective independent variables (attributes) to the preferes.

Many attempts have been made to model this decision process. The basic multi-attribute attitude model is:

$$A_{ij} = \sum_{k=1}^{n} (V_{ik} B_{ijk} - I_{ik}^r) \qquad 2$$

where:

$A_{ij} =$ the overall attitude score for brand j by individual i
$V_{ik} =$ the importance of attribute k to individual i
$B_{ijk} =$ individual i's belief about brand j on attribute k
$I_{ik} =$ the ideal point for individual i on attribute k
$r =$ the Minkowski metric ($r = 1$ city block; $r = 2$ Euclidean)
$n =$ the number of attributes.

Much effort is typically exerted in attempting to discover which form of the multi-attribute attitude model more accurately describes the decision process. Issues typically dealt with are: (1) usage of importance weights, V_{ik}, directly provided by the individuals or letting $V_{ik} = 1$ for all i and all k; (2) usage of ideal points, I_{ik}, provided by the individuals or letting I_{ik} be assumed at the extreme point ($I_{ik} = 0$) on the scale; and (3) should $r = 1$ or $r = 2$?

Depending on the purpose of the research, the model should be evaluated either in terms of its predictive ability or its descriptive ability.

The Data

Professors Bass, Pessemier, and Lehmann conducted an experiment in July 1969 at Purdue University, West Lafayette, Indiana.[2] They had 264 subjects (students and

[2]See Frank M. Bass, Edgar A. Pessemier, and Donald R. Lehmann, "An Experimental Study of Relationships between Attitudes, Brand Preference, and Choice," *Behavioral Science,* Vol. 17, No. 6 (November 1972), pp. 532–41.

secretaries) who ranked in terms of preference eight different soft drinks and provided belief scores on five attributes.

Importance scores and ideal points were also obtained for each of the attributes.
The format of the actual questions is shown below.

Ideal Point (I_{ik})

Assume you are given an opportunity to design a soft drink for your personal use.
Please indicate how it would be constructed with respect to each of the characteristics listed.

	High					Low
Carbonation	1	2	3	4	5	6
Calories	1	2	3	4	5	6
Sweetness	1	2	3	4	5	6
Thirst quenching	1	2	3	4	5	6
Popularity with others	1	2	3	4	5	6

Importance Score (V_{ik})

Please indicate how important each of these characteristics is to you in selecting a
soft drink by circling 1 if it would be very important, 6 if it would be very unimportant, or somewhere in between depending on how important it would be.

	Very Important					Very Unimportant
Carbonation	1	2	3	4	5	6
Calories	1	2	3	4	5	6
Sweetness	1	2	3	4	5	6
Thirst quenching	1	2	3	4	5	6
Popularity with others	1	2	3	4	5	6

Belief Score (B_{ijk})

Please indicate how much you think each of the eight brands of soft drinks has of
each of the characteristics by circling 1 if you believe the brand is high in the characteristic, 6 if you believe it is low in the characteristic or somewhere in between
depending on how much of the characteristic you believe the brand has.

Carbonation

	High				Low			High				Low
Coke	1	2	3	4	5	6	Pepsi	1	2	3	4	5	6
7-Up	1	2	3	4	5	6	Sprite	1	2	3	4	5	6
Tab	1	2	3	4	5	6	Diet Pepsi	1	2	3	4	5	6
Like	1	2	3	4	5	6	Fresca	1	2	3	4	5	6

Popularity with Others

	High				Low			High				Low
Coke	1	2	3	4	5	6	Pepsi	1	2	3	4	5	6
7-Up	1	2	3	4	5	6	Sprite	1	2	3	4	5	6
Tab	1	2	3	4	5	6	Diet Pepsi	1	2	3	4	5	6
Like	1	2	3	4	5	6	Fresca	1	2	3	4	5	6

Exhibit 1   Soft Drink Data

Subject No.	Attributes	Weights	\ Preference by Brand 1	2	3	4	5	6	7	8	\ Belief Scores by Brand 1	2	3	4	5	6	7	8	Ideal
1	No. 1	4	2	5	4	7	1	8	6	3	2	2	6	6	4	3	5	4	3
	No. 2	2									3	2	6	4	2	4	1	1	6
	No. 3	5									3	2	1	1	1	3	1	4	5
	No. 4	1									3	1	3	2	3	1	2	5	1
	No. 5	6									2	2	6	2	1	5	4	3	4
2	No. 1	2	3	1	7	6	2	4	5	8	3	2	2	2	1	1	3	4	3
	No. 2	1									2	3	5	1	1	3	2	1	5
	No. 3	3									3	2	2	2	2	3	1	2	3
	No. 4	2									2	2	2	2	2	1	1	4	2
	No. 5	6									3	3	5	2	1	1	4	5	1
3	No. 1	3	2	5	7	6	1	4	3	8	2	4	5	5	1	2	4	2	4
	No. 2	2									4	2	5	3	1	5	1	2	4
	No. 3	2									1	2	1	2	1	2	2	2	2
	No. 4	1									4	1	2	2	6	3	2	4	1
	No. 5	6									2	2	5	2	3	1	5	6	1
4	No. 1	3	6	3	8	4	2	1	7	5	2	3	5	5	3	3	4	4	4
	No. 2	2									3	3	3	3	3	4	4	2	5
	No. 3	2									4	3	2	3	4	3	2	4	3
	No. 4	2									3	2	2	3	3	3	3	4	1
	No. 5	3									2	2	5	2	4	3	4	4	3
5	No. 1	3	2	3	7	8	1	5	4	6	2	2	5	3	2	2	4	4	1
	No. 2	3									3	2	3	2	3	5	2	1	5
	No. 3	3									4	2	2	3	4	5	1	2	3
	No. 4	3									4	2	2	5	3	2	3	3	2
	No. 5	3									2	2	5	5	2	2	4	3	1
6	No. 1	3	8	1	6	4	5	2	7	3	1	3	5	4	4	2	4	4	3
	No. 2	5									4	5	4	4	2	5	2	3	3
	No. 3	4									4	2	2	3	4	4	5	2	3
	No. 4	1									5	2	3	3	2	3	3	6	1
	No. 5	4									2	3	6	3	6	3	6	2	2
7	No. 1	3	3	1	8	6	2	4	7	5	2	3	5	3	2	1	1	4	2
	No. 2	5									3	3	3	3	3	5	2	1	4
	No. 3	1									3	2	3	3	5	3	1	3	2
	No. 4	1									3	3	3	4	4	2	2	4	1
	No. 5	3									2	3	5	4	2	1	5	3	5
8	No. 1	2	1	2	8	6	4	3	7	5	2	4	6	4	2	2	3	4	2
	No. 2	6									3	5	4	5	3	4	2	3	1
	No. 3	3									6	5	2	3	2	2	2	3	4
	No. 4	3									4	2	4	3	3	3	2	4	2
	No. 5	6									3	4	5	3	3	2	5	4	1
9	No. 1	3	4	2	7	6	5	1	8	3	1	3	6	2	1	1	5	6	3
	No. 2	6									1	4	6	1	4	4	1	4	6
	No. 3	1									4	3	1	4	1	4	2	3	6
	No. 4	1									4	1	2	1	2	6	2	5	1
	No. 5	6									1	4	6	1	1	2	6	3	6
10	No. 1	5	3	5	6	8	2	4	7	1	1	3	4	5	2	3	4	6	2
	No. 2	5									4	6	4	1	3	4	1	2	4
	No. 3	1									5	5	2	3	1	3	1	4	5
	No. 4	1									3	1	3	1	4	3	3	4	1
	No. 5	3									2	3	6	3	4	2	5	2	2

The data for the first ten subjects are given in Exhibit 1. The attributes and brands are as follows:

Attribute 1:	Carbonation	Brand 1:	Coke
Attribute 2:	Calories	Brand 2:	7-Up
Attribute 3:	Sweetness	Brand 3:	Tab
Attribute 4:	Thirst quenching	Brand 4:	Like
Attribute 5:	Popularity with others	Brand 5:	Pepsi
		Brand 6:	Sprite
		Brand 7:	Diet Pepsi
		Brand 8:	Fresca

To compare a model's predictability of a ranking it is possible to use the Spearman rho rank correlation. This statistic measures the degree to which two rank orderings correlate with each other:

$$r_{RHO} = 1 - \frac{6\sum_{i=1}^{m} D_i^2}{m(m^2 - 1)}$$

where:

$$D_i = \text{rank } X_i - \text{rank } Y_i$$

(Stated preference rank of brand i—model's predicted rank of brand i; m = the number of brands being ranked.)

Questions

1. Using the model shown in equation (2), compute an attitude score for each brand for two individuals. This will enable you to rank the brands for these individuals. Comparing the attitude ranking with the stated preference rank, compute the Spearman rho rank correlation for each individual and then the average. Do this for alternative model forms (V_{ik} = stated versus V_{ik} = 1; I_{ik} = stated versus I_{ik} = 0; $r = 1$ versus $r = 2$) to determine which model is best in terms of predictability for two of the ten subjects.

2. Using the model shown in equation (1), compute the attribute importance weights by pooling all the observations and performing a regression for each brand. Interpret the meaning of the resulting coefficients and show what marketing implications can be derived.

24

ATTITUDE RESEARCH PROJECT (B): USING MULTIDIMENSIONAL SCALING IN MARKETING RESEARCH

As a consumer becomes more familiar with a product, he begins to associate a specific brand image in his mind which may change over a period of time as he is confronted with additional information and changing needs. Much of a firm's marketing effort, directed through its marketing decision variables, is aimed at the consumer's image of its brands. Frequently a company's advertising is focused on creating a particular image in the consumers' minds. For example, the Anheuser-Bush Brewing Company advertises one of its brands, Michelob, as a high-class status beer. Most of their advertisements show well-dressed, country-club types serving Michelob. Apparently, Anheuser-Bush hopes to generate the perception in the consumers' minds that Michelob is a high–quality, sophisticated beer.

The pricing variable can also be used to create a specific image of a product.[1] It has been generally shown that when a brand is priced higher than competing brands, it is perceived as having higher quality, more durability, etc. Likewise, the product variable is a tool available to the marketing manager which aids in the development of the product image. For instance, recognizing the need for a powerful mouthwash, the Listerine Company produced a product which was not only potent, but was also bitter tasting. Possibly the Listerine Company could have made the same mouthwash without the burning flavor, but it was felt that the flavor itself aided

---

[1] I. Robert Andrews and Enzo R. Valenzi, "The Relationship Between Price and Blind-Rated Quality for Margarines and Butter," *Journal of Marketing Research,* Vol. VII (November 1970), pp. 525–8; Ben M. Enis and James E. Stafford, "The Influence of Price and Store Information upon Price Quality Perception," *Southern Journal of Business,* Vol. 4 (April 1969), pp. 90–4; J. Douglass McConnell, "An Experimental Examination of the Price-Quality Relationship," *Journal of Business,* Vol. 41 (October 1968), pp. 439–44; James H. Myers and William H. Reynolds, *Consumer Behavior and Marketing Management* (Boston, Houghton-Mifflin Company, 1967), p. 47; and Robert A. Peterson, "The Price-Perceived Quality Relationship: Experimental Evidence," *Journal of Marketing Research,* Vol. VII (November 1970), pp. 525–8.

From *Cases in Marketing Research* by Randall L. Schultz, Gerald Zaltman, and Philip C. Burger. Copyright © 1975 by The Dryden Press, a division of Holt, Rinehart and Winston, Publishers. Reprinted by permission of Holt, Rinehart and Winston.

in the creation and maintenance of its desired image. If it tastes that bad, it must be doing something good!

In all, much effort, through a variety of means, is directed at the consumer's perception of the firm's brand.

Multidimensional Scaling

While the firm has attempted to portray a particular product image, it is necessary to determine how successful the effort has been; that is, how the consumers actually perceive the product. Multidimensional scaling is a tool which can be used for this purpose. A second aspect of multidimensional scaling is that it decomposes the overall image of the brands into major dimensions comprising the image. The technique provides a graphical representation which displays the relative proximity between the brands included in the analysis. The concept of a brand as a position on a set of dimensions has been recommended by economists,[2] mathematical psychologists,[3] and social psychologists.[4]

The managerial implications derived from multidimensional scaling vary, depending on the particular results. For an example of possible policy implications, assume there are three brands (*A*, *B*, and *C*) in the market and they can be represented through multidimensional scaling as shown in Exhibit 1. Also, let us assume that there are two segments in the market—segment 1 strongly prefers dimension 1 and segment 2 strongly prefers dimension 2.

The firm which produces brand *A* has several alternative strategies it could employ to try to increase its market share. First, it could change the product itself by including more of dimension 1 in the product consistency. This should result in a shift of brand *A* to the right if the consumers perceive the change, as indicated in Exhibit 2. Thus, for the segment of consumers who strongly prefer dimension 1, brand *A'* (the new and improved brand *A*) has more of dimension 1 than brands *B* and *C*, and hence, would be favored.

A second potential policy available to the manufacturer of brand *A* is to change the emphasis of its advertising to stressing dimension 1. Although the product itself has not been altered in nature, the intent is to influence the consumer to associate more of dimension 1 with their product than had previously been the case. If successful, a shift in the product space, similar to the shift with the preceding policy, should occur, and the reader is again referred to Figure 2. The same result of segment 1 preferring brand *A'* should occur.

In both of the first two policies it is assumed that it is possible to keep the same perceived level of dimension 2 while increasing the perceptions of dimension 1, thereby enabling brand *A* to maintain its strong appeal to segment 2 and increase its share of segment 1. However, in many instances this is difficult to do. In order to

[2]Kelvin J. Lancaster, "A New Approach to Consumer Theory," *Journal of Political Economy*, Vol. 74 (April 1966), pp. 132–57.

[3]J. B. Kruskal, "Multidimensional Scaling by Optimizing Goodness to Fit to a Nonmetric Hypothesis," *Psychometrika*, Vol. 29, (March 1964), pp. 1–27; Roger N. Shepard, "The Analysis of Proximities: Multidimensional Scaling with an Unknown Distance Function I," *Psychometrika*, Vol. 27 (June 1962), pp. 125–39; and "The Analysis of Proximities: Multidimensional Scaling with an Unknown Distance Function II," *Psychometrika*, Vol. 27 (September 1962), pp. 219–46.

[4]Martin Fishbein, "Attitude and the Prediction of Behavior," Martin Fishbein, ed., *Readings in Attitude Theory and Measurement* (New York, John Wiley & Sons, 1967), pp. 447–92; and M. J. Rosenberg, "Cognitive Structure and Attitudinal Affect," *Journal of Abnormal and Social Psychology*, Vol. 53 (November 1956), pp. 367–72.

Exhibit 1   Product Positioning of Three Brands in Two–Dimensional Space

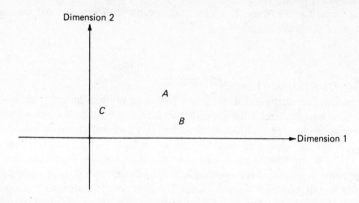

Exhibit 2   A Change in Product Positioning for Brand A

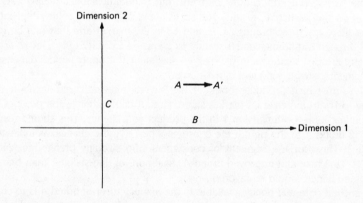

capture a large share of segment 1 without jeopardizing its dominating position with segment 2, a firm could possibly introduce a new product aimed specifically at segment 1 (shown as product *D* in Exhibit 3). Now the firm would have two brands on the market, *A* and *D,* each being the most preferred brand for the two different market segments.

There are different ways of introducing preferences into the product space. One way is called a Coombsian unfolding technique.[5] This is where a vector is introduced into the product space which is positioned such that a perpendicular trajectory of the most preferred brand, for the segment or for an individual, falls furthest out from the origin. For example, a preference of ABC is shown in Exhibit 4 for individual #1. (What are the projections, hence preferences, for #2 and #3?)

The individuals' vectors were fitted to the product space to maintain the preference rankings. For a large set of individuals with the same preference ranking, a

[5]Warren S. Torgerson, *Theory and Methods of Scaling* (New York: John Wiley & Sons, 1958), pp. 403–14.

Exhibit 3   Positioning of New Brand D

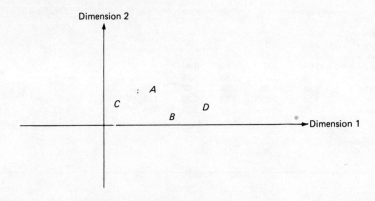

Exhibit 4   Product Preference Mapping for Individuals

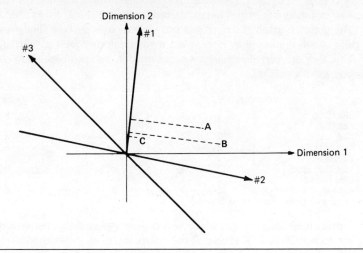

vector could be entered which would represent the entire segment. Based on the location of these vectors which represent the different segments, the marketing manager could develop his strategy.

The Data

The data necessary to perform multidimensional scaling are perceptual in nature. As discussed by Zaltman and Burger, there are numerous ways of obtaining the needed information.[6] For a decomposition model, that is, where one starts from an overall

[6]Gerald Zaltman and Philip C. Burger, *Marketing Research: Fundamentals and Dynamics* (Hinsdale, Illinois: The Dryden Press, 1975), Chapter 6.

Exhibit 5   Similarity Matrix*

	Coke	7-Up	Tab	Like	Pepsi	Sprite	Diet Pepsi	Fresca
A – Coke	0.0							
B – 7-Up	7.19	0.0						
C – Tab	3.93	6.63	0.0					
D – Like	7.08	2.83	6.00	0.0				
E – Pepsi	2.24	7.01	3.88	6.78	0.0			
F – Sprite	6.95	2.28	6.58	2.82	6.66	0.0		
G – Diet Pepsi	4.14	7.02	2.67	6.30	3.01	6.62	0.0	
H – Fresca	7.29	3.85	6.42	3.39	6.94	3.33	6.55	0.0

*1 = Very similar
 8 = Very dissimilar

perception and decomposes it into a set of dimensions, similarity data are used.[7] In the study conducted by Bass, Pessemier, and Lehmann which was described briefly in part A of this case, similarities were obtained for the set of soft drinks used in the study.[8] The question asked of the subject was, "please indicate how similar each of these pairs of soft drinks are by circling a 1 if you think they are very similar, an 8 if you think they are very dissimilar, or somewhere in between depending on how similar you feel the pair is."

	Similar							Dissimilar
Coke, 7-Up	1	2	3	4	5	6	7	8
Coke, Tab	1	2	3	4	5	6	7	8
Coke, Like	1	2	3	4	5	6	7	8
Coke, Pepsi	1	2	3	4	5	6	7	8
Coke, Sprite	1	2	3	4	5	6	7	8
Coke, Diet Pepsi	1	2	3	4	5	6	7	8
Coke, Fresca	1	2	3	4	5	6	7	8
7-Up,Tab	1	2	3	4	5	6	7	8

(etc., for all pairs of soft drink brands)

A matrix could be developed which would show the similarity between all the brands for each individual. By averaging the matrix across all individuals, you would have an overall group perceptual map of the soft drinks included in this study. The average matrix for the 264 subjects is shown in Exhibit 5.

Questions

1. Take the similarity data provided in Exhibit 5 and use a multidimensional scaling program to generate a product space.
2. Using the output derived for two dimensions, speculate what attributes the two dimensions represent. What would be a better way of determining the true representation of the dimensions in your product space?

[7]Donald R. Lehmann and Edgar A. Pessemier, "Market Structure Modeling Via Clustering and Discriminant Analysis. A Portrayal of the Soft Drink Market," Institute Paper No. 407, Institute for Research in the Behavioral, Economic, and Management Sciences, Krannert Graduate School of Industrial Administration, Purdue University, April, 1973.

[8]Frank M. Bass, Edgar A. Pessemier, and Donald R. Lehmann, "An Experimental Study of Relationships between Attitudes, Brand Preference, and Choice," *Behavioral Science,* Vol. 17, No. 6 (November 1972), pp. 532–41.

3.   Assume that there are three markets with preference rankings of the soft drink
     brands as follows:

Segment 1	Segment 2	Segment 3
Coke	Tab	7-Up
Pepsi	Diet Pepsi	Sprite
Diet Pepsi	Pepsi	Like
Tab	Coke	Fresca
7-Up	Fresca	Coke
Sprite	Like	Pepsi
Like	Sprite	Diet Pepsi
Fresca	7-Up	Tab

     Attempt to fit each of the segments preferences into the product space. Suggest
     different strategies which could be implemented to help improve a brand's
     share of the market.

4.   It would be possible for you to complete a paired comparison of all of the soft
     drink brands and use this in the multidimensional scaling program to compare
     your perception of the brands, or your product space, to that of the subjects in
     the experiment described in this case. How does your input compare?

25

AMERICAR (A): ATTITUDINAL AND ATTRIBUTE RESEARCH

Introduction

The economic situation faced by the automobile industry is the most controversial and unpredictable in history. The economic uncertainty being brought about by dwindling oil supplies and rising fuel costs has been forcing consumers to consider modes of transportation which were, to date, considered unfashionable or unnecessary. Smaller, more efficient automobiles are frequently replacing the large gas-guzzling models of earlier years. Some things have not changed, however, such as the desire for quality, comfort and style. Several automobile manufacturers are meeting the challenge of this new age with down-sized versions of many of their older models. The importance of this new, dynamic macroenvironment affecting the automobile industry is emphasized by the fact that little evidence exists to suggest that the current trend will not continue.

The automobile industry is an excellent example of a competitive environment that stresses consumer preferences in order to survive. The marketing concept is the key to this industry and, if success is to be had, consumer preferences must be understood. The highly competitive environment has resulted in continual product improvement, the development of a wide and diverse number of models to satisfy consumer needs, and advances in both technology and marketing practices. Competition stresses the development of an appropriate marketing mix and a better response to the demands of the marketplace. Because new product development requires large amounts of both time and monetary resources, to succeed in the automobile industry a marketer must be able to adapt to the dynamic environment by continually adjusting his marketing mix and be willing and able to take risks in order to do so.

Copyright © 1981 by Dr. William J. Lundstrom and Mark G. Dunn.

The Research Setting

U.S. Auto, a leading automobile manufacturer, was currently investigating the feasibility of introducing a new subcompact car to meet the changing needs of the marketplace. Although they currently were producing one subcompact, previous marketing mistakes had created an automobile with a poor brand image. With their current subcompact, they had been unable to capture a part of the continually rising subcompact market. Furthermore, all evidence lead to the conclusion that the trend for subcompact cars would persist for several years. The opportunity now existed for a new subcompact which would enable U.S. Auto to capitalize on the apparent growth trend. U.S. Auto wanted to pursue this opportunity.

The information collected in the initial research stages confirmed that the subcompact segment was strong and was indeed expected to grow at extraordinary rates over the next few years. As a result, the opportunity was translated into Americar, a new U.S. Auto subcompact.

The proposed Americar would be offered in a variety of models, including a four-door version, and would include a host of standard and optional features. Because of this, it was felt that the car would be appealing to many different consumer groups. The pricing strategy was developed to provide a distinct advantage over the dominant imports in the subcompact class. It was hoped, with a timely introduction, that Americar and its many benefits would enable U.S. Auto to become a dominant force in the subcompact market. The prospects for Americar certainly seemed promising.

As the marketing strategy was being prepared for Americar, it was felt that additional information was needed in order to better identify the prospective market. Therefore, top management referred the task to the marketing research department so that they could learn more about the subcompact target segment. It was most important to distinguish the consumers in this segment from other existing segments because consumer lifestyles of buyers tended to be correlated with different makes and models of automobiles. It was felt that any differences could provide valuable input into the development of marketing mix strategies for this potential group of automobile purchasers.

Based on past experience, U.S. Auto generally felt that once a market opportunity was perceived to exist, it was then necessary to develop a consumer profile of the appropriate target group. Traditionally, the organization viewed the automobile market from the standpoint of being composed of several subsegments identified by size of car. With the addition of Americar, U.S. Auto would now have cars covering four segments based on this method of automobile classification. These four segments include: (1) full–size, (2) intermediate, (3) compact, and (4) subcompact. The task was therefore obvious to top management of U.S. Auto. They felt it was necessary to determine the subcompact buyer's consumer profile and compare it with the profile of the other three segments.

The profile was to be composed of demographic variables, psychographic variables, and benefits sought, attempting to bring the consumer to life so that the company would almost be able to see and communicate with him or her. With the information that was to result from this profile, it was felt that U.S. Auto would be able to visualize exactly what the consumer of subcompact automobiles looked like. It was felt that this simulated visualization would enable the organization to develop a more effective marketing mix strategy.

The development of the necessary research program was turned over to a senior marketing research analyst. After several weeks of study and analysis, she developed and released her proposed marketing research program. It was her opinion

---

Exhibit 1   Project I Research Proposal: A Study of the Subcompact Market

In order to provide the information requested concerning the subcompact market, the following primary research projects are proposed:
1.   Automobile Attribute Project
2.   Projective Interview (telephone) Project
3.   Psychographic (AIO) Project
The purpose of the above proposed primary research is to provide information that would be useful in developing a consumer profile of the potential subcompact purchaser.
   The research is designed to answer the following questions:
1.   What are the salient benefits sought by the subcompact market?
2.   If a consumer profile can be developed for the subcompact owner which distinguishes this owner from other owners (e.g., the full-size car owner), what would this consumer look like?
This report provides a summary of the overall purposes and uses of the data obtained from the first of the three projects that will be conducted. The methodology of this project is briefly discussed, as well as the general objectives and purposes of the project.

Project I–Automobile Attribute Project

I. Introduction
An automobile attribute questionnaire was devised as an initial effort to identify those benefits which subcompact car owners or potential owners felt were most important when selecting a new automobile. With these benefits identified, product improvements can be approached with the confidence that such improvements will have a positive effect on consumers' attitudes. In addition, awareness of these benefits will be helpful in developing advertising copy, making media selection, and in other promotional considerations. (This questionnaire was also used to determine how respondents rated their own subcompacts relative to an "all others" standard.)

II. Purpose and Objective of the Automobile Attribute Project
A.   Identify the most salient benefits sought by subcompact purchasers.
B.   Have respondents rate their own subcompact along several attributes.

III. Methodology
   A. Design of Questionnaire. Members of the research group will choose 120 individuals from the population of subcompact car owners to complete a two-part questionnaire. The questionnaire will be given to the respondent personally, and is to be completed by the respondent without interviewer interference.
   The first part of the questionnaire asks respondents to rate, on a scale of one (very important) to five (not important at all), the importance of each of the eighteen attributes listed. This list of attributes was constructed using secondary sources as guidance. A section also requests respondents to rate their own car's performance on each of these same attributes. A section on demographics is used for classification of data.
   B. Analysis of Data. Computer programs for t-test, frequencies, and condescriptive are to be used to compile and analyze the data obtained from this study.

Exhibit 2   Automobile Attribute Study Questionnaire

```
                    (C)  Questionnaire  (see following)

                          AUTOMOBILE ATTRIBUTE STUDY

            SECTION I.

            The following are attributes of an automobile.  Please respond to the
            importance  of each in your selection of a new car.


                                    Very      Important   Somewhat   Not Very   Not Imp.
                                    Important             Important  Important  At all

SMOOTH RIDING                       _____   _____     _____    _____    _____

STYLING                             _____   _____     _____    _____    _____

OVERALL COMFORT                     _____   _____     _____    _____    _____

HIGH SPEED CAPABILITIES             _____   _____     _____    _____    _____

HANDLING                            _____   _____     _____    _____    _____

LUXURIOUS INTERIOR                  _____   _____     _____    _____    _____

QUALITY WORKMANSHIP                 _____   _____     _____    _____    _____

SMALL ENGINE                        _____   _____     _____    _____    _____

ADVANCED ENGINEERING                _____   _____     _____    _____    _____

PRESTIGE                            _____   _____     _____    _____    _____

LOW LEVEL OF POLLUTION EMISSION     _____   _____     _____    _____    _____

VALUE FOR MONEY                     _____   _____     _____    _____    _____

AMT OF SERVICE REQUIRED             _____   _____     _____    _____    _____

LOW HORSEPOWER                      _____   _____     _____    _____    _____

ECONOMY OF OPERATION                _____   _____     _____    _____    _____

QUALITY OF WARRANTY                 _____   _____     _____    _____    _____

LARGE SIZE                          _____   _____     _____    _____    _____

SPACIOUS INTERIOR                   _____   _____     _____    _____    _____
```

Exhibit 2   Automobile Attribute Study Questionnaire—Continued

SECTION II.

1) Please indicate the following concerning the subcompact car you
   personally own or operate:

   a. Was it purchased new or used? ____ New ____ Used

   b. What year is it? 19____

   c. What make? _____

   d. What model? _____

   e. What is the body type? ____ 2-door   ____ 4-door

                              ____ Hatchback   ____ Other

   f. In what month and year was it purchased? _____

2) Who made the final purchase decision for the automobile?

   ____ Myself

   ____ My spouse

   ____ My child

   ____ Joint family decision

   ____ other (please specify)

3) For what purpose was the automobile purchased?

   ____ Family car

   ____ Second car

   ____ Child's car

   ____ Other (please specify)

4) Which of the following sources of information was most influential
   in the purchase decision for your automobile? (please check only one)

   ____ Newspaper advertisement

   ____ Magazine advertisement

   ____ Television Advertisement

   ____ Salesperson

Exhibit 2   Automobile Attribute Study Questionnaire—Continued

```
5)  The next car I probably buy will probably be:
    ____  Full-size
    ____  Intermediate
    ____  Compact
    ____  Subcompact
    ____  Sport
    make and model: _____
```

Exhibit 2   Automobile Attribute Study Questionnaire—Continued

SECTION III.

Considering the following list of automobile attributes, I would rate
my small car, in relation to other small cars, to be:

	Much Better	Better Than	About the Same	Worse Than	Much Worse
SMOOTH RIDING	____	____	____	____	____
STYLING	____	____	____	____	____
OVERALL COMFORT	____	____	____	____	____
HIGHSPEED CAPABILITIES	____	____	____	____	____
HANDLING	____	____	____	____	____
LUXURIOUS INTERIOR	____	____	____	____	____
QUALITY WORKMANSHIP	____	____	____	____	____
SMALL ENGINE	____	____	____	____	____
ADVANCED ENGINEERING	____	____	____	____	____
PRESTIGE	____	____	____	____	____
LOW LEVEL OF POLLUTION EMISSION	____	____	____	____	____
VALUE FOR THE MONEY	____	____	____	____	____
AMT. OF SERVICE REQUIRED	____	____	____	____	____
LOW HORSEPOWER	____	____	____	____	____
ECONOMY OF OPERATION	____	____	____	____	____
QUALITY OF WARRANTY	____	____	____	____	____
LARGE SIZE	____	____	____	____	____
SPACIOUS INTERIOR	____	____	____	____	____

that each of the projects that were included in the proposal would be necessary to
supply top management with the profile information that was requested. The proposal can be found in Exhibit 1, and the corresponding questionnaire that was developed can be found in Exhibit 2.

The research report was turned over to several junior marketing research staff
members for critique.

Questions

1.   Evaluate each project in terms of proper research methodology for the problem
     at hand, making any suggestions that would improve the worth of the exercise.

Exhibit 2   Automobile Attribute Study Questionnaire—Continued

```
SECTION IV.  Demographics  (FOR CLASSIFICATION PURPOSES ONLY)

1.  Age _____ under 18      _____ 35-44       _____ 55 and over

            _____ 18-24      _____ 45-54

            _____ 25-34      _____ 55-64

2.  Your Sex: _____ Male      _____ Female

3.  Are you: _____ single       _____ separated
             _____ married      _____ surviving spouse
             _____ divorced

4.  Education: Number of years completed _____

5.  Ethnic Origin: _____ Caucasian     _____ Other (e.g. Indian, Mexican American)
                   _____ Black

6.  Number of Children: _____

7.  Residence: Own _____      Rent _____

8.  Occupation: _____

9.  Income:

        _____ Less than $5,000
        _____ $5,000 - $10,000
        _____ $10,000  - $15,000
        _____ $15,000  - $20,000
        _____ $20,000  - $25,000
        _____ over $25,000
```

2. Assuming that the research methodology is appropriate, evaluate the enclosed questionnaire.

3. How would you use the attitudinal information to position the Americar?

TULSA'S CENTRAL BUSINESS DISTRICT: A PSYCHOGRAPHIC ANALYSIS OF DOWNTOWN SHOPPERS

One research project in the program was to investigate downtown Tulsa shoppers in order to determine a psychographic profile of these people. Past research in consumer behavior has shown that, in many instances, demographic profiles can be enhanced by investigating psychographic information and thus, provide a richer description of the downtown shopper. Psychographic statements are a series of attitude, interest and opinion (AIO) statements that attempt to reflect consumer lifestyles.[1] Exploratory research to identify the primary areas for investigation was conducted using an open-ended personal interview.

Downtown Tulsa was changing. In 1977 a $2.6 central pedestrian system was under construction. Mayor Robert LaFortune said the pedestrian mall project reflects the solid "partnership of public and private interests" carrying out the downtown revitalization program. The concept of the central pedestrian system is expected to strengthen the "main street" segment as the prime rental area in Tulsa's downtown.

One of the most obvious symbols of what was happening downtown was the 52 story Bank of Oklahoma Tower, the focal point of the "new" Tulsa skyline. The Williams Companies have constructed the $18 million Bank of Oklahoma Tower, the state's tallest building, and office space was beginning to be leased. This was the first of several Williams Center projects to be completed. A downtown shopping mall was also planned. The first phase of retail construction in the new Williams Center planned 50 to 60 *small shops*—the largest with 10,000 square feet of floor area plus several restaurants and fast-food service spots. A *department store or major specialty store* will come in the second phase of construction.

Bob Griffin, Vice-president of Williams Reality Corporation, had asked Don Wolfe, Manager of Community Relations and John Piercey, Manager of Research for the Metropolitan Tulsa Chamber of Commerce, to meet with them in his office.

[1]William D. Wells and Douglas J. Tigert, "Activities, Interests and Opinions," *Journal of Advertising Research*, 1971.
Copyright © 1981 by Dr. William G. Zikmund

*Exhibit 1   Psychographic Analysis of Downtown Shoppers
(Percentage Agreeing With Statements)*

	Non-Shoppers (Percent)	Infrequent Shoppers (Percent)	Regular Shoppers (Percent)
Price Conscious			
1. A person can save a lot of money by shopping around for bargains.			
Strongly Agree	29.6	39.6	26.9
Mildly Agree	42.2	44.0	42.3
2. I shop a lot for "specials."			
Strongly Agree	17.8	26.7	15.4
Mildly Agree	39.0	36.7	34.6
3. I usually watch the advertisements for announcements of sales.			
Strongly Agree	34.3	37.4	30.8
Mildly Agree	43.2	40.7	57.7
Time Conscious			
4. I always shop where it saves me time.			
Strongly agree	30.8	28.1	30.8
Mildly Agree	38.2	34.8	19.2
5. I usually buy at the most convenient store.			
Strongly Agree	21.6	14.5	16.7
Mildly Agree	39.9	38.9	33.3
6. Shopping malls are the best place to shop.			
Strongly Agree	55.8	30.8	16.0
Mildly Agree	26.8	37.4	44.0
New Brand-Trier			
7. I often try new brands before my friends and neighbors do.			
Strongly Agree	12.7	13.5	19.2
Mildly Agree	25.5	29.2	26.9
8. When I see a new brand on the shelf I often buy it just to see what it's like.			
Strongly Agree	8.0	13.2	20.0
Mildly Agree	27.3	30.8	28.0
9. I like to try new and different things.			
Strongly Agree	26.5	27.8	16.0
Mildly Agree	47.9	51.1	60.0
Fashion Conscious			
10. When I must choose between the two, I usually dress for fashion, not for comfort.			
Strongly Agree	9.4	3.3	0.0
Mildly Agree	16.9	18.9	15.4

*Exhibit 1   Psychographic Analysis of Downtown Shoppers
(Percentage Agreeing With Statements)—Continued*

	Non-Shoppers (Percent)	Infrequent Shoppers (Percent)	Regular Shoppers (Percent)
Fashion Conscious—continued			
11. An important part of my life and activities is dressing smartly.			
Strongly Agree	16.5	8.8	24.0
Mildly Agree	36.3	36.3	20.0
12. I usually have one or more outfits that are of the very latest style.			
Strongly agree	28.2	18.7	15.4
Mildly Agree	39.0	38.5	38.5
Arts Enthusiast			
13. I often go out to dinner or to the theater.			
Strongly Agree	23.8	24.4	23.1
Mildly Agree	41.0	40.0	34.6
14. I enjoy going through an art gallery.			
Strongly Agree	32.1	36.3	34.6
Mildly Agree	40.6	28.6	42.3
Community-Minded			
15. I am an active member of more than one social or service organization.			
Strongly Agree	18.5	27.3	20.0
Mildly Agree	23.3	26.1	32.0
16. I like to work on community projects.			
Strongly Agree	7.1	13.5	11.5
Mildly Agree	30.8	29.2	34.6
17. I usually watch the advertisements for announcements of sales.			
Strongly Agree	14.0	18.9	15.4
Mildly Agree	19.8	30.0	26.9

At the meeting, after the normal informal chit-chat about goings on in the city, Bob Griffin addressed the group. "I've found out many things since the Williams Companies made the decision to develop the Williams Center. One is that we need to know more about the CBD. As I speak to perspective occupants of our space, one question almost universally asked is 'How many people work in the downtown area?' Knowing how many people work here is only the tip of the information iceberg. There are a number of other things we need to know about the downtown area. They also want to know about shoppers, worker traffic patterns and space occupancy in the CBD. I can't correctly answer their questions."

John Piercey commented "You know Bob, the future of Tulsa's central business district has been a topic of concern for many years. Its present conditions and its future are perceived to be an indication of the vitality and future of the entire city."

"Prior to 1970 Tulsa's CBD was in a state of decline. At that time there was every indication that Tulsa's downtown was going the way of those and so many other cities. But the Chamber of Commerce and Downtown Tulsa Unlimited started revitalization plans in the late 1960's and early 1970's hoping to reverse the declining trend. Many major private investments have been made in the last few years. But most of these efforts have been made on the bases of intuitive feelings about the CBD. I think you're right. The lack of timely information is hampered by industrial decision making and commercial marketing efforts in the downtown area. If the Chamber of Commerce is going to help the central business district, we have to eliminate the information gap about the central business district."

Later, several research projects were approved.

Methodology

A mail survey was utilized. A total of 770 questionnaires were mailed out, nine of which were not delivered. Of the 761 questionnaires distributed, 356 were returned, thus yielding a forty-seven percent response rate. The questionnaires were mailed to the "Mrs." of households listed in the Tulsa telephone directory. As anticipated, ninety percent of the respondents were women. The other ten percent of the sample presumably were households without female shoppers or where the male head of household was the primary shopper.

Exhibit 1 presents the psychographic profile of downtown shoppers.

The Instrument

A series of questions related to shopping activities, interests and opinions were measured. *Price consciousness* was measured using three statements: 1) "A person can save a lot of money by shopping around for bargains," 2) "I shop for a lot of 'specials'," and 3) "I usually watch the advertisements for the announcements of sales."

Consumers' *attitudes toward time* were measured with the statements: "I always shop where it saves me time," "I usually buy at the most convenient store," and "Shopping malls are the best place to shop."

Three statements made up the new brand-trier scale: 1) "I often try new brands before my friends and neighbors do," 2) "When I see a new brand on the shelf I often buy it just to see what it's like," and 3) "I like to try new and different things."

Three items composed the *fashion consciousness* scale: "When I must choose between the two, I usually dress for fashion not for comfort," "An important part of my life and activities is dressing smartly," and "I usually have one or more outfits of the latest style."

Two statements, "I often go out to dinner or to the theater," and "I enjoy going through an art gallery" made up the *art enthusiast* scale.

The *community-minded* scale was composed of three items: (1) "I am an active member of more than one social or service organization," (2) "I like to work on community projects," and (3) "I have personally worked on a project to better our town."

Results

Based on the question "How often do you shop at the following shopping centers (e.g., downtown Tulsa)," respondents were classified as either regular shoppers, infrequent shoppers or nonshoppers. Exhibit 1 presents the psychographic profile.

Questions

1. Profile the downtown shopper.
2. Evaluate psychographics as a means of measuring consumer attitudes and life-styles.

VII

FIELD METHODS AND CODING

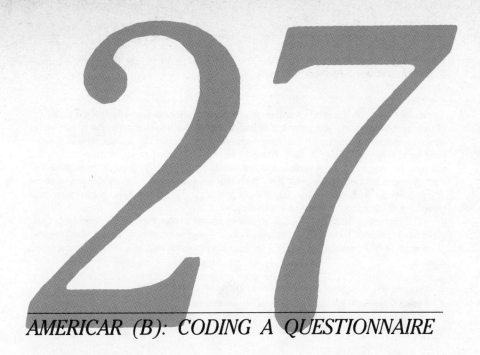

AMERICAR (B): CODING A QUESTIONNAIRE

Introduction

U.S. Auto, one of the largest U.S. automobile manufacturers, was convinced of the need to introduce another subcompact car to broaden its product offering. Its present subcompact, the Gemini, had been perceived by the public to have a split image—economy without quality. As the share of subcompacts was increasing at the expense of U.S. Auto's larger full and intermediate size models, the company felt the time was ripe to bring out another, improved version subcompact for the domestic public.

Code–named the Americar, the new offering would have a wider variety of models, better gas mileage and quality control, front-wheel drive, and more interior space than the Gemini. Through market research, the company wanted to avoid the mistakes made earlier on the Gemini and be better able to incorporate those features and benefits desired by potential buyers. In addition, the marketing staff wanted to know the underlying motives of potential purchasers and to develop a psychographic profile of these individuals based on activities, interests and opinions. These latter two studies were to be used in shaping the marketing strategy for the introduction and positioning of the Americar in the subcompact market.

Research Program

The research program proposed by the Marketing Research Department consisted of three individual projects which would provide management with the information needed to make their decision. These three projects were: (1) Automobile Attribute Project, (2) Projective Interview Project, (3) Psychographic (AIO) Project.

Copyright © 1981 by Dr. William J. Lundstrom and Mark G. Dunn

Exhibit 1   Project II Projection Interview

I. Introduction

Automobiles constitute a product category in which motivational forces behind purchase decisions are often varied and complex. Although a typical consumer could list a number of
concrete reasons supporting his purchase decision on a particular car, the deciding factor may
have been some psychological motive that he is either unwilling or unable to verbalize. For
example, he may purchase a certain make or model that conveys high social prestige or one
that enhances his own self-esteem. Many such motives lean toward varying degrees of social
acceptability; as such, the "image" that the car portrays, or the characteristics associated with
ownership of the car, is an important consideration.

The projection interview attempts to discover what people think of the subcompact and
subcompact owners. Projective techniques, including sentence completion, and word associations were used to reduce bias caused by respondents answering in a "socially acceptable"
manner.

II. Purposes and Objectives of the Projection Interview

A.   Identify potential competition by product awareness
B.   Identify potential competition along specified attributes
C.   Projected demographic profile of subcompact owner

III. Methodology

A. Design of Study—A structured questionnaire is to be administered over the telephone,
with each interview lasting approximately seven minutes. The sample will consist of a total of
165 respondents chosen randomly from the telephone directories in Birmingham, Alabama,
Memphis, Tennessee, and Jacksonville, Florida. Interviewing is to be conducted on five consecutive days (including one weekend) during the hours of 10 a.m.–12 p.m., 2 p.m.–4 p.m., and 8
p.m.–9 p.m.

B. Analysis of Data—The data is to be coded and compiled using the SPSS programs for
frequencies and crosstabulations.

C. Questionnaire—(See Exhibit 2 for the Telephone Projection Interview.)

Exhibit 2   Telephone Projection Interview

Introduction:

Hello, I'm _____, from the XYZ Research Company. We're
conducting a survey concerning small cars and small car owners and would appreciate having
your opinions on a few questions. (Get agreement.) Remember, there are no right or wrong
answers. What we need are *your opinions,* and preferably the thoughts that first come to your
mind.

1.   First of all, when you think of subcompact cars (pause), do you think of an American-

     made or foreign-made automobile?

                                   _____ American

                                   _____ Foreign

2.   What is the first make or model that comes to your mind when I say foreign subcom-

     pact? _____

Exhibit 2   Telephone Projection Interview—Continued

Can you name two others? _____

_____ no

3. What is the first make or model car that comes to mind when I say American subcom-

pact? _____

Can you name two others? _____

_____ no

4. Now I'd like you to tell me which make or model subcompact comes to mind when I say

each of the following words or phrases:

Economy _____

Serviceability _____

Quality Workmanship _____

Safety _____

Front Wheel Drive _____

Low Sticker Price _____

Many Standard Features _____

Diesel Fuel _____

5. What one word do you feel would adequately describe a typical subcompact? _____

6. Please complete the following sentence with *one* of the choices listed below:

When I see a subcompact on the Interstate,

A. _____ It's usually doing the speed limit.

B. _____ I usually pass it with little difficulty.

C. _____ It usually passes me and is out of sight in minutes.

D. _____ It's usually broken down on the side of the road.

7. How many adults can comfortably and safely fit into a subcompact?

Exhibit 2 Telephone Projection Interview—Continued

8. Now you're driving down the road, any road, and you see a subcompact. Please describe the person you would expect to see behind the wheel: (Record exactly and in detail) ___

___

(Probe) Any passengers? Please describe them, too. ___

___

___

___

9. Finally, how would you feel if you knew a member of your family were making a long trip in a subcompact? (Don't read list)

___ Uneasy

___ Secure (confident that they'd be safe, etc.)

___ Indifferent

Now I'd like to ask you a few questions about yourself for classification purposes. All information will be kept confidential, and none of it will be reported on an individual basis. (Get agreement.)

10. Do you own a subcompact, compact, or economy car?

        ___ No (Go to #12)

        ___ Yes

(If yes) What make? ___

      Model? ___

      Year? ___

11. Was it purchased new or used? ___ New ___ Used

12. Sex: ___ Male ___ Female

13. What is your marital status?

        ___ Single

        ___ Married

        ___ Separated

Exhibit 2   Telephone Projection Interview—Continued

_____ Divorced

_____ Widowed

14.   Do you have children? Please circle the number in each group:

         0–5 years   0   1   2   3   or more

         6–15 years   0   1   2   3   or more

         16–21 years   0   1   2   3   or more

         Over 21 years   0   1   2   3   or more

15.   What is your occupation? _____

16.   What was your age on your last birthday?

      _____ Under 18   _____ 45–54

      _____ 18–24   _____ 55–64

      _____ 25–34   _____ 65 and over

      _____ 35–44

17.   What is the highest level of education you completed?

      _____ Some high school

      _____ Completed high school

      _____ Vocational or technical training

      _____ Some college

      _____ Completed college

      _____ Some graduate study

18.   Please check the category that best describes your annual income:

      _____ $0–$4,999   _____ $20,000–$24,999

      _____ $5,000–$9,999   _____ $25,000–$29,999

      _____ $10,000–$14,999   _____ $30,000–$34,999

      _____ $15,000–$19,999   _____ $35,000 and over

19.   What is your race?

              _____ White

Exhibit 2   Telephone Projection Interview—Continued

_____ Black

_____ Other

Thank you for your cooperation.

Exhibit 3   Project III Psychographic Research–Activities, Interests and Opinions

I. Uses of Psychographic Research

The use of psychographic research in marketing is a relatively new concept in marketing management. Because of this, there has been much criticism concerning its use and the validity and reliability of this market segmentation and identification technique. Not dismissing these criticisms lightly, it is important for the researcher to realize it is necessary for the segmentation process to move beyond demographics into other more identifiable measures. This will enable the researcher to develop a more descriptive picture of the consumer, not only in demographic terms, but in psychographic terms as well. Therefore, in using psychographic research, marketing analysis can move into areas beyond mere demographic description and into a world that not only sees the consumer, but understands him as well.

The value of psychographic research lies in the very meaning of the term. Psychographic research implies an attempt to understand the consumer in terms of activities, interests, opinions, needs and values. The purpose underlying the use of psychographics, as well as benefit and demographic analysis, cannot be mistaken. Through psychographic research we operate under the assumption that, the more you know ad understand your customer, the more effectively you can develop your marketing-mix around the true needs of the marketplace. If your marketing-mix has been developed correctly, then your chances of success are improved.

Through lifestyle analysis, you not only can attempt to segment the market, but once segmented, you can also identify and make inferences about the lifestyle of that segment. With this in mind, the proposed research concentrates on gathering information concerning psychographic dimensions of automobile purchasers.

This project consists of twenty-eight statements, each concerned with one of three topics: (1) product-specific information (2) information-search information and (3) general lifestyle information. This research instrument provides information concerning the subcompact segment as well as information concerning automobile marketing in general.

II. Purpose and Objectives of Psychographic Questionnaire

A.   Provide a means of analysis of overall automobile market along product–specific items
B.   Provide a description of the subcompact market in psychographic terms
C.   Provide a basis for examining psychographic dimensions along demographic breakdowns

III. Methodology

A. Design of Questionnaire—Included in the questionnaire were twenty-eight lifestyle, seven benefit, as well as demographic and automobile ownership questions. With these questions it was possible to relate both psychographics and benefits to various car owners.

B. Sampling Procedure—The sample consisted of 186 respondents gathered by the conventional convenience sampling technique. Although major limitations exist in convenience sampling due to time constraints, it is deemed appropriate.

C. Analysis of Data—The analysis will be computer analyzed using appropriate programs found in SPSS. Among those used were Frequencies, T-Test and Analysis of Variance. With these statistical tests it will be possible to analyze and describe the automobile market in general and further describe the subcompact market in a more precise manner.

D. Questionnaire—(See Exhibit 4 for the Interests and Opinions Questionnaire used.)

Exhibit 4   Interests and Opinions Questionnaire

```
                        INTERESTS AND OPINIONS QUESTIONNAIRE


         SECTION I.

         Listed below are a number of interests and opinions.  For each
         statement, please indicate by placing a check mark ( ) in the space
         that best describes your feelings about the statement.

                                             neither
                                strongly  agree  agree or  disagree  strongly
                                agree            disagree            disagree

  1. In a car, economy is more
     important than power.       _____  _____  _____  _____  _____

  2. In a car, performance
     should be considered before
     styling.                    _____  _____  _____  _____  _____

  3. I am more practical in my
     car selection than the
     average automobile buyer.   _____  _____  _____  _____  _____

  4. The kind of car you have
     influences how people see you. _____  _____  _____  _____  _____

  5. I do a lot of driving.      _____  _____  _____  _____  _____

  6. I spend a lot of time
     comparing and inspecting dif-
     ferent brands before I make
     a final decision.           _____  _____  _____  _____  _____

  7. I normally read the newspaper
     everday.                    _____  _____  _____  _____  _____

  8. I look for the lowest prices
     when I shop.                _____  _____  _____  _____  _____

  9. Most car salesmen are dis-
     honest.                     _____  _____  _____  _____  _____

 10. I often ask my friends for
     advice before making a major
     purchase.                   _____  _____  _____  _____  _____

 11. When I receive mail adver-
     tising I normally will read
     most of it.                 _____  _____  _____  _____  _____

 12. The only function of a car is
     transportation.             _____  _____  _____  _____  _____
```

The first project, the Automobile Attribute Study, had already been assigned to a junior market research staff member for evaluation and a data coding system was developed for recording the information received from the questionnaire (see Americar (A) for the methodology and questionnaire design used for this project). Marketing management was pleased with design of the attribute study and had authorized that it be executed. Likewise, in an effort to gather the other information, management had given the preliminary go-ahead for the remaining two projects.

Preliminary authorization means that the projects should be evaluated by a research staff member, recommended changes should be made and the questionnaire should be coded for the ready transfer of raw data onto punch cards or computer-readable forms. These two proposed projects and their corresponding questionnaires are found in Exhibits 1 through 4 of this case.

Exhibit 4   Interests and Opinions Questionnaire—Continued

13. If I am satisfied with
    one make of car, I will
    buy the same one next time.

14. It is important to collect
    as much information as you
    can concerning a product
    before purchasing it.

15. A good looking car is very im-
    portant to me.

16. Americans should buy
    American made cars.

17. Ease of handling is more
    importanct to me than
    power or style.

18. Economy of operation should
    be the main consideration
    when purchasing a car.

19. I look at advertisements
    in magazines about as
    much as I read the articles.

20. Television advertising
    provides more information
    than radio or newspapers.

21. You can rely on information
    you receive from a friend
    more than you can that
    received from an ad.

22. Before making a major
    purchase, I consult
    Consumer Reports or a
    similar publication for
    product information.

23. Small, economical cars
    should be more popular.

24. Looks and styling are not
    important if the car
    functions properly.

25. A spacious interior is
    very important in my
    selection of a new car.

26. I don't pay too much
    attention to radio
    commercials.

Exhibit 4 Interests and Opinions Questionnaire—Continued

27. Quality is more important than price. _____ _____ _____ _____ _____

28. I have somewhat old-fashion tastes and habits. _____ _____ _____ _____ _____

Exhibit 4   Interests and Opinions Questionnaire—Continued

SECTION II.

Please answer the following questions concerning the car you drive
most regularly.

make _____   model _____   year _____

purchased   month/year
new or used _____   purchased _____

Before purchasing my present automobile I had a demostration ride.

yes _____   no _____

SECTION III.

Please indicate the importance of each of the following attributes in your
purchase decision for a car.

	very important	important	not important	not important at all
1. Economy	_____	_____	_____	_____
2. Quality	_____	_____	_____	_____
3. Price	_____	_____	_____	_____
4. Prestige	_____	_____	_____	_____
5. Servicability	_____	_____	_____	_____
6. Overall comfort	_____	_____	_____	_____
7. Smooth riding	_____	_____	_____	_____

Exhibit 4   Interests and Opinions Questionnaire—Continued

```
SECTION IV.  Demographics  (FOR CLASSIFICATION PURPOSES ONLY)

1.  Age _____ under 18      _____ 35-44      _____ 55 and over

        _____ 18-24         _____ 45-54

        _____ 25-34         _____ 55-64

2.  Your Sex: _____ Male      _____ Female

3.  Are you: _____ single       _____ separated
             _____ married      _____ surviving spouse
             _____ divorced

4.  Education:  Number of years completed _____

5.  Ethnic Origin: _____ Caucasian      _____ Other (e.g. Indian, Mexican American)
                   _____ Black

6.  Number of Children: _____

7.  Residence: Own _____      Rent _____

8.  Occupation: _____

9.  Income:

        _____ Less than $5,000
        _____ $5,000 - $10,000
        _____ $10,000  - $15,000
        _____ $15,000  - $20,000
        _____ $20,000  - $25,000
        _____ over $25,000
```

Questions

1. Evaluate the research methodology used in this case.
2. Evaluate each of the questionnaires following this case as to its ability to obtain the necessary information.
3. Prepare a detailed coding sheet for the efficient transfer of data onto computer cards.

MIAMI SOLAR WATER HEATER SURVEY: INTERVIEWER INSTRUCTIONS

In 1973, the National Science Foundation (NSF) launched a major investigation into the potential uses of new energy sources in the United States. Among the projects funded were studies by large firms such as Westinghouse, TRW and General Electric which evaluated the potential use of solar energy in heating and cooling buildings. Although use of solar heating and, to a lesser degree, solar cooling are now commonplace, few solar systems were commercially available at that time. Furthermore, an extremely limited number of homeowners had any real knowledge of solar applications or had any experience with solar heating systems.

As a part of a larger research project, NSF funded a study to investigate the use of solar water heaters in the Miami, Florida area. In Miami, and in other areas of Florida and California, builders in the 1920's and 1930's had built many homes with rudimentary solar water heaters. Typically, these hot water heaters were included in housing tracts where gas or electric service was either not yet available or was prohibitively expensive. As the cost of utility service became lower, fewer and fewer solar water heaters were installed and many of those previously installed were allowed to fall into disuse or were disconnected. By 1970, equipment surveys by the Florida Power Co., the local public utility, indicated that less than one percent of homes in the Miami area had a functioning solar water heater.

Research Project

NSF was interested in evaluating the attitudes of Miami area residents toward solar water heaters. Of particular interest were attitudes toward their reliability and performance, problems encountered (e.g., maintenance required) and the impact of so-

Copyright © 1981 by Dr. Donald Sciglimpaglia

Exhibit 1   Tally Form

Interview No. _____

Miami Solar Water Heater Survey

Check appropriate box after completing interview:

| Experience | | | Income Area | | Sex | | Survey Category Check When Complete |
Current User	Past User	Non-User	Low	High	Male	Female	
•			•		•		1 ( )
•			•			•	2 ( )
•				•	•		3 ( )
•				•		•	4 ( )
	•		•		•		5 ( )
	•		•			•	6 ( )
	•			•	•		7 ( )
	•			•		•	8 ( )
		•	•		•		9 ( )
		•	•			•	10 ( )
		•		•	•		11 ( )
		•		•		•	12 ( )

lar water heaters on lifestyle. A decision was made to conduct interviews with three groups: 1) current users, 2) former users who had discontinued use of the solar water heater, and 3) non-users who were aware of solar heaters. A total of 200 interviews were to be conducted with each group. In addition, the groups were to be further broken down such that each group contained equal numbers of respondents by sex and income area. A tally form prepared for use by interviewers which reflects these breakdowns is shown in Exhibit 1.

The only information available as to the location of households with solar heaters was obtained from Florida Power Co. and from the city of Miami. These sources were able to point out geographical areas where they were more likely to be found. Included were upper income areas such as Coral Gables and areas which were now lower income, such as Opalocka. Aerial photographs were available from local planning agencies which could be used to identify areas with solar panels on home roofs. However, it was impossible to determine from photographs whether or not the solar systems were in operation. Many of the areas identified had large percentages of Spanish-speaking or non-white households.

The research team prepared a sheet of instructions to be used in briefing interviewers. This is shown in Exhibit 2. Some concern was raised as to whether or not the instructions were sufficient.

Questions

1. Should this be a quota or a stratified random sampling plan? Why?
2. How should the households in the sample actually be selected for interviews?

Exhibit 2   Miami Solar Water Heater Survey: Notes to Interviewers

As part of a large scale effort to investigate the potential for application of alternative sources of energy for domestic use in the United States, the National Science Foundation has funded a number of studies to help ascertain the feasibility of using solar energy (heat from the sun's rays) to heat and cool homes and industrial buildings. Part of one of these studies, an analysis of how likely it would be for consumers to purchase solar heated and cooled homes, is a survey of Miami area residents which is intended to uncover their opinions of solar hot water heaters. These hot water heating units were quite common in the Miami area during the period of 1930–1950 and many are still in operation in older sections of the area.

Briefly, solar water heaters are located on the roof of the house and operate by heating water that flows through copper tubing in a solar collector, which absorbs the sun's heat. The heated water rises to a storage tank, usually located on the roof and covered by a false chimney, from which it is tapped for use in the home. The solar collector is usually found on the south-facing section of the roof and can be easily identified because it is covered by glass panels which gives it the appearance of being a "skylight" window. It is typically about four feet by eight feet. In order to maintain hot water during periods of cloudy weather, many solar water heaters utilize a booster heating unit, usually an electric heating coil, which is turned on manually or by an automatic thermostatic control unit.

Respondents

The investigators in this study are interested primarily in the opinions of three main classes of Miami area residents: current users, past users, and non-users.

1. *Current User—A Miami area resident head of household or spouse who currently uses a solar unit to heat all or part of the home's hot water.*
2. *Past User—A Miami area resident head of household or spouse who previously used a solar unit to heat all or part of their present or past home's hot water and whose household discontinued use of the solar unit by having it disconnected or removed. Potential respondents who discontinued use by moving from a home with a solar unit to one with a conventional gas or electric hot water heater (i.e. did not have the solar unit disconnected or removed) do not qualify as past users.*
3. *Non-User—A Miami area resident, of two or more years, head of household or spouse who has never used a solar hot water heater in their present or past home but who has some knowledge of what a solar water heater is. Potential respondents who indicate no knowledge of solar water heaters do not qualify as non-users.*

3. If an interviewing service needs to be selected, are there any special criteria or qualifications that it should possess?
4. From the information in the case, do you suggest personal or telephone interviews to collect the information required?
5. Are the interviewer instructions provided sufficient? Explain.
6. Do you foresee any specific problems in this research project? Explain.

29

CALIFORNIA PUBLIC OPINION COMPANY VIDEO RECORDER SURVEY: EVALUATION OF FIELD METHODS AND INTERVIEWER INSTRUCTIONS

California Public Opinion Company (CPO) was recently given the task of conducting a survey to evaluate the use of video cassette recorders and video programs. CPO is a full-service marketing research firm in Southern California. Sally Fisher, a marketing research analyst at CPO, was assigned the responsibility of project manager.

Background of the Video Cassette Industry

Introduced in 1976, video cassette recorders have now penetrated into an estimated 650,000 homes in the United States. This represents roughly one percent of the total television-equipped homes. The video industry estimates that by 1990 there will be seven million homes equipped with VCRs.

Video disc players were test marketed in the U.S. in Atlanta, Seattle and other cities between 1979–80. Initial full-scale introduction began in 1981 with RCA's entry into the market. Industry analysts forecast nearly seven million video discs will be in use by 1990.

Major differences between video disc players and video cassette recorders exist. Generally, VCRs are more expensive to purchase and prerecorded tapes are typically more costly than comparable video discs. However, with a VCR, the user can also record material straight from the television or by using a video camera. Video disc players are more compact and are designed only for playing prerecorded programs.

The Client: Nova Stores Corporation

CPO had been retained by Nova Stores Corporation, a large, diversified retailing firm, to conduct the video recorder survey. Nova department stores had television and

Copyright © 1981 by Dr. Donald Sciglimpaglia

VCR departments and so wished to know more about the market for video equipment and programs. Recently a large photo-processing retailer (Fotomat Corporation) had begun to sell and rent prerecorded video programs on a test basis using its booths in shopping center locations. Also a number of specialty stores had recently been opened which specialized in selling video equipment (e.g., Video World) or in the sales and rental of tapes (e.g., Video Library). In short, Nova Corporation's management wanted to keep abreast of developments in the video industry for future planning purposes. If warranted, management was considering the possibility of launching a chain of video specialty stores sometime in the future.

California is currently the biggest single market for electronic entertainment. Because San Diego was being utilized for the Fotomat test market, Nova Corporation elected to use that city as the area in which to conduct the research.

Research Objectives

Sally Fisher, in consultation with Nova personnel, formulated her objectives for the research project. They were as follows:

1. To gain insight into the size of the present and potential market in San Diego for home video equipment and programs.
2. To determine actual and projected purchases and uses of home video equipment programs.
3. To discover the profiles of video-oriented consumers in metropolitan San Diego.
4. To ascertain the changes and improvements needed in the home video field in order to penetrate a mass consumer market.

She identified her information needs as follows:

1. Identify current and potential users of home video recorders in metropolitan San Diego.
2. Determine reasons for present and potential purchases.
3. Obtain information about the positive and negative factors involved in owning equipment and in considering purchases.
4. Determine the uses of home video recorders.
5. Discover the attitudes toward and uses of prerecorded programs, including types and methods of acquisition.
6. Acquire data on demographic characteristics of present and potential users.
7. Ascertain awareness level of video disc equipment.

The Research Study

Based on existing secondary information and Nova sales records, Fisher profiled the VCR owner as being upper–income and, most likely, thirty-five years old or over. Since no comprehensive list of VCR owners was available, she decided to conduct a type of probability sampling. Fisher, using census data, selected specific areas which matched the VCR owner profile. She hoped to obtain a total of 200 completed interviews with VCR owners. Interviewers would be given telephone numbers in the selected areas and then instructed to add a digit to the assigned number in an attempt to reach unlisted numbers. Fisher thought that this would be a good way to make the household selection more random.

Exhibit 1   Video Recorder Survey: Instructions for Interviewers

Purpose: Residents in selected areas of metropolitan San Diego are being interviewed about owning or considering the purchase of the home video cassette recorder, a machine used to record television shows and play prerecorded program cassettes. In order to interview these people, the following is to be done:

1. Use the telephone questionnaire to interview an adult head of household, either male or female, about current or potential use of home video equipment. In your introduction, or at any time, if the respondent is hesitant, explain that the survey is not related to sales and no names or addresses are required. Due to the high degree of telephone sales or of theft in certain areas, this explanation may help create a rapport with respondents.

2. Contact the telephone numbers in your area assigned by the supervisor. Call the listed number and continue with random digit dialing through nine. If the number is a business, abandon, or if no response, record on call sheet and continue with next random telephone number. Use up to three call backs if needed for your area quota but change calling time.

3. Make your calls between 10 a.m. and 9 p.m. Calling on weekends is your choice. The total survey requires 200 completed interviews and each area has an assigned quota.

4. Follow directions exactly and read questions as written. If respondents do not understand, do not attempt to explain, just reread.

5. Read all capitalized copy and mark (X) in the answer blocks. In the "other" line, write the answers verbatim.

6. Record answers to questions, screening for useable respondents on Section I with pencil. If interviewee does not qualify, record on the tally sheet in the proper category. Erase questionnaire and reuse.

   A. Question 1: If respondent does not own a television set, stop the interview and record on tally sheet under "no television" category.

   B. If respondent is not familiar with video cassette recorders, stop interview and record mark on tally sheet under "not known" category.

   C. Questions 7 and 8: If respondent is familiar with video recorders but does not own one or is not planning on a purchase, ask the video disc questions and record on tally sheet. Erase and reuse screening page.

7. Follow directions exactly for each question in Section II—present owner, and in Section III—potential buyer. Each section ends with video disc and demographic data.

   A. For questions that state "Do not read," referring to the answer categories, mark the answer given in the correct blank. If you are not sure of the category, write the answer in "other." If necessary, probe using the answers as guides.

   B. For questions that say "Read," read the categories to respondent as written. Do say "other" in your reading so they feel free to comment.

   C. For questions that state "Read and rotate," read in order as written the first time. For the second reading, start at the second listing and read the first answer last. Continue this pattern. When you start with the last item, return to the top of the list and read through.

Exhibit 2   Video Equipment Survey: Interviewer Tally Sheet

Record data for nonrespondents

- Does not own television:

- Not familiar with video cassette recorder:

- Not familiar with video disc player:

- Familiar with video disc player:

- Considering purchase of video disc player:

- Not considering purchase of video disc player:

Exhibit 3   Video Recorder Survey: Questionnaire

Section I—Screening

Interviewer _____   Area _____
Head of Household: M( )   F( )   Telephone Number _____

Hello, my name is _____ of the California Public Opinion Company. We're surveying this area about equipment that changes television programming. You are a member of a select group chosen for your opinion. Could you take a few minutes to answer some important questions?

(Only proceed, if willing. If hesitant, explain no sales, no names, no addresses. If busy, schedule a call back on certain day and time.)

1. Do you own a television?   yes ( )1
                              no ( )2 (stop interview, thank)

2. Do you have a color television?   yes ( )1   black and white ( )2

3. How many sets do you own?   one ( )1   two ( )2   three ( )3   four + ( )4

4. What are the estimated total hours you watch television each day?
   Less than 1 hour ( )1 $5–6\frac{1}{2}$ ( )4
             $1–2\frac{1}{2}$ ( )2 $7–8\frac{1}{2}$ ( )5
             $3–4\frac{1}{2}$ ( )3 $9–10\frac{1}{2}$ ( )6
                              11 or more ( )7

Today you can watch television shows at your convenience by taping programs with recording equipment, known as home video cassette recorders.

5. Have you heard about the video recorder?   yes ( )1
                                              no ( )2 (stop interview)

6. Have you seen a recorder in operation?   yes ( )1
                                            no ( )2 (stop interview)

7. Do you own a video cassette recorder?   yes ( )1 (go to Question 9–Section II)
                                           no ( )2

Exhibit 3   Video Recorder Survey: Questionnaire—Continued

8. Are you considering the purchase of a home video cassette recorder within the next year?   yes (   )1 (go to Section III—potential buyer)
    no (   )2 (ask video disc questions and terminate)

(If answer no, ask question about video disc. If they are not familiar with video disc, mark tally sheet and reuse questionnaire form. If they are familiar and are considering a future purchase, mark tally sheet and reuse screen.)

Video Disc Data
(Mark the tally sheet according to answers. This page is only used with respondents familiar with video equipment, but not owning one or not considering a purchase of video cassette. This data is not coded since aggregate amount on the tally sheet will be the useable data.)

This year a new video machine that plays prerecorded television programs on a record will be available. Have you heard about the video disc player?

        yes (   ) (ask the next question and record on tally sheet)
        no (   ) (record in "not known" video disc on tally sheet)

Will you consider buying a video disc player when the equipment becomes available in this area?

        yes (   )
        no (   ) (record on tally sheet)
        don't know (   )

                      Section II—Present Owner

9. How long have you owned your video recorder? (Do not read.)
        6 months or less (   )1   2½ to 3 years   (   )4
        1 year   (   )2   more than 3 years (   )5
        1½ to 2 years   (   )3

10. Who made the decision to buy a video recorder? (Do not read.)
        head of household (   )1
        family/group   (   )2
        gift   (   )3

11. How did the buyer find out about video recorders? (Do not read.)
                friends/relatives   ( )1
                advertising   ( )2
                employment   ( )3
                television dealers   ( )4
                other _____ ( )5
                        (write in)

12. What was the key feature considered in choice of equipment? (Read and rotate.)
                quality of production   ( )1
                manufacturer reputation   ( )2
                recording time   ( )3
                price   ( )4
                other _____ ( )5
                        (write in)

Exhibit 3   Video Recorder Survey: Questionnaire—Continued

13. If you were to purchase video equipment today, what key feature would affect your choice? (Do not read.)

quality of production	( )1
manufacturer reputation	( )2
recording time	( )3
price	( )4
other _____	( )5
(write in)	

14. What type of tapes did you obtain with your original purchase? (Do not read.)

blank cassettes	( )1
prerecorded programs	( )2
none	( )3

15. Were the cassettes included in your purchase price?

yes	( )1
no	( )2

16. What is the major use of your video recorder? (Do not read.)

tape shows from television	( )1
play prerecorded cassettes	( )2
film home movies	( )3
other _____	( )4
(write in)	

17. What other ways do you use the recorder? (Do not read.)

tape shows from television	( )1
play prerecorded tapes	( )2
film home movies	( )3
other _____	( )4

18. Approximately how many television shows do you tape within a month? (Do not read.)

none ( )1	6–8 ( )4
1–2 ( )2	9 or more ( )5
3–5 ( )3	

19. What is the main method you use to record programs? (Read.)

watching the show	( )1
away from home	( )2
watching another show	( )3
other _____	( )4
(write in)	

20. What types of shows do you record? (Read and rotate.)

movies	( )1	weekly series	( )5
sports	( )2	children	( )6
education specials	( )3	music specials	( )7
(documentary)		talk shows	( )8
college credit	( )4	drama specials	( )9
other _____			( )10
(write in)			

Exhibit 3   *Video Recorder Survey: Questionnaire—Continued*

21. After viewing, what do you do with your tapes of television shows? (Do not read.)

library for replaying	( )1
erase and reuse	( )2
trade with friends	( )3
exchange club	( )4
business	( )5
other _____	( )6

22. Do you use prerecorded cassettes?

yes ( )1
no ( )2 (skip to Question 29)

23. Where do you obtain prerecorded cassettes? (Do not read.)

television dealers ( )1		video clubs	( )6
free with machine( )2		catalogs	( )7
discount stores ( )3		exchange clubs	( )8
department stores( )4		Fotomat	( )9
record shops ( )5		other _____ ( )10	

24. Are your prerecorded cassettes (read)

purchased	( )1
rented	( )2 (skip
borrowed	( )3 to
exchanged	( )4 Question 27)
other _____	( )5

25. How many times do you view purchased prerecorded tapes?

one ( )1   two ( )2   three ( )3   four+ ( )4

26. What do you do with purchased prerecorded tapes? (Do not read.)

trade with friends	( )1
file in library	( )2
exchange with club members	( )3
other _____	( )4

(write in)

27. What types of prerecorded programs do you watch? (Read and rotate.)

movies ( )1		how-to education	( )5
sports ( )2		musicals	( )6
comedies ( )3		adult	( )7
classics ( )4		other _____ ( )8	

28. In what types of situations do you use prerecorded tapes? (Do not read.)

group gatherings	( )1
family only	( )2
employment	( )3
other _____	( )4

(write in)

Exhibit 3   Video Recorder Survey: Questionnaire—Continued

29. What types of prerecorded programs need to become more available for home video users? (Do not read.)

how-to sports	( )1	children	( )7
how-to home help	( )2	science fiction	( )8
travel	( )3	adventure	( )9
general education	( )4	sports	( )10
remedial education	( )5	science	( )11
financial	( )6	college credit	( )12

other _____ ( )13

(write in)

30. Do you film home movies?   yes ( )1
                                no ( )2 (skip to Question 33)

31. What types of activities do you film? (Do not read.)

special occasions	( )1
everyday events	( )2
business	( )3
other _____	( )4

(write in)

32. What do you do with your filmed cassettes?

file in library for replaying	( )1
erase and reuse	( )2
send to relatives	( )3
use in business	( )4
other _____	( )5

(write in)

33. What suggestions or ideas could you offer to help improve or change home video equipment or programs? (Write as said.)

_____
_____
_____
_____

34. This year a new video machine that plays prerecorded television programs on a record will be available. Have you heard about the video disc?

                      yes ( )1 (ask Question 35)
                      no ( )2 (skip to Question 36)

35. Will you consider buying a video disc player when the equipment becomes available in this area?

yes	( )1
no	( )2
don't know	( )3

Exhibit 3   Video Recorder Survey: Questionnaire—Continued

Demographic Data
The following questions are to help classify data. In no way will you be identified with your answers.

36. How many members are in your household?

1 ( )1	6 ( )6
2 ( )2	7 ( )7
3 ( )3	8 ( )8
4 ( )4	9 ( )9
5 ( )5	10+ ( )10

37. How many are children under 18 years of age? (Do not read)

none ( )1	3 ( )4
1 ( )2	4 ( )5
2 ( )3	5+ ( )6

38. How many are adults age 65 or over? (Do not read.)

none ( )1
1   ( )2
2   ( )3
3+ ( )4

39. What is the life style of your household? (Read.)

Married with children	( )1
Childless married couple (include living together)	( )2
Group of singles	( )3
Single (include divorced, widowed, separated)	( )4
Other _____	( )5

(write in)

40. What is the highest grade of school or college the buyer of the video equipment has completed? (Do not read.)

grade school ( )1	some college ( )4
some high school ( )2	college graduate ( )5
high school graduate ( )3	postgraduate ( )6

41. What is the age group of the buyer (or potential buyer)? (Read.)

19–24 ( )1	41–45 ( )5	61–65 ( )9
25–30 ( )2	46–50 ( )6	66+ ( )10
31–35 ( )3	51–55 ( )7	
36–40 ( )4	56–60 ( )8	

42. What is the grouping for your annual family income please? (Read.)

$9,999 and below ( )1	$35,000 to $39,999 ( )7
$10,000 to $14,999 ( )2	$40,000 to $44,999 ( )8
$15,000 to $19,999 ( )3	$45,000 to $49,999 ( )9
$20,000 to $24,999 ( )4	$50,000 to $54,999 ( )10
$25,000 to $29,999 ( )5	$55,000 to $59,999 ( )11
$30,000 to $34,000 ( )6	$60,000 and above ( )12

Exhibit 3   Video Recorder Survey: Questionnaire—Continued

Thank you for helping us complete our survey. we appreciate your time and effort. Have a nice day (night). Good-bye.

Interviewer (initials) _____

Interview completed:
Date: _____
Time: _____

   Fisher then drew up an initial draft of a questionnaire for present owners and another for potential owners. In addition, she drafted a set of instructions for the interviewers. The instructions, the interviewer tally sheet, and the present owner questionnaire (section II) are shown in Exhibits 1, 2, and 3.

Questions

1.   Evaluate Fisher's research design and sampling plan.
2.   Evaluate the interviewer instructions. Are they sufficiently clear?
3.   Critique the questionnaire developed by Fisher. Are there any elements of the questionnaire which can be improved?

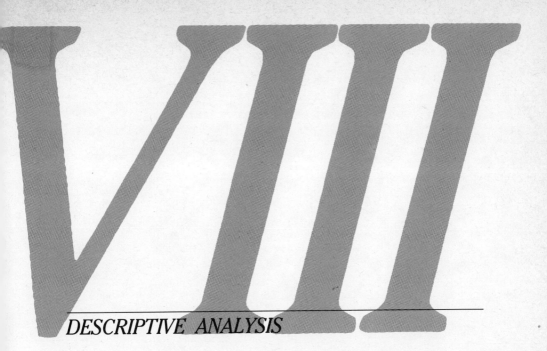

VIII

DESCRIPTIVE ANALYSIS

TLT (B): DESCRIPTIVE STATISTICS

In April 1979, the future officers of TLT (Tender Loving Transport) met to discuss the feasibility study conducted for the proposed limousine service. Present were Bill Ranford, maketing professor, Knox Gary, realtor and Jim Newman, thoroughbred breeder. This unlikely group meeting in Oxford, Mississippi, was seriously contemplating a limousine service to run from Oxford to Memphis International Airport. At this juncture, they were discussing the questions that were answered by the feasibility study and with new information, deciding whether it was a viable concept.

Background

Last January, these three potential entrepreneurs had agreed upon the need for a limousine service from Oxford to Memphis International Airport. All three had suffered from the poor airline service offered by Republic Airlines and believed that the community could support another public carrier to make connections at Memphis, which was a regional hub airport. Since Oxford was some eighty miles from the Memphis airport, private automobile use provided the major form of transportation and competition to such a service. Although a major busline, Continental Trailways, also served Oxford, it did not stop at the airport but went directly to the central downtown terminal which from there, was a ten–dollar cab ride to the airport. With the rising cost of gasoline and parking at the airport, the time seemed right for an additional public carrier.

As mentioned before, Oxford was eighty miles southeast of the Memphis airport. Although a university town with a population of 20,000 persons in the immediate metropolitan area, Oxford was not totally dependent on the University of Mississippi for employment. There were several industrial plants in the area which employed

Copyright © 1981 by Dr. William J. Lundstrom.

Exhibit 1   Estimated Cost of Operating Limousine Service

Fixed Costs	Per Year	Per Month
Vehicle $11,000 ÷ 2		
(2 year–life)	$5,500.00	$458.33
License-ICC	450.00	37.50
Attorney fees	1,100.00	91.66
State tags	200.00	16.67
Advertising (pre-start)	500.00	41.67
Total	$7,750.00	$645.83

Variable Costs (2 trips/day—30 day month)	Per Month
Driver salaries	$900.00
Fuel	900.00
Maintenance	100.00
Advertising	50.00
Printing	50.00
Commissions to travel agency	100.00
Total	$2,100.00

over 1,500 people. The Federal government had its regional headquarters for the state in Oxford and had a soil conservation lab and forestry service in the town. There were also a disproportionately large number of doctors serving the regional medical center and a large number of attorneys serving federal, state and local governments. All in all, Oxford was a unique environment with its mixture of professionals, as well as the many small business owners and retirees that it attracted.

It was in this setting that Ranford, a marketing professor, Newman and Gary had proposed initiating a limousine service for residents and visitors alike. The concept was to have comfortable (a customized van with captain's chairs and a couch) and convenient service between Oxford and the Memphis airport. A preliminary cost estimate was developed (see Exhibit 1) and they decided (or Ranford did) that they needed a feasibility study done on the demand side factor.

The April 10th Meeting

"Well, here it is," said Ranford as he dropped three copies of the feasibility study on the desk, "My marketing class spent over two months working on this project and I think it gives us the information we have been looking for."

"I am not well–versed in marketing research," responded Gary. "Could you go over how the study was done and who the people were that were interviewed to get the results?"

"I'd be glad to if you really want to know," said Ranford. "The project was fairly straightforward and really didn't involve anything very sophisticated. I'll be as brief as possible and then we can look at the results together."

Ranford went on and summarized the research methodology involved in the feasibility study as best he could to his uninitiated listeners.

Methodology

A questionnaire was developed that would hopefully hit on the major questions which needed to be answered (see Exhibit 2). The questionnaire was a structured

Exhibit 2   Telephone Marketing Questionnaire

Interviewer _____   Interviewee _____

Phone number _____

Date _____ Times called: Begin _____ End _____ No Contact _____
Date _____ Times called: Begin _____ End _____ No Contact _____
Date _____ Times called: Begin _____ End _____ No Contact _____

Hello. My name is _____. I am conducting a survey for the Small
Business Administration concerning transportation habits between Oxford and Memphis International Airport. May I speak to the person in your family who flies the most?

I.   How do you normally travel to Memphis International Airport?
     Car _____   Bus _____   Plane _____   Other _____

     If plane:
           Are you satisfied with the airline's dependability between Oxford and the Memphis
           airport?   Yes _____   No _____
           Are their flight times convenient for catching your connecting flights in
           Memphis?   Yes _____   No _____
           Do you feel that the airline's prices are reasonable between Oxford and
           Memphis?   Yes _____   No _____
II. How many times per month or year do you fly out of Memphis?   Per month _____
     Per year _____
     Do you normally travel alone?   Yes _____   No _____

     If no:
           How many people normally travel with you?
           Are these traveling companions friends _____family _____or business associ-
           ates _____?

     What percentage of your trips are business? _____
     What percentage of your trips are pleasure? _____
     What is your usual day of departure from Memphis?
     Monday _____   Tuesday _____   Wednesday _____   Thursday _____   Friday _____
     Saturday _____   Sunday _____
     What is your usual day of arrival in Memphis?   Monday _____   Tuesday _____
     Wednesday _____   Thursday _____   Friday _____   Saturday _____   Sunday _____

     What times of the day do your flights normally depart from Memphis? _____

     What times of the day do your flights normally arrive in Memphis? _____

     How much time do you allow yourself for check–in? _____
     How much luggage do you usually take? _____
III. Would you consider taking a limousine service between Oxford and Memphis?   Yes _____
     No _____

     Would you consider $30.00 a reasonable price for this round-trip service?   Yes _____
     No _____

     If no:
           Would you consider $25.00 a reasonable price for this round-trip service?   Yes _____
           No _____

Exhibit 2   Telephone Marketing Questionnaire—Continued

            If no:
                    Would you consider $20.00 a reasonable price for this round-trip
                    service?   Yes _____   No _____
IV   What is your age? Stop me when I reach your age bracket:

      18–25 _____ 26–35 _____ 36–45 _____ 46–55 _____ 56 and over _____.
      What is your occupation? _____
      Are you married?   Yes _____   No _____.
      How long have you lived in the Oxford area? _____

Thank you for your time and cooperation.

Exhibit 3   Mode of Travel

How do you normally travel to Memphis International Airport?

	Car	*Bus*	*Plane*	*Other*
Professors	75%	0%	10%	15%
Students	88	1	7	4
Professionals	82	0	5	13

Exhibit 4   Plane Travelers' Responses

Are you satisfied with the airline's dependability between Oxford and Memphis?

Professionals	55%	no	45%	yes
Students	100	no	0	yes
Professors	100	no	0	yes

Are the airline's flight times convenient for making your connecting flights?

Professionals	73%	no	27%	yes
Students	50	no	50	yes
Professors	100	no	0	yes

Do you feel that the airline's prices are reasonable between Oxford and Memphis?

Professionals	100%	no	0%	yes
Students	50	no	50	yes
Professors	72	no	28	yes

---

instrument and designed to be used either for personal or telephone interviewing.
The questions probed the level of satisfaction with present service, frequency of use,
time of departures and arrivals, usage of a limousine service, prices for fares and
other pertinent demographic characteristics.

The survey was conducted by telephone on three sample populations: (1) professors, (2) professionals, and (3) students. These groups were believed to make up
the bulk of travelers between Oxford and the Memphis airport. Sequential sampling
was used to reach the university population with the names having been drawn from
the university's directory. In a similar manner, the professionals were identified from
the local telephone directory and every third number was called. This sampling procedure resulted in 150 useable responses with the highest proportion coming from

---

Exhibit 5   Frequency of Travel

How many times per year do you fly out of Memphis?

Professors   6–8
Students   2–3
Professionals   3–4

What percentage of your trips are business–related?

Professors   90%
Students   7
Professionals   78

Do you normally travel alone?

Yes   63%
No   37%

How many people normally travel with you?

	Average
Professors	2.3
Students	4.7
Professionals	1.2

Exhibit 6   Time of Flight Departures

What times of the day do your flights normally depart from Memphis?

	12 a.m.–9 a.m.	9 a.m.–12 p.m.	12 p.m.–2 p.m.	2 p.m.–5 p.m.	5 p.m.–12 a.m.
Students	29%	25%	8%	29%	8%
Professionals	18	36	0	9	0
Professors	11	30	11	18	5
Total	58%	91%	19%	56%	13%

What times of the day do your flights normally arrive in Memphis?

	12 a.m.–9 a.m.	9 a.m.–12 p.m.	12 p.m.–2 p.m.	2 p.m.–5 p.m.	5 p.m.–12 a.m.
Students	0%	17%	8%	58%	16%
Professionals	0	18	9	18	18
Professors	0	2	7	43	21
Total	0%	37%	24%	119%	55%

---

professors (76), next from students (41) and least from professionals (33). Their responses to each question are presented in Exhibits 3–9.

Upon completing this portion of the presentation, Ranford sat back and opened the floor for discussion. Knowing that there would be a number of questions, he was prepared to answer those dealing with the research and analysis. However, he was somewhat unprepared for the response he received from Newman and Gary.

"That's a nice report," began Newman, "but my previous experience with Braniff does not give me a lot of faith in marketing research. Our research staff was wrong as many times as they were right. How much confidence do we put in these figures since our money is riding on the outcome?"

"Jim's got a point, Bill," chimed in Gary. What does this mean in terms of starting our business? Should we or shouldn't we make the 'go' decision?"

Exhibit 7   Airline Departures and Arrivals in Memphis

*Frequency of flight departures from Memphis per week**

	12 a.m.– 9 a.m.	9 a.m.– 12 p.m.	12 p.m.– 2 p.m.	2 p.m.– 5 p.m.	5 p.m.– 12 a.m.
Delta	82	73	39	62	93
Braniff	23	25	8	16	31
Allegheny	13	41	0	32	17
Piedmont	21	6	0	5	4
Republic	27	29	21	51	82

*Frequency of flight arrivals into Memphis per week**

	12 a.m.– 9 a.m.	9 a.m.– 12 p.m.	12 p.m.– 2 p.m.	2 p.m.– 5 p.m.	5 p.m.– 12 a.m.
Delta	68	41	48	60	126
Braniff	3	35	18	31	40
Allegheny	0	39	0	36	20
Piedmont	0	8	0	5	10
Republic	48	31	27	42	98

*This information has been taken from published airline schedules.

Exhibit 8   Days of Departure & Arrival

What is your usual day of departure from Memphis?

	Mon.– Wed.	Thurs.– Fri.	Sat.– Sun.	Varies
Students	8%	75%	21%	21%
Professionals	27	0	0	64
Professors	9	27	5	59
Total	44%	102%	26%	144%

What is your usual day of arrival in Memphis?

	Mon.– Wed.	Thurs.– Fri.	Sat.– Sun.	Varies
Students	13%	8%	58%	21%
Professionals	2	9	9	64
Professors	0	9	32	59
Total	15%	26%	99%	144%

Exhibit 9   Use and Cost of Proposed Service

Would you consider using a limousine service between Oxford and Memphis?

Yes   76%
No   24%

Would you pay $30, $25, $20 or under for round-trip service?

	$30	$25	$20	Under
Professors	43%	34%	19%	4%
Students	66	7	7	20
Professionals	66	0	11	23

Questions

1. How would you answer Newman?
2. What decision should be made on the limousine service based on the survey data presented in this report?
3. What other information should have been collected which would have made the decision easier?
4. How would you improve on the present study?

HAMILTON POWER TOOLS (B): INTERPRETING RESULTS FROM SURVEYS

Background

Prior to 1949, Hamilton Power Tools had been engaged in the manufacture and sale of industrial power tools to the construction industry. In 1949, John Hamilton, Sr., had acquired a small chain saw producer to broaden the product line offered to Hamilton Tool's existing customers. Some of the industrial buyers had found the Hamilton chain saw to be well designed and had begun using it around their own homes. From this simple beginning, Hamilton chain saws had been "pushed" into the consumer market without the company having prior knowledge of its customers.

Over the years, chain saws grew to be a sizable portion of Hamilton's business. In 1976, when the chain saw's marketing manager of twelve years retired and moved to Florida, Bill Campagna was promoted to executive status. When he took the job, he vowed he would change the Hamilton chain saw division from its sales orientation to a consumer orientation.

Shortly after his promotion, the new marketing executive included a short questionnaire on the warranty cards that purchasers returned after buying a Hamilton chain saw. On the basis of the warranty card "survey," the fastest growth in the chain saw market was in the homeowner or casual-user market segment. This market consisted of the "weekend woodcutter," who once or twice a year used a chain saw to cut firewood or to prune trees in the back yard.

In 1978, at Bill Campagna's urging, Consumer Metrics had been brought in to conduct Hamilton's first effort in consumer research. Their initial study was a consumer survey on chain saw users, followed by a Thematic Apperception Test (TAT) study of buyer motives.

A meeting was arranged with Consumer Metrics when the survey results had been tabulated. Dale Conway, vice-president of the research corporation, and Frank

Copyright © 1978 by Dr. William G. Zikmund

Baggins, a young research assistant, were to make the presentation for Consumer Metrics.

Mr. Conway began, "As you gentlemen know, the nonprofessional user has been a growing factor in the chain saw market. This user is a weekend woodcutter or a casual user, who once or a few times a year uses a chain saw to cut firewood or prune trees in the back yard. Beginning in March of this year, we conducted two research projects. The first was a survey of chain saw consumers, and the second was a Thematic Apperception Test (TAT). Today, Frank will give the results of the survey."

Frank stood up, thanked Mr. Conway, and began his presentation.

The West Coast is one of the faster growing markets for Hamilton chain saws. The number of retail outlets and servicing distributors in this area is in line with Hamilton marketing strategies. From a distribution standpoint, it is an excellent market. Therefore, we felt it would be best to sample people in California who purchased Hamilton chain saws between 1977 and 1978. Warranty cards that listed the purchasers during those years were used as a sampling frame. Cards that gave only institutional names and no individuals' names were omitted, as the purpose of the study was to learn about the behavior of the ultimate chain saw consumer rather than about the use of chain saws in private or public institutions. Of the 463 questionnaires mailed, 201 (43.4 percent) were returned and eighteen (3.9 percent) were not delivered.

The slides that Mr. Baggins showed are reproduced in Exhibit 1—15.

Consumer Profile

In Exhibit 1, the breakdown of age of Hamilton chain saw purchasers, we find that almost all purchasers of Hamilton chain saws are twenty-five years or older. The median age of a Hamilton chain saw owner is fifty.

More than two-thirds of the respondents had combined family incomes above $18,000 per year, and fifty-seven percent were above $20,000 per year. Exhibit 2 shows the actual family income dispersion of the California chain saw owner.

Almost seventy percent of the respondents had graduated from high school, and forty-one percent had attended college. Exhibit 3 shows the educational dispersion of chain saw customers.

Of all the people owning Hamilton chain saws in the California market, only 5.5 percent use a chain saw professionally. Twenty percent use chain saws on their farms. More than seventy percent of the respondents to the survey can be classified as casual users, as seen in Exhibit 4.[1]

Significant categories among the casual-user segment of the California market were:

1.   Workers, handicrafts workers, and skilled workers (16.5 percent)
2.   Professional and technical workers (12.0 percent)
3.   Operative workers and laborers (9.5 percent).

Almost as significant were:

4.   Managerial, official, and proprietary (including rental) personnel (12 percent)
5.   Government workers (9 percent)
6.   Retired persons (10 percent).

---

[1]Institutions, such as universities, municipalities, etc., were not sampled. However, this segment is estimated at less than five percent of the market.

Exhibit 1   Age of Hamilton Chain Saw Owners

Age Group	Total		1978		1977	
	No.	%	No.	%	No.	%
Under 25	4	2.0	1	1.0	3	3.1
25–34	26	13.0	16	15.4	10	10.4
35–44	48	24.0	24	23.0	24	25.0
45–54	65	32.5	37	35.6	28	29.2
55–64	38	19.0	18	17.3	20	20.8
65 and over	18	9.0	7	6.7	11	11.4
No answer	1	0.5	1	1.0	—	—
Base	200	100.0	104	100.0	96	100.0

Exhibit 2   Income of Hamilton Chain Saw Owners

Income	Total		1978		1977	
	No.	%	No.	%	No.	%
Under 15M	7	3.5	3	2.9	4	4.2
15M–17,999	35	17.5	17	16.4	18	18.8
18M–19,999	34	17.0	21	20.2	13	13.5
20M–24,999	64	32.0	33	31.7	31	32.3
25M and over	54	27.0	28	26.9	26	27.0
No answer	6	3.0	2	1.9	4	4.2
Base	200	100.0	104	100.0	96	100.0

Exhibit 3   Education of Hamilton Chain Saw Owners

Education	Total		1978		1977	
	No.	%	No.	%	No.	%
Attended grade school	8	4.0	4	3.8	4	4.2
Graduated grade school	26	13.0	12	11.5	14	14.6
Attended high school	28	14.0	14	13.5	14	14.6
Graduated high school	51	25.5	27	26.0	24	25.0
Attended college	44	22.0	21	20.2	23	24.0
Graduated college	42	21.0	25	24.0	17	17.6
No answer	1	0.5	1	1.0	—	—
Base	200	100.0	104	100.0	96	100.0

Exhibit 4   Occupations of Hamilton Chain Saw Owners

Occupation	Total		1978		1977	
	No.	%	No.	%	No.	%
Professional, technical	24	12.0	11	10.6	13	13.5
Managerial, official, proprietary	24	12.0	17	16.3	7	7.3
Clerical/sales	8	4.0	6	5.7	2	2.1
Worker, handicrafts, skilled	33	16.5	19	18.3	14	14.6
Operative and labor	19	9.5	14	13.5	5	5.2
Government	18	9.0	9	8.7	9	9.4
Farmer or rancher	40	20.0	16	15.4	24	25.0
Retired	20	10.0	7	6.7	13	13.5
Student	2	1.0	—	—	2	2.1
Tree surgeon/professional cutter	11	5.5	4	3.8	7	7.3
No answer	1	0.5	1	1.0	—	—
Base	200	100.0	104	100.0	96	100.0

Exhibit 5   Opinion of Owners of Quality of Hamilton Chain Saws

Quality	No.	%
Excellent	81	40.5
Good	90	45.0
Fair	15	7.5
Poor	7	3.5
No answer	7	3.5
Base	200	100.0

Exhibit 6   Retail Outlets Where Hamilton Chain Saws Are Purchased

Outlet	No.	%
Chain saw specialty	70	35.0
Equipment/tools	41	20.5
Hardware	19	9.5
Department	16	8.0
Farm	14	7.0
Sports	10	5.0
Catalog	8	4.0
Marine	2	1.0
Other	15	7.5
No answer	5	2.5
Base	200	100.0

Exhibit 7   Number of Times Visited Chain Saw Dealer

Times Visited	No.	%
0	7	3.5
1	53	26.5
2	40	20.0
3	39	19.5
4	16	8.0
5	7	3.5
6 or more	25	12.5
No answer	13	6.5
Base	200	100.0

As Exhibit 5 shows, the quality of Hamilton chain saws is considered to be good or excellent by more than eighty-five percent of the respondents. Slightly more than one-third of the respondents have had their chain saws repaired, and seventy-five percent of these people were satisfied with the repair work.

Retail Activity

Exhibit 6 shows Hamilton receives thirty-five percent of its retail sales from chain saw specialty stores, 20.5 percent from equipment or tool stores, and 9.5 percent from hardware stores. Only seven percent of the respondents mentioned purchasing their chain saws from farm stores and only five percent from sports stores.

Exhibit 8   Number of Different Chain Saw Dealers Visited

Number of Dealers	No.	%
0	9	4.5
1	50	25.0
2	51	25.5
3	47	23.5
4 or more	28	14.0
No answer	15	7.5
Base	200	100.0

Exhibit 9   Time Respondents Had Been Thinking About Chain Saw Purchase

Length of Time	No.	%
Less than 1 week	7	3.5
1 week to 1 month	25	12.5
Over 1 to 3 months	24	12.0
Over 3 to 6 months	37	18.5
Over 6 months to 1 year	35	17.5
Over 1 year	33	16.5
Owned chain saw previously	20	10.0
Don't know/no answer	14	7.0
Part of inventory	2	1.0
Not long	3	1.5
Base	200	100.0

Exhibit 10   Respondents' Ratings of Familiarity with Chain Saws

Response	No.	%
Completely familiar	64	32.0
Somewhat familiar	88	44.0
Unfamiliar	39	19.5
No answer/don't know	9	4.5
Base	200	100.0

*Exhibit 11   Respondents Had Specific Brand in Mind
on First Visit to Chain Saw Dealer*

Response	No.	%
Yes	129	64.5
No	67	33.5
No answer	4	2.0
Base	200	100.0

Exhibits 7 and 8 show the number of times Hamilton chain saw purchasers visited a chain saw dealer and the number of different chain saw dealers they visited before purchasing their first chain saw. More than sixty percent of the respondents visited two or more *different* chain saw dealers before purchasing a Hamilton chain saw. Two, three, four, or more trips to chain saw dealers were the general rule for potential buyers.

Exhibit 12   Brand of Chain Saw Planned to Purchase

Brand	No.	%
Homelite	59	45.7
Hamilton	41	31.8
McCulloch	41	31.8
Stihl	2	1.5
Pioneer	1	0.8
Other	5	3.9
Base	129	*

*Multiple answers possible; base exceeds 100 percent.

Exhibit 13   Dealer Influence

Amount of Influence	No.	%
Great	54	27.0
Quite a bit	36	18.0
Some	32	16.0
Hardly any	13	6.5
None	53	26.5
No answer	12	6.0
Base	200	100.0

Exhibit 14   Activities on First Visit to Chain Saw Dealer

Activity That Took Place	No.	%
Talked to salesperson or owner about chain saws	123	61.5
Looked at chain saws	116	58.0
Learned the price of the chain saws	114	57.0
Picked up information about chain saws	71	35.5
Learned proper model of saw for own needs	57	28.5
Watched chain saw demonstrated	43	21.5
Rented or borrowed a chain saw	11	5.5
No answer	13	6.5
Base	200	*

*Multiple mentions; base exceeds 100 percent.

Buying Behavior

More than one-half of all respondents thought for three months or more about purchasing a chain saw (see Exhibit 9).

Exhibit 10 shows that only thirty-two percent of the respondents rating their familiarity with chain saws said they were completely familiar with them when they first visited a dealer. "Somewhat familiar" (forty-four percent) was the most common response, and 19.5 percent stated they were unfamiliar with chain saws when they first visited a dealer. Therefore, it can be concluded that at least 63.5 percent of potential chain saw purchasers could use more knowledge about (familiarity with) chain saws.

Almost two-thirds of the respondents had a specific brand or brands of chain

Exhibit 15   How Purchaser Learned Store Carried Chain Saws

Response	No.	%
Previous visit	101	50.5
Friend/relative recommended	18	9.0
Magazine/newspaper advertising	14	7.0
Yellow pages	12	6.0
Radio/TV	6	3.0
Outside store identification/driving by	6	3.0
Other	24	12.0
No answer	19	9.5
Base	200	100.0

saw in mind when they first visited a dealer. Only twenty percent of all respondents had planned to buy Hamilton (Exhibits 11 and 12).

An important finding from this question is that all these people purchased Hamilton chain saws even though more than fifty percent had another brand name in mind before they first visited a chain saw dealer. Although we have no measurement of name brand preference, we can conclude that it is possible to sway some people who have preconceived purchasing plans. The other side of the coin is that thirty percent of the people planned to purchase a Hamilton and actually did. However, perhaps even more significant, we do not know how many people who had planned to purchase other leading brands actually did purchase one of these competitive saws.

The amount of influence a chain saw dealer's recommendation had on the purchasing decision of the consumer is given in Exhibit 13.

We can see that in forty-five percent of the cases the dealer had considerable influence on the purchasing decision. In at least sixteen percent more cases, the dealer exerted some influence. Thus, the dealer can be an important part of the marketing of chain saws. But we see that there are other influencing factors involved, as 26.5 percent of the respondents mentioned that the dealer had no influence on their decision, sixteen percent said only some influence, and 6.5 percent said the dealer hardly influenced their decision.

What happened when the respondents first visited a chain saw dealer? Exhibit 14 shows the activities respondents stated happened. When analyzing the information, it appears significant to look at what did *not* happen at the dealer level. More than one-third of all respondents did not *talk* to a dealer the *first* time they visited. Only 21.5 percent saw the chain saw demonstrated and only 28.5 percent learned the proper model of chain saw for their needs. In most cases, it looks as if the first visit was a *passive* buying visit to a chain saw dealer. The responses indicate that most potential customers talked to a salesperson rather than looked at chain saws. Thus, with some nonstocking dealers a customer would have to go to another store to see a chain saw.

Finally, Exhibit 15 shows how Hamilton purchasers first learned of the stores where they purchased their chain saws.

Questions

1.   Why would a company such as Hamilton wait so long before conducting consumer research?

2.   Is this an exploratory, descriptive or causal study?
3.   Evaluate the sampling frame used by Consumer Metrics. What possible sources of error exist in this study?
4.   What further information would be needed before a complete plan could be submitted to Hamilton's management?

32

U.S. DEPARTMENT OF ENERGY: THE LOW COST/NO COST ENERGY CONSERVATION PROGRAM IN NEW ENGLAND

The Low Cost/No Cost Energy Conservation Program was developed by the U.S. Department of Energy (DOE) to inform New England homeowners of eleven inexpensive actions they could take to save up to twenty-five percent on their home energy bills.

During the month of November 1979, DOE conducted the Low Cost/No Cost Program in Massachusetts, Vermont, Connecticut, Rhode Island, Maine and New Hampshire. The purpose of the program was to motivate consumers to take the recommended low cost/no actions, which would save energy and help control increasing energy costs. The $2.6 million program consisted of a strong multimedia marketing effort with the following components:

1. An integrated, $1 million paid advertising campaign which included television, radio and print. Approximately ninety percent of the New England population were reached during the Low Cost/No Cost campaign.
2. Direct distribution to 4.5 million New England households, through the U.S. Postal Service, of the Low Cost/No Cost Energy Savers booklet and a water flow controller for use in the shower.
3. Strong public awareness activities, including press conferences with governors in five of the six states, television and radio public affairs talk shows, and newspaper articles and editorials.

The program was initially developed by DOE during the Spring of 1979 in response to the projected shortage of heating oil stock in New England and the likelihood of higher heating oil prices. The six New England states were chosen to test the program because of the region's heavy dependence on heating oil and severe winter weather. If a typical New England household followed the eleven low cost/no cost actions referred to in the booklet, DOE estimated they could save up to twenty-five

Copyright © 1981 by Dr. William G. Zikmund

percent of their home energy bill. Yet, all of the LC/NC actions could be completed for less than a total of $100; some actions could be completed without any cost.

The Almost One Million Dollar DOE Advertising Program

The LC/NC Program was advertised through a coordinated television, radio and newspaper campaign which totaled $909,000 over a 3½ week period. The media plan was designed to attain the greatest reach and frequency levels possible including:

- 300 Gross Rating Points (GRP's) for television with emphasis on wide coverage from stations broadcasting from major cities. TV ads were heavier during the first ten days.
- 300 GRP's for radio in all the major A markets (large cities).
- 200 GRP's for radio in thirteen markets; smaller cities over 35,000.
- 2,000 line ads twice a week in larger cities (papers with over 50,000 circulation); once a week in smaller papers with circulations between 25,000–50,000.

Heavy emphasis was placed on TV and print including:

- Newspaper expenditures of $374,000, constituting forty-one percent of the advertising budget.
- Radio expenditures of $161,000, equaling eighteen percent of the total advertising budget.
- Television expenditures of $374,000 or 41 percent of the budget.

The public awareness efforts began on November 8th with heavy concentration during the early days of the media effort. This initial effort involved press conferences with five of the six New England governors to kick off the program and to gain positive follow-up in the various markets by news coverage. In addition, the public awareness efforts included securing media time for public service announcements, appearances on TV and radio talk shows, and news stories and editorials in print media.

In November 1979, DOE initiated an evaluation of the Low Cost/No Cost Program. The purpose of the evaluation was to determine the effectiveness of the program in motivating New England households to adopt the LC/NC conservation actions. One aspect of the evaluation consisted of day-after recall tests of a sample of 305 households in order to determine the memorability of television advertising. Recall studies measure how well the public remembers program advertising, and what advertising messages are remembered.

A syndicated service—Burke Market Research—was used to measure recall of the LC/NC television advertising. The methodology used by Burke allowed for "real world" exposure to the ad, recall tests to see what messages were actually remembered, and comparison to norms to evaluate the recall results. The tests were conducted for the two versions of the LC/NC television advertisement the day after the first airing of these commercials on November 8th. A random sample of potential viewers was developed from viewers in the greater Boston-metropolitan area. The sample was selected by screening for the potential audience of the commerical, by determining if the members of the sample had their televisions on and tuned to the appropriate channel, and were themselves in the room and awake when the LC/NC commercial was aired. The samples for each ad contained approximately an equal percentage of males and females who responded to a standardized set of questions. The questions were designed to examine what the individual remembered about the commercial and to probe the extent to which specific advertising messages were remembered. The answers were recorded verbatim and then compared to the actual content of the commercial and coded as either correct or incorrect recall.

The levels of recall were evaluated two ways:

1. The relative importance of the messages that were remembered—the level of memorability—was compared to the goals or intended messages of the commercials.

2. The levels of recall for the overall advertising and for the individual messages are compared to the level of recall that is commonly achieved for thirty-second commercials. Specifically, the level of recall of the first, second and third messages contained in the LC/NC advertising were compared to levels of recall commonly obtained for thirty-second commercials.

Thus, the results of this study can help determine the potential effectiveness of the commercial in communicating the LC/NC message.

The day-after recall test results suggest that the LC/NC television advertising copy was comparable—in quality and viewer impact—to commercial advertising. Two copy tests were run on the LC/NC advertising. Both these tests were conducted on November 9th and were tested the first prime time airing for the shower flow device and the mailman commercials. A sample was drawn for each commercial separately, since these commercials were shown at slightly different times (within the same hour) on different channels. The sample sizes were: shower flow device sample size was 76 men and 76 women, or 152, and the mailman sample size was 78 men and 75 women, or 153. Results from each of these commercials will be presented separately.

*The Shower Flow Commerical Recall**

The Shower Flow Commercial achieved a recall equivalent to the Burke norms of commercial advertising. Briefly, this commercial had the storyline of a young man helping his mother save energy (and money) by installing the shower flow device which was received in the mail with the LC/NC booklet.

Correct recall of this ad was given by twenty-one percent of the sample. This was composed of twenty-two percent of the males (Burke norm = twenty-one percent) and twenty percent of the females (Burke norm = twenty-four percent). These levels of achieved recall are not significantly different than the norms.

With regard to the advertising messages in the shower flow commercial, males exhibited the following recall:

- "Variety of ways to save energy"—sixteen percent (norm = twelve percent)
- "Offers energy saving booklet/directions/actions"—14 percent (norm = eight percent)
- "Can save twenty-five percent on the fuel bill"—seven percent (norm = five percent).

For the females the same advertising messages were recalled, but in a slightly different order:

- "Offers energy saving booklet/directions/actions"—seventeen percent (norm = fifteen percent)
- "Variety of ways to save energy"—thirteen percent (norm = eleven percent)
- "Can save 25 percent on the fuel bill"—5 percent (norm = 8 percent).

*(Exhibit 1 provides a more detailed description of the results of the day-after recall study.)

Exhibit 1   Research Summary

Purpose

The purpose of these tests is to measure the communications effectiveness, under normal viewing conditions, of the thirty-second U.S. Department of Energy "Shower Device" and "Mailman" commercials.

Program Carriers

"Shower Device"   "Mailman"

   "Quincy"   Spot Between "Benson" and
                                                   "Barney Miller"

Location

Boston, Massachussetts

Date of Telecast

November 8, 1979

Date of Interviewing

November 9, 1979

Method

Day-after recall, conducted by telephone, among male and female heads of household who were program viewers. No more than fifty percent of the respondents were fifty years of age or older.

Samples

Shower Device

   187 program viewers, 152 (81 percent) in the commercial audience
    95 male program viewers, 76 (80 percent) in the commercial audience
    92 female program viewers, 76 (83 percent) in the commercial audience

Mailman

   234 program viewers, 153 (65 percent) in the commercial audience.
   120 male program viewers, 78 (65 percent) in the commercial audience.
   114 female program viewers, 75 (65 percent) in the commercial audience.

Interpretation of Data

Net percentages represent respondents who made one or more comments in a category.

Exhibit 1   Research Summary—Continued

Table 1

	Males Percent of Commercial Audience	
	"Shower Device" (76)	Burke Norms
Sales Messages (Net)	21	18
Variety of Ways to Save Energy (Net)	16	12[1]
Offers Energy Saving Booklet/Directions/Tips	14	8[2]
Can Save 25 Percent of Energy/On Fuel Bill (Net)	7	5[3]

Table 2

	Females Percent of Commercial Audience	
	"Shower Device" (76)	Burke Norms
Sales Messages (Net)	20	22
Offers Energy Saving Booklet/Directions/Tips	17	15[1]
Variety of Ways to Save Energy (Net)	13	11[2]
Can Save 25 Percent of Energy/On Fuel Bill (Net)	5	8[3]

Table 3

	Males Percent of Commercial Audience	
	"Mailman" (78)	Burke Norms
Sales Message (Net)	19	18
Offers Energy Saving Booklet/Directions/Tips	10	12[1]
Variety of Ways to Save Energy (Net)	8	8[2]
Can Save 25 Percent of Energy/On Fuel Bill (Net)	6	5[3]
Save Money—General (Net)	6	

Table 4

	Females Percent of Commercial Audience	
	"Mailman" (75)	Burke Norms
Sales Messages (Net)	20	22
Offers Energy Saving Booklet/Directions/Tips	17	15[1]
Variety of Ways to Save Energy (Net)	13	11[2]
Can Save 25 Percent of Energy/On Fuel Bill (Net)	7	8[3]

[1] Norm for category recalled most often.
[2] Norm for category recalled second most often.
[3] Norm for category recalled third most often.

Exhibit 1   Research Summary—Continued

Table 5

	Percent of Commercial Audience			
	Males		Females	
	"Shower Device" (76)	"Mail- man" (78)	"Shower Device" (76)	"Mail- man" (75)
Gave Related Recall	22	19	20	21
Sales Messages (Net)	21	19	20	20
Variety of Ways to Save Energy (Net)	16	8	13	13
Offers Energy Saving Booklet/Directions/Tips	14	10	17	17
Can Save 25 Percent of Energy/On Fuel Bill	7	6	5	7
Save Money—General (Net)	3	6	1	4

The recall of specific advertising messages is slightly higher for males than females as is the overall recall, but statistically these levels are not different from the Burke norm for message recall. In terms of both the level and the order of recall, the twenty-five percent savings claim appears a poor third for both males and females.

In addition, the respondents were asked to describe the scenes and actions for this commercial. Both males and females cited visual details at the level statistically equivalent to the Burke norms.

The Mailman Commercial Recall

Recall of the mailman commercial achieved Burke norms, but did not achieve the same level of recall reached by the shower flow commercial. This commercial presented a mailman making deliveries of the LC/NC Booklet. In addition, the mailman shows how to insulate ductwork and describes the potential energy savings from insulating exposed ductwork.

Correct recall was given by nineteen percent of the males (norm is twenty-one percent) and twenty-one percent of the females (norm is twenty-four percent) for a total sample recall of twenty percent. This level of recall is not statistically different from the norms.

The recall level of advertising messages for males was:

■ "Offers energy saving booklet/directions/actions"—ten percent (norm is twelve percent)
■ "Variety of ways to save energy"—eight percent (norm is eight percent)
■ "Can save twenty-five percent on the fuel bill"—seven percent (norm is five percent)

For females the pattern and level of message recall was:

■ "Offers energy saving booklet/directions/actions"—thirteen percent (norm is eleven percent)
■ "Variety of ways to save energy"—thirteen percent (norm is eleven percent)
■ "Can save twenty-five percent on the fuel bill"—seven percent (norm is eight percent)

These recall levels are not significantly different than the Burke norms. However, when asked to recall visual details of the mailman advertising, females were statistically equal to the norm, and males were significantly below the norm.

Questions

1. Interpret recall test results for the Low Cost/No Cost advertising program for overall memorability and copy point registration.
2. Is there a difference between men and women on recall?
3. Evaluate the day-after recall technique as a means of measuring advertising effectiveness.

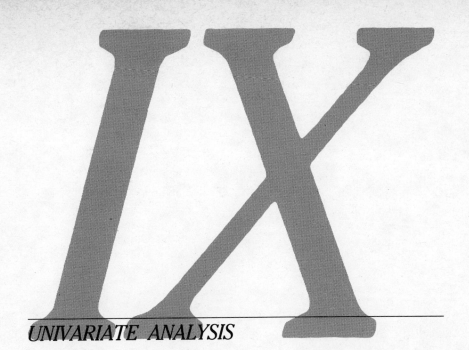

IX

UNIVARIATE ANALYSIS

AMERICAR (C): TEST OF GROUP DIFFERENCES

U.S. Auto, in an attempt to capitalize on a potentially strong automobile consumer market, embarked on a campaign to develop and introduce a new subcompact automobile, the Americar. As a result, U.S. Auto began preliminary investigations into the subcompact market. The Americar was to be a dominant force among U.S. subcompacts, as well as an automobile that could regain some of the automobile market that was being lost to foreign competition in recent years.

Preliminary Research

The information collected in the preliminary research of the market suggested that the subcompact market was indeed strong and appeared to offer excellent growth potential for U.S. Auto. In this initial investigation, it was felt that further information was necessary in order to delineate subcompact owners from owners of larger sized automobiles.

With this in mind, U.S. Auto's Corporate Planning Division suggested that it was necessary to develop a consumer profile for each of the four groups of automobile owners. These groups included: (1) full size, (2) intermediate, (3) compact, and (4) subcompact owners. The profile consisted of demographic characteristics, psychographic (lifestyle) characteristics and benefits sought by members in each general class. The profile, it was hoped, was to provide information that would bring the consumer to life. With this information, better marketing-mix strategies could be developed.

The primary research consisted of an Interests and Opinions Questionnaire. Included in the questionnaire were twenty-eight lifestyle questions, seven benefit questions, automobile ownership information, and demographic information. A copy of

Copyright © 1981, Dr. William J. Lundstrom and Mark G. Dunn

Exhibit 1   Comparison of Subcompact and All Other Automobile Owners

Section 1

Item	Sub-compact x̄	All Others x̄	F-Value	2-tail Prob.	Pooled Variance T-Value	Pooled Variance 2-tail Prob.	Separate Variance T-Value	Separate Variance 2-tail Prob.
1	2.0333	2.3548	1.02	.908	-2.08	.039	-2.07	.041
2	2.05	2.096	1.14	.53	-.32	.751	-.31	.757
3	1.9167	2.584	1.13	.614	-4.59	.000	-4.69	.000
4	2.55	2.75	1.25	.348	-1.24	.215	-1.29	.198
5	1.0333	3.096	1.49	.089	-1.04	.298	-1.12	.266
6	1.0333	2.424	1.12	.634	-3.15	.002	-3.21	.002
7	2.1833	1.952	1.41	.111	1.54	.124	1.45	.149
8	2.2167	2.624	1.26	.315	-2.45	.015	-2.55	.012
9	3.1833	3.24	1.12	.646	-.41	.684	-.14	.679
10	2.35	2.776	1.38	.168	-2.59	.01	-2.74	.007
11	3.1833	3.464	1.06	.809	-1.67	.097	-1.69	.094
12	3.0	3.312	1.05	.817	-1.85	.066	-1.84	.069
13	2.3333	2.656	1.31	.243	-1.89	.06	-1.99	.049
14	1.85	1.888	1.99	.001	-.32	.751	-.28	.778
15	2.25	2.4	1.4	.146	-1.09	.275	-1.16	.247
16	3.1	3.056	1.28	.257	.26	.794	.25	.803
17	2.6167	2.536	1.02	.894	.55	.583	.55	.585

18	2.2333	2.704	1.17	.50	-2.12	.002	-3.21	.002
19	2.6	2.52	1.43	.128	.56	.579	.59	.555
20	2.7667	2.736	1.08	.768	.18	.856	.18	.854
21	2.7167	2.536	1.22	.355	1.2	.233	1.15	.251
22	2.8644	3.16	1.46	.084	-1.79	.076	-1.67	.098
23	1.8833	2.712	1.85	.009	-5.87	.000	-6.53	.000
24	3.2833	3.176	1.16	.49	.63	.528	.62	.54
25	2.55	2.496	1.15	.554	.37	.714	.38	.707
26	3.0833	2.936	1.09	.726	.93	.353	.94	.347
27	2.5333	2.336	1.3	.228	1.32	.187	1.26	.209
28	2.8833	2.568	1.19	.456	2.01	.046	2.07	.04
Section 3								
1	1.25	1.7742	2.46	.000	-5.42	.000	-6.28	.000
2	1.35	1.384	1.17	.505	-.43	.67	-.44	.662
3	1.4333	15968	1.49	.091	-1.69	.092	-1.81	.072
4	2.6102	2.4959	1.09	.725	.94	.348	.95	.342
5	1.45	1.4435	1.02	.916	.07	.942	.07	.942
6	1.7167	1.6452	1.20	.443	.713	.466	.75	.453
7	1.7333	1.626	1.17	.513	1.18	.24	1.21	.228

Exhibit 2 Demographic Characteristics:
Psychographic Research and Results

Demographic	Subcompact	Compact	Intermediate	Full
Age				
18–24	50.8%	70.0%	45.2%	26.2%
25–34	25.4	16.7	11.9	9.5
35–44	15.3	3.3	11.9	14.3
45–54				33.3
Sex				
Male	67.2	53.3	45.2	45.2
Female	32.8	46.7	54.8	54.8
Marital Status				
Single	49.1	83.3	42.9	27.9
Married	45.6	16.7	50.0	60.5
Education				
High School	16.9	10.0	14.6	
Some Collete	37.3	63.3	41.5	46.5
College	22.0	23.3	22.0	25.6
Predominantly				
White	96.4	100.0	90.2	93.2
Children				
None	60.0	76.7	52.4	30.2
One	15.0	16.7	9.5	11.6
Two	15.0		28.6	30.2
Three	8.3			16.3
Occupation				
Professional	19.3	6.7	7.9	33.3
White Collar	15.8	20.0	13.2	26.2
Clerical	7.0	10.0	2.6	4.8
Retail	10.5	6.7	2.6	4.8
Blue Collar	15.8		15.8	
Student	29.8		50.0	21.4
Income				
Less than $4999	29.3	56.7	43.2	28.9
$5000–$9999	19.3	10.0	16.2	10.5
$10,000–$14,999	17.5	20.0	8.1	7.9
$15,000–$19,999	10.5	3.3	8.1	5.3
$20,000–$24,999	7.0	3.3	5.4	10.5
Greater than $25,000	15.8	6.7	18.9	36.8

the questionnaire appears in Case 28, Exhibit 4. The purpose of the research project was to provide useful information for developing the consumer profile. More specifically, the following objectives were stated in the research procedure:

1. To provide a means of analysis of overall automobile market along product specific items and benefits sought by each major group.
2. To provide information concerning the demographic make-up of each group.

The sample consisted of 186 respondents, chosen randomly, from a northern metropolitan area. The sample breakdown for each subgroup was a follows:

(1) Subcompact owners $n = 60$
(2) Compact owners $n = 30$
(3) Intermediate owners $n = 42$
(4) Full-size owners $n = 43$

The analysis consisted of T-test between subcompact owners and all other owners for all items in sections one and three of the questionnaire and the results are seen in Exhibit 1. In addition, means were reported for all items in sections one and three for the total group. The demographic section of the questionnaire was analyzed in terms of frequencies and percentages and is presented in Exhibit 2. This information was then turned over to a marketing analyst whose task was to develop a consumer profile for each subgroup and distinguish any differences that may appear.

Questions

1. Isolate those items that differentiate between subcompact owners and all other automobile owners.
2. Develop a profile of the subcompact owner using the interest and opinion responses, automobile attribute importance and demographic characteristics.

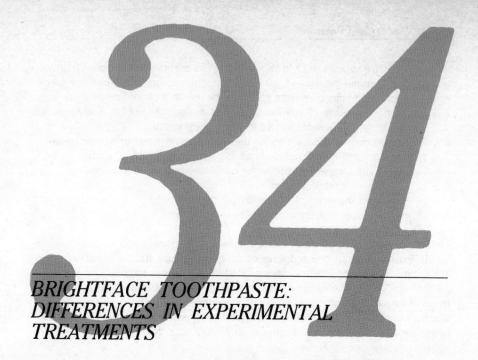

BRIGHTFACE TOOTHPASTE: DIFFERENCES IN EXPERIMENTAL TREATMENTS

The manufacturers of Brightface toothpaste enjoyed a dominant position in the market for many years. While they had active competition, Brightface maintained a forty percent share of market. The closest competing brand had only half that level. When an occasional new competitor entered, Brightface increased their promotional activity and maintained the prominence of the brand. Competing brands primarily fought for market position among themselves. Any temporary market share decline for Brightface never exceeded three percent for the first few months of new product trial. The relatively loyal Brightface users came back after trying one or two tubes of the new products.

In the first and second quarter of 1960, however, they watched their market share decline a total of eight points. Competitors—as their market share information showed—were also losing position both in dollar and unit volume. The cause for changes was a new brand, Pinnacle, which had a tooth decay fighting ingredient which was endorsed by the American Dental Association. Brightface management, research and development personnel, as well as top management, knew the efficacy of the new ingredient; had reviewed all of the ADA's clinical studies; and had decided to develop a similar ingredient which would have similar properties.

One year after the introduction of Pinnacle, Brightface was almost ready to introduce Brightface II, a formulation which also had properties of dental cavity prevention if used consistently in a strict hygiene regimen. For the following six months, various flavor strengths and formulations were tested for flavor characteristics and preferences. Promotional materials and advertising themes were developed. During this period, Pinnacle had gained one of the major positions in the dentifrice market,

Prepared by F.P. Tobolski. From *Cases in Marketing Research* by Randall L. Schultz, Gerald Zaltman, and Philip C. Burger. Copyright © 1975 by The Dryden Press, a division of Holt, Rinehart and Winston, Publishers. Reprinted by permission of Holt, Rinehart and Winston.

commanding 25 percent of the total market, fifteen points obtained from the Brightface share. Brightface had dropped to twenty-five percent!

The Brightface product management, however, was optimistic. While they knew that they might not regain their prior dominance, Brightface II had good product acceptance in blind tests due to its superior flavor. They continued their planning to reposition the brand to cover both their prior whiteness-oriented market and the new clinically-oriented anticavity market.

A major strategy of the reposition plan related to the Brightface packaging. The current Brightface package was easily identified, having been changed only slightly in the last five years. It was well accepted by their current and former users; could be located on the shelf with ease; and projected the fun and brightfaced gaiety of their former positioning in its "fun" design. Not knowing whether copy additions announcing their new ingredient would be sufficient to change the product/package imagery of the brand, they commissioned a prominent package design firm to create new packaging graphics. Given the new marketing platform, the design firm developed three graphic approaches. One of these was a minor modification of the current design with the copy additions. The second was a major change toward a more therapeutic clinical design. The third was also a major change which, however, used many of the current design elements, especially color, organized in a more creative format. These three designs which were to be tested for recognition and imagery positioning by consumer/users were named "Copy," "White," and "Bi-Segment" by the eager Brightface product management. The research department of the design firm was commissioned to evaluate the three designs.

Package Graphics Evaluation Methods and Procedures

Since a variety of product tests had already been accomplished, the Brightface research director in conjunction with the research department developed a procedure which would focus only on the package designs' communications of the product. The following test design was agreed upon.

Each graphic approach was to be tested in a laboratory situation, simulating an in-store condition of shelved toothpaste. The newly printed packages used to construct the displays were prepared in the same manner as the other stimuli. Nine separate sub-samples of consumers were to be employed. Since there was, and still is, a high incidence of toothpaste usage, it was not difficult to obtain respondents. These were blind screened with a selection questionnaire which covered the product and brand usage on a wide range of products. Users of the different brands were randomly assigned to the separate samples using the quota system below. Since the various locations of the shopping centers in which the research was conducted were known to have shoppers from a wide area, the samples were assumed to be representative of this single most important Brightface market. The locations also allowed management and advertising agency personnel visitations to the test sites.

"Current" Sample a. $N = 500$
"Current" Design and
New Concept Statement
"Current" Sample b. $N = 500$
   "Current" Design
   versus three competitors

"Copy" Sample a. $N = 500$
"Copy" Design and
New Concept Statement
"Copy" Sample b. $N = 500$
   "Copy" Design
   versus three competitors

"White" Sample a. N = 500	"Bi-Segment" Sample a. N = 500
"White" Design and	"Bi-Segment" Design and
Concept Statement	Copy Statement
"White" Design Sample b. N = 500	"Bi-Segment" Sample b. N = 500
"White" Design	"Bi-Segment" Design
versus three competitors	versus three competitors

"Load-Up" Sample N = 300
Current and Three New Brightface
Designs with Concept Statement

The samples—except for the load-up sample which was comprised of all Brightface users—were quota grouped to include 200 Brightface users, and 100 users of each of the three competitive brands. Stimuli were to be the displays built from the various Brightface designs and packaging of the competing brands in the study. The concept statement, developed by the advertising agency, was a print ad which was to be used in the introductory campaign for Brightface II and was used only in the a. sections of the samples.

All of the interviewing was accomplished within a one-week period. Since the interviews were conducted every day of that week, and since the respondents were randomly assigned, a review of the samples disclosed no significant differences in the predetermined matching demographics of age, sex, occupational level, educational level, and toothpaste usage frequency and amount, etc.

A tachistoscopic[1] test was performed with the respondents in all of the b. sub-samples. Presenting designs at limited viewing durations, it was possible to determine the percentages of consumer/respondents recognizing the brand and product for each of the Brightface designs and the competitors' designs. In the multi-speed tachistoscopic test and in the imagery evaluation which was to follow, a strict stimulus presentation procedure (size, order of presentation, etc.) was used.

A series of semantic differential[2] items were used by all respondents in all of the sub-samples to rate either the packages/displays or the Concept Statement. The Concept Statement sub-samples–that is, all of the a. sections–used the series of bipolar scales to rate the statement and the graphic design/display. With the resultant data, it was possible to determine the imagery match or mismatch of the design with the new positioning covered in the statement. The same type of comparisons were made in the b. sections. The stimuli compared in these samples were the various competitive brands. In the "Load-Up" sample, both the statement and various Brightface II design ratings were compared.

Findings and Analysis: Recognition Levels

The tachistoscopic test results were carefully analyzed. Product management did not wish to lose any recognition equity which the prior Brightface package had established. Two of the proposed designs disclosed levels of brand and product recogni-

---

[1] A tachistoscopic test is one where visual stimuli are presented at various speeds. It is a standard psychometric procedure.

[2] For discussion of the use of semantic differentials in attitude research, see C. E. Osgood, G. J. Suci, and P. H. Tannenbaum, *The Measurement of Meaning* (Chicago: University of Illinois Press, 1957), p. 5; and J. G. Snider and C. E. Osgood, *Semantic Differential Technique* (Chicago: Aldine Publishing Co., 1969), p. 50.

tion equal to the current Brightface package graphics. When these cross-sample comparisons were made, no significant differences in share of brand recognition were found. Product recognition was also at the prior high levels for these two designs when compared to the current graphics and competitive designs.

The "White" Design, however, had significantly lower recognition. It was recognized as Brightface by only ten percent of the total sample in White Design Sample b. Due to the confusion generated by the new design, product recognition suffered and no one reported any of the new ingredient copy. A subsequent analysis of the imagery data (see below) also indicated the nonacceptability of this design.

Attitude and Imagery Results: Concept Statement Comparisons

The Current Brightface design, utilized as a reference design, did not compare favorably with the Concept Statement. This was expected since the Concept Statement was defining a new product with cavity prevention features.

The Copy Design, with its additional copy defining the new Brightface II, however, compared favorably with the Concept Statement, indicating effective communications and image projection for this design.

The findings comparing the Bi-Segment Design scale results with the Concept Statement data also were positive. In this comparative analysis, the best match with the Concept Statement ratings was found.

The White Design was found to have some ratings in the correct direction—high in perceived dentist recommendation and effectiveness—but it was more negative than the Concept Statement on unpleasant taste, weak, a product for older people, unattractive, etc. Because of this concept mismatch, its poor comparison with competitive packaging and its low recognition, the White Design was not considered as a good package design for Brightness II.

Competitive Package Graphics Comparisons

All of the various combinations of Brightface II and the competitive package design ratings were made. These various tables, together with the cross-sample comparisons, comprised a major portion of the analysis. These, overall, showed strong image profiles and good comparisons of the Copy and Bi-Segment Designs with the competitors, Pinnacle included.

For these reasons, product management and research personnel focused on the comparisons of the ratings by Brightface users of the Copy Design and those of the Bi-Segment Design. In addition, their comparisons with the Current Design benchmark were reviewed.[3]

Following are the three semantic differential image comparison exhibits which show the mean ratings, the mean differences, and those criteria scales (underscored) where the differences between the means were significant. The seven point scales had a maximum of 7 and a minimum of 1 with a midpoint of 4. This midpoint is a pivotal position, indicating neutrality; ratings in either direction above or below the

---

[3]For purposes of this case, the data analysis has been simplified. Overall, more than ninety tables of rating scale data comparisons were studied, including those of the total samples, Brightface user sub-samples and other brand user ratings.

Exhibit 1   The Differential Image of the Current and Copy Designs

Current Graphics	Mean*	Difference	Mean	Copy Design
Not recommended by dentists	3.70	2.51S	6.21	Recommended by dentists
Not expensive	4.01	2.10S	6.11	Expensive
Not effective	4.73	1.97S	6.70	Effective
Cosmetic	6.91	1.90S	5.01	Not cosmetic
Feminine	5.87	1.67S	4.20	Masculine
Does not help prevent cavities	4.20	1.63S	5.83	Helps prevent cavities
Lower quality	5.97	.63S	6.60	Higher quality
Weak	5.30	.61S	5.91	Strong
A youthful product	5.70	.60S	5.10	Not a youthful product
Not as good as others	4.70	.58S	5.28	Better than others
Bad	5.02	.45S	5.47	Good
Not distinctive	3.60	.29	3.89	Distinctive
Would have pleasant taste	5.60	.15	5.45	Would not have pleasant taste
For me	6.10	.11	5.99	Not for me
Cleans teeth well	5.15	.05	5.10	Does not clean teeth well
Not attractive	4.11	.04	4.15	Attractive
Brightens teeth	5.45	.05	5.40	Does not brighten teeth
Refreshing	6.01	.04	5.97	Not refreshing
Modern	5.23	.03	5.20	Old fashioned
A product for younger people	5.76	.02	5.74	Not a product for younger people

Brightface Users—*N* = 200

*Underscored means are significantly higher than compared means at the .05 level. Significant differences are denoted by S. Standard errors of differences between the means have been deleted.

Exhibit 2   The Differential Image of the Current and Bi-Segment Designs

Current Graphics	Mean*	Difference	Mean	Bi-Segment Design
Not recommended by dentists	3.70	2.56S	6.26	Recommended by dentists
Not expensive	4.01	2.44S	6.45	Expensive
Not distinctive	3.60	2.29S	5.89	Distinctive
Not effective	4.73	2.17S	6.90	Effective
Feminine	5.87	1.87S	4.00	Masculine
Does not help prevent cavities	4.20	1.73S	5.93	Helps prevent cavities
A youthful product	5.70	1.60S	4.10	Not a youthful product
Bad	5.02	1.45S	6.47	Good
A product for younger people	5.76	1.16S	4.60	Not a product for younger people
Not as good as others	4.70	1.08S	5.78	Better than others
Not attractive	4.11	1.04S	5.15	Attractive
Old fashioned	5.23	.97S	6.20	Modern
Weak	5.30	.91S	6.21	Strong
Lower quality	5.97	.72S	6.69	Higher quality
Would have pleasant taste	5.60	.55S	5.05	Would not have pleasant taste
Brightens teeth	5.45	.25	5.20	Does not brighten teeth
Refreshing	6.01	.14	5.87	Not refreshing
Does not clean teeth well	5.15	.30	5.45	Cleans teeth well
Cosmetic	6.91	.10	6.81	Not cosmetic
For me	6.10	.02	6.12	Not for me

Brightface User—*N* = 200

*Underscored means are significantly higher than compared means at the .05 level. Significant differences are denoted by S. Standard errors of differences between the means have been deleted.

midpoint are given the positive or negative scale end position by the computer. Further, since direction is important, the computer also had been programmed to give the negative end of the scale to the lower mean even though it may not be below the neutral 4 position of the scale.

Questions

1.   What other experimental design would you have suggested to meet the objectives? How would you formulate the sampling plan differently? What are some

Exhibit 3   The Differential Image of the Copy and Bi-Segment Designs

Copy Design	Mean*	Difference	Mean	Bi-Segment Design
Not distinctive	3.89	2.00S	5.89	Distinctive
Not cosmetic	5.01	1.80S	6.81	Cosmetic
A product for younger people	5.74	1.14S	4.60	Not a product for younger people
Bad	5.47	1.00S	6.47	Good
A youthful product	5.10	1.00S	4.10	Not a youthful product
Not attractive	4.15	1.00S	5.15	Attractive
Old fashioned	5.20	1.00S	6.20	Modern
Not as good as others	5.28	.50S	5.78	Better than others
Would have a pleasant taste	5.45	.40S	5.05	Would not have a pleasant taste
Does not clean teeth well	5.10	.35S	5.45	Cleans teeth well
Not expensive	6.11	.34S	6.45	Expensive
Weak	5.91	.30S	6.21	Strong
Feminine	4.20	.20	4.00	Masculine
Not effective	6.70	.20	6.90	Effective
Brightens teeth	5.40	.20	5.20	Does not brighten teeth
Not for me	5.99	.13	6.12	For me
Refreshing	5.97	.10	5.87	Not refreshing
Does not help prevent cavities	5.83	.10	5.93	Helps prevent cavities
Lower quality	6.60	.09	6.69	Higher quality
Not recommended by dentists	6.21	.05	6.26	Recommended by dentists

Brightface Users—*N* = 200

*Underscored means are significantly higher than compared means at the .05 level. Significant differences are denoted by S. Standard errors of differences between the means have been deleted.

of the other ways of handling the independent variables? What other dependent variable measurement approaches could have been used?

2. Based on the information you have been given, which of the two remaining package graphics approaches would you select for Brightface II? Why?

3. What additional data would you have been interested in analyzing to help you make the selection or the recommendation for the more correct design?

4. What would be your recommendation for the next step in the product introduction? Would you suggest a field experiment such as a controlled store test? What variable should be controlled in such a test?

35

CENTER FOR AMERICAN ENTERPRISE (A): A STUDY OF PSYCHOLOGICAL AND DEMOGRAPHIC CONTRIBUTORS TO CONSUMERISM

In the summer of 1979, the Center for American Enterprise commissioned a study to determine the causes of consumerism. This was done in an effort to stem the tide of growing disenchantment with American business and its practices among a wide number of consumers.

The Center, located in Dallas, Texas, was a private foundation funded by a large number of corporations to spread the ideal of the free enterprise system. It conducted a number of projects to better understand what Americans knew about business and published numerous brochures that were sent to high schools and elementary schools throughout the U.S. Although consumerism had taken a back seat to the oil embargo and the hostage situation in Iran, the Center realized that it was still a major problem facing business and wished to pursue it as an area of study.

Since the Center did not have the expertise to properly formulate the research problem and its accompanying theory, it decided to seek outside assistance for this project. Commissioned to do the study were three professors, Thomas, Rogers and Michaels at Southern Methodist University who had done considerable research on the topic. The report they generated follows.

Report on Psychological and Demographic Correlates of Consumer Discontent

The study of consumerism and the allied psychological state of consumer discontent has been theoretically and empirically examined within the confines of the economic system. Although these market interfaces provide discrete areas for analyzing consumerism or consumer discontent, they may be only symptomatic of broader psy-

Copyright © 1981, Dr. William J. Lundstrom

chological states currently existing in society. With the exception of one study relating consumer alienation to marketing activities, little research has actively explored potential relationships between psychological states and discontent with the market system. Identification of those psychological states and demographic characteristics associated with consumer discontent would provide valuable insight into the dynamics of this phenomenon and assist in the development of constructive approaches for dealing with it from a public policy perspective.

Study Purpose

The purpose of this study is to examine the relationships between selected psychological states, demographic variables and consumer discontent. Specific objectives of this study are threefold:

1. To determine if consumer discontent with the marketplace is rooted in more basic conceptions of an individual's life-space.
2. To determine the appropriateness of psychological constructs as potential contributors and explanatory states for investigating consumer discontent.
3. To identify demographic correlates of consumer discontent.

Method

A two-stage area sampling procedure was used to select 228 individuals from the Dallas, Texas, metropolitan area. A subsequent analysis of demographic data indicated that the sample represented a cross section of the area. Individuals were personally contacted in their homes by trained interviewers.

Respondents were given a self-administered questionnaire containing a list of 145 statements designed to measure life satisfaction, powerlessness, anomie, alienation, normlessness, social isolation, aggression and consumer discontent. All statements were scored on a five-point Likert-type scale except for the consumer discontent scale which had a six-point Likert-type scale. Demographic data on the respondent were also collected.

Results

Results of the study are shown in Exhibits 1 and 2. Exhibit 1 presents the correlation matrix between the measures of psychological states and the consumer discontent scale. The correlations indicate that consumer discontent is indeed related to basic psychological states.

Exhibit 2 presents the correlation matrix between demographic variables and the consumer discontent scale. Examination of demographic variables also reveals that discontent is related to certain characteristics of the populace.

Together, the psychological and demographic correlates of consumer discontent provide a profile of the discontented consumer. Consumer discontent may be an outgrowth of more basic psychological states reflecting disassociation with society in general and specifically with the marketplace. One may speculate that dislocation in society will produce consumer discontent. Given the growing complexity of business and society, it appears that this may become an even more pervasive problem in the future and thus warrants further research at this time.

Exhibit 1   Correlation Matrix of Scale Responses

(N=228)

	CD	LS	AN	AL	Po	No	SI	Ag
Consumer Discontent (CD)	1.00	−.11[b]	.37[a]	.42[a]	.37[a]	.28[a]	.34[a]	.21[a]
Life Satisfaction (LS)		1.00	−.44[a]	−.44[a]	−.33[a]	−.25[a]	−.44[a]	−.27[a]
Anomie (AN)			1.00	.66[a]	.56[a]	.47[a]	.54[a]	.25[a]
Alienation (AL)				1.00	.80[a]	.77[a]	.79[a]	.31[a]
Powerlessness (Po)					1.00	.46[a]	.42[a]	.15[b]
Normlessness (No)						1.00	.42[a]	.32[a]
Social Isolation (SI)							1.00	.28[a]
Aggression (Ag)								1.00

[a]$p<.01$
[b]$p<.05$; Pearson Product-Moment Correlation Coefficients

*Exhibit 2   Correlation of Scale Responses
with Demographic Characteristics*

(N=228)

	CP	LS	AN	AL	Po	No	SI	Ag
Age	.13[b]	.14[b]	.10	.31[a]	.07	.29[a]	37[a]	.13[b]
Sex[1]	−.13[b]	−.05	.02	−.15[b]	−.11	−.06	−.18[b]	.11
Race[2]	−.06	.08	.04	−.15[b]	−.13[b]	−.21[a]	−.03	−.06
Family Size	.02	−.16[a]	.21[a]	.24[a]	.11[b]	.17[b]	.27[a]	.09[c]
Income	.31[a]	−.29[a]	.22[a]	.37[a]	.30[a]	.31[a]	.30[a]	.17[b]
Occupation[3]	−.26[a]	.08	−.20[a]	−.26[a]	−.23[a]	−.15[b]	−.23[a]	.01
Education	.15[b]	−.03	−.11	.20[a]	.27[a]	.16[b]	.06	.11

[a]$p<.01$
[b]$p<.05$
[1]Scored: Male = 1, Female = 2
[2]Scored: Caucasian = 1, Black = 2, Mexican American = 3, Other = 4
[3]Scored: Professional = 1, Skilled Worker = 2, Unskilled Worker = 3, Unemployed = 4, Retired = 5

Questions

1. Interpret the results of the correlation matrices.
2. Develop a profile of the discontented and contented consumer.
3. What policy implications would you suggest based on these results?

CENTER FOR AMERICAN ENTERPRISE (B): ANALYSIS OF CONTINGENCY TABLES

The results from the pilot study on the relation of certain psychological and demographic variables to consumer discontent had been turned into the Center for American Enterprise. The findings presented from the study showed that there were certain variables that had a relatively strong and significant correlation with a measure of consumer dissatisfaction (see Case 35 for details). However, since the study results showed only the correlation between the variables and not the actual scores across each segment of the population, the Center did not know the factors on which it should focus its attention.

Background

The Center for American Enterprise was established in Dallas, Texas, to be a watchdog for the free enterprise system. One of its primary missions was to enhance the understanding of a free-market economy and to come to its defense in times of challenge. The late 60's and early 70's had seen an erosion in the belief that business was doing its best to provide the U.S. public with goods and services that were both safe and reasonably priced. This erosion—known as consumerism—became a focal point for the Center in an effort to bolster its defenses against forces that were undermining its basic purpose. As a first step in this initiative, the Center contracted for a pilot study to determine what psychological and demographic variables were related to consumerism. The results of this study showed that there were several demographic factors which correlated with consumer discontent but, it was not evident where in the population the problem was to be found.

Copyright © 1981 by Dr. William J. Lundstrom.

Exhibit 1   Age by Consumer Discontent

		Low	Medium	High	Total
	Under 25	8	8	9	25
Age	25–45	14	15	16	45
	Over 45	16	12	14	42
	Total	38	35	39	

Exhibit 2   Sex by Consumer Discontent

		CDScale			
		Low	Medium	High	Total
Sex	Male	32	23	29	84
	Female	6	12	9	27
	Total	38	35	38	

Exhibit 3   Race by Consumer Discontent

		CDScale			
		Low	Medium	High	Total
Race	Black	0	4	6	10
	Caucasian	37	31	33	101
	Total	37	35	39	

Exhibit 4   Income by Consumer Discontent

		CDScale			
		Low	Medium	High	Total
	Low	7	11	20	38
Income	Moderate	8	15	12	35
	High	23	9	7	39
	Total	38	35	39	

Exhibit 5   Education by Consumer Discontent

		CDScale			
		Low	Medium	High	Total
	High School	6	5	13	24
Education	Some College	21	21	14	56
	College	11	9	12	32
	Total	38	35	39	

The Present Study

In the present study commissioned by the Center, the research team of Professors Thomas, Rogers and Michaels from the University, concentrated on demographic variables and how they were present in the population. A small sample of 112 people were selected at random and administered the Consumer Discontent Scale

(CDScale). For purposes of cross-tabulating the results, the CDScale scores were condensed into three categories: (1) content; (2) moderately discontent; and (3) discontent. The results of this survey are presented in the contingency tables in Exhibits 1–5.

Questions

1. Determine whether there is a systematic relationship between each demographic variable and consumer discontent.
2. What problems do you see in some of the contingency tables that may bias the results?

X

MULTIVARIATE ANALYSIS

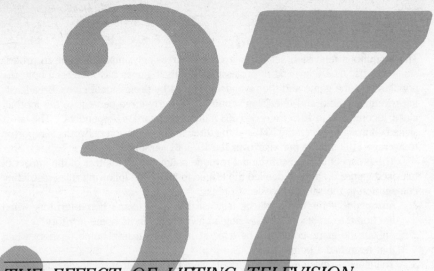

THE EFFECT OF LIFTING TELEVISION BLACKOUTS ON PROFESSIONAL FOOTBALL NO-SHOWS: REGRESSION

Background

In 1973 Congress legislated against television blackout agreements. These agreements prohibited the live telecasting of sold-out home games in the home area of professional sports clubs.[1] The law was opposed strenuously by National Football League (NFL) officials on grounds that such agreements were necessary to maintain the long-run economic viability of professional football. Pete Rozelle, Commissioner of the NFL, stated that the law without question would cause economic damage to the sport. "The only realistic issue is *how* damaging . . . and how soon." [10, pp. 2–3]. The League's opposition to the legislation was based, in part, on the NFL's prediction of an increasing number of no-shows, i.e., people who buy tickets but do not attend the game. No-shows contribute to lost parking and concession revenues. Ultimately, it was claimed that no-shows become no-buys.

Public Law 93–107 expired after the 1975 football season. Since that time the NFL annually has agreed to comply with the spirit of the law which includes televising home games into home territories when the games are sold out at least seventy-two hours in advance, as well as providing data to the Federal Communications Commission for continued analysis of the law's effects.

This study evaluates the impact of the antiblackout legislation on no-shows for professional football games that were televised locally, as a result of the law, during the 1973 through 1977 seasons. The analysis is limited to football because the law has had minimal application to other major sports.

---

[1]The act (P.L. 93–107) provided that if any game of a professional sports club was to be televised on a network pursuant to a league contract and all tickets offered for sale had been sold seventy-two hours before game time, blackout agreements prohibiting the simultaneous telecast of the game in the home territory were invalid. The definition of "home territory" was ambiguous. It included generally the area seventy-five miles from the game site, but did not specify whether the telecast had to originate outside the seventy-five mile limit or whether the signal was not allowed to penetrate the limit. For a detailed review of the act see Shooshan [12]. All references are listed by number at the back of the case.

This case was prepared by John J. Siegfried and C. Elton Hinshaw, both of Vanderbilt University.

Legislative Background

The ubiquitous television set has played an increasingly important role in professional sports.[2] The televising of professional football games has increased both the popularity of the game and the revenues received by professional clubs. Broadcasting revenues (radio and television) contributed thirty-three percent of the football clubs' income and in 1975 exceeded $63 million per year [14, Appendix C]. The latest signed contract between the NFL and the three major television networks is reported to average $162 million per year over the 1978–81 seasons [1, p. 5].

The prospect of such substantial revenue coupled with the fear of the impact of televised games on attendance led the league to adopt the following rules restricting competition in the sale of broadcast rights:

1. An outside game could not be telecast in a third team's home territory when the home team also was televising an away game in its home territory.
2. An outside game could not be telecast in a third team's home territory when that team had a home game.
3. The clubs' television broadcast rights were pooled so that the league negotiated with the television networks for the sale of the collective rights.
4. Blackout agreements were made under the pooled arrangement which prevented the telecasting of a game at the same time and in the same area in which the game was being played.

When these rules and practices came into conflict with anti-trust legislation and the courts, professional sports teams appealed to Congress for relief. In 1961 Congress amended the anti-trust laws to allow professional sports teams to pool broadcast rights, to negotiate with the networks as a cartel, and to blackout home games in home territories. Congress amended this legislation in 1973 to prohibit blackout agreements for a three-year trial period.[3] Since the expiration of the Anti-Blackout Law, an extension of the bill has been tied up in Congressional committees, but the NFL annually has agreed to abide by the provisions of the former law.

The NFL's Arguments

Rozelle argued, on behalf of the NFL, that the principal immediate impact of the 1973 legislation probably would be on the number of no-shows. Although no-shows do not affect gate receipts, the NFL is concerned about them because "full crowds are a major element in the atmosphere of every game. Such crowds are even an element in the performance of the home team." [10, pp. 10–11]. The reasoning was that a large number of no-shows affect the appeal of professional football and adversely affect revenues from parking and concessions.

Rozelle also predicted that revenues from the sale of radio broadcast rights would be jeopardized. Radio broadcasters presumably purchased the rights on the assumption that they would have exclusive rights for all home games. When confronted by direct competition with television, the radio audience would be reduced drastically, as would the value of the radio broadcast rights [10, p. 12].

Rozelle concluded that the Anti-Blackout Law would be highly detrimental to the long-run future of professional football. As fans learn that they have a guaranteed option of either seeing the game in person or watching it on television, Rozelle

---

[2]For a detailed economic analysis of the sale of broadcast rights see Horowitz [5].
[3]For a comprehensive review of the historical background see Hochberg [4].

argued, demand for tickets will decline steadily. This guaranteed option would fundamentally alter the demand for tickets by changing the ticket-buying habits of NFL fans. TV oversaturation and changed attendance habits could eventually destroy professional football in the same manner that they had largely destroyed professional boxing [10, p. 26]. Football thus faced the danger of becoming a studio sport. In the Commissioner's view, blackout agreements are essential for the economic viability of professional football.

Empirical Tests of the No-Show Hypothesis

The possibility of long-run economic injury to professional football convinced Congress initially to repeal automatically the Anti-Blackout Law (in the absence of further legislation) after a trial period of three seasons and to request annual evaluations of the Law's impact by the Federal Communications Commission (FCC). Three such reports were made pursuant to the Law, and two subsequent reports have been issued as a result of requests by the Senate Committee on Commerce, Science, and Transportation. The first report, made after the 1973 football season, concluded that "based on limited data and experience available to the commission, . . . the law's overall effect on the NFL member clubs was minimal . . ." [9, p. 35].

The report for 1974 stated that, "Given the players' strike and the general state of the economy, plus the competitive threat of the World Football League, the NFL would appear to have had a 'good' year . . ." and that "there is no indication that professional football is about to become a 'studio sport'." [11, p. 86][4]

The third report said that "it must be concluded that Public Law 93–107 has not adversely affected the sale of season tickets to professional football games" [15, p. 29]. The report further concluded that "there is no evidence of oversaturation of the sport" [p. 40].

In 1977, after a team-by-team analysis of the effects of the Anti-Blackout Law, the FCC estimated that the league-wide impact of increased no-shows was about $700,000 for each of the first four years of televising home games locally. The FCC, however, conceded that this amount was not significant since it was less than one-half of one percent of total annual revenues accruing to NFL teams. In addition, the FCC estimated the increased value of advertising (from larger audiences if home teams are televised locally) to be about $1.4 million per year, although it is not evident how that amount is divided (or will be divided in the future), among advertisers, television networks, and the NFL [3, pp. xi and xii].

The results of the fifth annual FCC report did not change the previous year's conclusions. Although the enactment of the Anti-Blackout Law occurred simultaneously with the beginning of a decline in season ticket sales and with increased no-shows, these trends appear to have stabilized quickly, and it is difficult to associate the law conclusively with these phenomena. In fact, the report revealed that the average level of no-shows for televised games since 1974 was 2.5 percentage points

---

[4]The second report refers to a statistical analysis developed to explain attendance. The analysis is not contained in the report. The FCC concluded that "precipitation and team standings are much more important influences on the number of no-shows than is the Anti-Blackout Law," and that "the number of games televised locally had no statistically significant effect." [11, p. 87]. The third through fifth reports assess the impact of the Law on the number of no-shows on a team–by–team basis. Such methodology takes into account differences in fan response to the various factors across cities that can affect no-shows. The authors' methodology permits an assessment of fan response over time. Since Congress is more interested in the overall effect of the Law than the city-by-city effect, this analysis is more appropriate for public policy purposes.

below the average level for blacked-out games. The FCC acknowledged that this surprising finding could be explained by the fact that the televised games are the most popular, although the analysis later in this study indicates that this explanation is insufficient [14, pp. 2, 3, 14].

Since the NFL's opposition to the Law is predicated on an increasing number of no-shows with a resulting adverse effect on the long-run demand for tickets, a statistical analysis of the causes of no-shows is appropriate to evaluate the relationship between the local telecast of sold-out games and the number of no-shows for those games.[5] Prior to the Anti-Blackout Law, no regular-season home games were televised in the home team's territory. In the 1973 season, 109 regular-season games were televised locally; in the four subsequent years, eighty-six, seventy-five, eighty-six, and eighty-six games, respectively, were televised. The no-show total for all games was 1,035,831 in 1973, 1,124,879 in 1974, and 874,733 in 1975. For the corresponding 182 home games involving non-expansion teams the number of no-shows was 942,654 in 1976 and 868,542 in 1977 [14, p.11].

Since the mean number of no-shows per game increased from 5,691 in 1973 to 6,181 in 1974, initial support was lent to the NFL's argument that lifting blackouts slowly discourages attendance. The Commissioner argued that the quality of the show deteriorates as no-shows increase, and, over time, fewer people attend or watch the game on TV. However, the average number of no-shows per game decreased subsequently to 4,806 in 1975, 4,841 in 1976, and 4,772 in 1977.

The NFL has argued that the relevant comparison is between no-shows in 1972, the last complete season during which home games were blacked out, and subsequent years. In 1972 the average reported number of no-shows per game, excluding the Dallas and the New Orleans games (not reported), was 3,447. Although the subsequent no-show figures exceed the 1972 average, the authors attach little significance to this trend. First, the 1972 data are incomplete and were not collected under the more rigorous requirements in effect subsequent to that time. Second, since many other things have happened since 1972, changes in no-shows could be attributable to other factors. For example, the 1972 season may have had unusually good weather, close championship races, etc. Indeed, it was about that time that NFL stadiums were selling out for most of their games; 97.6 percent of total stadium capacity was sold in 1972, and it has declined steadily to 88.0 percent in 1977 [14, p. 11]. Given such popularity, the number of sold seats and tickets used has but one direction to go—down.

To test whether no-shows are affected significantly by the Anti-Blackout Law, a multiple regression analysis is used. The dependent variable is no-shows as a percent of total tickets distributed (tickets sold plus complimentary tickets) for each game. Percentage no-shows is used instead of the absolute number of no-shows to adjust for stadium size. The larger the seating capacity of the stadium, the greater is the number of no-shows if the inclination not to show is equal across ticket holders in the various cities. Using no-shows as a percent of tickets distributed avoids this problem.

Cross-sectional regressions are used for each of the five seasons since the Anti-Blackout Law was first in effect. Cross-sectional analysis is superior to a comparison

---

[5]This study does not analyze the impact of the law on revenues derived from parking, concessions, or radio broadcast rights. An assessment of these factors is contained in the FCC reports. The probable effect on parking and concession revenues can be inferred directly from the analysis of no-shows since those revenues are related strongly to live attendance. The third FCC report points out that parking revenues are not likely to be affected at most stadiums even if no-shows increase because of the acute shortage of available parking [15, p. 13].

of time-trends in no-shows since it factors out the impact of general interest trends in professional football over time.[6] Because some teams have sold out many of their games and therefore televised them locally, and other teams have sold out few or no games and consequently televised only a few games locally, the impact of televising local games on no-shows can be compared. Differences in the attractiveness of various games do exist, and these are taken into account by considering the effects of weather and game quality separately.

Since the NFL's predictions of impending doom in the presence of the Anti-Blackout Law forecasted patterns of behavior over time, the behavior patterns as they actually change over time should be examined closely. This study used separate regressions for each of the last five NFL seasons 1973–1977. The interaction effects of various explanatory factors on the percent of ticket holders not attending the games are explicitly considered. For example, it is postulated that televising a home game into the local area has a greater impact on no-shows if it rains during the game than if the weather is clear. The FCC models are not sensitive to such combined effects.

The explanatory factors considered in the analysis include weather conditions, quality of the game, and local television status. The specific variables and description of measures used to represent each are:

1.   Weather Quality Variables

   a.   Precipitation   Precipitation is measured by a binary variable that equals one if there was any rain or snow reported by the home club on the day of the game, and zero otherwise. The expectation is that no-shows are related positively to this variable since precipitation causes sufficient discomfort for some ticket holders to raise the disadvantages of attendance above the advantages.

   b.   Coldness   The measure of coldness is the squared difference between the thirty-year average of the October and November mean temperatures in each city and any lower temperature on game day. The mean seasonal temperature for each NFL city is used as a base because it is assumed that "blood freezes at different temperatures" in different cities. Fans acclimated to and prepared for cold weather are more likely to attend games in low temperatures than are fans accustomed to warmer climates. A temperature of thirty-two degrees has a different impact on Miami Dolphin fans than on Green Bay Packer fans.[7] Coldness is specified to have a non-linear effect on

---

[6]The Federal Communications Commission also has undertaken regression analyses of the effect of blackouts on the percentage of ticket holders who attend games, but the methodology of this study is superior for several reasons. First, the FCC has conducted its analyses on a team-by-team basis in order to determine which teams were affected most by the lifting of blackouts. This technique has several disadvantages. It necessitates the inclusion of 1972 data into the model since otherwise certain teams would have televised all of their home games and the regression could not discriminate for teams that have televised no home games. For those that have televised only one or two games over the period, the impact of the blackout relies heavily on the behavior of fans at relatively few games. By running the regressions across all of the games of each team for the six-year period 1972–1977 the FCC model forces the parameters relating weather, game quality, and TV blackouts to be the same each year. Only shifts in the average number of no-shows are permitted in the FCC model. In contrast, a model across all games in the league for each year separately forces the parameters relating weather, game quality, and blackout status to be the same across all teams, but permits them to vary across time. The authors believe that the latter formulation of the problem is more realistic since Congress is unlikely to pass legislation specifying special rules for individual teams, and consequently it should be interested in the overall impact of the legislation on the league.

[7]Temperatures above the mean are assumed to have no effect on no-shows.

no-shows—a temperature of ten degrees below the October and November average temperature has more than twice the effect of a temperature five degrees below the mean. A positive sign on the coefficient of coldness is expected for reasons analogous to those presented for precipitation.

    c. *Coldness-Precipitation Interaction* Some fans may not attend if it is either cold or if there is precipitation. In the case of such behavior, if both precipitation and cold occur simultaneously, the effect of the two variables on no-shows cannot be additive. People who stay home if it is either cold or precipitating cannot stay home twice if it is both cold and raining (or snowing). However, some fans may attend games if it is only cold or only wet but stay home if both conditions occur simultaneously. Therefore, a variable is included that is the product of the precipitation and coldness variables. Because of the conflicting hypotheses a two-tail test is necessary to test for significance.

2. *Game Quality Variables*

    a. *Home Team* The divisional standing of the home team at the time the game is played is employed to measure quality of the home team.[8] (For the first three games of the season, the final divisional standing of the previous season is used.) The hypothesis is that the better the home team (the lower the rank value), the fewer no-shows occur, and a positive coefficient is expected on the home team divisional standing variable.

    b. *Visiting Team* Divisional standing of the visiting team at the time of the game is used to measure the quality of the opposition. (For the first three games of the season, the final divisional standing of the previous season is used.) The hypothesis is that the better the visiting team, the fewer no-shows occur, and a positive coefficient is expected for the visiting team's divisional standing variable.

    c. *Competition* To measure the degree of competitiveness of the game, the absolute value of the difference in the divisional standings of the home and visiting teams is used. Lower values indicate more evenly matched teams and are expected to be associated with fewer no-shows. The hypothesis is that this variable has a positive coefficient in the regressions.

3. *Television Status Variables*

    a. *Blackout Lifted* Lifting of the local blackout is incorporated into the model as a binary variable that is assigned a value of one if the game was televised locally, or zero if the blackout remained in effect. Televised games are expected to have more no-shows because some ticket holders may exercise the option of staying home and watching the game on TV.

---

[8]Previous studies of attendance at professional sports events have found that a measure of home team quality is significant. See for example Demmert [2] and Noll [8].

b. *Blackout Lifted and Precipitation Interaction* Some no-shows may be related directly to the televising of the game into the home area. Since most tickets are purchased prior to the day of the game, people who desire intensely to see the game in some form, either live or on television, cannot base their ticket purchase decision on game-time weather. Though they definitely want to see the game, they may be relatively indifferent to viewing the game live or on TV, and their slight preference for live viewing causes them to purchase tickets. Poor weather on game day might easily persuade such people to stay home and watch the game on television. These people would attend in person regardless of the weather if the game were not televised. In order to distinguish this interactive effect of weather and television from the separate effects of each, interaction variables are included. The first is the product of the blackout lifted variable and the precipitation variable. The sign of the coefficient of this variable is expected to be positive.

c. *Blackout Lifted and Coldness Interaction* For reasons similar to those for precipitation, one expects an interaction effect of coldness and television status. To distinguish this effect, a variable that is the product of the blackout lifted variable and the coldness variable is included. The expected sign of the coefficient is positive.

d. *Blackout Lifted, Precipitation, and Coldness Interaction* This variable is the product of the blackout lifted, precipitation, and coldness variables. For reasons similar to those discussed for the precipitation-coldness interaction, the sign of the coefficient of this variable cannot be predicted. In order to control for this interaction effect and to get unbiased estimates of the coefficients on other weather and television status variables, it is imperative to include it in the analysis.

Empirical Results

The results of the multiple linear regressions testing the hypotheses outlined above are reported in Exhibit 1. There are 182 games per season. Data for four games from the 1973 season were unavailable to the authors.[9] The statistical significance of each coefficient is indicated with the appropriate tailed t-test. Columns (1) through (5) report the results for the simplest model in which only the single television variable is included. The interactions between television status and weather are included in the results reported in columns (6) through (10).

In the simple model, the measures of precipitation, coldness, and divisional standing of the home team are significant statistically at the five percent level for all five years and have the expected sign. Lifting the blackout, and televising the game locally, does not have a significant positive effect on the percent of no-shows in any season.

[9]With the expansion of the NFL to include Seattle and Tampa Bay in 1976, the number of games increased to 196. The home games of these two expansion teams are excluded because fan behavior during the introductory years of a team may be different from that in other league cities. Therefore, the analysis covers 182 games for the 1974 through 1977 seasons.

Exhibit 1   Regressions of NFL No-Shows/Tickets Distributed On Explanatory Variables

Explanatory Variables	Expected Sign	1973 (1)	1974 (2)	1975 (3)	1976 (4)	1977 (5)	1973 (6)	1974 (7)	1975 (8)	1976 (9)	1977 (10)
Constant		.0038	.0301	.0443	.0092	.0034	.0034	−.0170	.0377	.0128	.0021
Weather Quality Variables											
Precipitation	+	.0585* (3.05)	.1215* (5.58)	.0691* (4.41)	.0767* (4.63)	.0661* (3.80)	.0695* (2.11)	.1128* (3.97)	.0686* (3.12)	.0792* (3.56)	.0541* (2.24)
Coldness	+	.0003* (5.89)	.0004* (5.32)	.0002* (6.25)	.0001* (2.93)	.0002* (7.93)	.0003* (5.03)	.0002* (1.57)	.0002* (5.35)	.0001 (1.29)	.0002* (4.80)
Precipitation · Coldness	±	−.0001 (−1.57)	−.0001 (−0.63)	.0000 (0.13)	−.0000 (−0.04)	.0000 (0.31)	−.0003* (−2.07)	.0012* (3.09)	.0001 (0.41)	.0001 (0.99)	.0003* (3.02)
Game Quality Variables											
Division Standing— home team	+	.0133* (2.65)	.0307* (4.89)	.0130* (2.56)	.0153* (2.82)	.0146* (2.86)	.0140* (2.79)	.0278* (4.65)	.0135* (2.62)	.0137* (2.53)	.0141* (2.83)
Division Standing— visiting team	+	.0095* (1.96)	.0074 (1.28)	.0003 (0.07)	.0091* (1.86)	.0135* (2.99)	.0098* (2.00)	.0083 (1.52)	.0012 (0.27)	.0084* (1.73)	.0123* (2.77)
Closeness of Division Standings	+	−.0035 (−0.59)	−.0050 (−0.66)	−.0037 (−0.70)	.0011 (0.19)	−.0076 (−1.34)	−.0032 (−0.54)	−.0063 (0.87)	−.0032 (−0.59)	.0018 (0.30)	−.0052 (−0.94)
Television Status Variables											
Blackout Lifted	+	.0191 (1.49)	.0036 (0.23)	−.0278 (−2.66)	−.0280 (−2.32)	−.0267 (−2.07)	.0129 (0.91)	−.0084 (−0.50)	−.0220 (−1.83)	−.0250 (−1.78)	−.0211 (−1.52)
Blackout Lifted · Precipitation	+						−.0156 (−0.39)	.0029 (0.07)	−.0017 (−0.06)	.0037 (0.11)	.0165 (0.49)
Blackout Lifted · Coldness	+						.0002 (1.06)	.0006* (3.77)	−.0001 (−1.03)	.0000 (0.30)	.0000 (0.28)
Blackout Lifted · Precipitation · Coldness	±						.0001 (0.31)	−.0017 (−3.86)	−.0000 (−0.23)	−.0003* (−2.13)	−.0004* (−3.31)
F		11.3*	18.0*	14.8*	9.5*	18.5*	8.4*	16.4*	10.5*	7.5*	15.1*
R^2		.319	.419	.374	.276	.426	.337	.490	.381	.306	.469
n		178	182	182	182	182	178	182	182	182	182

t-ratios are in parentheses.

* = statistically significant at .05 level

When the television status-weather interaction variables are added to the model, the precipitation and divisional standing of the home team continue to be significant at the five percent level in all five years, but the index of coldness remains significant at the same level only for the 1973, 1975, and 1977 seasons. The precipitation-coldness interaction variable is significant at the five percent level for the 1973, 1974, and 1977 seasons in the expanded model, but it switches signs from negative in 1973 to positive in 1974 and 1977; it was not significant in 1975 or 1976. Apparently people with different behavioral reactions to the combination of rain and cold owned tickets in the five years, or there was a change in the behavior pattern of fans who owned tickets. The television status variable remains insignificant in all five seasons.[10]

In alternative specifications of the model, individual city binary variables (New York is the control city) are added to each of the first two models. These city binary variables are included to control for systematic differences in fan behavior across cities caused by various factors: ease of access to stadium, traffic congestion, location of the stadium, entertainment alternatives, winning traditions, proportion of complimentary tickets, proportion of tickets sold as season tickets, etc. Houston, for example, has a domed stadium, and fans there presumably would be less sensitive to weather conditions. These city dummy variables are intended to control for the multitude of factors that cause the relative advantages and disadvantages of attending games to vary across cities.[11] The diversity of influences that can affect attendance by city is too complex to yield a simple interpretation. Thus the authors do not formulate hypotheses regarding the coefficients of the city binary variables.[12] However, their inclusion in the model does help to identify the unbiased impact of televising home games on no-shows by controlling for these various factors that are city specific and unrelated to television status. The coefficients of the city binary variables are omitted from Exhibit 2 because the interpretation is ambiguous, and reporting them requires considerable space.

A brief discussion of Atlanta, which had statistically significantly more no-shows than New York in both the 1973 and 1974 seasons, illustrates the usefulness of the city dummy variables. Atlanta led the NFL in no-shows in both seasons with 64,361 in 1973 and 143,488 in 1974, an increase of almost 80,000, or over 75 percent of the total increase for the League [11, p. 30]. Slightly over 89,000 ticket holders failed to attend the last two home games of the 1974 season. The weather was miserable and the Falcons were out of contention for the playoffs. Their performance was substantially below preseason expectations. These are reasonable alternative explanations to lifting the local television blackout for Atlanta's substantial contribution to increasing NFL no-shows.

Empirical results of the multiple linear regressions including city dummy variables are reported in Exhibit 2. Columns (1) through (5) contain the results without the television status-weather interaction variables, and columns (6) through (10) present the results of the expanded model.

---

[10]Although the *t*-value for the blackout lifted variable exceeds the critical level in absolute value for the 1975 and 1976 regressions, the appropriate test is a one-tail positive test, and, therefore, the coefficient is not statistically significantly different from zero.

[11]Running the regressions separately for each year, plus inserting individual city binary variables, also controls for changes in outside conditions over time, e.g., the moving of the Detroit team from an open to an enclosed stadium.

[12]Caution must be exercised in interpreting the coefficients of the city dummy variables. Trends in no-shows for cities are not revealed by a comparison of the coefficients. The coefficients on the dummy variables are deviations from the New York base (included in the intercept) for each year. But the New York base probably changes from year to year. The authors cannot identify even the direction of this change because it is embedded, with numerous other factors, in the intercept term. The city binary variable coefficients are available from the authors on request.

Exhibit 2   Regressions of NFL No-Show/Tickets Distributed On Explanatory Variables and City Dummy Variables

Explanatory Variables	Expected Sign	1973 (1)	1974 (2)	1975 (3)	1976 (4)	1977 (5)	1973 (6)	1974 (7)	1975 (8)	1976 (9)	1977 (10)
Constant		−.0720	−.0121	.0896	.1311	.0053	−.0660	.0092	.0819	.1406	−.0033
Weather Quality Variables											
Precipitation	+	.0688* (4.35)	.1301* (5.81)	.0586* (4.45)	.0654 (4.40)	.0620* (3.77)	.0730* (2.79)	.1195* (3.85)	.0647* (3.51)	.0786* (3.98)	.0743* (3.08)
Coldness	+	.0003* (6.79)	.0004* (4.93)	.0002* (7.73)	.0001* (3.64)	.0002* (7.93)	.0003* (5.53)	.0002* (1.77)	.0003* (6.11)	.0002* (2.67)	.0002* (4.96)
Precipitation · Coldness	±	−.0001* (−2.01)	−.0000 (−0.13)	.0001 (0.96)	−.0000 (−0.39)	.0000 (0.78)	−.0002* (−2.54)	.0014* (4.04)	.0001 (0.84)	.0000 (0.23)	.0002* (2.24)
Game Quality Variables											
Division Standing—home team	+	.0251* (3.56)	.0269* (2.67)	.0089 (1.14)	−.0075 (−0.84)	.0225* (2.43)	.0267* (3.87)	.0234* (2.50)	.0096 (1.22)	−.0103 (−1.18)	.0209* (2.27)
Division Standing—visiting team	+	.0138* (3.53)	.0060 (1.18)	.0029 (0.77)	.0132* (3.05)	.0155* (3.54)	.0138* (3.58)	.0062 (1.29)	.0036 (0.89)	.0126* (2.98)	.0142* (3.26)
Closeness of Division Standings	+	.0021 (0.44)	.0060 (0.85)	−.0014 (−2.51)	−.0050 (−0.91)	−.0018 (−2.14)	.0023 (0.49)	.0052 (0.80)	−.0110 (−2.40)	−.0053 (−1.01)	−.0088 (−1.60)
Television Status Variables											
Blackout Lifted	+	.0231 (1.44)	−.0070 (−0.32)	−.0034 (0.28)	−.0174 (−1.16)	−.0206 (−1.24)	.0098 (0.57)	−.0106 (−0.50)	.0021 (0.15)	−.0058 (−0.36)	.0115 (−0.65)
Blackout Lifted · Precipitation	+						−.0052 (−0.16)	−.0037 (−0.09)	−.0135 (−0.51)	−.0151 (−0.51)	−.0196 (−0.57)
Blackout Lifted · Coldness	+						.0003 (−1.95)	.0004* (3.03)	−.0000 (−0.65)	−.0001 (−0.99)	−.0000 (−0.51)
Blackout Lifted · Coldness · Precipitation	±						−.0000 (−0.05)	−.0017* (−4.44)	−.0000 (−0.15)	−.0002* (−1.84)	−.0003* (−2.04)
F		9.0*	9.0*	9.7*	6.2*	7.0*	9.0*	10.2*	8.8*	6.5*	6.9*
R^2		.659	.649	.668	.563	.592	.682	.703	.671	.600	.615
n		178	182	182	182	182	178	182	182	182	182

t-rations are in parentheses.
* = statistically significant at .05 level

Exhibit 3   Tests of Significance of Four Television Variables Simultaneously
(F-Ratio)

Model	1973	1974	1975	1976	1977
Without City Dummy Variables	1.70	23.69*	2.20	12.75*	18.29*
With City Dummy Variables	3.15*	26.45*	0.32	15.08*	11.92*

Critical Values: $F_{05}(4,171) = 2.41$
$F_{05}(4,147) = 2.43$
See J. Johnston, *Econometric Methods*, pp. 123–30, New York, McGraw-Hill Book Company, Inc., 1963.

In each of the ten regressions, precipitation and coldness are significant at the five percent level. The television status variable has no significant explanatory power in any of the regressions. The television status-precipitation interaction variable is not significantly different from zero in any of the ten equations it enters [columns (6) through (10) of Exhibits 1 and 2]. Apparently those ticket holders that stay home when it rains do so independently of whether the game is televised or not. However, the television status-coldness interaction is significant statistically in two of the ten regressions in which it appears. The coldness variable generally decreases and in two cases [columns (7) and (9) of Exhibit 1] becomes insignificant when the television status-coldness interaction variable is added to the model. Evidently failure to account for the interaction between lifting the blackout and weather may underestimate the effect of televising games on no-shows.

Half of the reported regressions include a set of variables that reflect the impact of local television on no-shows; blackout lifted, blackout lifted/precipitation, blackout lifted/coldness, and blackout lifted/precipitation/coldness. Results of a joint F-test for these variables taken together are reported in Exhibit 3. The joint F-statistic tests whether the coefficients of the four television–related variables are equal simultaneously to zero. In three of the ten cases, even the combined impact of the television variables is insignificant at the five percent level. There is no statistical test to determine the direction of the total impact of the television variable set, and since there are both positive and negative coefficients of at least one television variable in seven of the ten regressions, there also is no straightforward way of assessing the qualitative impact.

Exhibit 4   Estimated Percentage Point Increase in No-Shows as a Result of Lifting
the Blackout

Model	1973	1974	1975	1976	1977
Without City Dummy Variables	1.8%	−1.3%*	−2.6%	−2.9%*	−2.6%*
With City Dummy Variables	2.0%*	−2.5%*	−0.2%	−2.1%*	−2.3%*

*Corresponds to models with significant F-ratios for the television status variable set

A crude estimate of the practical importance of lifting blackouts on the percent of no-shows can be obtained by summing the product of the mean values of the weather variables (precipitation, coldness, and precipitation·coldness) and the coefficient of each of the respective four television variables. Exhibit 4 reports the percentage point increases in the no-show percentages resulting from lifting the blackout for the ten models containing the interaction variables.

A simple average of the seven significant estimates of the estimated contribution of lifting the television blackout is less than zero. The simple average of the combined distribution of the television status variables for all ten specifications of this model is also negative. This would reflect fewer no-shows when the blackout is lifted and when variations in weather and game quality are controlled. In the judgment of the authors, the impact of televised home games in the local area has no practical effect on the number of ticket holders that attend professional football games.[13]

Question

1.   Review the methodology in this case. What conclusions can be drawn from this study?

References

1. *Broadcasting Magazine* (November 14, 1977).

2. H. G. Demmert, *The Economics of Professional Team Sports,* Lexington, Mass., Lexington Books, 1973.

3. *Fourth Annual Report of the Federal Communications Commission on the Effect of Public Law 93-107, The Sports Anti-blackout Law, on the Broadcasting of Sold-Out Home Games of Professional Football, Baseball, Basketball, and Hockey,* Washington, D.C., U.S. Government Printing Office, 1977.

4. P. Hockberg, "Second and Goal to Go: The Legislation Attack in the 92nd Congress on Sports Broadcasting Practices," *N.Y.L.F.,* 18:841 (1973).

5. I. Horowitz, "Sports Broadcasting," *Government and the Sports Business,* ed. R. G. Noll, Washington, D.C., The Brookings Institution, 1974.

6. ————, "Pay TV and Sports Siphoning," *Inquiry into Professional Sports,* Appendix III-E-2, Final Report of the Select Committee on Professional Sports, pp. 644–56, Washington, D.C., U.S. House of Representatives, 94th Congress, 2nd Session, H.R. 94-1786, January 3, 1977.

7. L. R. Klein, *An Introduction to Econometrics,* Englewood Cliffs, N.J., Prentice-Hall, 1962.

8. R. G. Noll, "Attendance and Price Setting," *Government and the Sports Business,* ed. R. G. Noll, Washington, D.C., The Brookings Institution, 1974.

[13]There is a possibility that multicollinearity among the independent variables has caused inflation of the standard errors and, consequently, the acceptance of the null hypothesis when, in fact, the alternative it true. Although there is no definitive test for multicollinearity, Klein [7, p. 101] suggests as a rule of thumb that multicollinearity is "tolerable" if $r_{ij} < R$, where R is the square root of the coefficient of multiple determination and r_{ij} are the absolute values of the simple correlation coefficients among independent variables i and j. When applying this test to the 1975 data, all of the simple correlations among non-interaction terms pass Klein's test. Three interaction terms are questionable for the regressions excluding the city binary variables, but even these pass Klein's test for the regressions including the city binaries. Even if multicollinearity exists, it appears to be "tolerable." Low simple correlation coefficients are a necessary but not sufficient condition for the absence of multicollinearity. It is conceivable that linear combinations of independent variables are equivalent approximately to another independent variable. However, the authors specified the model on the basis of the theoretically preferred form, and they believe that the interaction terms are necessary to describe properly the expected behavior of football ticket holders. If multicollinearity arises from linear combinations of the blackout interaction variables, the substantive conclusions are not distorted because the authors test the statistical significance of the blackout variables as a group (using a joint F-test). Some of the variables one might have expected to be highly correlated are, in fact, not so. There is surprisingly low correlation between the game quality variables and the television status variables: $-.216$ between home team standing and television status; $-.104$ between visiting team standing and television status; and $.018$ between competitiveness and television status for 1976. Similar findings are obtained for the other years. Finally, even if multicollinearity is present, the conclusions stand. The authors have based their conclusion that the lifting of the blackout variable does not affect no-shows principally on the magnitude of the coefficients of the television status variables rather than on whether they are significant statistically. Since the presence of multicollinearity does not bias the coefficients, the estimates of the no-show effect of televising home games should be the best point estimate available.

9. *Report of the Federal Communications Commission on the Effect of Public Law 93–107, the Sports Anti-Blackout Law, on the Broadcasting of Sold-Out Home Games of Professional Football, Baseball, Basketball, and Hockey,* Washington, D.C., U.S. Government Printing Office, 1974.

10. P. Rozelle, "Statement of Commissioner Rozelle of the National Football League," mimeographed paper issued by the National Football League, 1973.

11. *Second Annual Report of the Federal Communications Commission on the Effect of Public Law 93–107, The Sports Anti-Blackout Law, on the Broadcasting of Sold-Out Home Games of Professional Football, Baseball, Basketball, and Hockey,* Washington, D.C., U.S. Government Printing Office, 1975.

12. H. M. Shooshan, III, "Confrontation with Congress: Professional Sports and the Television Anti-Blackout Law," *Syracuse Law Review,* 25:713 (1974).

13. J. J. Siegfried and C. E. Hinshaw, "The Professional Sports Television Anti-Blackout Law," *Inquiry into Professional Sports,* Appendix III–E–1, Final Report of the Select Committee on Professional Sports, pp. 644–56, Washington, D.C., U.S. House of Representatives, 94th Congress, 2nd Session, H.R 94–1786, January 3, 1977.

14. *The Effect of the Sports Anti-Blackout Law: Fifth Annual Report,* Washington, D.C., Federal Communications Commission, June 1978.

15. *Third Annual Report of the Federal Communications Commission on the Effect of Public Law 93–107, The Sports Anti-Blackout Law, on the Broadcasting of Sold-Out Home Games of Professional Football, Baseball, Basketball, and Hockey,* Washington, D.C., U.S. Government Printing Office, 1976.

AMERICAR (D): ANALYSIS OF VARIANCE

In its continuing effort to pinpoint the exact characteristics and differences between subcompact car buyers and larger size car buyers, U.S. Auto, a major manufacturer of automobiles, had embarked upon a research project. The purpose of the research program was to identify specific needs, attributes and differences among these car segments and develop the Americar, a new subcompact, to compete with domestic and foreign imports.

Preliminary research studies indicated a strong market for subcompact autos, so there was substantial room for U.S. Auto's new entry. These earlier research studies suggested the company go ahead with the project. However, company management, always rather cautious, felt that more research was needed on the specifics of the ownership characteristics of the market segments in the industry.

The corporate planning division authorized several studies which involved developing consumer profiles of the major automobile segments. These included: subcompact, compact, intermediate, and full-size automobile owners. The profile was to be developed by using demographic and psychographic measures and by the benefits each group of buyers were seeking in an automobile. The completed profiles would be used in designing the Americar and in creating a marketing strategy for the initial marketing program.

Research Project and Results
The field research was undertaken in a major metropolitan area and involved 186 respondents from the following market segments:
- Full–size owners   43
- Intermediate owners   42

Copyright © 1980, Dr. William Lundstrom and Mark G. Dunn.

- Compact owners   30
- Subcompact owners   60

The respondents were randomly chosen from people shopping at several malls throughout the region.

A questionnaire was administered to each person and consisted of twenty-eight lifestyle question, seven benefits questions, automobile ownership information and demographic information (see Case 28, Exhibit 4). While comparisons were made between subcompact owners and the aggregate group of other buyers (see Case 34), further analysis was needed to see how the four groups differed from one another.

The analysis used to do the four group comparisons was one-way analysis of variance. The comparisons were made on each of the twenty-eight lifestyle factors and seven automobile attributes and are presented in Exhibit 1. Demographic information for each of the groups is found in Case 34, Exhibit 2.

The results from the statistical analysis section were turned over to a market analyst to complete a consumer profile of each group and make recommendations for developing a marketing strategy.

Questions

1. Interpret the results of the analysis of variance.
2. Develop a profile of each market segment.
3. Based on your findings, what would you recommend as a marketing strategy for the Americar?

Exhibit 1   Interests and Opinions Questionnaire—Psychographic Variables

Item	Sub-compact x̄	Compact x̄	Inter-mediate x̄	Full-size x̄	Sum of Squares Between Groups	D.F SSB	Sum of Squares Within Groups	D.F SSW
1	2.0333	2.1333	2.3415	2.3953	4.2336	3	160.8986	170
2	2.05	1.9	2.2619	2.1628	2.6191	3	149.5295	171
3	1.9167	2.3000	2.6905	2.6279	19.5225	3	143.906	171
4	2.55	2.7667	2.561	2.907	4.0349	3	169.9421	170
5	1.9333	2.0667	1.9524	2.2326	2.6151	3	171.1792	171
6	1.9333	1.9333	2.50	2.6744	19.3953	3	157.5419	171
7	2.1833	2.1333	1.8095	1.8372	5.2133	3	152.7867	171
8	2.2167	2.2667	2.7381	2.7907	12.4518	3	189.2853	171
9	3.1833	3.3333	3.2857	3.186	.6612	3	132.7331	171
10	2.3500	2.2333	2.881	3.0465	19.5287	3	175.3284	171
11	3.1833	3.500	3.3810	3.5581	4.1158	3	194.9927	171
12	3.0	3.2333	3.5714	3.1163	8.487	3	2.8269	170
13	2.3333	2.7667	2.8810	2.3953	9.8505	3	199.3838	171
14	1.85	1.8	1.881	2.0	.8598	3	102.8548	171
15	2.25	2.667	2.5	2.4186	1.9525	3	126.0818	171
16	3.1	3.3333	2.9524	3.0233	2.7661	3	198.9482	171
17	2.6167	2.5000	2.5714	2.5116	.4068	3	150.7132	171
18	2.2333	2.4	2.9524	2.6047	13.5171	3	156.1172	171
19	2.6	2.433	2.5476	2.6279	.7763	3	150.2179	171
20	2.7667	2.7667	2.8095	2.6977	.2741	3	205.646	171
21	2.7167	2.2667	2.667	2.4884	4.7296	3	150.1275	171
22	2.8644	3.0667	3.1190	3.2326	3.6734	3	186.8611	170
23	1.8823	2.1667	3.1190	2.7209	43.5884	3	125.4059	171
24	3.2833	3.100	3.3571	3.093	2.1545	3	202.1541	171
25	2.55	2.8	2.4524	2.2791	5.0426	3	144.7059	171
26	3.0833	3.0	2.8571	2.8605	1.831	3	174.889	171
27	2.5333	2.4	2.3333	2.2791	1.8833	3	150.1178	171
28	2.8833	2.9	2.5	2.3256	10.6034	3	168.8252	171

Exhibit 1 Interests and Opinions Questionnaire—Psychographic Variables—Continued

Attributes	SC	C	I	FS				
1	1.25	1.5	1.7857	1.9048	12.9331	3	59.4405	170
2	1.35	1.3	1.3751	1.5116	1.0115	3	44.337	171
3	1.433	1.4	1.6585	1.6512	2.3728	3	62.9203	170
4	2.6102	2.6	2.4359	2.5476	.7951	3	95.2284	166
5	1.45	1.4667	1.4146	1.4651	.0689	3	54.9656	170
6	1.7167	1.7333	1.5366	1.6047	1.0908	3	60.5242	170
7	1.7333	1.7	1.4878	1.6474	1.5712	3	49.9201	169

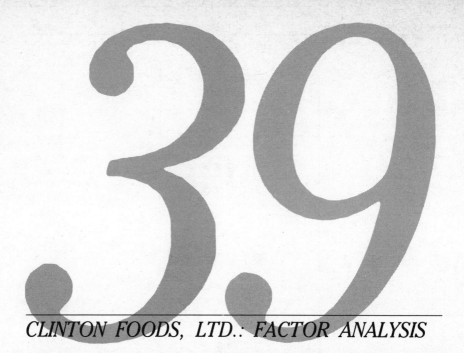

CLINTON FOODS, LTD.: FACTOR ANALYSIS

Clinton Foods Ltd., a leading food processor in the United States and abroad, was planning to launch a new dairy-like product, synthetic eggs. A competing egg substitute produced by another firm was already on the market and, despite its being only recently available (it had been on the market four and one-half months), was proving successful saleswise. As the Clinton Foods' product was being readied for introduction on a national level, the promotions manager, Mr. Albert Stonder, was asked to prepare promotional material for both point-of-purchase and mass media advertising.

Stonder had had several years' experience in the food industry, particularly dealing with new product introduction. As a result of long experience in developing marketing strategy for new products, he tended to place major importance on the consumers' perception of new products. He customarily used this information by stressing through advertising those attributes perceived as positive and minimizing through advertising any negative attributes. Accordingly, in his first strategic planning meeting with his department, he asked three people from his six-member staff to develop a set of questions which could be used to determine what attributes of the egg substitute were perceived as important in both positive and negative ways. The instrument Stonder's staff developed to measure consumers' perceptions of the new product is shown in Exhibit 1. Stonder was advised by a staff statistician that a factor analysis of the data would be appropriate, although Stonder was not fully convinced of this. Stonder and some of his staff felt it desirable to differentiate among respondents according to their awareness and experience with this type of product. Some staff felt the competing brand had not been available long enough for desirable and meaningful attitudes and impressions to develop in the market. In fact,

This case is based on an actual situation, but the names are disguised. From *Cases in Marketing Research* by Randall L. Schultz, Gerald Zaltman, and Philip C. Burger. Copyright © 1975 by The Dryden Press, a division of Holt, Rinehart and Winston, Publishers. Reprinted by permission of Holt, Rinehart and Winston.

Exhibit 1   Consumer Questionnaire

Please answer *all* the questions below with the following product in mind. Make sure that you remember what the product is. You may go back to the description of the product whenever you feel it necessary to refresh your memory.

PRODUCT DESCRIPTION

> The product is a substitute for eggs, costing about the same as regular eggs. The product claims to be cholesterol free, to have the same taste, egg yolk color and nutritional value as regular eggs. The product comes packaged in small cartons, such as those used for milk and is kept frozen until ready for use.

1. Have you heard of this product?

   Yes   (1)   No   (2)

   If yes, answer the following questions . . . . .If no, go on to question #4d.

2. Where or from whom have you heard of this product?

Television	(1)
Neighbors or friends	(2)
Newspapers or magazines	(3)
Relatives (including your immediate family)	(4)
In the store	(5)
Radio	(6)
Other	(7)

   (Please specify)

3. Do you know what this product is called?

   Yes   (1)   No   (2)

   If yes, please specify

4. Have you already tried this product?

   Yes   (1)   No   (2)

YES	NO
If yes, answer the 3 questions below, then go on to question #5.	*If no*, answer the 2 questions below, then go on to question #5.

4a. Do you currently use or own this product?	**4c.** In my opinion, the claims about this product are accurate.
yes (1) no (2)	strongly agree (1)
	moderately agree (2)
4b. How do you like it?	slightly agree (3)
like very much (1)	slightly disagree (4)
like moderately (2)	moderately disagree (5)
like slightly (3)	strongly disagree (6)
dislike slightly (4)	
dislike moderately (5)	
dislike strongly (6)	
4d. I will try it in the near future.	**4e.** In my opinion, the claims about this product are accurate.
strongly agree (1)	strongly agree (1)
moderately agree (2)	moderately agree (2)
slightly agree (3)	slightly agree (3)
slightly disagree (4)	slightly disagree (4)
moderately disagree (5)	moderately disagree (5)
strongly disagree (6)	strongly disagree (6)

5. Please indicate how you feel about the statement below by checking "strongly agree", "moderately agree", "slightly agree", "slightly disagree", "moderately disagree" or "strongly disagree":

	strongly agree	moderately agree	slightly agree	slightly disagree	moderately disagree	strongly disagree
1. This product is not intended for a woman like me.	——	——	——	——	——	——
2. I would not feel badly about the money which was spent on it if it does not perform properly.	——	——	——	——	——	——
3. I do not understand how to use it.	——	——	——	——	——	——

Exhibit 1   Consumer Questionnaire—Continued

	strongly agree	moderately agree	slightly agree	slightly disagree	moderately disagree	strongly disagree
4. It would not be difficult for me to evaluate the claims about it.	—	—	—	—	—	—
5. I would make a special effort to tell my friends about a product like this one.	—	—	—	—	—	—
6. I usually try out this sort of product before telling my friends about it.	—	—	—	—	—	—
7. I would have no difficulty in describing what this product is like to a friend who is not familiar with it.	—	—	—	—	—	—
8. I usually search for all relevant information before deciding to buy a product like this one.	—	—	—	—	—	—
9. I generally discuss this sort of product with my family before buying.	—	—	—	—	—	—
10. Other people would certainly notice if I were using it.	—	—	—	—	—	—
11. I would be afraid of any dangerous or ill effects from using it.	—	—	—	—	—	—
12. Most of my friends are likely to use this product.	—	—	—	—	—	—
13. I am confident that such a product is based upon sound technological knowledge.	—	—	—	—	—	—
14. If it does not give me full satisfaction I can still easily go back to my old product.	—	—	—	—	—	—
15. I really do not understand what is so special about this product.	—	—	—	—	—	—
16. My family is not likely to approve my using it.	—	—	—	—	—	—
17. A product like this one could really change one's ways of doing things.	—	—	—	—	—	—
18. This product seems very unique to me.	—	—	—	—	—	—
19. I do not understand at all the scientific and technological basis for this product.	—	—	—	—	—	—
20. This product has been on the market a long time.	—	—	—	—	—	—
21. This product has been widely accepted by consumers.	—	—	—	—	—	—

there was considerable uncertainty as to who constituted the market. Senior management, including the brand manager for the egg substitute, felt that all egg users could legitimately be considered good prospects as users. Stonder felt otherwise, believing the market should be segmented according to such benefits as low cholesterol, storage ease, etc. Several staff members, particularly those responsible for developing the questionnaire, disagreed, siding with senior management.

Factor Analysis

A major container manufacturer located in the midwest United States allowed Stonder to use their consumer panel of housewives. The cost of using the panel was

Exhibit 2   A.   Eigenvalues and Percent of Variance Explained for Unrotated Factors Concerning all Respondents (n = 273)

Factor	Eigenvale	PCT of Var	Cum PCT
1	3.21842	15.3	15.3
2	2.08701	9.9	25.3
3	1.66131	7.9	33.2
4	1.43827	6.8	40.0
5	1.30825	6.2	46.3
6	1.14575	5.5	51.7
7	1.07899	5.1	56.8
8	1.04201	5.0	61.8
9	.93870	4.5	66.3
10	.90517	4.3	70.6
11	.81930	3.9	74.5
12	.76612	3.6	78.1
13	.68636	3.3	81.4
14	.64355	3.1	84.5
15	.56942	2.7	87.2
16	.53660	2.6	89.7
17	.50659	2.4	92.2
18	.49374	2.4	94.5
19	.42441	2.0	96.5
20	.38817	1.8	98.4
21	.34185	1.6	100.0

B.   Eigenvalues and Percent of Variance Explained for Unrotated Factors Concerning Respondents Who Have Tried the Product (n = 44)

Factor	Eigenvalue	PCT of Var	Cum PCT
1	4.29663	20.5	20.5
2	2.07191	9.9	30.3
3	1.72085	8.2	38.5
4	1.66842	7.9	46.5
5	1.47194	7.0	53.5
6	1.39028	6.6	60.1
7	1.23696	5.9	66.0
8	1.04182	5.0	70.9
9	.97932	4.7	75.6
10	.90302	4.3	79.9
11	.75849	3.6	83.5
12	.71318	3.4	86.9
13	.59346	2.8	89.7
14	.44875	2.1	91.9
15	.41177	2.0	93.8
16	.31438	1.5	95.3
17	.26736	1.3	96.6
18	.24457	1.2	97.8
19	.20654	1.0	98.8
20	.15767	.8	99.5
21	.10271	.5	100.0

minimal and a response rate of eighty-three percent was obtained. This represented 273 respondents. A factor analysis was performed for all respondents, that is, for those who had tried synthetic eggs; for those who had heard of the product but had not tried it; and for those who had not heard of the product.

The factor analysis for each group is presented in Exhibit 2. Unrotated factors with eigenvalues less than 1.00 were deleted from the analysis. Eigenvalues for rotated factors and percentage of variance explained for each of the factors retained are presented at the bottom of the column for each factor. The percentage of the

C. *Factor Analysis for all Respondents (n = 273)*

Variable No.	Factor 1	Factor 2	Factor 3	Factor 4	Factor 5	Factor 6	Factor 7	Factor 8	Communality
1	-.15098	.00662	.00206	.10133	-.01496	.42365	.15112	.01443	.23586
2	-.01893	-.15003	.04104	-.07341	-.01245	.00313	-.07554	.39596	.19260
3	-.32056	.15427	.16150	.38612	-.15456	.14039	.09817	.08944	.36297
4	.52939	.09852	.04881	-.03150	-.04659	-.09952	.01895	.00974	.30587
5	.39344	.26520	.10123	.08088	.02047	-.48950	-.04837	.13651	.50292
6	.15363	.02615	.50611	.03567	-.08846	-.01842	-.08014	-.12830	.32255
7	.51597	.81389	.17780	-.15843	-.02642	-.15913	-.06603	.01310	.35368
8	.05191	-.07258	.65165	.01723	.01386	-.14893	.14893	.13432	.48084
9	-.08169	.11384	.34860	.03976	.00750	.15886	.16345	.33361	.30604
10	-.08281	.14416	.29430	-.02975	.00385	.27916	.08875	.17679	.23221
11	.01315	.08056	.11836	.10936	-.03628	.12432	.58622	.00576	.39309
12	.24857	.20835	-.03612	.22605	-.02040	-.23919	-.05248	.45139	.42173
13	.18157	.29265	.01191	.05939	.07740	-.17558	.47822	.20907	.43150
14	.14559	-.09451	-.05977	.03196	.00977	.14825	.05093	.00097	.05885
15	-.17316	-.23567	.02287	.45393	-.36250	.48346	-.04167	.00571	.65873
16	-.06866	.05670	.03456	.14382	-.06082	.72421	.14163	-.04913	.57981
17	.06937	.63467	.07123	.07139	-.07198	.13335	.06092	-.00706	.44448
18	.01568	.73169	-.03865	-.09970	-.05590	-.18842	-.08238	-.08679	.59912
19	-.04427	-.02556	-.00516	.66624	-.01799	.10195	.05971	-.03896	.46278
20	-.09643	-.10870	.02149	-.07315	.54101	.03896	-.02385	.07546	.32740
21	.05326	.26416	-.13122	.01631	.55686	-.19891	-.07366	.11116	.45754
Eigenvalue	2.69176	1.48565	1.09320	.85907	.66643	.66643	.49290	.39220	
PCT. of variance	33.1	51.4	64.8	75.4	83.6	89.6	95.2	100.0	

D.   Eigenvalues and Percent of Variance Explained for Unrotated Factors Concerning Respondents Who Have Heard of the Product but Not Tried It ($n = 192$)

Factor	Eigenvalue	PCT of Var	Cum PCT
1	3.03915	14.5	14.5
2	2.18793	10.4	24.9
3	1.86363	8.9	33.8
4	1.41615	6.7	40.5
5	1.36473	6.5	47.0
6	1.22411	5.8	52.8
7	1.08198	5.2	58.0
8	1.02402	4.9	62.9
9	.96730	4.6	67.5
10	.86856	4.1	71.6
11	.84125	4.0	75.6
12	.73141	3.5	79.1
13	.68260	3.3	82.3
14	.66237	3.2	85.5
15	.54330	2.6	88.1
16	.52972	2.5	90.6
17	.49702	2.4	93.0
18	.43927	2.1	95.1
19	.37701	1.8	96.9
20	.36039	1.7	98.6
21	.29808	1.4	100.0

E.   Eigenvalues and Percent of Variance Explained for Unrotated Factors Concerning Respondents Who Have Not Heard of the Product ($n = 37$)

Factor	Eigenvalue	PCT of Var	Cum PCT
1	3.73768	17.8	17.8
2	2.89125	13.8	31.6
3	2.47874	11.8	43.4
4	1.69124	8.1	51.4
5	1.43711	6.8	58.3
6	1.33404	6.4	64.6
7	1.10890	5.3	69.9
8	1.01673	4.8	74.7
9	1.00084	4.8	79.5
10	.85760	4.1	83.6
11	.65749	3.1	86.7
12	.60693	2.9	89.6
13	.52491	2.5	92.1
14	.42448	2.0	94.1
15	.30890	1.5	95.6
16	.25191	1.2	96.8
17	.20485	1.0	97.8
18	.14867	.7	98.5
19	.12680	.6	99.1
20	.11285	.5	99.6
21	.07810	.4	100.0

variance explained in this case will always add to 100 percent since the results have been normalized.

One task facing Stonder and his staff was to determine first what variables to retain as defining each factor, what to label each factor or newly constructed variable, and how to use the information in promotional campaigns. Another task was to decide where the various respondent groupings differed significantly among themselves in terms of the kinds of factors or new relevant variables and the sequence of

F. *Factor Analysis for Respondents Who Have Tried the Product (n = 44)*

Variable No.	Factor 1	Factor 2	Factor 3	Factor 4	Factor 5	Factor 6	Factor 7	Factor 8	Communality
1	-.52323	-.00260	-.08528	.11420	.07813	.11953	.03658	.03100	.31678
2	.05796	-.07256	-.01567	-.05632	.05150	.07114	.11800	.82966	.72201
3	-.61133	-.90656	.00069	-.00683	.09335	.30924	.06730	-.02356	.48324
4	.52587	.03926	.11420	-.03123	.33051	-.28801	-.25902	-.07080	.55638
5	.58583	.19149	-.11218	-.07413	.05940	.04447	-.47516	.05410	.63215
6	.17587	.56708	.01781	.25205	-.01265	-.12495	.06222	-.22434	.48632
7	.28441	.16508	.29344	.30703	-.05641	-.48149	.05349	-.01431	.52660
8	.05903	.92223	.04653	-.13041	.07385	-.01276	-.06027	.10129	.89268
9	-.11416	.30519	.22930	-.13227	.18213	.30286	-.01656	.03089	.30237
10	-.23037	.10916	.68859	-.14797	-.06882	.16040	.16821	-.03279	.62086
11	-.08897	.04831	.02099	.11182	.81699	.12787	.05871	.05679	.71369
12	.58978	.07646	-.28310	-.07454	.12788	.22638	-.00990	.12640	.43510
13	.61793	.02513	.11813	.27743	-.36279	.12994	-.15665	.13996	.66602
14	-.03433	-.35869	.00217	.18541	.16632	-.03741	.43710	.16255	.41076
15	-.59060	-.09229	.02505	.14521	.05074	.28628	.49826	.06564	.71615
16	-.41059	.01423	.30573	-.04935	.15098	.12473	.71957	-.08941	.82882
17	.18844	-.01055	.54081	.09217	.07183	-.09217	-.03918	.00007	.35178
18	-.12561	-.10465	.10998	.66221	.04457	-.09341	-.24201	.04577	.54873
19	-.06385	-.01526	.04081	.12376	.03163	.50869	.11283	-.05340	.29664
20	.06228	.08105	.12845	-.54425	-.05736	-.17625	-.16406	.12230	.39939
21	.10750	-.23811	.13424	-.00189	.14355	-.13781	-.48876	-.30188	.45590
Eigenvalue	3.89894	1.67028	1.27178	1.18494	1.03329	.97906	.71711	.60695	
PCT. of variance	34.3	14.7	11.2	10.4	9.1	8.6	6.3	5.3	

G. *Factor Analysis for Respondents Who Have Heard of Product But Not Tried It* ($n = 192$)

Variable No.	Factor 1	Factor 2	Factor 3	Factor 4	Factor 5	Factor 6	Factor 7	Factor 8	Communality
1	.19386	−.08860	−.04258	−.05768	.09331	.66607	−.08989	.12153	.52578
2	−.04243	.03275	−.31717	.17830	.21940	−.06057	.10470	.00294	.19804
3	.19832	−.03374	.15553	.03482	.12789	.11452	.01834	.69784	.58266
4	.05272	.58242	−.00320	.11703	−.00151	.10045	−.01357	−.12562	.38175
5	−.31102	.47271	.19513	.34981	−.05659	−.09638	.11956	.14755	.52919
6	.00174	.31091	.14330	−.19219	.32199	−.00022	.07961	.01710	.26444
7	−.17277	.50562	−.00881	.04708	.05791	−.05437	−.00078	−.09892	.30389
8	−.10339	.15415	.00437	−.05057	.53710	−.04088	−.09993	.01653	.33743
9	.03876	.03066	−.10512	.08941	.50428	.11360	−.09743	.24954	.36045
10	.08375	−.08225	.06315	.07542	.51432	.05962	−.02510	−.03332	.29327
11	.05007	.03563	.12858	−.00975	.17057	.16889	−.57067	.03260	.40475
12	.04854	.19764	.05647	.62369	.15268	−.20077	.09466	.03485	.50740
13	−.11277	.11646	.15220	.31043	.01320	.08658	.53279	.02120	.43779
14	−.04141	.20758	.03854	−.00194	−.03224	.22041	.20287	−.23439	.19210
15	.73860	−.11368	−.16489	−.23275	.04085	.05169	−.02461	.13382	.66266
16	.48433	−.18032	.13233	−.10860	.16255	.31746	−.14458	−.03219	.44555
17	.13880	−.01282	.66438	.21325	.20215	−.02879	−.07785	.05568	.56004
18	−.35090	.05194	.67074	.12342	−.02478	−.03842	.18863	.13145	.64590
19	.44133	−.04084	.07775	.15607	−.13337	.07365	−.05472	.21479	.29919
20	.02782	−.31848	.03955	.06602	−.03767	.08376	−.02246	−.07579	.12281
21	−.29959	−.21935	.12527	.56124	.06848	.16238	.15272	.01551	.52318
Eigenvalue	2.54798	1.64033	1.24105	.81478	.75993	.61647	.49544	.46219	
PCT. of variance	29.7	19.1	14.5	9.5	8.9	7.2	5.8	5.4	

H. *Factor Analysis for Respondents Who Have Not Heard of the Product (n = 37)*

Variable No.	Factor 1	Factor 2	Factor 3	Factor 4	Factor 5	Factor 6	Factor 7	Factor 8	Factor 9	Communality
1	−.02930	.74400	−.19857	.02662	.06509	.06974	−.08628	.11322	−.29626	.71167
2	−.07420	−.10389	−.06723	−.00168	.11409	−.27825	.02916	.53203	−.12678	.41125
3	.00290	.29098	−.35591	.15841	.44643	.06963	.02107	.20151	−.12060	.49618
4	.13133	−.06343	.07175	−.01357	−.09721	.87480	−.02447	−.10280	−.04036	.81412
5	.22736	−.28407	.57103	.12892	.00768	.40298	.24748	−.16842	.30416	.81966
6	−.15647	−.06300	.21111	.22760	.02648	.05011	.78963	.15349	.06766	.77968
7	−.09648	−.11278	.80837	−.01443	−.25972	−.01512	.09642	−.00036	.02970	.75356
8	−.41364	.00321	.57156	.15300	.31279	.26789	.11836	.18556	.09918	.74908
9	.28308	.21635	.04475	.17895	.52264	−.29567	.20556	.28216	.19418	.68112
10	.01468	.63895	−.01955	.01324	.24278	.01556	.07745	−.16668	−.00264	.50201
11	.03606	.07828	−.08133	.06735	.75323	−.06064	−.02537	−.05320	.07621	.59890
12	.30350	−.20909	.39751	.29138	.00862	.14259	−.56947	.38340	.03652	.87178
13	.20111	−.14922	.15478	.21717	.31213	.15353	−.02189	.40813	.04635	.42403
14	−.01466	−.11214	.10834	−.11920	.02925	−.03458	.16469	−.11383	−.00075	.08087
15	.12929	.17765	−.02532	.92591	−.01605	−.02794	.04366	.17671	−.10624	.95168
16	.21729	.67667	−.05637	.02185	−.02861	−.24784	−.08705	−.13382	−.04387	.59345
17	.76642	.29743	−.12883	−.04753	.00278	.03287	−.12473	.12343	.21048	.77090
18	.80890	−.04647	−.16788	.06102	.07563	.20232	−.14917	.07450	−.18114	.79566
19	−.00910	−.14156	.10776	.66944	.41224	.01067	.06552	−.10310	−.03620	.66617
20	−.64895	−.00929	−.24971	−.23404	−.07017	.00524	−.00572	.21746	.28641	.67294
21	−.14185	−.22959	.11744	−.11327	−.06062	−.01720	.03832	−.11872	.70667	.61837
Eigenvalue	3.4566	2.64999	2.19556	1.29819	1.11296	1.01201	.83052	.67865	.56953	
PCT. of variance	24.8	19.3	16.0	9.4	8.1	7.4	6.0	4.9	4.1	

their importance. Stonder found his staff very divided among themselves in their own responses to these issues. After three large sessions failed to yield any meaningful consensus among his staff as to what the different factors really were, how they should be used, etc., Stonder decided to make all the necessary decisions for the final report himself.

Questions

1. What factor labels would you attach to the factors presented in Exhibit 2?
2. Are the major factors in each table sufficiently different to a market segmentation approach based on different degrees of familiarity with the product, that is, should different appeals or themes be directed to people who differ in their awareness of and experience with the product?
3. What promotional themes or messages are suggested by each factor in Exhibit 2?
4. How much reliability can be placed on the data and statistical method of analysis?

OKLAHOMA HEALTH PLANNING COMMISSION: A FACTOR ANALYSIS INVESTIGATION

The Oklahoma Health Planning Commission is a state agency that aids in the planning of health care facilities and programs within the state of Oklahoma.

The agency had realized that access to health care through traditional health care facilities (especially physicians) was a problem for a number of rural Oklahomans. In some Oklahoma counties, there was only one physician and in some communities there was a complete absence of health care facilities. One possible solution to the lack of physicians in other health care facilities in rural areas is to substitute a nurse practitioner in appropriate situations. The Oklahoma Health Planning Commission had defined a nurse practitioner in the following manner:

The nurse practitioner is used as a medically trained person who has passed the state licensing examination for registered nurse and has one additional year of special study in "medicine." This person would treat common illnesses, minor injury, and patients with chronic diseases, such as diabetes and high blood pressure. He or she might also treat children who are well and ill, and other health problems, when the patient is not seriously ill.

A pair of university research consultants were invited to a meeting to help the Oklahoma Health Planning Commission investigate the "consumer" decision–making process for nurse practitioners. When the two researchers met with the Health Planning Commission staff, they explained that the marketing of non-profit organizations was not *conceptually* too much different from the marketing of the product of goods and services. They explained that conceptually a nurse practitioner could be viewed as a "new product" or "new service" available to consumers. The researchers felt that the key to determining if nurse practitioners would be utilized in the state was one of finding and satisfying the consumer's need.

The staff and the researchers agreed that a survey needed to be taken. One aspect of the research was to identify consumer attitude. The purpose of this was to identify the important cognitive dimensions.

Copyright © 1981 by Dr. William G. Zikmund.

Sample

In conjunction with representatives from the Oklahoma Health Planning Commission staff, a judgment sample of ten rural health communities in Oklahoma was selected for study. Criteria in the selection were communities of approximately 2,500 or fewer residents without a physician or with only one physician, capacity for diverse health care delivery systems, and geographic and socioeconomic diversity among communities. The actual sampling was in multistage processes. Visual surveys of housing types and conditions were conducted within each community; these factors are surrogate indicants of socioeconomic status. Then, residential blocks were randomly selected from each distinguishable socioeconomic area for each community. Finally, based on a systematic random sample, households were selected from each block.

The subjects of the study were 220 adults; women were sampled more heavily since they have traditionally played the greater role in household health care decisions. From the original sample, 205 usable questionnaires (containing answers to all relevant questions) were obtained. The sample included 148 women and 57 men. The refusal rate among subjects was less than five percent, with those who refused to participate being replaced by subjects in contiguous houses.

Procedure

Personal interviews were conducted in the subjects' homes. Pretesting of the questionnaire for clarity and ease of administration was conducted in a nonsurveyed community. Before interview questions about attitudes were asked, a description of the nurse practitioner concept as presented above was read to the subjects. In addition, they were informed that the nurse practitioner's office would be located in the community and that the nurse practitioner would be maintaining liaison with a physician in the nearest community where a practice existed.

Instrument

Attitudes were measured on five-point Likert-type scales that reflected the extent of agreement with statements about nurse practitioners. Scales ranged from "strongly agree" (5) to "strongly disagree" (1), with a midpoint of "neither agree nor disagree" (3). For example, one statement was, "Going to a nurse practitioner in this community rather than a doctor in another community would be extremely convenient." The items included in the research were generated from a larger number of attitudinal statements that were generated by the researchers and the Health Planning Commission staff. In total, fifteen belief statements were included in the measurement. These fifteen items were selected as the most appropriate.

Analysis

To delineate the principal dimensions of consumer attitudes toward nurse practitioners, the fifteen attitude variables were factor analyzed. The investigation proceeded by examining the eigenvalues associated with the initial unrotated factors. Three eigenvalues of 1.0 or more were observed. Orthogonal (varimax) simple structure solutions were examined for rotations of three, four, and five factors. Under the criteria of interpretability and meaningfulness, the initial three-factor solution was selected. The researchers believed variables selected as definers of the factors should have a minimal loading of at least .45 on the factor.

Exhibit 1   Factor Loadings for Attitude Variables with Rotated Factor Matrix (N = 205)

	Factor Loading			
Attitude Statement	*Factor 1*	*Factor 2*	*Factor 3*	*h^2*
A nurse practitioner would be qualified to care for minor injuries and minor illnesses.	.77	.09	.22	.66
A nurse practitioner would be available when needed.	.72	.13	.09	.55
I would respect the medical opinions of a nurse practitioner.	.66	.21	.41	.64
A nurse practitioner would explain things so patients could understand the nature of their illness.	.54	.37	.01	.43
Going to a nurse practitioner in this community rather than to a doctor in another community would be extremely convenient.	.49	.31	.24	.40
A nurse practitioner would make a right diagnosis about as often as a doctor would make a right diagnosis	.51	.08	.47	.49
A nurse practitioner would take more personal interest in the patient than would a doctor.	−.02	.79	.27	.69
A nurse practitioner would spend more time with a patient than would a doctor.	.18	.78	.01	.63
Using a nurse practitioner rather than a doctor would save on medical bills.	.30	.56	−.03	.40
I would expect a nurse practitioner to provide health counseling.	.34	.49	.15	.38
I would not trust a nurse practitioner to prescribe drugs for me or my family.	.03	.01	.75	.56
A nurse practitioner would not be able to detect the symptoms of a serious disease that should be referred to a physician.	.12	−.01	.69	.49
I would obey the advice of a nurse practitioner as much as I would a doctor's advice.	.07	.32	.64	.52
Nurse practitioners would not treat most minor health problems as well as a doctor.	.29	.08	.60	.45
A nurse practitioner should only work in a physician's office where a doctor can be consulted immediately.	.24	.10	.56	.38
Eigenvalue	4.9	1.6	1.1	
Total variance	33.0%	11.0%	7.0%	
Cumulative total variance	33.0%	44.0%	51.0%	
Common variance	35.8%	28.9%	35.3%	

Exhibit 2   Means and Standard Deviations for the Attitudes About Nurse Practitioners

Attitude Statement	*M*	*SD*
A nurse practitioner would be qualified to care for minor injuries and minor illnesses.	4.5	0.62
A nurse practitioner would be available when needed.	4.0	0.81
I would respect the medical opinions of a nurse practitioner.	4.3	0.72
A nurse practitioner would explain things so patients could understand the nature of their illness.	3.9	0.89
Going to a nurse practitioner in this community rather than to a doctor in another community would be extremely convenient.	4.1	1.11
A nurse practitioner would make a right diagnosis about as often as a doctor would make a right diagnosis.	3.3	1.23

Exhibit 2   Means and Standard Deviations for the Attitudes About Nurse Practitioners—Continued

Attitude Statement	M	SD
A nurse practitioner would take more personal interest in the patient than would a doctor.	3.1	1.28
A nurse practitioner would spend more time with a patient than would a doctor.	3.7	1.07
Using a nurse practitioner rather than a doctor would save on medical bills.	3.6	1.10
I would expect a nurse practitioner to provide health counseling.	4.2	0.87
I would not trust a nurse practitioner to prescribe drugs for me or my family.	2.9	1.44
A nurse practitioner would not be able to detect the symptoms of a serious disease that should be referred to a physician.	3.2	1.30
I would obey the advice of a nurse practitioner as much as I would a doctor's advice.	3.5	1.31
Nurse practitioners would not treat most minor health problems as well as a doctor.	3.5	1.27
A nurse practitioner should work only in a physician's office where a doctor can be consulted immediately.	3.2	1.38

Note: 5 = Strongly agree, 3 = Neither agree nor disagree, 1 = Strongly disagree.

Results

The 15 attitudes measured in the research are listed in Exhibit 1 according to saliency in the rotated factor matrix. The factor loadings are given for each variable. The three–factor matrix accounted for fifty-one percent of the total variance in the data. Exhibit 2 gives the mean responses and standard deviations for each of the attitude statements.

Question
1.   Interpret the three-factor solution.

XI

EXPERIMENTAL RESEARCH

AMERICAN HEART ASSOCIATION:
MAIL RESPONSE EXPERIMENT

Like many other charitable organizations, the American Heart Association raises a good deal of it total donations through direct mail. In this regard, it works very closely with direct mail advertising firms and mailing list brokerages to refine its mail campaign. An overriding objective is to be able to generate the most response (in dollar contributions) for the budgeted expenditure.

Factors in Need of Testing

Virtually every conceivable element of the direct mail campaign is tested periodically in an attempt to optimize returns. Tests are run of old and prospective mailing lists in an attempt to identify the right prospects. Frequency of mailings, follow-ups and reminder mailings are evaluated to determine how often to correspond with prospective donors. The entire mailing package itself (including the letter, envelopes and enclosures) is tested frequently to determine if it can be improved. Even such "trivial" items as color of paper, manner of affixing postage, use of commemorative stamps, personification, titles and headlines have been shown to significantly alter the response rates to mailings of this sort.

The American Heart Association has had recent success with a mailing package which consisted of an outer #10 envelope with panels which show the name and address of the addressee and that of the sender. Previous research had shown that local mailings (from the chairman of the local heart association) drew better than national mailings. Enclosed with the rest of the mailing was a two-color letter from the local chairman soliciting a donation, a pledge card and a colored #9 return envelope.

This case is based on materials made available by the Direct Mail/Marketing Educational Foundation. Copyright © 1981 by Dr. Donald Sciglimpaglia.

Exhibit 1   Teaser Line Samples

 AMERICAN HEART ASSOCIATION

NON-PROFIT ORG.
U.S POSTAGE
PAID
Permit No. 35193
Los Angeles, Calif.

4 years ago, Billy Thompson's dad would have died...

YOUR
AMERICAN HEART ASSOCIATION

NON-PROFIT ORG.
U.S POSTAGE
PAID
Permit No. 35193
Los Angeles, Calif.

We'd like to show you how you can help save a life. YOURS.

ADDRESS CORRECTION REQUESTED

 AMERICAN HEART ASSOCIATION

NON-PROFIT ORG.
U.S POSTAGE
PAID
Permit No. 35193
Los Angeles, Calif.

Use the enclosed FREE GIFT.
ADDRESS CORRECTION REQUESTED

You may save a life!

Exhibit 1   Teaser Line Samples—continued

 AMERICAN HEART ASSOCIATION

NON-PROFIT ORG.
U.S POSTAGE
PAID
Permit No. 35193
Los Angeles, Calif.

If you have ever worried about having a heart attack—

We have important news for you!

 AMERICAN HEART ASSOCIATION

NON-PROFIT ORG.
U.S POSTAGE
PAID
Permit No. 35193
Los Angeles, Calif.

Emergency Heart Attack Card Enclosed.

Read it and you may SAVE A LIFE!

NON-PROFIT ORG.
U.S POSTAGE
PAID
Permit No. 35193
Los Angeles, Calif.

Exhibit 1   Teaser Line Samples—continued

YOU hold lives
in your hands...TODAY...

  AND THAT'S IMPORTANT!

NON-PROFIT ORG.
U.S POSTAGE
PAID
Permit No. 35193
Los Angeles, Calif.

YOUR
AMERICAN HEART ASSOCIATION

AMERICAN HEART ASSOCIATION
3640 Fifth Avenue
San Diego, CA 92103

NON-PROFIT ORG.
U.S. POSTAGE
PAID
AMERICAN HEART
ASSOCIATION

We'd like to show you how you
can help save a life. YOURS.

We have important news for you!

Although this basic mailing package had been successful in the past, the account representative of the heart association's direct response advertising firm suggested that results might be increased by adding a "teaser line" to the outer envelope. The teaser line is a device used to generate interest among prospects so that they would be more likely to open and read the direct mail piece.

The Test

The direct response firm suggested the use of six potential teaser lines. Test mailing packages were prepared which contained the different messages. The contents of the mailing packages were essentially the same, the only real difference being the teaser line on the outer envelope. To make the teaser fit the mailing package, the contents were modified slightly so that the enclosures tied in with the appropriate teaser. Examples of different test envelopes and contents are shown in Exhibits 1–3.

Exhibit 2   Example of Donation Letter

YOUR
AMERICAN HEART ASSOCIATION

Today's heart attack victim
has a much better chance for survival
than ever before.

Dear Neighbor:

Heart disease is still the nation's #1 killer. But we
have it on the run. The incidence of heart attack
deaths is decreasing--thank goodness.

Why? Because of better prevention, treatment & education
...all made possible by community support.

Thanks to community support, your Heart Association was
able to establish the first paramedic training programs.
Paramedics now save the lives of hundreds of heart
attack victims each year.

Thanks to community support, your Heart Association
has been able to teach the Cardiopulmonary Resuscitation
method throughout the country. Time after time, CPR
has made the difference between life and death when
heart attacks have occurred.

We've been putting your money to work. And we've
gained valuable ground. But heart disease is far from
licked.

Please help us continue our research, treatment, and
education by contributing to your Heart Association.
Send your donation today. And help us keep heart
disease on the run!

Sincerely,

Joseph V. O'Donnell

Joseph V. O'Donnell
Campaign Chairman

P.S. We want to make your chance of survival even
      greater. Your donation of $10, $25 or $50 will
      be greatly appreciated and put to good use.
      I promise it.

Exhibit 3   Example of Return Mailing

```
 _____                                    ┌──────────┐
 _____                                    │  THANK   │
 _____                                    │  YOU     │
                                                        └──────────┘


                               AMERICAN HEART ASSOCIATION




 ┌──────────────────────────────────────────────────────────────────────┐
 │  ❤                                          Here is my contribution    │
 │      YOUR    2405 West 8th Street           of $_____          │
 │  ® AMERICAN HEART ASSOCIATION                                          │
 │  ══════════════════════════════════════════════════════════════════   │
 │  We are beating America's number 1 killer.                            │
 │  If your name or address is not right, please correct here.            │
 │       FROM:                                    TO:                     │
 │                                                                        │
 │                                                                        │
 │  Please mail your check along with this donor record card in the enclosed reply envelope. YOUR DONATION IS TAX DEDUCTIBLE. │
 │        □ Please send me information on tax benefits and providing a life income for myself. │
 └──────────────────────────────────────────────────────────────────────┘
```

The following seven envelope packages were to be tested with the following teaser lines:

- Control   —No teaser copy
- Test Number 1—"Use the Enclosed Free Gift" (Gift was a pocket card on CPR emergency rules)
- Test Number 2—"Emergency Heart Attack Card Enclosed"
- Test Number 3—"4 Years Ago Billy Thompson's Dad Would Have Died . . ."
- Test Number 4—"If you have ever worried about having a heart attack—"
- Test Number 5—"You hold lives in your hands . . . TODAY . . . AND THAT'S IMPORTANT"
- Test Number 6—"We'd like to show you how to save a life . . . Yours."

Each was to be sent to a matched sample of names stratified so that it contained both prospects (those who had not previously donated) and donors. The total sample size of each of the seven test panels (six test plus control) was to be the same. Overall, roughly ten percent of the heart association's mailing list was used for the test.

Questions

1. Why was only one element tested? Why not test lists, copy and graphics simultaneously?
2. What is the purpose of the control package?
3. How should the results be analyzed? What statistical tests could be applied?

TRANSIT DISPLAY ADVERTISING, INC.: EXPERIMENT IN TRANSIT ADVERTISING

Transit Display Advertising, Inc. (TDA) specializes in outdoor advertising, especially transit ads on cabs and buses. TDA works in two separate capacities: 1) it designs and places advertising for clients and 2) it represents a number of metropolitan taxi and bus companies in selling advertising space to other advertisers.

Bob Martin was the general manager for Florida of TDA. A former general manager for several South Florida radio stations, Martin had always been bothered that he had difficulty in showing the effectiveness of bus ads compared to other media. In radio, for example, advertising research was often conducted to show the media's effectiveness in reaching various demographic targets. As Martin often said, "I've been in radio all of my life, and I'm used to numbers."

The Research Project

Martin was familiar with effectiveness studies which were conducted for billboard advertising. Some used a before/after interview technique for specific test billboards in certain locations. Martin decided to adapt this research technique to bus advertising. Basically, he planned to first determine people's awareness or knowledge of a subject, run ads on buses for a specified period of time, and then determine their awareness after the campaign. The positive change would show how bus advertising could be effectively utilized.

Rather than use a product or an advertising slogan for the test, Martin went to an encyclopedia and searched for a suitable subject. He thought that it would be good to use something unambiguous and simple, such as questions concerning

This case is based on "Floridians 'Pass' Bus Test," *Advertising Age*, October 15, 1979, pg. 76. Copyright © 1981 by Dr. Donald Sciglimpaglia.

world capitals or history. Martin turned to the section on American presidents and found his answer.

Martin commissioned Advanced Market Research (AMR) to conduct telephone interviews in the Miami area with persons eighteen or older, in category groups which reflected the general population breakdown in that area. In addition to pinpointing the demographics, AMR was to ask two questions: "Who was the 30th President of the U.S." and, "Who was Eisenhower's vice-president?" The first (Calvin Coolidge) was Martin's test question and the second (Richard Nixon) was a control question.

Pre-Test Results

In June AMR interviewed 1,524 persons ages eighteen and older. Roughly four percent of the persons interviewed knew that Coolidge was the 30th President. About twenty-six percent knew that Nixon was the correct answer to the other question.

Next, Martin placed a somewhat cryptic twelve-foot long banner on 130 buses in the greater Miami area in early July. It read, "Calvin Coolidge, 30th President of the U.S." (See Exhibit 1.) Within a few days after the "ads" were put on buses, however, the local media gave the story extensive coverage. Stories, including pictures of the buses, appeared in local newspapers on the front page. Several television stations also picked up the story. Concerned about the immediate impact of the media coverage on the test, Martin commissioned AMR to do an intermediate study covering the last two weeks of July. AMR found that the results had not changed significantly. As Martin explained, "Either people didn't read the papers or watch TV, or they forgot about it right away." The Coolidge message was left on the buses for about six weeks.

Post-Test Results

In late August, AMR interviewed 1,184 persons asking the same questions. Among men, those knowing that Coolidge was the 30th U.S. President had increased from 4.3 percent to 13.2 percent. Among those 18 to 34, the percentage increased from 0.4 to 9.8. The most impressive gain was among men ages 35 to 54. That figure went from 1.4 percent to 16.3 percent two months later.

Among all women, there was a 100 percent increase, going from 3.6 to 7.1 percent. Among females eighteen to thirty-four, the results went from 0.7 percent to 6.1 percent. In the thirty-five to fourty-four group, the pre-ad result was 1.7 percent versus 7.0 afterward. The percentage of correct answers in the fifty-five plus category dropped from 4.2 percent to 2.8 percent.

Overall Results

Inexplicably, the results of the control question also increased from 25.6 percent overall to 37.3 percent. Martin had overlooked the fact that it had been the fifth anniversary of the Watergate affair and that Richard Nixon's name had frequently been in the news lately.

Overall, Martin was pleased with the results. Now, he was prepared to present

Exhibit 1   Miami Bus Advertising Message

quantitative evidence of the effectiveness of transit advertising. He was quoted as saying that the project "has been about as successful as I could wish it to be. It has really raised our level of believability."

Questions
1.   How would you describe this test as an experimental design?
2.   What major factors could affect the validity of this test?
3.   How could you explain the reduction in correct recall among older women?
4.   Overall, do you agree with Martin concerning the believability of the results?

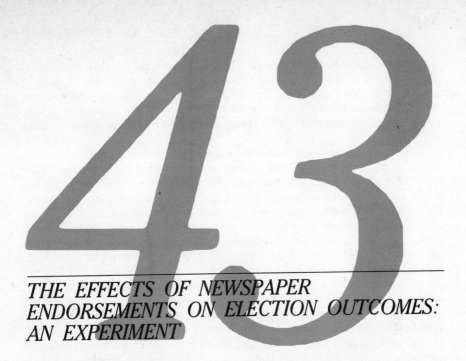

THE EFFECTS OF NEWSPAPER ENDORSEMENTS ON ELECTION OUTCOMES: AN EXPERIMENT

The decline of party and the rise of candidate-oriented election campaigns have underscored the importance of the question of what impact campaign events have on election outcomes. This reports the results of a study of a newspaper's candidate endorsements.

Background

The election we focus attention on is the November 1977 contest in Suffolk County, New York, for the office of County District Attorney. Located on eastern Long Island, Suffolk County is classified as a suburb of New York City, and its one and one-third million residents make it the second most populous county in the state outside the city. Because the population is scattered over hundreds of small communities (school districts, hamlets, housing developments), because city newspapers are read each morning, and because most radio and television sets are tuned to city stations, there is no easy way of communication for the local office holder or candidate.

The 1977 district attorney race was characterized by two unusual circumstances. First, the incumbent district attorney, Henry O'Brien, was a Democrat, an extraordinary occurrence in a county which traditionally has been heavily Republican. Second, O'Brien's three years in office had been marked by a running feud with the county police commissioner. After O'Brien publicly levied charges of "corruption" against the commissioner and his department, the police produced a witness who swore that O'Brien was a homosexual. Although the witness subsequently recanted his testimony, the charge of homosexuality against O'Brien, a bachelor, was not easily forgotten.

This case was prepared by Howard A. Scarrow with Steve Borman. Reprinted by permission of the publisher by Howard A. Scarrow and Steve Borman, *Public Opinion Quarterly*, vol. 43 (3), pp. 388–393. Copyright © 1979 by The Trustees of Columbia University.

Since neither *Newsday,* the island's only newspaper, nor the *New York Times,* which includes occasional but brief coverage of Suffolk County, took an editorial position or endorsed one of the candidates, the general newspaper reader had to decide for himself whether to vote for the reelection of O'Brien, or whether to vote for his Republican opponent, Patrick Henry, a name which added additional color to the contest.

There was one newspaper, however, whose editorial stand throughout the feud had been outspokenly pro-O'Brien. *Suffolk Life* is a twice-weekly newspaper published from offices located in the extreme eastern part of the county. The paper has a high circulation because, sustained by advertisements, it is delivered *free* to the doorstep of virtually every house—the paper claims 98 percent coverage—in the six eastern-most towns and small parts of two of the other four towns. Altogether, the circulation covers an area which contained 43.9 percent of the November 1977 registered voters. The hallmark of the paper is its blatantly outspoken editorials which, although often seemingly conservative (e.g., it opposed the Panama Canal Treaty), are best described as anti-establishment (unions, corporations, government). The editor is scathing in his denunciation of many Republican officials, yet nothing angers him more than "liberal Democrats." The editor happened to be a long-time friend of O'Brien. Hence, throughout O'Brien's feud with the police, editorials decried the fact that a district attorney who "had the courage to expose corruption in high places" was paying the price of having his personal morality questioned. Several times the full details of O'Brien's family life were spelled out, details which were said to explain why O'Brien had never married. On the weekend preceeding the election the paper's front–page editorial carried the headline "IS O'BRIEN QUEER?" Anyone who had read the paper over the preceeding months knew the editor's negative answer to that question.

The Experiment

We have, then, the beginnings of an unusually good set of experimental conditions to test the effectiveness of a newspaper's candidate endorsement: an election for an office about which the public usually knows or cares very little, the absence of any countywide media endorsements, and the circulation within one part of the electorate and only one part, of a newspaper which carried a well-publicized endorsement. Two additional factors complete the experimental setting: the basic similarity of the two parts of the county, and the presence of a control variable.

Both sections of the county are heavily Republican in voter registration. In the eastern part of the county where *Suffolk Life* circulates—hereafter referred to as the east—the ratio of registered Republicans to registered Democrats was, at the time of the election, 65 percent to 35 percent in the western part of the county the ratio was 59 percent Republican to 41 percent Democratic. There is another method of measuring the partisan complexion of the two parts of the county, made possible by the fact that on the same ballot as the district attorney race was the contest for two vacancies on the family court. As sometimes happens in these judicial races, the Republican and Democratic parties backed the same two candidates. For each vacancy on the court, therefore, the one name appeared on the ballot twice—once on the Republican row and once again on the Democratic row. It may be presumed that when a voter recorded his preference for the name as it appeared on the Republican row, that voter was Republican in orientation. Similarly, if he voted for that candidate as the name appeared on the Democratic row, that voter may be presumed to be a

Democrat. Using this method, then, the ratio of Republicans to Democrats was identical in both parts of the county, viz., 53 percent to 47 percent.

Finally, the conditions for an experimental setting are completed by the presence of a control variable. There was one additional countywide office to be filled in the November election—the office of county clerk. Like the office of district attorney, this post is usually of low visibility and tends to be lost among the many other local offices which clutter the election machine. For our purposes, however, it presents a valuable control: *Suffolk Life* made no endorsement among the competing candidates. If *Suffolk Life's* endorsement of O'Brien made a difference in the district attorney contest, we would expect that difference to be reflected *only* in that contest and *not* in the county clerk contest.

Results

The election was won by the Republican Patrick Henry, who polled 53.4 percent of the valid vote.[1] *Suffolk Life's* favored candidate, Henry O'Brien, thus lost the election. But for our purposes the important question is whether the election outcome differed in the two parts of the county in such a way that we may infer that the newspaper's efforts on behalf of O'Brien made a difference. And if it made a difference, how much of a difference?

There are two ways we can compare the election outcomes in the two parts of the county: (1) comparison of the raw vote totals, and (2) comparison of the extent to which each district attorney candidate "ran ahead" or "ran behind" the average of his party's totals in the two family court races.

In terms of raw percentages of the two-party totals,[2] within *Suffolk Life's* circulation area O'Brien beat Henry 54.9 percent to 45.1 percent. In the western end of the county the result was nearly the exact opposite: Henry beat O'Brien 54.5 percent to 45.5 percent. In terms of the candidates "excess" or "deficit" votes, the same pattern was apparent. In the east there was a plus eight percentage point difference between O'Brien's share of the two-party vote (54.9 percent) and the Democratic court candidates' vote share (46.9 percent). In contrast, in the west the difference between O'Brien's vote share and the judicial candidates' vote share was a minus 1.8 percentage points (45.5 percent contrasted to 47.3 percent). Henry's vote percentages were, of course, the reciprocals of these figures. By both methods of analysis, therefore, the conclusion seems inescapable that *Suffolk Life's* endorsement of O'Brien made a difference.[3]

How much difference? We note that in the western part of the county, where *Suffolk Life's* influence could *not* be felt, O'Brien still managed to outpoll his fellow judicial candidates by 2 percent (59,481 compared to 58,292). If we assume that in the east, without *Suffolk Life,* there still would have been this 2 percent difference, and then if we compare this hypothetical eastern result with the actual eastern result, we may infer that *Suffolk Life* accounted for over 20 percent of O'Brien's eastern

---

[1]Henry's total was 143,961, made up of 122,498 on the Republican row, and 21,463 on the Conservative row. O'Brien's total was 125,812, made up of 121,904 on the Democratic row, and an additional 4,908 on a separate Independent row.

[2]To facilitate comparisons with the family court totals, these and the following percentages are based on the Republican and Democratic votes only. The Conservatives put up only one candidate in the two family court posts.

[3]An analysis of Henry's 21,000 Conservative votes reveals the same pattern as his 122,000 Republican votes, i.e., a better performance in the west (relative to one Conservative judicial candidate) than in the east.

vote.[4] That percentage "boost" is sufficiently large that had it been present in the west as well, O'Brien would easily have won the election.

But, the skeptic may well ask, how do we know that these east-west differentials are not the result of some other factor common to all Democratic candidates, and not the influence of *Suffolk Life*'s pro-O'Brien editorials? The best way to answer this question is to look at the east-west totals for the office of county clerk, an office for which *Suffolk Life* made no candidate endorsement. These results show that the Democratic candidate for county clerk lost out to his Republican opponent in both parts of the county, the margins of defeat being about the same in both areas.[5]

There seems no question, therefore, that O'Brien's exceptionally strong showing in the east stemmed from some factor which was peculiar to the district attorney contest.

Questions
1.   Evaluate this experiment. What type of experiment is it?
2.   What types of experimental controls were utilized?
3.   What other factors might have accounted for the difference between Henry and O'Brien?

---

[4]The arithmetic is as follows:
   2 percent of 47,596 (Democratic judicial vote in east) = 952
   O'Brien's hypothetical eastern vote = 47,596 + 952 = 48,548
   O'Brien's actual eastern vote = 62,423
   Difference = 13,875, or 22.2 percent of 62,424

[5]44.9 percent to 55.1 percent in the east; 47.6 percent to 52.4 percent in the west. In terms of "excess" or "deficit," the Democratic clerk performance was a minus 2.0 percentage points in the east, a plus 0.3 percentage points in the west.

ETHICS IN MARKETING RESEARCH

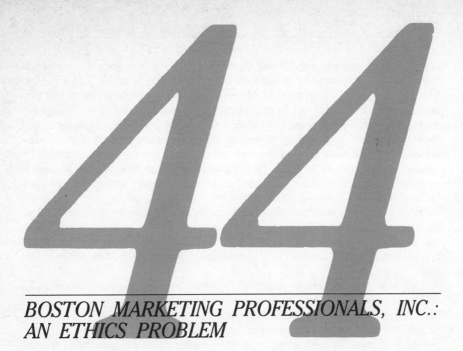

BOSTON MARKETING PROFESSIONALS, INC.: AN ETHICS PROBLEM

Background

Boston Marketing Professionals, Inc. (BMP) was a small marketing consulting and research firm in Boston. Their president, Mike Johnson, had been employed by several major corporations headquartered in Boston since his graduation from Harvard in 1968 with an MBA degree. Though he had gained substantial experience and training at each firm and had always been very rapidly promoted, Johnson left his last position as Marketing Research Director of Magna Corporation to start BMP. He was always quick to discuss his reasons for leaving his former high-paying positions, frequently citing certain business practices which he considered unethical. As he often said of these practices, "If you're ashamed to mention it outside the board room, you shouldn't adopt it as a viable business option."

He had performed well in his most recent position at Magna Corporation and the firm realized that they would have difficulty finding a replacement. But he did not leave without a certain amount of unpleasant feelings on both sides. So intense were these feelings that Johnson was almost paranoid about the actions he thought certain people would take against him after he left. But, as he told his wife Sharon, "I think it will be worth it in the long run. Now I can plan my own work and conduct business in the manner in which I feel it should be conducted."

Johnson felt that most of the practices he viewed as unethical at Magna and at other firms could have been avoided. He believed that the situations which forced these types of practices to be adopted often arose because someone hadn't worked hard enough at some point prior to the event. In addition, he was quick to point out the lack of moral and ethical values in many of those persons with whom he had been in contact at Magna and elsewhere.

Now that he was on his own, Johnson looked forward to the challenges facing

All names are fictitious. Any resemblance to real persons or companies is strictly coincidental. Copyright © 1981 by Dr. Donald Sciglimpaglia.

him as a small businessman. He had been fortunate enough to have been active in many of Boston's community events such as the Chamber of Commerce, United Way, Junior Achievement, and in his own church. In addition to people whom he had met professionally, this meant he had the opportunity to come in contact with business–people from a variety of firms. Even while he was employed by Magna, several bus-inesspeople asked him for help in various decision–making aspects of their busi-nesses. He turned down most of these offers because he felt they were in conflict of interest with his position at Magna. He gladly accepted other opportunities to consult as an aid in building up the capital he knew he would require when he would start his own business. These activities, which were performed on his own time, were tolerated by his superiors at Magna because they did not interfere with his job and because they knew of his interest in helping "small, struggling businesses." It was one of these businesses that became his first client after he formed BMP, providing him with enough monthly cash flow to help cover most of the fixed expenses of the firm.

Johnson was repeatedly tested during the first few months in operation. Whereas before he had always been responsible for one functional area, he was now "wearing all of the hats" essential to the success of a small business. Not only was he the chief salesperson and consultant, he was also responsible for hiring and firing personnel, monitoring their personal conflicts, setting up bookkeeping and account-ing systems, and even considering acquisitions. He had taken responsibility for pur-chasing office equipment (when he could afford it) and planning work loads so he knew when to hire additional temporary help. Needless to say, Mike worked harder and longer than he had ever worked before.

Since Mike considered his employees' salaries to be a fixed instead of a variable cost, as many large firms do, he felt that his primary responsibility to the firm was to bring in enough business each month so that he could pay his employees and cover all of the fixed expenses. Whatever was left was used to pay the few variable expenses and, if anything was left after that, he would take a salary of his own. Real profit was unknown in the early days of BMP.

This work situation affected Mike's wife Sharon as well. Despite seeing him even less often than when he was employed by Magna, Mike's "salary" had decreased from close to $50,000 a year to almost $14,000. To help even out the unsteady flow of his salary, Mike accepted a part-time teaching position at a local community col-lege and also conducted a series of business seminars in the Boston area.

After almost two years of attempting to build his business, Mike started to feel an increasing distance between himself and his wife. Formerly a marketing research professional herself, she had left her job in 1974 when the Johnsons had their first child. It was this family pressure more than anything else that drove Mike to bring his business under control. He was striving for a contract large enough to meet his monthly cash flow needs. Then he could quit his sideline jobs and take a more prominent role as a family man. This contract came from a very unexpected source.

First New England Pilgrim Project

It was after one of the business seminars on corporate planning that Mike was ap-proached by Scott McMurphy, Vice-President of Marketing of a large Boston-based insurance company, First New England Pilgrim Corporation (FNEP). McMurphy had been impressed with what Mike had to say about planning in the seminar and was interested in seeing if BMP might be able to assess a new business venture that his firm was working on. Although FNEP was well managed and highly successful, its management was very much aware of the problems that can be encountered when entering a new business area. McMurphy wanted to talk to Johnson about a new concept associated with franchising independent automobile insurance agents. McMurphy had been approached by Bruce Bantom, owner of a local insurance agency, who was interested in getting FNEP involved in setting up a franchised approach to auto insurance. Bantom believed that this concept could be promoted and spread nationwide by franchising major metorpolitan areas on an exclusive basis. His plan was to offer services similar to those of Century 21 in real estate, which tie local, independent real estate brokers into a well-promoted "umbrella" organization. After his meetings with Bantom, McMurphy recognized that such a program could be seen as very attractive to local insurance brokers. He also knew that it was an idea which could be easily copied by another firm, possibly even preempting the venture.

So when McMurphy spoke to Johnson, it was about researching the feasibility of this highly confidential new venture. Confidentiality was the key to the whole project, since McMurphy had heard rumors that a major insurance brokerage firm was looking at a somewhat similar concept. Under these strict conditions, Johnson was awarded a contract to research the feasibility of this potentially multi-million dollar venture.

Finally the pressure at BPM was lightened. Now that cash flow was assured for a year, additional projects that came in would add to the firm's first real profits. Although Johnson was happy to have additional time at home without worrying about the next day's receipts, he was now aware of the pressure to perform well for this highly demanding client. McMurphy and various members of his staff were at each checkpoint meeting and they were always anxious to hear how the research was progressing.

Johnson had delegated much of the project to Bill Clerkin, a BMP staff member and recent marketing graduate. Clerkin's father was an insurance agent in Kansas City, so Bill thought he had a fair understanding of the target market. Clerkin was in the process of designing the field research for the project when his father called and happened to mention that one of his associates in Kansas City had recently been interviewed concerning a concept which sounded surprisingly similar to the First New England Pilgrim project.

It was at this time that Johnson also caught wind of similar activities being undertaken by another firm, whose identity was unknown. Although Johnson's project was one of fairly sizable budget, the unknown firm had reportedly hired Major Market Ventures (MMV) to conduct the marketing research. MMV was a nationally recognized marketing research and consulting organization.

It was obvious to Johnson that the other sponsoring firm might plan to develop the concept as rapidly as possible. He referred to his and FNEP's situations as ". . . running a race blindfolded. You can't see where your opponent is, but you know he's bigger and stronger than you are and that you wouldn't have a hope if you hadn't had a sizable headstart!"

It was during the presentation of the results from the initial research that McMurphy asked whether or not anything was known about their competitor's progress. Neither Clerkin nor Johnson could provide an adequate response and they left the meeting wondering what MMV's research would turn up. Their question was answered that afternoon when Johnson received the following phone call from a leading field research firm:

S. F.   Hello, is this Michael Johnson?

M. J.   Yes it is, how can I help you?

S. F.   Mike, my name is Scott Farber and I work for Professional Interviewers in New York. We plan on doing some interviewing of independent automobile insurance agents, and we need to subcontract a firm to help recruit respondents in the Boston area. We also need a facility that we can use for the interviews. Can your firm help us out on this?

M. H.   Just a minute Scott, let me bring my assistant, Bill Clerkin, in on another line to talk to you about this.

B. C.   Hello, Scott? Bill Clerkin. What type of interview will you be conducting?

S. F.   Well, Bill, all I can tell you is that we will be conducting a twenty to thirty minute interview with auto insurance agents across the country. I will be in Boston for interviews on next Tuesday and I need about fifty agents from the area. We can offer them $25 apiece. We can offer you $1000 to recruit them and another $500 to use your facility for the interviewing. Can you handle that for me? I'm under a lot of time pressure.

B. C.   Sure, Scott, I don't think that will be a problem.

M. J.   Scott, who is your client for this job?

S. F.   We've been hired by Major Market Ventures to conduct the interviews, but they aren't the originator of the survey and they won't say who is. In fact, confidentiality is so important on this job that we have to insist that you and the agents not talk about the survey to anybody.

M. J.   No problem, Scott, we treat all of our clients with the utmost confidentiality.

B.C.   Scott, it might be helpful if we knew what the survey was like before we try to recruit any respondents. Can you mail one to us?

S. F.   No way. In fact, this survey isn't even conducted on paper. I will be bringing along a minicomputer terminal that has been preprogrammed with the survey and we will just enter the respondent's remarks directly into the data bank. We find this procedure not only helps with elaborate skip patterns, but aids in confidentiality.

M. J.   Well that certainly sounds interesting Scott! I'm looking forward to the day when we can afford that kind of technology here at BMP. We'll begin recruiting today and we'll have everything set up to begin at, say, 9:30 a.m. next Tuesday.

S. F.   Done. Just invoice us after we're finished.

After the call, Mike Johnson felt a little uneasy that he hadn't spoken up during the telephone conversation to tell Scott Farber that they were already involved in a project concerning automobile insurance agents. After all, Farber did stress that confidentiality was important for this project. But, he rationalized, Farber had never even asked him whether or not there might be a conflict of interest problem. And, of course, he would get a look at the competitive research project which would help him keep McMurphy happy.

Johnson phoned McMurphy to tell him of these developments and immediately recognized that he was in trouble. McMurphy had suggested (half jokingly) that ". . . to participate in our competitor's study would be unethical as hell." Johnson agreed but it was obvious that this was what they were going to do. McMurphy continued, "As long as you're going to do that, plan on interviewing some of the agents to find out more about the questions that they've asked. Better yet, call Bantom and get him and some of his friends into the sessions. Not only can we find out about the project, but maybe we can produce some discouraging results by having Bantom's guys give them some negative comments. If we're lucky we might even be able to influence the results of the project and kill off a potential future competitor."

Johnson protested, but weakly. McMurphy reminded him of the monetary value of First New England First Pilgrim's contract and of the future marketing planning project which may be coming his way if things turned out positively. Mike Johnson knew he had some serious thinking to do before next Tuesday.

Questions

1. What could Johnson have done to avoid this problem?
2. Should Johnson have volunteered to Scott Farber that his firm was already doing a project which involved automobile insurance agents?
3. What care should have been taken by Major Market Ventures or its interviewing company to insure confidentiality?
4. What should Johnson do now?

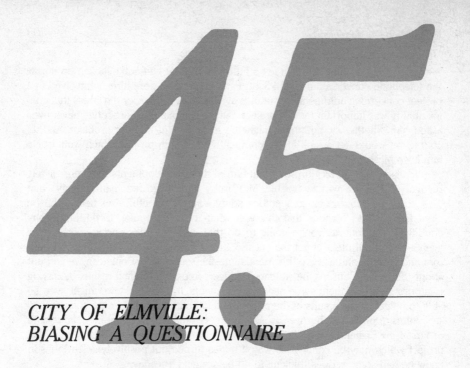

CITY OF ELMVILLE:
BIASING A QUESTIONNAIRE

It was one of those cold, blustery November mornings when Bill Crockett drove through the park on his way to Zeller and Fitzpatrick Advertising. The day had not started well and Crockett hoped that his next assignment would at least pull him out of his doldrums. As the Marketing Research Director of Z & F, he had enjoyed working on many projects for the diverse client base of the agency ranging from concept testing to marketing penetration studies. His eleven years in the agency business had taught him the rules of survival and he had always managed to keep his job even when a major client decided to switch agencies. This day was to prove whether he had learned his lessons well.

Upon entering the office, Mr. Zeller's personal secretary asked Crockett if he could see the boss as soon as possible. Although it was not unusual to be asked to see Zeller on such short notice, Crockett sensed that something was out of the ordinary.

As Crockett entered the office, he heard the tailend of Jack Zeller's conversation with a client. "No problem H.O., I'm putting my Research Director on it this morning and we'll get the results you want in two to three weeks."

"Bill, shut the door and sit down over here," said Zeller. "I've got an interesting problem that we need to discuss. That was Harry Oliver of the Industrial Development Board from the City of Elmville. The ID Board has been a steady, although not big, client of ours for the last five years."

"OK, Jack," said Crockett, "What do they want us to do for them?"

"The Board had a big meeting last night," said Zeller, "and have decided to promote industrialization in Elmville in a big way. They could turn into one of our largest clients and, if they are successful in getting new firms to locate in Elmville, we'll have the inside track on their advertising business."

Copyright © 1981 by Dr. William J. Lundstrom.

"Sounds great. What's the catch?" asked Crockett.

"It appears that all the citizens of Elmville are not as enthusiastic about growth and having new firms in the city as the ID board is," responded Zeller. "Our job is to do a research study before we run the ads in *Business Week* showing that the good people of Elmville would welcome new industry with open arms. If we can do that for the ID Board, we get the one year campaign in the mass media and a strong recommendation by the board for new firms to use our agency."

"And you want me to design a questionnaire that will insure that the citizens of Elmville say they will embrace any new industry—is that right?" asked Crockett.

"Partially right," said Zeller. "The ID Board does not want dirty or polluting industry. Only light industry, high technology, finance and distribution firms. Nothing that would hurt the environment. Can you do it?"

"It is not a question whether I can do it or not, but whether we should do it," Crockett replied. "I know I can get the results you want by wording the questions in a certain way so that they are 'motherhood questions' and people can't say no."

"What do you mean?" asked Zeller.

"For instance," said Crockett, "Do you favor new industry in Elmville that will help to lower your taxes? Do you favor attracting new firms that will provide new jobs and help to increase your standard of living? And so on. The people responding to questions like these almost have to say yes."

"I see what you're driving at," winked Zeller.

"Is the account important to us?" asked Crockett.

"Potentially, very important," replied Zeller.

"Let me think it over and I'll get back with you this afternoon," said Crockett as he got up to leave.

"Remember, Bill, accounts like this can either make or break the future of Zeller and Fitzpatrick and yours as well," Zeller commented as Crockett walked out the door.

Epilogue

In the summer of 1980, a series of advertisements were run in *Business Week* and *Fortune* extolling the virtues of locating in the City of Elmville, a remote suburban community of Houston, Texas. One of the biggest selling points highlighted in the copy of the ad was the warm, friendly and reliable people in the community who heartily supported relocation to their city. A research study, used to substantiate this claim, maintained that over ninety-four percent of the citizens surveyed would gladly welcome any and all new firms to the City of Elmville.

Some twenty-three companies took up the offer. Elmville is now fifty-five percent larger than it was prior to the advertisements and faces serious problems with housing, traffic, overcrowded schools, water and sanitation, and an increasing crime rate.

Questions

1. What would you have done if you were Crockett?
2. How should the research have been conducted to be unbiased?

XIII

COMPREHENSIVE CASES IN MARKETING RESEARCH

PACIFIC COASTAL FEDERAL SAVINGS AND LOAN: EVALUATING A COMPLETE RESEARCH PROPOSAL

Pacific Coastal Federal Savings and Loan Association is one of the largest savings and loan associations in the United States. Headquartered in San Francisco, it has fifty-six offices throughout California. In 1980, Pacific Coastal Federal's management was making preparations for offering NOW account service. NOW accounts are basically checking accounts which pay interest on the account balance. Pacific Coastal Federal's management knew that the Federal government would shortly authorize banks and savings and loans to offer such accounts. Previously, Pacific Coastal (and all other California S&L's) had been prohibited from offering any form of consumer checking accounts.

Although Pacific Coastal Federal's annual advertising budget was about $4,000,000, its management had historically spent little on marketing or advertising research. When research was conducted, it was usually directed by a staff person in either the marketing or advertising department. Lisa McClean, an assistant to the vice-president of marketing, was given the task of developing a consumer research project to study the area of NOW accounts. After a week's work she submitted the following research proposal.

NOW Account Research

I. *Problem Situation*

    1. *Definition*

        NOW accounts are interest-paying transaction accounts. The public views them as simply interest-paying checking accounts.

    2. *National Situation*

        It is believed that sometime in 1980 Congress will allow NOW accounts to be offered by savings and loans throughout the United States, including California. If legislated, the tentative date for allowed offering will be Janu-

Copyright © 1981 by Dr. Donald Sciglimpaglia.

ary 1, 1981. Presently NOW accounts are authorized only in New York, New Jersey and the New England states.

3.   *California Public*

The greatest problem surrounding NOW accounts is that much of the general California public does not know what NOW accounts are. To motivate consumers to open NOW accounts at Pacific Coastal Federal, the association must first build awareness, educate, show advantages of NOW accounts over other types of traditional checking accounts or telephone-transfer savings accounts, and show advantages of Pacific Coastal Federal's NOW accounts over other local financial institutions' NOW accounts.

4.   *Secondary Research*

a.   *Demographics*

A January 1979 survey of persons in 1,714 locations outside of New England, New York and New Jersey revealed that the idea of a savings and loan checking account appealed to younger, more educated, higher income customers. Six in ten with family income of more than $30,000 preferred an interest-bearing checking account to transferring funds back and forth between checking and savings. White–collar workers and professionals found the interest-bearing checking accounts more attractive than did blue–collar workers or retired persons. Those in cities with populations over 500,000 found NOW accounts more attractive than did those living in towns under 15,000— with the percentage of appeal growing in relation to size of the city.

In a survey by the U.S. League of Savings Associations, data showed that savings and loan association savings customers are heavier users of most types of financial services than are other Americans. For instance, only fifty-eight percent of all adult Americans have checking accounts as compared with eighty-eight percent of association savers. Twenty percent of Americans have stocks or bonds compared with sixty percent of association savers. Savers are heavier purchasers of mutual fund shares (twenty percent vs. three percent), U.S. Savings bonds (forty percent vs. twenty-three percent), and life insurance (eighty-one percent vs. fifty-one percent). According to the league's survey, the income difference between Americans and American savers at savings and loans is not large enough to explain the much heavier usage of checking accounts, etc. The league attributes this greater usage to personal factors, such as greater financial sophistication, more commitment to investment or more concern with financial security. Along with other demographic information, this leads us to believe that our own customers will be a good market and we can hypothesize that savings and loan customers' awareness levels of NOW accounts will be higher than those of non-customers.

Do the UNIDEX demographics of persons interested in NOW accounts differ from those of checking account users? In a U.S. League survey of savings and loan customers who have checking accounts, the highest percentage of persons with checking accounts were persons between the ages of twenty-five and sixty-five who held professional, executive, managerial, supervisory or self-employed jobs. The percentage of persons holding checking accounts increased directly with age (for example, eighty-eight percent with incomes $5,000–9,999, ninety-four percent with income $15,000–19,999 and ninety-seven percent with incomes over $25,000).

Pacific Coastal Federal's California research may be able to determine any specific demographic differences between current checking account holders and persons interested in NOW accounts.

b.   *Competition*
Research in existing NOW markets (by the Federal Reserve Bank, the Federal Home Loan Bank, the Federal Deposit Insurance Corporation and "local" institutions such as the New York Reserve Bank) show that savings and loans are holding smaller market shares on NOWs than banks, and smaller average account balances.

However, according to a 1979 survey done by Anita Miller, a recently resigned member of the Federal Home Loan Bank Board, the savings and loans currently offering NOWs are relatively small both in terms of asset size and market share. She felt that California savings and loans would get a much larger share of the market (in comparison with banks) than the current savings and loans.

In addition to local banking competition, Pacific Coastal Federal will receive competition from other savings and loans. Because the start-up costs of NOW accounts are predicted to be substantial, and because 1980 is not expected to be a very profitable year for the savings and loan industry in general, only the larger savings and loans in the state will provide strong competition in the battle for NOW account market shares.

II.   *Research Objectives*
1.   Evaluate high potential markets for NOW accounts.
2.   Determine consumer awareness levels of NOW accounts to estimate amount of consumer education needed in advertising, promotion and publicity.
3.   Determine characteristics of California consumers most receptive to NOW accounts (age, income, sex, profession and residence).
4.   Determine competitive pricing strategy for NOW accounts and consumer preferences for NOW account features.
5.   Determine nature of trade-offs consumers will make in selection of NOW accounts.
6.   Determine best "image" of NOW accounts to be promoted.

Information Needs
1.   Determine inadequacies of checking accounts.
2.   Determine popular types of checking accounts.
3.   Determine whether NOW accounts represent improvement over inadequacies of checking accounts.
4.   Determine whether other types of accounts are competitive. Determine what may affect use of the account.
5.   Determine important features of NOW accounts and rank of importance.
6.   Determine demographics profile of respondents interested in NOW accounts.
7.   Determine what percentage of persons are aware of NOW accounts.
8.   Determine awareness levels towards NOW accounts.

9.   Determine differences between customers and non-customers in views to-
     wards NOW accounts.

III.   *Sampling*

Telephone surveys allow each of the three major sampling groups to be surveyed in the same way, because sampling units for each one include phone
numbers. The three major sampling frames are: a) Pacific Coastal Federal customers, b) other savings and loan customers, and c) non–savings and loan customers.

Categories "a" and "b" must be broken down into *loan* customers and *savings*
customers because exploratory research showed that the two groups are often
mutually exclusive. Two hundred persons from each group will be interviewed
with the first two groups being broken down further into 100 savings customer
interviews and 100 loan customer interviews. This is more simply explained by
the diagram:

Pacific Coastal Federal Customers	*Other S&L Customers*	*Non S&L Customers*
Random sample from savings list: quota—100	Random sample digit dialing—100 savings	Random sample digit dialing—200
Random sample from loan list: quota—100	Random sample digit dialing—100 loan	

1.   Because some savings list customers have loans and *vice versa,* any sav-
     ings list customer who also has (a) loan(s) is a valid interviewee. This is
     true of the opposite circumstance as well.

2.   Because savings and loan customers in general may have both savings
     accounts and loans at savings and loans, up to thirty-five persons in each
     category may be interviewed if they have both savings accounts and loans
     at a savings and loan.

3.   The third category is limited to persons who do not, at *the time of the
     interview,* have an account or a loan at a savings and loan.

Six hundred persons were decided upon because it allows a large enough number of interviews in each category breakdown for purposes of comparison. Precision in sample size is not needed here because this is a general survey of
attitudes towards NOW accounts as opposed to a projection of number of persons intending to purchase, etc.

The sampling plan is basically a stratified sampling of each group, accomplished
through random sampling of a list of loan customers and savings customers
(until quota is reached) and random digit dialing to get a quota of other savings
and loan customers and non-savings and loan customers. (See Exhibit 1 for the
Proposed Data Collection Form.)

IV.   *Time Schedule and Budget*

1.   *Budget*

     Six hundred interviews at $12 each totals $7,200. This cost includes staff
     costs, research time, computer time costs, coding costs, secretarial costs
     and printing of code manuals and surveys. Any sophisticated training tools
     (such as an audio-visual presentation on telephone interviewing, etc.)
     would be an extra incurred cost.

2.   *Time Schedule*

     Two telephone interviewers working three, forty-hour weeks should be able
     to complete the quota of 600 surveys. (Approximately ten to twenty extra
     surveys in each of the five sampling categories will be completed to use as

Exhibit 1   Proposed Data Collection Form*

HELLO, THIS IS M_____ OF THE FINANCIAL SURVEY COMPANY. I AM DOING A CONSUMER SURVEY ON A NEW FINANCIAL SERVICE THAT THE FEDERAL GOVERNMENT MAY ALLOW TO BE OFFERED IN CALIFORNIA WITHIN THE NEXT YEAR. HAVE YOU BEEN APPROACHED IN THE LAST THREE WEEKS BY ANYONE DOING A SIMILAR SURVEY? WOULD YOU CONSENT TO ANSWERING A FEW QUESTIONS FOR ME ABOUT BANKING SERVICES? THIS SURVEY IS DESIGNED TO TAKE ONLY A FEW MINUTES OF YOUR TIME AND WILL GIVE YOU AN OPPORTUNITY TO EXPRESS YOUR OPINIONS OF CURRENT BANKING SERVICES.

Screening:

1.   DO YOU HAVE A SAVINGS ACCOUNT AT A SAVINGS & LOAN ASSOCIATION?

_____ yes
_____ no
_____ more than one account
_____ don't know

2.   DO YOU HAVE A LOAN AT A SAVINGS & LOAN ASSOCIATION?

_____ yes
_____ no
_____ don't know

Interviewer: If on Pacific Coastal Federal list, category A.
             If answer to any question is *yes,* category B.
             If answer is *no,* then category C.

		(POSSIBLE)	
Interviewer Check One	1–100	0–70	1–100
Category A _____	loan _____	both _____	savings _____
Category B _____	loan _____	both _____	savings _____
Category C _____			

Questions
1.   CURRENTLY, SAVINGS & LOANS ARE NOT AUTHORIZED TO OFFER CHECKING ACCOUNTS. DO YOU HAVE A CHECKING ACCOUNT AT ANOTHER FINANCIAL INSTITUTION?

_____ no (skip to Q12)
_____ don't know (skip to Q12)
_____ says has one at S&L (skip to Q12)
_____ yes (continue)

2.   (if yes) DO YOU KNOW AT WHAT TYPE OF FINANCIAL INSTITUTION IT IS?

_____ bank   _____ don't know   _____ other
_____ credit union

*Material printed in capital letters is to be read out loud by the interviewer to the interviewee.

Exhibit 1   Proposed Data Collection Form*—continued

3. (if no) HAVE YOU HAD A CHECKING ACCOUNT IN THE PAST?

    If no, continue to question 13.
    If yes, WHY DID YOU CLOSE IT?
    _____ not used enough   _____ no response/don't know
    _____ charges too much
    _____ minimum too much
    _____ didn't like the bank (or credit union)

4. DO YOU HAVE A TYPE OF CHECKING ACCOUNT WHICH, WHEN A MINIMUM BALANCE IS
    MAINTAINED, NO MONTHLY SERVICE CHARGE OR OTHER FEE IS CHARGED?

    _____ no   _____ don't know
    _____ yes

If yes,

5. WHAT IS THE MINIMUM BALANCE REQUIRED?

    _____ less than $100   _____ $1,500–$2,000
    _____ $100–$499   _____ more than $2,000
    _____ $500–$999   _____ don't know
    _____ $1,000–$1,499

If no,

6. DO YOU HAVE A CHECKING ACCOUNT WITH A MONTHLY SERVICE CHARGE OR OTHER
    FEE?

    _____ no   _____ don't know
    _____ yes

If yes,

7. IS IT A SET FEE PER MONTH OR IS IT DETERMINED BY THE NUMBER OF CHECKS YOU
    WRITE?

    _____ set fee
    _____ number of checks
    _____ other
    _____ don't know

If set fee,

8. HOW MUCH IS THE FEE?

    _____ $0–$3   _____ don't know
    _____ $3.01–$5
    _____ $5.01–$10
    _____ more than $10

If number of checks,

Exhibit 1   Proposed Data Collection Form—continued*

9. IF IT IS CALCULATED BY THE NUMBER OF CHECKS YOU WRITE, WHAT IS THE CHARGE
    PER CHECK?

    _____ 0–5¢
    _____ 6¢–10¢
    _____ 11¢–15¢   _____ don't know
    _____ 16¢–20¢
    _____ more than 20¢

If don't know,

10. WELL, CAN YOU ESTIMATE WHAT THE AVERAGE MONTHLY SERVICE CHARGE HAS BEEN
    DURING THE LAST TWO OR THREE MONTHS ON YOUR CHECKING ACCOUNT?

    _____ 0–$3 per month
    _____ $3.01–$5 per month
    _____ $5.01–$10 per month   _____ don't know
    _____ more than $10 per month

11. IF YOU COULD CHANGE ANYTHING ABOUT YOUR CHECKING ACCOUNT, WHAT WOULD
    YOU LIKE TO SEE CHANGED?
    Interviewer: Write in comments or check. _____

    _____

    _____

    _____ make it free
    _____ pay interest on it
    _____ change cosmetically (shape/color of checks)
    _____ change monthly statement to bimonthly, semimonthly, etc.

    AT THIS POINT, I WOULD LIKE TO ASK YOU A FEW SHORT QUESTIONS ABOUT NOW
    ACCOUNTS. NOW ACCOUNTS ARE CURRENTLY OFFERED IN BANKS, SAVINGS BANKS
    AND SAVINGS & LOAN ASSOCIATIONS IN NEW YORK, NEW JERSEY AND THE NEW EN-
    GLAND STATES. CONGRESS IS CONSIDERING MAKING THEM LEGAL FOR ALL FINANCIAL
    INSTITUTIONS IN THE U.S., INCLUDING CALIFORNIA. BASICALLY, NOW ACCOUNTS ARE
    LIKE CHECKING ACCOUNTS, EXCEPT THAT THE CUSTOMER ALSO RECEIVES INTEREST
    PAYMENTS—AS YOU DO ON A SAVINGS ACCOUNT—RANGING FROM THREE PERCENT
    TO SIX PERCENT.

Interviewer: Write any comments made: _____

    _____

    _____

12. DO YOU THINK MOST PEOPLE HAVE HEARD OF NOW ACCOUNTS?

    _____ yes
    _____ don't know
    _____ no
    _____ not sure

Exhibit 1   Proposed Data Collection Form*—continued

13. HOW ATTRACTIVE DO NOW ACCOUNTS SEEM TO YOU?

_____ VERY ATTRACTIVE
_____ SOMEWHAT ATTRACTIVE
_____ SOMEWHAT UNATTRACTIVE
_____ VERY ATTRACTIVE
_____ not sure/don't know

14. WHICH WOULD YOU PREFER? (1) A NOW ACCOUNT WITH THE MAXIMUM INTEREST
ALLOWED PAID, SAY FIVE PERCENT, AND A MINIMUM BALANCE REQUIREMENT OR (2)
A SMALLER AMOUNT OF INTEREST PAID, SAY THREE PERCENT, AND NO MINIMUM BAL-
ANCE.

_____ (1)
_____ (2)
_____ no preference

15. IF YOUR NOW ACCOUNT PAID FIVE PERCENT INTEREST WOULD YOU BE WILLING TO
KEEP IN IT. . . .

_____ A $500 MINIMUM BALANCE
_____ A $1,000 MINIMUM BALANCE
_____ A $2,000 MINIMUM BALANCE
_____ A $2,500 MINIMUM BALANCE
_____ no minimum balance
_____ don't know/unsure

16. IF YOUR NOW ACCOUNT PAID FIVE PERCENT INTEREST, WHICH OF THESE, IF ANY,
WOULD YOU BE WILLING TO PAY IN CHECK CHARGES?

_____ 10¢ PER CHECK   _____ don't know
_____ 15¢ PER CHECK
_____ 20¢ PER CHECK

17. AN ALTERNATIVE TO PAYING PER CHECK, OR TO MINIMUM BALANCES, WOULD BE TO
PAY A MONTHLY FEE. WHICH OF THESE, IF ANY, WOULD YOU BE WILLING TO PAY?

_____ $2 PER MONTH
_____ $3.50 PER MONTH
_____ $5 PER MONTH
_____ none
_____ don't know

18. IN GENERAL, WHICH OF THESE THREE WOULD YOU PREFER ON A NOW ACCOUNT
PAYING FIVE PERCENT?

_____ FEE PER CHECK
_____ SET MONTHLY FEE
_____ MINIMUM BALANCE
_____ all would be same
_____ not sure/don't know

Exhibit 1   Proposed Data Collection Form*—continued

19. IF NOW ACCOUNTS WERE OFFERED IN YOUR BANK OR SAVINGS & LOAN, WOULD YOU BE INTERESTED IN OPENING ONE?

   _____ yes   Why? _____
   _____ no

20. IF A SAVINGS & LOAN NOW ACCOUNT PAID HIGHER INTEREST OR HAD LOWER OR NO MINIMUM BALANCE REQUIREMENTS COMPARED TO BANKS, WOULD YOU OPEN A NOW ACCOUNT AT A SAVINGS & LOAN?

   _____ yes   Why? _____
   _____ no
   _____ don't know

21. DO YOU THINK YOU WOULD CHANGE FINANCIAL INSTITUTIONS TO DO SO?

   _____ yes
   _____ no
   _____ don't know

22. IF YOU HAD A TRADITIONAL CHECKING ACCOUNT, WOULD YOU CLOSE IT TO OPEN A NOW ACCOUNT?

   _____ yes
   _____ no
   _____ don't know

THANK YOU. THE FOLLOWING QUESTIONS ARE FOR STATISTICAL PURPOSES ONLY. THEY ARE SOLELY TO HELP US ANALYZE THE DATA FROM THE SURVEY AND WILL NOT BE IDENTIFIED WITH YOUR ANSWERS.

1. WHERE DO YOU GET MOST OF YOUR INFORMATION ABOUT BANKING SERVICES?

   _____ newspaper & magazines
   _____ radio and/or TV
   _____ word of mouth
   _____ professional consultation (lawyer, accountant)

2. WHAT IS YOUR MARITAL STATUS?
   _____ married   _____ separated
   _____ widowed   _____ other
   _____ divorced
   _____ single

3. DO YOU HAVE ANY CHILDREN? _____ yes _____ no

4. WHAT IS THE HIGHEST GRADE OF SCHOOL OR COLLEGE YOU HAVE COMPLETED?

   _____ grade school   _____ some college, technical or trade school
   _____ some high school   _____ college graduate
   _____ high school   _____ postgraduate

Exhibit 1   Proposed Data Collection Form—Continued*

5. PLEASE TELL ME WHICH OF THESE AGE GROUPS YOU ARE IN.

    _____ 18–24   _____ 45–54
    _____ 25–34   _____ 44–64
    _____ 35–44   _____ 65 OR OVER

6. WHICH ONE OF THESE INCOME GROUPS DOES YOUR TOTAL FAMILY INCOME FALL
    INTO?

    _____ LESS THAN $5,000
    _____ $5,000–$9,999
    _____ $10,000–$14,999
    _____ $15,000–$19,999
    _____ $20,000–$24,999
    _____ $25,000–$30,000
    _____ OVER $30,000

replacement surveys where needed.) This estimate is based on three completed surveys per hour, allowing extra time per hour for no response/
wrong numbers/etc.

Prior to that, the interviewers should be given a one-day seminar in data
collection training, including training in telephone interview techniques and
specific background about NOW accounts and what this survey is attempting to accomplish. The interviewer should be provided with an easy-to-read
manual on NOW accounts, so that any respondent questions about NOW
accounts may be answered.

Questions

1. Based on the information in the case, evaluate McClean's research objectives
    and information needs.
2. Evaluate the sampling plan, interviewer instructions and data collection proce-
    dure.
3. Evaluate the survey questionnaire.
4. Comment on the proposed time schedule and budget.

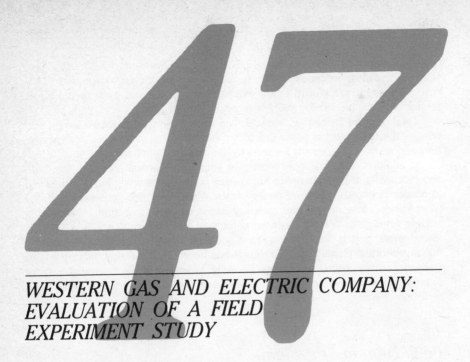

WESTERN GAS AND ELECTRIC COMPANY: EVALUATION OF A FIELD EXPERIMENT STUDY

Western Gas and Electric Company (W G & E) is a moderately large investor-owned public utility serving roughly 720,000 residential and commercial customers. Its service area includes a major metropolitan area in Southern California, surrounding suburban areas, and small towns and rural areas in three counties. In all, the service territory includes ninety different communities. Although the number of customers served is small in relation to some other public utilities, W G & E services a geographical area larger than the states of Rhode Island and Delaware combined. Included is one of ten largest metropolitan areas in the United States.

W G & E provides gas and electric service to customers in this service area. Although it also markets energy conservation products and services (such as home insulation material), nearly all of its revenues are derived from the sale of electric power and natural gas.

W G & E's Overall Situation
In one aspect, W G & E's situation is similar to that of other public utilities. Operating costs (particularly those associated with purchasing fuel oil and other fossil fuels) continue to rise dramatically. Revenues, on the other hand, are restricted by state and local government and have risen more slowly. The net result for most utilities has been a reduction in earnings and profits to stockholders.

In other ways, W G & E's situation is rather unique. Its service area has been growing at a farily consistent rate. The total population in the area has increased roughly by forty percent in the past ten years and forecasts estimate a growth rate of thirty percent over the next ten years.

Copyright © 1981 by Dr. Donald Sciglimpaglia

This population expansion is reflected in W G & E's customer base. In the past year, the company extended service to 33,981 new electric customers and 15,427 new gas customers, a growth rate of five percent over the past year. The customer service base for the past five years is shown in Exhibit 1.

Total demand for energy, however, has been growing even more rapidly. Last year, total sales of electric power (9.5 billion kilowatt hours) rose seven percent over the previous year. The results for recent years are shown in Exhibit 2.

In addition, W G & E faces a complex situation regarding energy supply. With reduced profits, it has experienced increasing difficulty attracting funds with which to finance new construction of power plants. While some new generating capacity has recently come on-line, the company has been prevented from expanding its nuclear generating capacity (now ten percent of total capacity), which W G & E's management feels is the best long-term solution. Moreover, planning for conventional generating plants (i.e., oil or coal) has become exceedingly difficult due to costs and environmental constraints. Recently, management has given high priority to projects involving solar and geothermal energy and to those oriented toward conservation of energy.

Peak Demand Problem

As demand for power has grown more rapidly than the ability to supply it, W G & E now faces a serious problem with its electric reserve margin (the difference between supply and demand for electricity). Most utilities aim for a margin of seventeen percent to twenty percent to protect against power plant shutdowns or exceedingly heavy demand. At W G & E, the reserve margin for the past year was only nine percent. Forecasts indicated that peak demand (i.e., maximum demand on the system) would increase from the present 2019 megawatts to 3148 megawatts in the next ten years—an increase of over fifty percent.

The pattern of demand for energy on W G & E's system also is a problem. In actuality, there are two demand patterns which are problematic. First, there is a yearly demand pattern which shows highest average consumption in the summer months (due to heavy air conditioning loads). In addition, there is a daily demand pattern, as shown in Exhibit 3.

On an average summer day, demand for energy is relatively low in the later evening and early morning, but increases rapidly to peak in the late afternoon. This peak load pattern is troublesome for two reasons. First, the peak loads subtract from the overall reserve margin (increasing the threat of inability to meet demand). Second, the power plants brought on line to generate electric power in peak demand periods are the most costly to operate, driving up W G & E's operating costs.

Load Management Program

In an effort to "level" these energy demand peaks, W G & E instituted a load management program. The overall goal of the program was to attempt to even out energy consumption during the summer months so that its power plants could be used more efficiently.

Part of the program was directed toward commercial customers where W G & E recommended such actions as reducing air conditioning use late in the day. The rest of the program was directed towards residential customers. A heavy

Exhibit 1   W G & E's Total Consumer Base

	Current Year	One Year Ago	Two Years Ago	Three Years Ago	Four Years Ago	Five Years Ago
Customers (End of Year)						
Residential	654,137	613,886	579,968	553,045	532,800	508,914
Commercial and industrial	67,802	65,018	51,514	60,973	58,873	56,657
Agricultural	3,142	3,213	3,175	3,138	3,133	3,114
Street and Highway Lighting	840	824	755	725	651	612
Other Sales	6	5	5	5	5	5
Total Customers	716,927	682,946	645,417	617,886	595,462	569,302

Exhibit 2   W G & E's Total Demand for Electric Power

	Current Year	One Year Ago	Two Years Ago	Three Years Ago	Four Years Ago	Five Years Ago
Sales-KWHR (Millions)						
Residential	3,728	3,437	3,295	3,102	2,913	2,880
Commercial and Industrial	5,341	5,023	4,940	4,842	4,545	4,720
Agricultural	133	145	135	124	125	118
Street and Highway Lighting	76	71	70	67	64	60
Other Sales	185	255	206	183	118	125
Total Sales	9,463	8,931	8,646	8,318	7,765	7,903

advertising campaign was mounted in an attempt to increase consumer awareness of the peak load problem and affect changes in consumption behavior. Chief among these suggested changes in behavior were to restrict dishwashing, clothes washing and swimming pool filtering to early morning or late evening. Consumers were also asked to control their use of air conditioning during the late afternoon and early evening.

In addition, W G & E felt that creative pricing might be an effective tool which could be used to get consumers to change their behavior. To test this concept, W G & E elected to conduct a pilot program called Peakshift.

The Peakshift Program

The Peakshift Program was designed to test consumer reaction to reduction in electric rates in return for a change in behavior related to energy use. The program had two separate components which W G & E wished to evaluate: 1) automatic load deferment, and 2) voluntary time-of-use rate reductions.

The automatic load deferment project involved the use of a small computer at a W G & E substation. On demand, the computer was capable of sending coded FM radio signals to a small circuit box which could be attached to a residential air conditioner or hot water heater. The coded signal could shut off the appliance for a specified period of time per hour. In return for a reduction in rates, W G & E could

Exhibit 3   W G & E's Daily Demand for Electricity

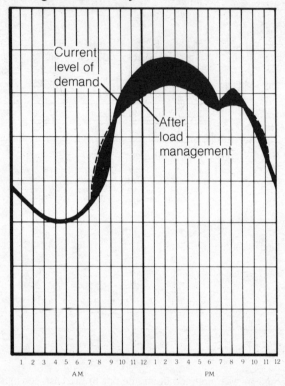

Average Summer Day

help manage peak demand by cycling off heavily used appliances in participating homes.

The time-of-use project was designed to see if consumers would voluntarily shift their consumption to off-peak periods in return for reduced rates. Essentially, participants would pay more than current rates if the energy was used during peak hours. They would pay substantially less if it was used before 9:00 a.m. or after 9:00 p.m. and would pay about the same as they were currently paying during the remaining hours of the day.

W G & E planned to attach a small device to the existing meter which would indicate when electricity is used as well as how much. Since participants would pay more than regular rates for on-peak electricity, they would hopefully be motivated to shift as much usage as possible to off-peak hours.

The Pilot Test
W G & E planned to use Peakshift as an experimental study to test both voluntary versus involuntary load management approaches and differences in rate savings. The

load deferment project was designed so that homes could have air conditioners or hot water heaters shut off for a maximum of either fifteen minutes or thirty minutes per hour. The time-of-use project was used to test two different levels of overall rate reductions for voluntary changes in consumption—ten percent and thirty percent.

A special notice was mailed to 50,000 households in two adjoining geographic areas along with their monthly bills. The notice described the energy experiment and asked for volunteers. Consumers were told in the mailer that special meters would be attached to specified appliances in the home or to the electric meter. Also, W G & E informed them that temperature probes would have to be installed in the home so that a record of changes in temperature could be kept.

The mailer went on to indicate that the project would continue for twenty-eight months. In addition to the rate reductions in the test programs, W G & E offered an extra incentive to all participants in that no general rate increases would be applied to them during the experiment. Although encouraged to remain in the study for the entire period, a household could leave the experiment at any time without penalty.

W G & E hoped to be able to form four separate test groups plus one statistical control group. It was anticipated that each group was to have 125 households. These five groups were:

Group	Description	Projected Size
1. Load Deferment A	Maximum shut-off time of fifteen minutes per hour. Rate reduction of five percent.	125
2. Load Deferment B	Maximum shut-off time of thirty minutes per hour. Rate reduction of five percent.	125
3. Time-of-Use A	On–peak rates increased five percent. Off-peak rates reduced ten percent.	125
4. Time-of-Use B	On-peak rates increased ten percent. Off-peak rates reduced thirty percent.	125
5. Control Group	Standard rates.	125

A total of 2,613 households returned postcards indicating that they would be interested in participating in the project. The marketing research department now faced the task of limiting the participating households to 625, assigning the test groups, determining what should be evaluated in the test and how it should be conducted.

Questions

1. How should the participating households be selected and how should they be assigned to groups?
2. What extraneous factors (i.e., potential confounding aspects of the experiment) should be considered?
3. What should W G & E measure or evaluate as the dependent variable(s) in this situation?
4. How should the results be analyzed?
5. What would affect the ability to generalize the results of the study to the entire residential customer base?

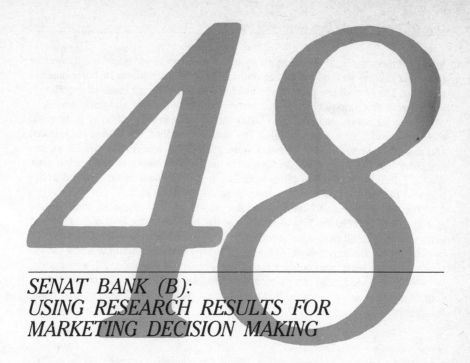

SENAT BANK (B):
USING RESEARCH RESULTS FOR
MARKETING DECISION MAKING

On John White's desk was the report that he had commissioned from High Performance Research (HPR) in Chicago. In it, he knew he had much of the information he needed to make the changes necessary to move Senat Bank from a stodgy country bank into one that embraced the marketing concept. The key to unlocking this wealth of information was the correct interpretation of the results and whether he would agree with the options presented by Jack Grisham of HPR. Since the Board of Directors was meeting in two days and they would expect some leadership from their new president, White pondered what to do and then eagerly reread the HPR report to develop his plan for redirecting the Bank's efforts.

Recent History of Senat Bank

It had only been a few short months since John White assumed the reins as President and Chief Executive Officer of Senat Bank. White was tapped by the bank after an executive search firm presented three solid candidates to the bank's Board of Directors. His past experience at Continental Illinois Bank of Chicago during its transition to a marketing orientation, made White the board's first choice. Recognizing that changing the direction of an old-line, country bank to a modern one following the marketing concept was not an easy task, White accepted the challenge and the opportunity to live in the bucolic Indiana countryside.

White's past experience at Continental had taught him that marketing research *prior* to making a major policy change was the prudent thing to do. Recalling that High Performance Research had performed a satisfactory image and positioning study for his previous bank, he called upon Jack Grisham of HPR to do the same for Senat Bank. The study commissioned used a multiattribute attitude model measuring twenty-five attributes of Senat and competing banks. The research was conducted

Copyright © 1981 by Dr. William J. Lundstrom.

through the use of random-digit dialing and telephone interviews of people residing in the immediate county (the primary bank trading area). When the research was completed, Grisham sent White a copy of the report along with certain options that Senat Bank might follow in order to change its image and become more customer oriented than it had been in the past.

The Senat Bank Study
I. Awareness of Banks in Clark County

When asked what banks in Clark County come to mind, seventy-three percent of the 250 survey respondents indicated awareness of Senat Bank.

Peoples Bank had about the same awareness level (seventy-seven percent) as that of Senat. Slightly over half (fifty-seven percent) of the respondents indicated awareness of Citizens Bank. About three percent mentioned some other bank.

Awareness of Banks

Bank	Percent of Total (Unaided Awareness)
Peoples	77%
Senat	73
Citizens	57
Other	3

Survey respondents who were customers of Peoples Bank indicated a high level of awareness for Senat Bank. About eighty-three percent of this group indicated top-of-mind awareness of Senat Bank while only fifty-one percent indicated awareness of Citizens Bank.

Account Relationship and Awareness of Other Banks

Aware of:	Total	Citizens	Any Account Relationship With Peoples	Senat
Citizens	57%	100%	55%	51%
Peoples	77	73	100	87
Senat	73	65	83	100
Other	3	5	4	1

Survey respondents were asked if they had recently seen or heard any advertisements for Clark County Banks. Only about half of the respondents mentioned a specific bank advertisement. Of the respondents who indicated awareness of bank advertising, only a small portion mentioned any source other than the newspaper. In addition, almost all respondents who recalled *any* bank advertising mentioned *all three* banks. Further details follow.

Advertising Awareness

	Total*	Peoples	Aware of Advertising for Senat	Citizens
Newspaper	40%	41%	38%	40%
Radio	5	7	5	3
Other	1	1	2	1

*Percent of respondents who recalled one or more types of advertising for each bank.

It is interesting to note the extremely low incidence of awareness of billboard bank advertising. This may be due to the fact that the respondents do not view bank billboards as advertisements.

II. Predisposition

All survey respondents were asked to name the one bank they most preferred. This was particularly important in this study since a large portion of respondents maintained accounts with more than one bank in Clark County. Peoples Bank was preferred by thirty-nine percent of the respondents, followed by Senat Bank with thirty-two percent, and Citizens with twenty-eight percent. Only one percent of the respondents indicated they did not like a particular bank. Senat Bank had the highest percentage of "also liked" responses, indicating that eighty-five percent of all respondents were favorably disposed to it.

Bank Preference and Liking

	One Bank Most Preferred	A Bank Also Liked	A Bank Neither Liked Nor Disliked	A Bank Not Liked
Peoples	39%	49	12	–
Senat	32	53	14	1
Citizens	28	46	25	1
Other	1	1	–	–

Predisposition toward Senat Bank is graphically shown following this paragraph. It shows a strong showing for Senat since experience suggests that a financial institution which desires to appeal to a mass market needs favorable predisposition in the range of forty to sixty percent. Since Senat Bank has already generated eighty-eight percent favorable predisposition, the thrust should be in increasing the share-of-market with that segment which already feels favorably toward the institution rather than targeting those who neither like nor dislike or don't currently like the bank.

From this illustration, it is obvious that a significant percentage of respondents who currently prefer Peoples and Citizens also like Senat.

III. Account Relationship

Slightly over half (fifty-two percent) of the respondents maintained an account relationship with Peoples Bank, followed by forty-five percent with Senat, thirty-one percent with Citizens, and three percent with other banks. Overall, approximately twenty-three percent had an account relationship with two or more of the three banks in the county.

Households with Any Account Relationship

Peoples	52%
Senat	45
Citizens	31
Other	3

Although Peoples Bank had slightly over half of the survey respondents as customers, their share of the total number of customers and accounts was somewhat

Exhibit 1   Predisposition Toward Senat Bank Don't like Senat

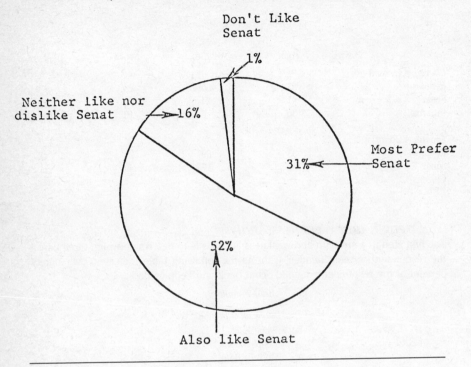

As previously mentioned, a significant portion of the survey respondents maintain accounts with two or three different Clark County banks. It is interesting to note that about half (forty-nine percent) of the respondents who had checking accounts at Citizens and Senat also maintained savings accounts at their respective banks. For Peoples Bank checking customers, sixty-nine percent maintained a savings account at Peoples Bank. It is also significant that thirty percent of Senat checking customers

less. As shown in the following table, the survey indicates that Peoples has a forty-two percent share of the market followed by Senat Bank with thirty-four percent and Citizens with twenty-four percent. By type of service, Peoples has nearly half of the savings accounts (forty-eight percent) and auto loans (fifty percent). For survey respondents, Senat Bank's largest share is in checking accounts with thirty-five percent of the total. The 125 survey respondents who bank with Peoples maintain 246 accounts, an average of about two accounts per person. The 101 Senat Bank customers maintain a total of 170 accounts for an average of 1.7 per person.

| | | Bank Share of Households | | | |
| | | Checking | Savings | Auto | |
	Total	Account	Account	Loan	Other
Peoples	42%	40%	48%	50%	44%
Senat	34	45	30	31	32
Citizens	24	25	22	19	24

As previously mentioned, a significant portion of the survey respondents maintain accounts with two or three different Clark County banks. It is interesting to note that about half (forty-nine percent) of the respondents who had checking accounts at Citizens and Senat also maintained savings accounts at their respective banks. For Peoples Bank checking customers, sixty-nine percent maintained a savings account at Peoples Bank. It is also significant that thirty percent of Senat checking customers maintained savings accounts at Peoples or Citizens while thirty-eight percent maintained checking accounts at the two other banks.

Type of Account Relationships

	Total	Peoples	Checking Account at: Senat	Citizens
Checking Account at:				
Peoples	52%	100%	28%	13%
Senat	41	24	100	13
Citizens	30	9	10	100
Savings Account at:				
Peoples	35	69	23	11
Senat	22	17	49	11
Citizens	16	7	7	44

IV. Strength and Weakness Analysis

The first step in a strength and weakness analysis is to determine which three banks the respondent is most familiar with. As the following table indicates, over ninety percent of the respondents named Senat Bank and Peoples Bank.

Bank Familiarity

Three Banks Most Familiar With

Senat Bank	93%
Peoples Bank	91
Citizens Bank	64
Other*	6

*Excluding Independence Bank Branch

In analyzing the strength and weakness information it is important to remember that respondents only rated the three banks they were most familiar with.

Respondents were then asked to compare the three banks they were most familiar with on 25 attributes which could influence financial customers to pick one institution over another. The responses are processed by a proprietary computer program which analyzes them in terms of where the respondent currently banks and where he/she is favorably/unfavorably predisposed to bank in order to determine their relative influence. This is plotted on what we call a Motivational Profile, which ranks the 25 attributes from most influential *(convenient to home)* to least influential *(community minded)*. (See Exhibit 2.)

Having previously determined the relative importance of the 25 attributes in influencing financial behavior and predisposition, we now need to determine which of the attributes are *product class expectations*—that is, attributes on which the major banks are seen as being "pretty much the same." As the following table indicates, four of the seven most influential attributes are product class expectations. So, for example, while *friendly employees* is the fourth most important attribute, no individual bank has a significant advantage in this area among the aggregate market.

Product Class Expectations of All Banks

Importance Rank		Motivational Profile Score
3	Easy to get waited on	176
4	Friendly employees	167
5	Easy to obtain a loan	138
7	Sympathetic and understanding attitude when dealing with problems	135
12	Makes least mistakes	102
12	Auto loans	102
14	Knowledgeable employees	99
15	Service charge on checking account	82
19	Variety of savings plans	61
20	Attractive facilities	50
21	Parking	47
21	Interest paid on savings	47
25	Community minded	20

Options

Just as financial customers see all banks as being "pretty much the same" in various areas, so also do they believe individual banks to have particular strengths and/or weaknesses. The objective is to have key strengths (attributes on which the bank is seen as being "clearly better" than other financial institutions) among the largest and most desirable market segment available. To accomplish this, several options must be evaluated.

A.   *Option 1* would be to optimize current strengths and minimize current weaknesses in the aggregate market (*all* respondents who rated Senat Bank). Among this group, Senat Bank evidenced no key strengths and four key weaknesses.

Key Weaknesses for Senat Bank

Importance Rank		Distance from Motivational Profile
16	Offers new services	−22
8	Sympathetic and understanding attitude when dealing with problems	−26
3	Easy to get waited on	−33
1	Convenient to home	−39

Overall, Option 1 does not appear all that promising for Senat Bank. First of all, Senat Bank has no key strengths to optimize. As shown by the Image Profile in Exhibit 3, there are four strengths (*friendly employees, makes fewest mistakes, service charge, and attractive facilities*). However, none of the four are significantly above the motivational profile line and all four are product class expectations.

While the four key weaknesses can be impacted, one (*easy to get waited on*) is a product class expectation. Key strengths and weaknesses for competitors are shown in the image profiles in Exhibits 4 and 5.

Between the two major competitors, Citizens Bank had by far the largest number of key weaknesses with eleven. Of this number, seven were key strengths for Peoples Bank. The only key weaknesses for Peoples Bank included *convenience to home, work and shopping*. As was the case with Senat Bank, these weaknesses are primarily due to the exceptionally high scores for Citizens Bank on corresponding attributes. Key weaknesses for competitors of Senat Bank are shown on the following page and,

Exhibit 2   Motivational Profile

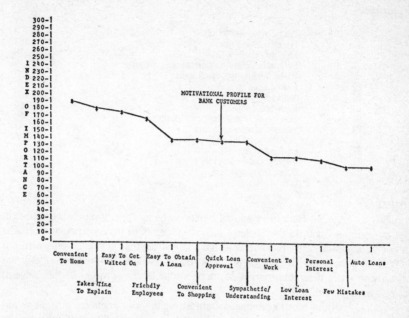

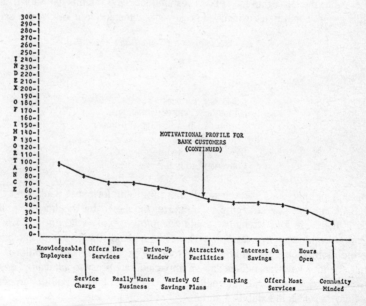

Exhibit 3   Image Profile

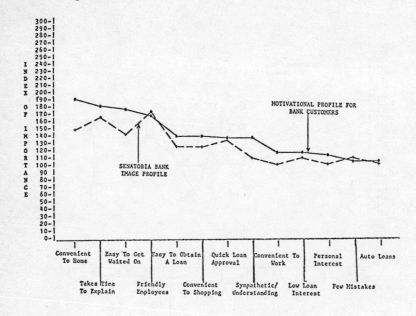

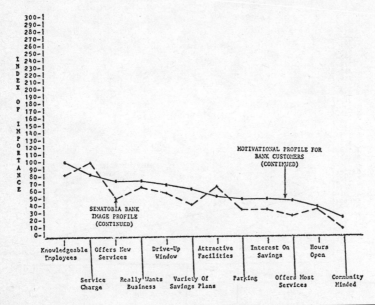

Exhibit 4   Image Profile

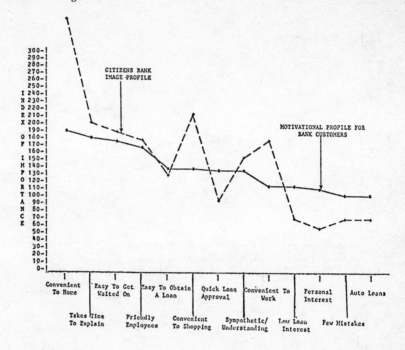

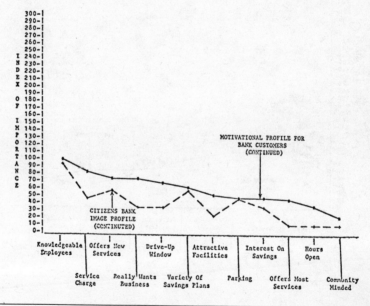

Exhibit 5   Image Profile

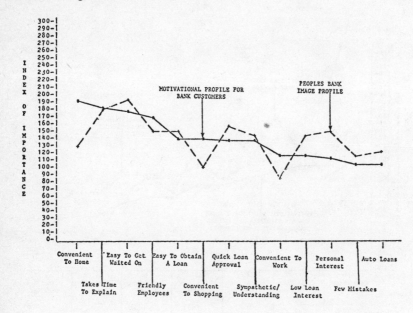

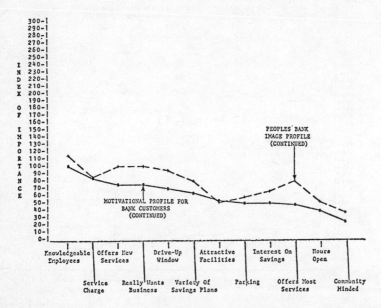

Exhibit 6 Image Profile

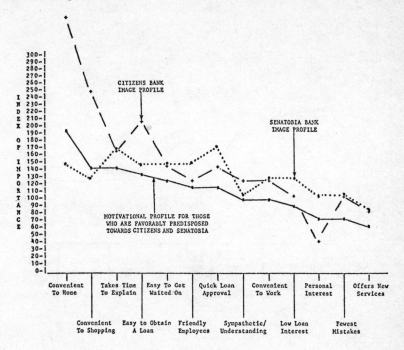

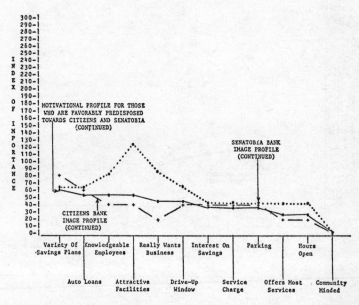

as with key strengths, indicate those attributes for which scores deviated significantly from the motivational profile for bank customers in general.

Competitors' Key Weaknesses

Peoples Bank	*Citizens Bank*
Convenient to work	Hours open
Convenient to shopping	Attractive facilities
Convenient to home	Makes fewest mistakes
	Auto loans
	Drive-up window service
	Offers the most services
	Service charge on checking account
	Really wants your business
	Quick approval on loans
	Low interest on loans
	Personal interest in customers

Image Profiles for Citizens Bank and Peoples Bank will be found on the following four pages.

B.   *Option 2* is for Senat Bank to emphasize the attributes which are currently most influential in the marketplace. However, Senat Bank does not currently have key strengths on any of the eight most influential attributes.

Option 2
Emphasize Most Important Attributes

Importance Rank		*SB Rank*	*Ranked First*
1	Convenient to home	2	CB
2	Takes time to explain accounts and services	3	CB
3	Easy to get waited on	3	PB
4	Friendly employees	2	CB
5	Easy to obtain a loan	3	PB
6	Convenient to shopping	2	CB
7	Quick approval on loans	2	PB
8	Sympathetic and understanding attitude	3	CB

Taking advantage of *Option 2* will require emphasis on consumer loans and personal attention to bank customers. Peoples Bank ranked first on the following attributes: *easy to obtain a loan, quick approval on loans,* and *easy to get waited on.* Citizens Bank ranked first in the following: *takes time to explain accounts/services, friendly employees,* and *sympathetic/understanding attitude.*

C.   *Option 3* would be to concentrate on areas where Senat Bank ranked significantly lower than the other two Clark County banks. Although Senat Bank ranked third on eleven of the twenty-five attributes, only three were considered to be key weaknesses.

Option 3
Areas Where Senat Bank Ranked Third

Importance Rank		*Distance From Motivational Profile*
2	Takes time to explain accounts/services	−13
3	Easy to get waited on	−33*

Option 3—continued
Areas Where Senat Bank Ranked Third

Importance Rank		Motivational Profile
5	Easy to obtain a loan	−12
8	Sympathetic/understanding attitude	−26*
12	Makes fewest mistakes	−18
14	Knowledgeable employees	−15
16	Offers new services	−22*
19	Variety of savings plans	−19
21	Parking	−13
21	Interest paid on savings	−13
25	Community minded	−12

* Denotes Key Weakness

D.   *Option 4* involves targeting against Citizens Bank by appealing more to those respondents who are favorably disposed toward both Senat and Citizens. Following are key strengths for each financial institution in this segment (see complete Image Profiles in Exhibits).

Option 4
Consumers Favorably Predisposed Toward SB and CB

Importance Rank	Major Strengths for Senat Bank	Distance From Motivational Profile
17	Attractive facilities	+72
7	Quick approval on loans	+52
18	Really wants your business	+39
10	Low interest on loans	+37
12	Makes fewest mistakes	+34
6	Friendly employees	+32
16	Knowledgeable employees	+30
	Major Strengths for Citizens Bank	
1	Convenient to home	+161
2	Convenient to shopping	+109
4	Easy to obtain a loan	+76
12	Makes fewest mistakes	+34
7	Quick approval on loans	+32

E.   *Option 5* involves targeting against Peoples Bank by appealing more to those respondents who are favorably predisposed toward both Senat Bank and Peoples Bank. Following are key strengths for Peoples Bank. There were no key strengths for Senat. The complete Image Profile for Senat and Peoples is found in Exhibit 7.

Option 5
Consumers Favorably Disposed Toward SB and PB

Importance Rank	Major Strengths for Peoples Bank	Difference From Motivational Profile
3	Quick approval on loans	+86
4	Easy to obtain a loan	+83

Option 5—continued
Consumers Favorably Disposed Toward SB and PB

Importance Rank	Major Strengths for Peoples Bank	Difference From Motivational Profile
6	Low interest on loans	+77
11	Personal interest in customers	+77
1	Easy to get waited on	+76
16	Drive–up window service	+68
12	Knowledgeable employees	+57
20	Offers most services	+57
21	Parking	+57
2	Takes time to explain accounts/services	+51
16	Really wants your business	+45
12	Convenient to shopping	+38
19	Variety of savings plans	+36
12	Offers new services	+35

F.   *Option 6* is to concentrate on image improvement among those most influenced by *really wants your business*. For the more important attributes, Senat Bank's Image Profile compared favorably with the Motivational Profile for this particular segment of survey respondents. This is shown in more detail in the following Exhibit 8.

The following table lists those attributes where the Senat Bank Image Profile is significantly *above* the Motivational Profile line for those respondents most influenced by *really wants your business*. In other words, Senat Bank has a significantly good image in four attributes as viewed by this particular group.

Importance Rank*	Good Image	Distance From Motivational Profile**
1	Convenient to home	+49
20	Attractive facilities	+47
9	Convenient to work	+46
4	Friendly employees	+43

* For bank customers
** For those most influenced by *really wants your business*.

To the group most influenced by *really wants your business*, Senat Bank had a relatively poor image in the following areas:

Importance Rank*	Poor Image	Distance From Motivational Profile**
16	Really wants your business	−70
22	Interest on savings	−61
19	Variety of savings plans	−60
23	Offers most services	−57
11	Personal interest in customers	−50
24	Hours open	−41
25	Community minded	−33
16	Offers new services	−31

* For bank customers
** For those most influenced by *really wants your business*.

Exhibit 7   Image Profile

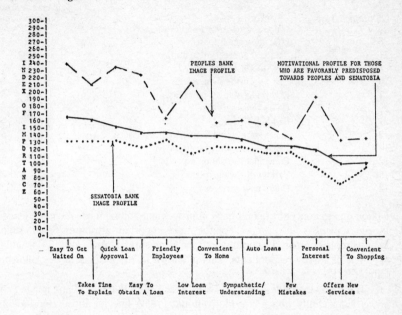

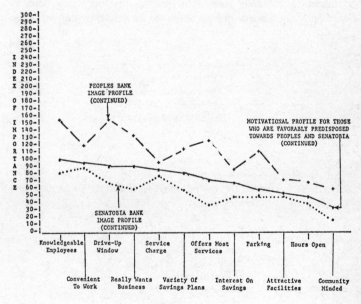

Exhibit 8   Image Profile

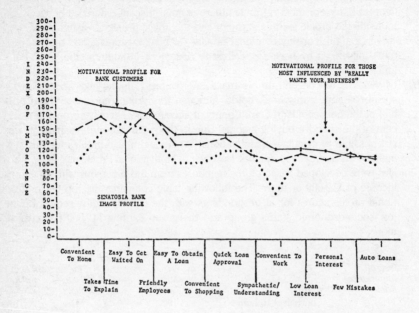

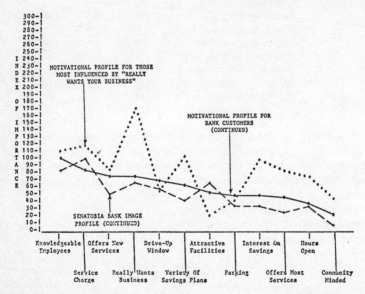

G.   *Option 7* is to appeal to those most influenced by *personal interest in customers.* Overall, this was the eleventh most important attribute and a key strength for Peoples Bank. For most attributes there is no significant difference between the motivational profile for this segment and the image profile for Senat Bank.

   In Exhibit 8 are motivational profiles for bank customers and the segment most influenced by *personal interest in customers.* In addition, the Senat Bank Image Profile is shown.

H.   *Option 8* is to concentrate on image improvement among high and moderate socioeconomic status households. Although this group represents about one-half of the households in Clark County, it accounts for roughly seventy-five percent of the effective buying income. Due to the small size of the sample, it was not possible to calculate a Motivational Profile and Image Profiles for this segment of the survey respondents. However, a Motivational Profile and Image Profiles were developed based on the responses from those persons with an annual income of $12,000 or more. The following table compares the top ten motivational profile scores for all respondents with the corresponding scores for the low socio-economic status group and the group earning $12,000 per year or more.

Overall Importance Rank	Attribute	MP Score	MP Score for $12,000+ Group	MP Score for low S.E.S.
1	Convenient to home	190	141	161
2	Takes time to explain	181	156	200
3	Easy to get waited on	176	141	187
4	Friendly employees	167	117	168
5	Easy to obtain a loan	138	149	181
5	Convenient to shopping	138	102	142
7	Quick approval on loans	135	141	178
7	Sympathetic/understanding	135	110	161
9	Convenient to work	114	117	142
9	Low interest on loans	114	117	155

The scores of the low S.E.S. group were consistently highest for all attributes. The $12,000+ group had higher scores than the overall Motivational Profile for the three loan-related attributes and *convenient to work.* "Easy to get waited on"—Although this is a product class expectation, it is a key weakness of Senat Bank.

V.   *Characteristics of Survey Respondents*
   Four of every five respondents were white, and they were fairly evenly divided between men and women:

Characteristics of Survey Respondents
(Race & Sex)

	Total	Citizens	Any Account Relationship With Peoples	Senat
Race				
White	81%	87%	79%	73%
Black	19	13	21	27
Sex				
Male	48	43	49	51
Female	52	57	51	49

Exhibit 9   Image Profile

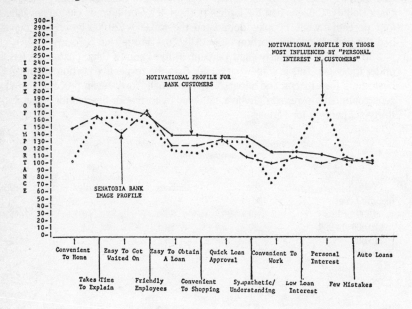

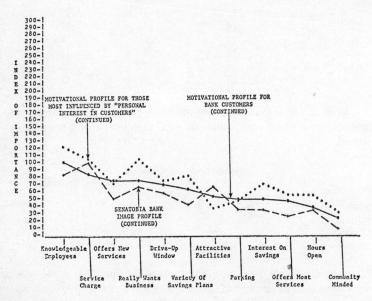

About half of the respondents surveyed had annual household incomes of less than $10,000. This is consistent with the recent median income figure for Clark County. Citizens had the largest portion of lower–income customers (fifty-four percent), while Peoples dominated the $10,000–$20,000 group and Senat had the highest relative portion of the $20,000 + group (ten percent).

In terms of age, thirty-eight percent of the Peoples Bank customers were under thirty-six. This is somewhat higher than the respective portion of younger customers for Citizens and Senat. Nearly one-half (forty-seven percent) of Citizens customers were over fifty-five, followed by forty-four percent for Senat, and thirty-six percent for Peoples.

Characteristics of Survey Respondents
(Income & Age)

	Total	Citizens	Age Account Relationship With Peoples	Senat
Income Level				
$9,999 or less	49%	54%	40%	49%
$10,000–14,999	30	29	33	29
$15,000–19,999	14	15	20	12
$20,000 or more	7	2	7	10
Age				
25 or younger	13	9	13	12
26–35	18	13	25	17
36–45	10	15	8	6
46–55	18	15	18	21
56–65	18	17	19	23
65 or older	23	30	17	21

Most survey respondents (seventy-seven percent) were married. The next most common group was "widowed." Less than ten percent were single or divorced.

Marital Status of Respondents

	Total	Citizens	Bank Most Preferred Peoples	Senat
Single	7%	7%	5%	11%
Married	77	79	79	70
Divorced	1	–	2	2
Widowed	15	14	14	17

Overall, slightly over one-fourth (twenty-eight percent) of the respondents were retired or unemployed. Of those employed, the largest part were blue-collar workers, a group which comprised twenty-eight percent of the total. Executives and white-collar workers accounted for forty-three percent of those who most preferred Senat Bank. Relatively speaking, Citizens Bank had the largest proportion of blue-collar and farm workers with forty-four percent. Details appear in the following table.

Bank Preference by Occupation

	Total	Peoples	Bank Most Preferred Senat	Citizens
Head-of-Household Occupation:				
Executive	21%	28%	13%	19%
White–Collar	10	15	13	2
Blue–Collar	28	30	30	22
Farm	13	8	10	22
Retired/unemployed	28	19	34	35

Survey respondents were grouped by life cycle category. Life cycle is based on age, marital/child status, and employment status. The eight life cycle categories are subdivided into *under 35* and *over 35* for convenience. As previously indicated, Peoples has the largest share of younger persons. Of those who most prefer Peoples Bank, over one-third were under thirty-five. Peoples also had the largest relative proportion of households containing children with twenty-eight percent, compared to twenty-two percent for Citizens and fifteen percent for Senat. Details appear in the following table.

	Total	Citizens	Bank Most Preferred Peoples	Senat
Under 35				
Bachelor	7%	5%	5%	13%
Young couple/no children	4	3	12	–
Young couple/children	16	14	19	13
Subtotal	30	22	36	26
35 or Older				
Mature family/children	6	8	9	2
Older couple*	30	29	30	30
Retired couple*	16	24	6	23
Older single/employed	5	3	8	4
Older single/retired	13	14	11	15
Subtotal	70	78	64	74

* No children at home

The Decision

As White closed the report, he sat back and reflected on the voluminous material. He felt that he had certainly gotten his money's worth from HPR. Now, all he had to do was decipher what it meant, how he would act on it and what changes he would propose to the board based on the research.

Questions

1. What do you see as the major strengths of Senat Bank? The major weaknesses?
2. Comment on the completeness of the research.
3. Develop a detailed marketing plan for Senat Bank using the information presented in the report.
4. What assumptions or additional information would you need to make your marketing plan better?